Real Thoughts from Real People about *On This Day in History Sh!t*

Shawn Hawley
Ok ima have to quit reading your shit for a while . . . just had a heart attack this past Monday and all the laughing made my ticker tremble. I'll catch up in a couple weeks.

Chrissy Santic Linford
Absolutely love bite sized history but had some explaining to do when my 2.5 year old used the word 'Cocktoboggan' to name his latest monster truck.

Ashley Bedford
Your writing made my dyslexic 12 year old kid give a shit about reading history. I'm sure he's not the only one. And his vocabulary is growing by the day alongside his history knowledge. I owe you a debt of gratitude.

Mitch James
I bought your first book a few days ago. I need to buy a new copy as a few pages are now covered in coffee.
That I spat out.
Through my nose.

Lisa M. Parks
You had me at 'fucktacular shitnado of ass'.

Arvilla Rothe
My 29 year old special needs son and my 81 year old mother think you're fucking hilarious!

Roxanne Rizzo
My neighbor came over to ask "just what's so funny?!?!" Apparently they were mowing and my cackling was louder than the machine.

Mary Ann Slaughter Ray
I laughed so hard I scared my cats.

Julia Creadore
Listen, motherfu... your books and posts are in large part responsible for me learning and laughing til I pee myself almost daily for the last few years, and I'm goddamn grateful for you!

Jamie Stidger
I'm a high school English teacher in Hawaii with mostly kids who never read. I got both volumes, and the kids fight over who gets to read today's story to the class! Life changing!

Kimberly Collier
Just so you know, "dropped out of middle school to pursue a career in competitive cousin fucking" is now part of my daily vernacular.

Ami Segna Jones
My biggest complaint is that, after reading your book, my kids now have a way better repertoire of swear words than I do.

Lynn Flanagan Clark
I've genuinely learned some really cool things about history from your books, and laughed until I could not freaking breathe while doing it!

Don Webster
I once laughed so hard I had to leave my office building to collect myself. I had disrupted the entire area of cubicles, and was getting the HR friendly version of dirty looks.

Dina Taibi
The gals in the office think I'm up to something sinister or something dirty because of the way James Fell makes me laugh out loud.

On
This
Day in
History
Sh!t
Went
Down

James Fell

On This Day in History Sh!t Went Down

BANTAM

NEW YORK, NEW YORK

2023 Bantam Books Trade Paperback Edition

Copyright © 2021, 2023 by James Fell

Published in the United States by Bantam Books, an imprint of Random House, a division of Penguin Random House LLC, New York.

BANTAM BOOKS and B colophon are registered trademarks of Penguin Random House LLC.

Originally published in paperback in Canada and in different form by BFW Publishing, Calgary, Alberta, Canada in 2021.

Library of Congress Cataloging-in-Publication Data
Names: Fell, James (Motivation, health, and fitness writer), author.
Title: On this day in history sh!t went down / James Fell.
Other titles: On this day in history shit went down
Description: New York, New York: Bantam, [2023] |
Identifiers: LCCN 2023016854 (print) | LCCN 2023016855 (ebook) |
ISBN 9780593724088 (trade paperback) | ISBN 9781777574215 (ebook)
Subjects: LCSH: Chronology, Historical. | History—Miscellanea.
Classification: LCC D11.5 .F45 2023 (print) | LCC D11.5 (ebook) |
DDC 902/.02—dc23/eng/20230503
LC record available at https://lccn.loc.gov/2023016854
LC ebook record available at https://lccn.loc.gov/2023016855

Printed in the United States of America on acid-free paper

randomhousebooks.com

9 8 7 6 5 4 3 2 1

1st Printing

Book design by Ralph Fowler

For my two dads,
a couple of cool motherfuckers.

Contents

Author's Note

I can't believe I have to say this, but Nazis are bad.

Bad before World War II. Bad during. Still bad now.

The worst kind of bad.

There are no "very fine people" among them.

If you disagree, you won't like this book. Also, fuck you.

Still here? Cool.

The idea for this sweary history project arrived on a bike ride on April 17, 2020, and launched on Facebook the following day. Being published on Facebook, which is owned by someone who doesn't like it when anyone uses his platform to speak ill of white men, I had to be careful when poking fun at the frequent fuckery of that demographic, lest I spend a month in Facebook jail. This led to some creative euphemisms for pasty-skinned penis possessors, of which I am one. I've largely left these in for the book.

It is possible you'll be vexed by how I have exposed some historical and religious figures as less than perfect. To that end, I'll quote from the entry for December 10:

> *Everyone is flawed. Some aren't just flawed, they're evil. We should not praise people as heroes, because we will always find reason to be disappointed, crushed, or aghast. However, we can praise heroic acts. Admire the deeds you deem worthy rather than the person behind them. Alternatively, feel free to say fuck them and cancel them from your life. No one is owed your admiration. No one.*

P.S. You'll notice no shortage of Trump hate in this book. Fuck that guy.

On This Day in History Sh!t Went Down

January

Does a bear shit in the woods? Duh. Does a horse shit in the house? If you don't want it stolen by mutineers during the American Revolution and the best place to hide said horse is in a second-floor bedroom, then yeah, the horse shits in your house. This, in part, is the story of Tempe Wick.

Tempe was a woman, not a horse. The horse's name was Colonel. Anyfuckingway, mutiny.

The Pennsylvania Line Mutiny began on January 1, 1781, among Continental Army soldiers. If you're American, those were the good guys. Regardless, they were pissed about not getting paid for being shot at by those tea-drinking asswipes in the red coats.

The Pennsylvania soldiers were treated like shit. In addition to no pay, the housing conditions were deplorable. Even General George Washington agreed. Literally, their rights were being violated; the state of Pennsylvania disregarded their terms of enlistment. So, they mutinied in Morristown, New Jersey, shooting one of their captains in the process, and headed for Philadelphia on New Year's Day. Yes, alcohol was involved.

Why Philadelphia? Because that's where the Continental Congress was located. They intended to confront the assembled Founding Fathers and other rich white dudes and say hey motherfuckers army life sucks make it suck less please. For anyone paying attention on January 6, 2021, such banging on the doors of Congress may seem eerily familiar. Except not really. Unlike the deranged followers of Tangerine Palpatine, the 1781 mutineers had no intention of actually harming any members of Congress.

So, a horse shits in a house. The mutineers raided supplies for their journey, including horses. Tempe Wick, age twenty-two, lived in Jockey Hollow, New Jersey. Her father recently deceased, she cared for her sick mother and mentally ill brother. Her mother's health took a downward turn, and Tempe rode Colonel to fetch the doctor. Along the way, three mutineers intercepted her and said give us that fucking horse. She said okay, asking the soldier holding Colonel's bridle to help her dismount. Chivalry not being dead, he said sure and the moment he let go of the bridle she said, "Psych!" and kicked Colonel into a gallop.

January 1, 1781

The soldiers knew where she lived, so putting Colonel in the barn wouldn't suffice. She led the equine upstairs and had him stand on a feather mattress to muffle his hooves, hiding him there for three weeks. Three weeks? That's a whole mess of horseshit. Fortunately, the soldiers never thought to search the second floor and she got to keep the family quadruped.

And the mutineers? The British said hey come fight for us we'll pay you. They said we're mutineers not *traitor* traitors, so get fornicated. Then the Pennsylvania government cut a deal with the mutineers in mid-January that brought an end to the crisis. Inspired by this, the New Jersey Line mutinied days later and Washington said not this bullshit again and crushed the mutiny by force.

Lotta crazy shit happened in Spain in 1492. The crown financed Columbus raping a continent, they kicked out the Jews, and they also *finally* kicked out the Muslims. I say "finally" because they had been fighting since the Muslims invaded the region over seven centuries earlier. The Spanish victory was deemed a reconquering of their own territory. That's why they called it the *Reconquista*.

January 2, 1492

By 711, a mere century after it had begun, Islam had spread across North Africa and crossed the Strait of Gibraltar to invade the Iberian Peninsula. How did it spread so far so fast? The same way many religions spread, not through peaceful explanation of the revelations of the prophet but by the sword. Convert, or die.

At the time of the Muslim conquest, the region that would come to be known as Spain and Portugal was a divided Visigoth kingdom that could not mount a unified defense against Muslim invaders, and over the next fifteen years the invaders conquered most of the peninsula, with the exception of the northwest corner. And it was from that corner the *Reconquista* launched, pretty much right away, but wow was it slow going.

Almost eight motherfucking centuries of fighting to take back the territory, which of course involved the forcible conversion of Muslims (and Jews) to Christianity. On January 2, 1492, the Emirate of Granada in the southeast of Spain, the final Muslim stronghold on the peninsula, surrendered to the Christian forces.

The interesting thing is that during the Islamic occupation of Spain, the invaders had been pretty tolerant of other religions, and many Christians and Jews and Muslims lived side by side, mostly in peace. Muslims had little tolerance for polytheists because *ONE GOD!* But since Jews and Christians are monotheists (mostly), you could keep those faiths if you were willing to pay extra taxes for the privilege.

But as the reconquest moved south, the tolerance for anything not Christian was paltry, and this included Jews. A few months after the surrender at Granada, there was a decree that any Jews remaining in the country had to convert to Christianity or get the fuck out.

And many did convert, but others refused. Approximately 100,000 Jews were expelled, and thousands died during their flight.

They say no one expects the Spanish Inquisition, but they kinda telegraphed that shit.

> **A few months after the surrender at Granada, there was a decree that any Jews remaining in the country had to convert to Christianity or get the fuck out.**

The focus of this story takes place a decade previous, but I must begin by saying that the end of the shogunate in Japan deserved a better Hollywood telling than Tom Cruise as a white savior for a lost cause in *The Last Samurai*. Watching that movie, I kind of wanted the samurai to lose. And lose they did, because they brought knives to a gunfight. They were really big and very sharp knives, but the guys fighting for the Meiji Empire had rapid-firing rifles. Some putz with a few weeks' rifle training can kill the shit out of almost anyone who's spent their life studying the blade, so long as they keep their distance.

Now to our story. In 1600, after winning the Battle of Sekigahara, the Tokugawa Shogunate came to rule Japan by ending the period of civil wars that had lasted over a century. One of the first things they did was kick out all the dirty foreigners, especially the Christians trying to convert their population. Thus began a period of over two centuries of peace, prosperity, and isolation from Western influences.

By the mid-nineteenth century, the shogunate was in decline, and in 1853 the American navy showed up to negotiate a treaty to open the country to trade. The Japanese took one look at how technologically advanced these foreign ships were and went oh fuck we need to get some of that. And so, there was a revolution to overthrow the isolationist factions of the shogunate and restore imperial rule in Japan and open the country to foreign technology so it wouldn't be colonized by countries with far superior weaponry.

January 3, 1868

This was done in the name of Emperor Meiji, who was only fifteen years old at the time, and it became known as the Meiji Restoration. The emperor made an official acknowledgment of his line's return to power on January 3, 1868, but the resistant factions of the shogunate, while weakened, hadn't given up just yet. War followed within a few weeks. But with foreign assistance and new weapons, the imperial forces prevailed within eighteen months. Those fighting on the side of preserving the shogunate did have guns, but Emperor Meiji's forces had better guns.

As for the Tom Cruise "sword to a gunfight" stuff, that happened during the Satsuma Rebellion almost a decade later. Disaffected samurai, who had their value to society made obsolete after the modernization of Japan's military, decided to go out in suicidal style in September 1877 with a sword-wielding charge against the modern Imperial Army. It went about as well as you might expect, and the samurai class effectively came to an end.

People are fucking sick. Here is an idea: Let's abuse the shit out of an elephant for the amusement of others, give her over to some drunk asshole of a handler, and when she acts out, we can electrocute her to death and make a movie out of it. Fun!

January 4, 1903

Topsy the elephant was born in the wild around 1875 in Southeast Asia, captured, smuggled into the United States, and proclaimed to be the first elephant born in America. They named her after an enslaved girl character in *Uncle Tom's Cabin,* which was devastatingly appropriate considering that chattel slavery gave people the legal right to murder their enslaved people if they so desired.

Because she was abused, Topsy gained a reputation as a "bad" elephant. Then, in 1902, she killed a spectator. But the fucker was asking for it. James Blount was pissed to the gills and wandered his drunken belligerent ass into the tent where the elephants were tied up. He teased the elephants and threw sand in Topsy's face. Then he burned the sensitive tip of her trunk with a lit cigar. She reacted by throwing him to the ground with her trunk and crushing him. Because fuck that guy.

She'd never killed before, but the newspapers made her out to be a serial murderer of men, proclaiming that she'd already killed a dozen times. Topsy was sold and moved to Coney Island. There were two incidents involving her drunken handler, William Alt, letting her run loose and using her to terrorize a police station. I've been plenty drunk, but I've never been fuck-da-police-elephant-ride-rampage drunk. Anyway, Alt was fired, and the park was all the fuck do we do with her now? They tried to give her away, but no one wanted the poor abused creature. Not even zoos.

Then they said, "Hey, let's kill her and sell tickets!"

They were going to do it via hanging, but the president of the ASPCA said are you fucking kidding? No! They wanted to make sure she didn't suffer too much, or that the execution wouldn't be botched, so they went for the triple threat: electrocution, poison, and strangulation. Fifteen hundred spectators and a hundred photographers and press showed up to the horrid spectacle on January 4, 1903. They fed Topsy a bunch of cyanide-laced carrots, and then hit her with 6,600 volts for ten seconds, which toppled her over. Then a steam-powered winch tightened two nooses around her neck to make sure she was dead.

The Edison Film Company recorded it as a 74-second documentary titled *Electrocuting an Elephant.* Terrible film. Two thumbs down.

In the days before television, public executions were considered great entertainment. Life was mostly misery and suffering anyway, so why not watch some poor bastard who tried to kill the king writhe in agony while getting pulled apart by horses to take your mind off your own horrible shit?

Our would-be-assassin, Robert-François Damiens, nicknamed "Robert the Devil," was forty-two, and had trouble keeping a job due to several instances of misconduct. Looking at his last name, I wonder if the screenwriter for *The Omen* knew the story. Anyway, dude decided to kill King Louis XV on January 5, 1757. With a penknife. It was a pretty pathetic assassination attempt, and many historians surmise that Damiens was dealing with some type of mental illness.

Just outside the Palace of Versailles, Damiens charged past the king's bodyguards (who totally must have sucked at their jobs) just as King Louis was getting into his carriage, and stabbed him in the chest. Being that it was winter, the king's thick clothing stopped most of the thrust and the blade only penetrated Louis's torso by half an inch. After he stabbed the king, Damiens just stood there and said arrest me motherfuckers, and so they did.

The king was a total wimp and thought he was dying, like that kid who had to see the school nurse after getting grazed by a dodgeball. He called for a confessor and when his queen arrived at his side, he begged her forgiveness for all the other women he'd slept with. Good thing she didn't have a knife too, or she might have finished the job.

January 5, 1757

Damiens was taken away for some torturing to get him to name his accomplices, but he said nope it was just me because fuck that king guy. So, they tried him as a regicide, even though the king didn't die, and sentenced him to horrible public execution.

They did all sorts of nasty shit to him while people cheered it on. They crushed his feet, used red-hot pincers, burned him with molten lead and boiling oil, and then, to finish him off, he was quartered. That involves tying each limb to a different horse and whipping them to run, resulting in ripped-off limbs. But it didn't always work that well, and this was one of those times. They had to sever Damiens's tendons and try again to complete the dismemberment. Then his still-living head and torso were burnt at the stake. Ick.

Damiens was the last person in France to be executed in such a manner. Guess it triggered those liberal snowflakes too much.

> **They had to sever Damiens's tendons and try again to complete the dismemberment. Then his still-living head and torso were burnt at the stake. Ick.**

The movement called "Freedom Summer" was a volunteer effort in 1964 to register as many Black people to vote in Mississippi as possible. Of course, there were plenty of alabastards who didn't like that idea. Some didn't like it so much that they turned to murder.

Three men, one of them Black and two of them Jewish, were members of the civil rights group Congress of Racial Equality and had been talking with members of Mount Zion Methodist Church, a Black church in the community of Long-dale that had been burned. The civil rights workers' names were James Chaney, Andrew Goodman, and Michael Schwerner. After they drove away from the church, they were pulled over for speeding and ar-rested. Taken to the jail in Philadelphia, Mississippi, they were held for several hours then released. As they left town in their vehi-cle, they were followed by a posse of cars that included law enforcement.

The cops pulled them over a second time, and this time abducted the three men, drove them to another location, shot them all to death, and buried them. Local law enforce-ment didn't investigate shit, so the FBI got involved to make sure a modicum of justice was done. Eighteen men were alleged to have participated in the crime. Seven of them were convicted. One was deputy sher-iff and KKK member Cecil Price, who served less than five years. None of the seven convicted served more than six years.

Edgar Killen was a KKK member and minister who incited and led the murders. He was arrested after the crime, but his trial resulted in an 11–1 hung jury because one juror said she couldn't convict a preacher. The puddle of pus went on to live as a free man for another four decades. Yet some would not give up on the quest for justice.

Edgar Killen in 1964

A group of people from Neshoba County called the Philadelphia Coalition gathered evidence and lob-bied state lawmakers to reopen the case, and Mis-sissippi attorney general Jim Hood was convinced. On January 6, 2005, Killen was arrested for the mur-ders a second time. The following June 21, forty-one years to the day after the murders, he was con-victed of three counts of manslaughter and sentenced to sixty years' incarceration.

He died in prison in 2018 at the age of ninety-two.

English actor and comedian Stephen Fry's opinion of people being offended is "So fucking what?" Unfortunately, Islamic extremists decided being offended gave them license to murder a dozen employees of a magazine.

French satirical magazine *Charlie Hebdo* has a long history of doing its best to offend. Nothing is sacred. Since its founding in 1960, it has lampooned everything from victims of Covid, to dead children trying to immigrate to France, to Jewish people, to the pope. Its circulation is small, and most people in France consider the magazine extreme or just plain disgusting. But they defend its right to exist cuz freeze peach.

The same opinions are not held by some Islamic extremists. *Charlie Hebdo* claims not to be anti-Islam, but rather anti-extremism. Its writers rightfully go after intolerance, oppression, and violence done in the name of Islam, but in the use of shock value to provoke a reaction and promote their anti-extremist message, they push the limits of France's hate-speech laws.

Although it is not strictly banned by the Quran, many Islamic leaders proclaim that creating images of the prophet Muhammad is blasphemy. In September of 2012 *Charlie Hebdo* published a series of satirical cartoons that depicted Muhammad in unflattering ways. One cartoon showed him nude on all fours with a star over his ass. There was outcry over the publication across the political and religious spectrum. Even President Obama, while not mentioning the magazine specifically, made a condemnation of "those who slander the prophet of Islam" the following week, while addressing the UN.

January 7, 2015

On January 7, 2015, two French Muslim brothers of Algerian descent, whose names I won't acknowledge, entered the Paris headquarters of the magazine and went on a murder spree. They killed a dozen people and wounded eleven others. During the attack the men shouted *"Allahu akbar,"* which is Arabic for "God is great." Over the next three days there were similar attacks across Paris that killed five more people and wounded another eleven. On January 9, the brothers were killed in a shootout with French Armed Forces.

A week after the shooting, *Charlie Hebdo* published "the survivors' issue." Normally the magazine's print run was sixty thousand, but demand was so high that they ended up printing five million copies. Revenue from the issue went toward the families of the victims. After the attack, the phrase *Je suis Charlie* ("I am Charlie") became a rallying cry for freedom of expression.

I'm a bad person, because the deaths of these five men strikes me as rather hilarious. It's the epitome of "fuck around and find out." What these men found out was that a tribe living in isolation in the Ecuadoran rainforest had earned its reputation for violence, and they weren't interested in converting to Christianity. Eat spears, Jesus freaks!

January 8, 1956

The arrogance is just fucking astounding. "Oh, hey. Here is a group of uncontacted people just minding their own fucking business, but we Christian missionaries are totes justified in contacting them because they just *have* to hear about the glorious word of Jesus!"

The missionaries' target was the Huaorani people in the Amazonian region of Ecuador. In the 1950s the Huaorani numbered around six hundred people, divided into three mutually hostile groups. They were known to be cannibals who viciously defended their territory. Sounds like plenty good reason to leave them the fuck alone. But nope, five Christian missionaries from the United States wanted to make first contact and save their souls.

The proselytizing mission was called "Operation Auca." Why was it called that? Because the missionaries were bigoted dicks. "Auca" is a pejorative term for the Huaorani, and is a modification of *awqa,* which is Quechua for "savages."

The five men flew a small plane in tight circles around the tribe while lowering gifts of things like machetes, pots, and clothing. The Huaorani seemed pleased with the gifts and tied their own reciprocal gifts to the rope to give back to sky Santa. This was interpreted as "They are ready to receive the Lord!"

But they weren't receiving shit.

The missionaries landed their plane on a sandbar near the riverbank. They shouted basic Huaorani phrases into the jungle, and three days later four Huaorani showed up and said 'sup. The missionaries offered more presents and even gave one a ride in the plane. Things seemed fine until the guy who went for a plane ride, Nankiwi, started walking back to his tribe with his girlfriend and encountered their fellow tribe members, including the girlfriend's furious brother, who asked, "Where the fuck is your chaperone?" because patriarchal bullshit exists everywhere. And Nankiwi was all oh fuck better think of a lie quick and said, "Those fuckers attacked us and we had to run away and got separated." And the Huaorani said oh well if that's the case let's go fuck their shit up.

And so, on January 8, 1956, the Huaorani killed the five invading Christian evangelists and destroyed their devil sky machine, too. And it taught Christians an important lesson about leaving people alone. Kidding! It made international news and money poured into Christian evangelizing efforts worldwide. And they kept pestering the Huaorani and ended up converting a bunch of them.

Jesus Christ.

The Black Death, now *there* was a plague. Worldwide it killed perhaps as many as 200 million people in only seven years, at a time when humanity had fewer than half a billion people. All that death made people crazy, and angry. So what did they do? They blamed the Jews.

Basel is a nice little city in northwest Switzerland on the banks of the Rhine River. And like most places on the entire goddamn planet, because humans are awful, it has a dark history. In the late twelfth century a small Jewish community formed in Basel. In 1346 the plague began to ravage Europe, and people, being superstitious and hateful idiots, decided it must have been the Jews who were the cause. Antisemitism had been a thing since forever, and Jewish people were always a favorite scapegoat. Across Western Europe a rumor spread that Jewish people were poisoning wells with the plague to kill all the good little Christians. Because . . . reasons?

In December 1348 the plague still had not reached Basel, but the townsfolk decided fuck those Jews and destroyed the Jewish cemetery. Some of the Jewish population then fled, but most remained. On January 9, 1349, a mob formed in Basel and went in search of the Jewish people in their town. They were always easy to find, because in 1215 the pope had decreed that Jews had to wear a yellow badge at all times to identify themselves. Hitler didn't invent that shit.

January 9, 1349

The mob in Basel captured all the Jewish people who remained in the town. They decided not to kill the children, but to kill their heritage by forcefully baptizing them into Christianity and placing them in monasteries. The townsfolk constructed a wooden hut on an island in the Rhine and forced all the adult Jewish people inside, approximately seventy human beings, then set it on fire.

The massacre of Jews in Basel was only one of many such mass murders. A month later in the French city of Strasbourg, about eighty miles north of Basel, several hundred Jewish people met a similar fate.

Jews had nothing to do with the plague. But these medieval fucknuts were way too clueless to understand a bacterium called *Yersinia pestus* that was spread mostly by fleas.

In December 1348 the plague still had not reached Basel, but the townsfolk decided fuck those Jews and destroyed the Jewish cemetery.

The die has been cast." It's a statement that means *Welp, no turning back now. We're committed.* And it's what Julius Caesar said—the die-casting stuff—when he crossed the Rubicon, because doing so was a violation of Roman law. And not today's blank-skinned billionaires raping the environment kind of lawbreaking, but a law that the government actually cared about.

January 10, 49 B.C.E.

What the fuck is a Rubicon? Since many suck at geography: It's a river in Northern Italy. About a half century before Jesus, Caesar was conquering the shit out of Gaul, a region that can be described as "big-ass chunk of Western Europe" but on a modern map is mostly East France/West Germany. Philosopher Plutarch said Caesar's forces killed a million people and enslaved a million more during his Gaul campaign. There may have been some hyperbole with those numbers.

That nice bit of invasion-rape-murder-enslavement complete, Rome said okay Jules, it's time to come home, but leave your army behind. They were pretty fucking explicit about it, because they didn't want some super-popular returning hero doing that returning with a big-ass battle-hardened ultra-loyal military force at his back. Because he might decide to, you know, take over.

The Rubicon River is more like a shallow stream that marked the border of Italy. Caesar was supposed to leave all his bloodthirsty armored dudes with pointy implements of death on the north side of it. But on January 10, 49 B.C.E., he said what the fuck boys why don't you come with me? And they did. He disobeyed a direct order from the Roman Republic and therefore achieved a point of no return and now we have a saying about it.

He didn't bring his entire army, just one legion. He brought it because he feared that without such protection, he would be arrested for the crime of being popular. And the Senate, in alliance with the Roman general Pompey, didn't want him stealing their power. So he brought his legion and stole it anyway.

When they saw Caesar coming with troops at his back, a bunch of senators said "Oh, fuck!" and ran away. A civil war followed, which Julius won, making him the unchallenged military dictator of Rome. He was proclaimed "dictator for life," which the Senate took literally and stabbed the life out of him five years later. Die. Cast.

Imagine this: Your child is in a coma, lying in a hospital ward with several other comatose children. All of them are dying, expected to never wake up. Then three doctors come in and start injecting all the children with a new drug. Suddenly, before the physicians finish treating all the young patients, the first kids to receive the drug begin to wake up.

For most of human history, diabetes was a death sentence. Once a person was diagnosed with Type 1 diabetes, which usually happened in childhood, they had maybe a year or two to live. But a Canadian physician was determined to change that.

Frederick Banting was born in the province of Ontario in 1891. In 1910 he enrolled in a general arts program at the University of Toronto, and they failed his ass. But he said no wait please can I be a doctor instead? And they were all yeah sure I guess, and in 1912 he was accepted into their medical school.

Ten years later, he changed the world.

After serving with distinction as a doctor in World War I, Banting then returned to

Frederick Banting (right) and Charles Best

Toronto to complete his surgical training. He became interested in diabetes after reading an article about the pancreas. He delved into the research, trying to solve the problem of extracting insulin from a pancreas to treat diabetes without destroying the organ during the extraction. How he and his lab assistant Charles Best eventually isolated and extracted insulin is complicated medical shit you can google if you want. For our purposes: They found a way to do it.

January 11, 1922

On January 11, 1922, a fourteen-year-old boy named Leonard Thompson lay dying from Type 1 diabetes. Banting and Best tested their insulin extract—taken from the pancreas of an ox—on the boy, but it was full of impurities and Thompson suffered a severe allergic reaction. They canceled further treatment, and biochemist James Collip worked diligently to purify the insulin extract over the next several days. Physiology professor J. J. R. Macleod, whose lab was used for the experiments, also helped with the process.

A second, purified dose was injected into Thompson on January 23, with amazing results (insulin would keep him alive another thirteen years, until pneumonia took his life at age twenty-six). The following year, Banting and Macleod were awarded a Nobel Prize. Banting shared his winnings with Best, and Macleod subsequently shared his with Collip. They sold the patent for insulin to the University of Toronto.

The price? One dollar.

It was a historically stupid speech that nearly ruined Abraham Lincoln's political career, and instead somehow led to him becoming president. The war with Mexico was won and everyone was all "America fuck yeah" and junior congressman Abe was "Fuck no, that was a shitty thing to do" and other people were all "Shut the fuck up Abe, let us have this."

January 12, 1848

Some called it "Polk's War," named after President Polk, who wanted some of that sweet Mexican territory to make more 'Murica. The official name of the conflict, north of the border, is the Mexican-American War. South of the border they have different opinions and call it the "U.S. intervention in Mexico." Whatever you call it, between 1845 and 1848 the United States bit off some big chunks of Mexico and said this shit is ours now.

On January 12, 1848, the war was all but over. Most Americans were planning victory celebrations. Then wet-behind-the-ears Congressman Lincoln stood up and gave a blistering antiwar renunciation of President Polk, referring to the war as "unnecessary" and "unconstitutional" and "half insane." In his lengthy tirade he referred to Polk as "a bewildered, confounded, and miserably perplexed man."

The general response was "Fuck you, Abe." One historian proclaimed that the speech "cast him into the political wilderness." That ended up being a good thing for Lincoln, since the early 1850s were a poop storm of political fuckery as the country grew more divided on the issue of slavery. While political careers were being murdered to death over the keeping of humans as property, Lincoln was off in the corner licking his wounds and staying pretty invisible and therefore insulated from it all.

In the 1850s, when he reemerged as a leader, the experience of being outcast taught Lincoln that he should not only be moralistic, but also pragmatic. This combination of events and education helped take him to the White House and preserve the Union in the face of secession by traitorous states over the matter of thinking skin tone was a reason to deny a person their freedom.

Abraham Lincoln in 1846

Country singer Johnny Cash cultivated a bad-boy image, and was so good at it that many thought he was a hardened criminal who did time behind bars. He was a guest at a few different prisons, but always as a performer, not an inmate. And while prison destroys many lives, it was a performance at California's Folsom Prison that saved Cash.

Cash wrote the song "Folsom Prison Blues" in 1955 after watching a documentary about the place, and had pondered the idea of recording a performance at a prison. But it was the 1950s and people were really fucking uptight, so it was another thirteen years before the album finally happened. And when it did, ol' Johnny was circling the drain.

Like a lot of musicians, Cash was frequently drunk and drugged up. He popped uppers and downers like they were Skittles (except those wouldn't exist until 1974). In 1965 he was on a fishing trip and was so baked off his ass, he started a campfire that burned down five hundred acres of California forest. Cash blamed it on his truck's exhaust system.

He never spent more than a night in jail, for various misdemeanors, but he nurtured the outlaw narrative. He'd played prisons before, including Folsom, but never recorded it. On January 13, 1968, he performed for some actual outlaws at Folsom and turned out a live album.

January 13, 1968

At the time of the recording, his addictions were spiraling out of control, his record label was threatening to punt his ass, and he was considering taking his own life. But Folsom turned things around. He performed two shows that became the sixteen-track *Johnny Cash at Folsom Prison.* The following year he did another live prison album, *Johnny Cash at San Quentin.* Both albums hit #1 on the *Billboard* country chart.

Afterward, Cash would become a champion for prison reform. He continued to battle his addictions, but with the help of his new wife, June Carter, whom he married just six weeks after the Folsom show, and his strong faith, his career flourished for decades. June Carter Cash died in 2003, and Johnny followed her four months later.

> But it was the 1950s and people were really fucking uptight, so it was another thirteen years before the album finally happened. And when it did, ol' Johnny was circling the drain.

The event that launched the "Summer of Love" was the Human Be-In, which is an almost-clever play on words that probably could have used some corporate communications tweaking, but the organizers were all about "fuck that neoliberal capitalist bullshit." The happening was held in San Francisco's Golden Gate Park on January 14, 1967, and smelled of incense, marijuana, and unwashed hippie.

January 14, 1967

Fired Harvard psychologist–slash–space cadet pretending to be profound "neuronaut" Timothy Leary was there, and probably stoned out of his mind. So was poet Allen Ginsberg, *Howl*ing about capitalism and conformity. Comedian Dick Gregory made people laugh about how fucking racist America was (I mean, still is). Jerry Rubin was there too, one of the Chicago Seven in that Netflix movie. Bands present included Jefferson Airplane, the Grateful Dead, as well as Santana and the Steve Miller Band. Two years later Steve wrote about space cowboys, which makes sense.

Anyway, Reagan was the new governor of California and it should surprise no one that the husband of Mrs. Just Say No did not like

hippies. This be-in was a counterculture statement at a time when the stodgy white mainstream had little tolerance. Leary was facing a potential thirty-year prison term for a tiny amount of pot, and two other speakers, poet Lenore Kandel and playwright Michael McClure, had recently been arrested on obscenity charges.

What made this be-in such a big deal was the massive crowd. About 30,000 showed up, by far the largest gathering ever for such an event. The media kind of freaked out. Like, what the fuck is going on? These people should be getting haircuts and going to church and getting married and having missionary-position sex once a week and only taking amphetamines and barbiturates properly prescribed by their cigarette-smoking doctor. Don't forget to mix with alcohol and vote for Nixon.

The Human Be-In spread a message of peace and love and civil rights, and it took off. The resulting Summer of Love got national attention; it was of course exploited and sensationalized to the point that by the fall, hippies themselves proclaimed the "Death of the Hippie" in order to get the media to stop covering it. They even held a mock funeral in Haight-Ashbury on October 6. Bummer, man.

Her name was Elizabeth Short. She was an aspiring actress who was brutally murdered in Los Angeles when she was only twenty-two. The media gave her the nickname "Black Dahlia," and despite there being more than 150 suspects, no one was ever arrested for the crime. It remains one of the most famous unsolved murders in American history.

Elizabeth was born in 1924 in Boston, and when she was six her father, having lost all his money in the 1929 stock market crash, abandoned his car on the Charlestown Bridge. It was assumed he had taken his own life by jumping into the river. When Short was eighteen, her mother received a letter of apology from her father, saying he'd not killed himself but had started a new life in California. His daughter, not imagining that a guy who deserted a wife and his five girls might be a piece of shit, traveled there to live with him. Big surprise, the happy reunion didn't last long, and she moved out soon after.

She moved around, was engaged to an Air Commando who died in a plane crash five days before the war with Japan ended, and then landed in L.A. to try her hand at acting. She had been working as a waitress to support herself, and living on Hollywood Boulevard for six months, when her mutilated body was found on January 15, 1947, in Leimert Park. She wasn't just mutilated, but cut completely in half at the waist. Yikes.

There are a lot of other grisly details you

Elizabeth Short in 1947

can google, but I'll only share that the poor woman's body had been washed and "posed" by the murderer. Although no semen was present, there was evidence of rape. The nickname Black Dahlia came from a pharmacy owner who said that's how the male customers referred to her.

January 15, 1947

The media shitstorm by the Hearst-owned newspaper *Los Angeles Examiner* was disgusting. They phoned Short's mother in Boston and said that her daughter had won a beauty contest, in order to wring information out of her for their scoop. The *Examiner* and another Hearst paper, the *Herald-Express,* slut-shamed Short and falsely characterized her as a woman who prowled Hollywood Boulevard for sex.

A week later, the killer taunted the *Examiner* by mailing them items including Short's birth certificate, and two months later an alleged suicide note was found tucked into some men's clothing near the ocean. The note claimed responsibility for the murder, but there was no evidence of its veracity. Over the years, hundreds of men have claimed to be the killer. Many hypotheses have been generated, with a physician named George Hodel becoming a prime suspect after his death, but there's no certainty about who killed Elizabeth Short.

What kind of shit do you have to pull to get "the Terrible" added to your name, especially in Russia, where their rulers aren't exactly known for their sunny dispositions? Here is the story of some nasty shit that Ivan did.

Ivan IV Vasilyevich was only three when his dad, the Grand Prince of Moscow, ate his last bowl of borscht. Ivan didn't do much other than have toddler tantrums for a bit, but when he was sixteen, his council proclaimed the Tsardom of Russia with Ivan as first-ever tsar. He was crowned on January 16, 1547. (That date is in the Gregorian calendar, which Russia didn't use yet, but never mind that.)

Ivan the Terrible and his son

The translation from Russian of his nickname *"Ivan Grozny"* isn't the best. It's not "terrible" as in "holy fucking shit, Trump was a terrible president." It's more about inspiring fear and obedience through the wielding of power. Ivan got the moniker because he was considered formidable in some ways and shitty in others.

The word "tsar" is derived from the Latin *Caesar,* meaning "emperor." As tsar of all Russia, Ivan sought to establish an empire by expanding Russia to include non-Slavic states. As was common in pretty much all of world history, there was famine and plague and Russia got its ass kicked in some wars, and that didn't do much to improve Ivan's disposition. After his wife was (probably) murdered, Ivan was additionally pissed and used his newly created secret police to take revenge, killing and exiling some of the nobility. It was that police force—loyal only to him—and the centralization of power that would be his lasting legacy.

It had to be, because he killed the other legacy. He beat his pregnant daughter-in-law, the wife of his oldest son and heir, and killed the child she was carrying. When his son was all "Hey Dad what the fuck?" he beat his son to death as well. That left his younger son Feodor in charge when Ivan died at the age of fifty-three. Feodor was a total fucking putz who died childless, launching what is called the "Time of Troubles" in Russia. The next century was a fucktacular shitnado of ass for Russia, a period of anarchy and lawlessness finally rectified after Peter the Great became tsar in 1682.

Her name was Lili'uokalani, and she was queen regnant of the Hawaiian Islands. That is, until the United States decided the islands, with their beautiful sunsets and amazing beaches, were a little too fine to be left to self-rule, and stole them in a coup d'état.

Born in 1838, she became queen in 1891 when her brother died. Then she had the audacity to examine this thing called "the Bayonet Constitution," which had been forced on her brother and her nation in 1887 to give a bunch of power to American and European elites living in Hawai'i, and she said, "This is some major fucking bullshit."

And it was. It was named after an implement of death because they threatened to murder her brother if he didn't adopt it. And it disenfranchised two-thirds of the native Hawaiian population of their right to vote. Lili'uokalani proposed a new constitution that would bring back power to the monarchy and the general Hawaiian population by restoring their voting ability. The people were all "That's totally awesome. Please do it!"

Queen Regnant Lili'uokalani of Hawai'i

But the wealthy foreigners and native elites who made their living exploiting Hawai'i and her people were hellbent on stopping this reform. So they said "Fuck no" and formed a "Committee of Safety," which was a fancy term for "Protect the Rich People."

And those loyal to Queen Lili'uokalani responded by forming their own "No, fuck *you*" committee and gave some speeches to a couple thousand people in the palace square saying hey the queen is awesome and we love her, and the people cheered that shit.

January 17, 1893

Then the elites said, "Fuck this, it's coup time" and they called out, "'Murica, li'l help?" And 'Murica was all "Oh yeah, we love to steal islands," as they would prove in places like Samoa, the Philippines, Puerto Rico, Guam, and many other places. President Grover Cleveland authorized the loan of a bunch of Marines and sailors from the USS *Boston,* which was moored nearby purely by coincidence, I'm sure, to march around and be all intimidating. The royalists were all well shit that's an assload of guns they got I guess we're boned, and they gave up. Queen Lili'uokalani was deposed as monarch on January 17, 1893.

Two years later there was a rebellion to restore her to power, but it failed and Lili'uokalani abdicated her throne in order to save the lives of her supporters who had been sentenced to death. She was sentenced to five years' hard labor for the rebellion, but it was commuted to imprisonment in the palace; she received a pardon the following year. Hawai'i was annexed by the United States in 1898 and became a state in 1959.

And that's the story of how Americans got a place where they could travel to surf and drink mai tais and harass sea turtles without needing a passport.

Seriously, don't touch the fucking sea turtles.

You know how in some movies about grand battles there is a challenge between leaders to single combat to settle it without thousands having to die? That pretty much never happens. One account said it did actually happen in 1593, between the king of Siam and the crown prince of Burma, but other historians called bullshit. Still, the clash was a big deal as far as battles go, and one of those two guys *did* die in it. On a fucking elephant, no less.

In 1590, Naresuan became king of the Ayutthaya Kingdom, which was a precursor to modern Thailand, which used to be called Siam. Mingyi Swa was heir apparent of Burma (now called Myanmar), and he led three invasions of Siam during his life. The last one killed him. Thanks a lot, Dad.

Yeah, it was Mingyi's father, King Nanda, who told him to invade Siam yet again. And so he did, in November 1592. Part of their arsenal for making war, on both sides, involved fighting atop elephants. It was a sixteenth-century arms race, I guess. "They have elephants? We need elephants. We must not allow an elephant gap!"

Anyway, the romanticized Thai version is that on January 18, 1593, the Siamese were

> **Most historians proclaim that the epic throwdown "accept my fucking challenge" formal duel never actually happened.**

facing certain death and so Naresuan said to Mingyi in an act of desperation: You and me throw down, motherfucker. And Mingyi said: Bring it, ya Siamese fucknut. And they fought atop their elephants, which would probably much rather have been eating grass, and both armies just stopped killing each other to watch shit go down.

As the story goes, Mingyi hit Naresuan with his spear/sword thing (a "glaive") in the head, but his helmet took the blow. Then Naresuan cleaved Mingyi through the shoulder and he died. Historically, all we know is that Mingyi died that day, possibly from a bullet or a mortar round. Or maybe it was ten days earlier. The Burmese say it happened on January 8. Whatever, it happened. Maybe.

Most historians proclaim that the epic throwdown "accept my fucking challenge" formal duel never actually happened. After the battle, Naresuan and the Siamese forces were in retreat, because they'd been losing. The likely scenario is that after retreating, they learned of Mingyi's death and said hey let's hold back and see what happens now that their leader is taking a dirt nap. That was wise, because with Mingyi's death the Burmese were bummed and fucked off back home.

The victory of Naresuan over Mingyi is why Thailand celebrates January 18 as Royal Thai Armed Forces Day.

When President Ford pardoned Nixon in 1974, a lot of people said, "Really, dude? Fuck that guy." Ford tried to make up for it, a little, by pardoning the infamous radio broadcaster "Tokyo Rose" on his last full day in office.

Her real name was Iva Toguri, and her radio handle was "Orphan Ann." The name Tokyo Rose predated her broadcasts; it was the moniker given by Allied troops to *all* English-speaking female radio personalities who broadcast Japanese propaganda as part of their "psychological warfare." But because of her trial and imprisonment, Toguri came to epitomize the Tokyo Rose handle.

She was born in Los Angeles in 1916, the daughter of Japanese immigrants, and attained a degree in zoology from UCLA in 1940. In 1941 she sailed to Japan to visit a sick relative, but when she tried to come home Pearl Harbor had happened, and the United States said, "Nope, not you. No Japanese allowed." It didn't matter that she was FUCKING BORN THERE.

Iva Toguri at Radio Tokyo, 1944

Japan was a dick to her as well. They told her to renounce her American citizenship. She refused and they said, "Fine, you're an enemy alien then." Since they already considered her the enemy, she embraced the role and smuggled food to starving Allied POWs. Speaking of which, POWs were often forced to broadcast propaganda. Toguri wasn't forced, but she needed work to survive, so when asked to be a broadcaster for the *Zero*

Hour radio show, she agreed. However, she refused to broadcast anti-American propaganda, and she fucking didn't.

January 19, 1977

That didn't save Toguri from getting sent to prison after the war, though. After Japan's surrender, she was detained in Yokohama by the U.S. military for a year, and eventually released when they determined her broadcasts to be "innocuous." Yet when she tried to return to the United States, a bunch of Americans freaked out. The FBI decided to screw her over to appease the racists. In 1949 they charged her with eight counts of treason. She was found guilty of one count and served more than six years of a ten-year sentence. As part of the conviction, they also yanked her U.S. citizenship. Again: BORN THERE!

In 1976 the *Chicago Tribune* investigated and discovered the FBI and the U.S. occupation police had coached the primary witnesses against Toguri. The witnesses had been threatened with charges of treason if they didn't cooperate, so they perjured themselves at her trial to secure a conviction. That story led to President Ford's pardon on January 19, 1977, which also restored her citizenship. Iva Toguri died in Chicago in 2006 at age ninety.

Before Emperor Theodosius proclaimed Christianity to be the official state religion of the Roman Empire in 380, Roman emperors were not so welcoming of the followers of Jesus. In 250 Emperor Decius decided some persecution of Christians was in order, and one of the first people killed was the pope.

January 20, 250

Decius had been emperor for a few months when he decided there weren't enough people kissing his imperial ass. He wanted his subjects to pledge a loyalty oath that was sanctified by the polytheistic Roman religion rather than the monotheistic Christian belief system. Decius said they had to burn some smelly shit and sacrifice some poor critter to the Roman gods in front of an image of the emperor, or else.

For once, Jews weren't the target. Julius Caesar had proclaimed Judaism a "permitted religion," so they got a bye on wringing some chicken's neck over incense praise be to the pantheon shit. But fuck those Christians. We're gonna make them do this ritual and loyalty oath that has to be witnessed by a Roman magistrate and get a certificate saying they did it and holy shit you thought vaccine mandates were bad. (Side note: Vaccine mandates are good and only necessary because of all the anti-vaccine fuckwaffles so get the fucking shots.)

The Christian faith prohibited them from doing this ritual because "Thou shalt have no other gods before me. I'm a petty jealous beyotch god and you better be monogamous in your monotheism. Also, none of that graven image shit or I'll wreck your shit." And so, many refused.

Then the killing started.

You won't do the loyalty oath to exalted Emperor Decius? You sure about that? We Romans practically invented creative ways to make people die. The very real threat of imminent execution had lots of Christians saying screw it I don't wanna die I'll do your ritual. Many others fled, but a lot stuck around and stuck to their Jesus guns and paid the price. Some were executed, some died in prison. We don't know how many. One of the first to die was Pope Fabian, on January 20, 250. It is uncertain if he died via execution or in prison. I mean, the whole Decian persecution had just begun and if it was in prison then he went off to the great popely beyond pretty damn fast so it's likely someone hastened his earthly departure in one way or another.

Wasn't all bad for the guy. He got to be a martyr and the Church made him a saint and he got a feast day and everything.

It's unknown how many Christians apostatized to save their own asses, but it was a lot, so many that there ended up being a backlog for those who wanted the "please don't kill me" certificate. They were shunned by the faithful, but who can blame them? Things were about to get worse for Christians in the Roman Empire before they got better, but that's another tale.

> **Wasn't all bad for the guy. He got to be a martyr and the Church made him a saint and he got a feast day and everything.**

"**G**rab them by the pussy," he said. When Trump won the presidency in 2016 by negative three million votes, a lot of women were righteously pissed. Not all women. Some believed Trump was their kind of guy, their Jaundiced Jesus. But plenty others were angry, and the day after his inauguration they took to the streets.

In 2016, 39 percent of women voters cast their ballot for the blatant misogynist with a couple dozen sexual assault and rape accusations against him. While 47 percent of white women voted for him, the average percentage was pulled down by Hispanic women's 28 percent support and Black women, whose support for Trump was so fucking low it didn't even register as a single percentage point.

The Women's March took place on January 21, 2017, but its planning began on the saddest day of 2016, the day after that pumpkin pustule won the electoral college. On November 9, retired lawyer Teresa Shook created a Facebook event for a march on Washington, and within a day hundreds of thousands of people said fuck yes we need to let that semi-sentient skin disease know just what we think of him and his bullshit. The massive level of interest became the impetus for organizing the Women's March, with the involvement of numerous activists.

It wasn't dubbed an "anti-Trump" march. At least, not technically. One leader, Linda Sarsour, proclaimed it was "a stand on social justice and human rights issues ranging from race, ethnicity, gender, religion, immigration and healthcare." Put that way, it sure sounds like an anti-Trump march. He hates that stuff.

January 21, 2017

The Washington march had almost half a million attendees. Vice President Kamala Harris, then senator of California, and Senator Tammy Duckworth spoke, as did several celebrities, and for some reason people thought inviting Michael Moore was a good idea. Across the rest of the country about 5 million people marched. Worldwide marches tallied up another few million. People around the world were fucking pissed that this guy was now president, and rightfully so.

It needs to be mentioned that originator Teresa Shook accused four of the march's leaders, including Sarsour, of antisemitism and called for them to step down. Shook ended up dissociating herself from the march.

Nevertheless, the marches on that day sent a powerful message that there were a lot of people who weren't pleased with Trump and would not tolerate his presidency a day longer than necessary. And many of those people showed up to vote him out in 2020.

Three decades prior to playing the best Scrooge ever, alongside a bunch of Muppets, Michael Caine starred as a young officer in the 1964 film *Zulu,* which tells the tale of the Battle of Rorke's Drift in somewhat accurate detail. That detail being that a small number of men with guns in a fortified position can hold off thousands of enemy soldiers bearing only spears and flimsy shields.

January 22, 1879

In 1879, Britain was doing its thing invading places that didn't belong to them and the Zulu warriors were less than pleased. On January 22 at midday, 20,000 Zulu attacked 1,800 British troops (and their African auxiliaries) in what would later be called South Africa, and massacred the fuck out of them in the Battle of Isandlwana. The Brits were overwhelmed because they were caught in the open and they couldn't set up a defensive perimeter, and about three-quarters of them did the dirt nap. Most of the survivors were from the auxiliaries. Fewer than half a dozen Europeans lived to colonize another day.

The Battle of Rorke's Drift began later the same day. This time, the Brits knew they were going to be attacked and had time to prepare their fortification at the mission station they occupied.

The clash was 150 British defenders vs. close to 4,000 Zulus. It was a brutal engagement that lasted through the night, into early morning. Although, let's be honest; it was the Zulus who were defending their homeland. Fuck colonialism.

It is difficult to describe the chaos, which is why I mention the movie, because it delivers a good representation of the scene. Zulus considered the rifle to be "the weapon of a coward." Instead, they charged into death wielding their spears toward the British lines again and again and again, only to be shot down repeatedly. I'm not sure bravery is the right word to describe that.

By the morning of the 23rd, the Zulus had left the field. The battle left 351 Zulu dead, and approximately 500 wounded. It is rumored that most of the Zulu wounded left behind were then murdered by the British as payback for Isandlwana. One trooper's account proclaimed, "We were very bitter and did not spare wounded Zulus." The defenders at Rorke's Drift had only 17 killed, and 15 wounded.

For those at home in England, in the wake of the massive defeat at Isandlwana, it was important to proclaim as heroes the defenders of Rorke's Drift, to perpetuate the idea of the superiority of the British soldier. As a result, a whopping eleven Victoria Crosses (the highest award in the British military system) were given out to soldiers who fought there. In the aftermath, the British took the Zulu much more seriously as a foe and sent a far more heavily reinforced second invasion that led to a decisive defeat of the Zulu, enabling Britain to fuck over yet another portion of Africa for decades to come.

Have you ever wondered what might be the single deadliest day in world history? It was a whopper, shattering, quite literally, every other recording of deadly days for us mostly hairless bipeds by a wide margin. If you were in the province of Shaanxi in China on January 23, 1556, then it sucked to be you.

The cause was the motherfucker of all earthquakes. Its epicenter was in the Wei River Valley, but it destroyed an area over five hundred miles in diameter, killing approximately 60 percent of the population in that region. The death toll resulted in part from the type of dwelling that people in the area lived in. Called a *yaodong,* it is still popular today in China. *Yaodongs* are part cave, part house, carved out of a hillside. During the earthquake, many of these collapsed and crushed or suffocated those inside.

It is believed that 830,000 people died.

Modern estimates put the quake at an 8.0 or higher on the Richter scale. In addition to collapsing homes, it caused massive landslides. Mountains and rivers moved. New hills were formed, and others fell. There have been many more powerful earthquakes in history, but this one hit a densely populated area filled with homes that were easily destroyed, resulting in the terrible toll.

January 23, 1556

And being that Christians are so tolerant and understanding (sarcasm), a Portuguese friar of the Dominican order named Gaspar da Cruz visited China later in the year and said that the earthquake was a punishment for their sins. He wrote that the Chinese were guilty of "a filthy abomination, which is that they are so given to the accursed sin of unnatural vice." Basically, the Chinese had sex in a way that he, and supposedly Jesus, didn't approve of, and so the Lord sent a mighty shaking of the earth in his rage over some anal and oral sex.

A month later there was a great comet that flew over Europe. Da Cruz saw it as a sign of more bad shit to come for the world, including the birth of the Antichrist, probably because people were doing it in the butt too much.

There have been many more powerful earthquakes in history, but this one hit a densely populated area filled with homes that were easily destroyed, resulting in the terrible toll.

Film critic Roger Ebert called the 1979 film *Caligula* "sickening" and a "travesty." Thing is, the actual reign of Roman emperor Caligula was both those things and much worse. That's why his own Praetorian Guards said "Fuck this guy" and killed his ass less than four years after he took power.

January 24, 41

"Caligula" was a nickname; it references a diminutive soldier's boot. He got the moniker because as a child he accompanied his father on campaigns in Germania and liked to dress in miniature versions of soldier's attire. His real name was Gaius Julius Caesar, after a famous relative of his you may have heard of.

Being a Roman noble did not always come with a long life expectancy, because of all the murderous political fuckery, and almost everyone in Caligula's family got snuffed. But the lad ingratiated himself to his grandfather Tiberius, the Roman Emperor, and was spared. He didn't return the favor, however. When Tiberius was seventy-seven, which was way fucking old for ancient times, Caligula got tired of waiting for Grandpa to croak and got his friend Macro, head of the

The Assassination of the Emperor Caligula

Praetorian Guard, to accelerate his departure into the next life. Probably.

Caligula took the throne in March of the year 37 at age twenty-four and wow was he a dick. Not at first. People loved him, but the honeymoon was short-lived. Six months into his reign he fell ill, possibly due to poison, and emerged from his sickness a murderous motherfucker.

He executed a bunch of people without trial, including several senators, and even forced his old friend Macro to commit suicide when he imagined he might not be completely loyal. He killed for fun and spent money like a drunken sailor on shore leave, triggering both a financial crisis and a famine. He claimed to be a god and fucked/raped other men's wives, then bragged about it.

Tired of his shit, on January 24, 41 A.D., a group of Praetorian Guards, with the blessing of the Senate, went repeatedly stabby on Caligula, bringing his short reign of terror to an end. They also killed his wife and one-year-old daughter. The Senate then wanted to restore the republic that Julius Caesar had ended, but the Praetorians were all haha nope and installed Caligula's uncle Claudius as emperor the same day. Comparatively speaking, Claudius was a pretty good ruler.

People don't usually receive the nickname "Butcher" without earning it, and Idi Amin definitely earned "Butcher of Uganda," killing as many as half a million of his own people during his reign as "president."

We have British colonialism to thank for teaching Amin how to kill, as he joined the Colonial Army in 1946. As a cook. Well, not even a cook, an assistant cook. The following year he was transferred to an infantry unit as a private and saw plenty of action, working his way up the ranks as high as they would permit someone with his skin color, which was warrant officer. In 1962, when Uganda achieved independence, he began his meteoric rise to the top of their military, eventually attaining the rank of field marshal. His military nickname was "the Machete."

In 1965 he and the prime minister, Milton Obote, were investigated in an "arms for ivory" deal with the Congo and rather than atone, they decided "Fuck it. We're in charge now." Obote declared himself executive president, and Amin's forces attacked the palace and sent the sitting president into exile.

But Amin and Obote's friendship didn't last. Half a dozen years later Amin decided I'm the one with the loyal army, so fuck Obote. On January 25, 1971, he staged a coup and Obote fled to Tanzania. Amin established military rule and declared himself High Overlord of Everything aka You Mess with Me You Die. He also fucked around a lot, having at least six wives and over forty children.

January 25, 1971

He ruled by decree. Amin basically got what he wanted, and what he wanted was murder. He purged Obote supporters from the military and massacred ethnic groups he felt didn't support his regime. He murdered journalists and educators and preachers and bureaucrats and lawyers and judges and students and . . . anyone he surmised was the remotest threat. Many of the slain were ignobly disposed of in the Nile River. And yet, he proclaimed, "I am the hero of Africa." He also praised Hitler and had one-liners like "You cannot run faster than a bullet."

After eight years and half a million murders, he picked a fight with Tanzania and they fought back, with the help of Ugandan exiles, ousting him from power. The following year the exiled Obote was returned to power in a (probably rigged) election, and Amin lived the rest of his life in Saudi Arabia, expressing no remorse for what he'd done.

Being that it was born six centuries after Christianity, we know a fair bit of the real history of how Islam began, and there was quite a bit of death involved. Not that Christianity hasn't had its share of killing, it's just that for the early days of Islam there was better record-keeping on who was snuffed and when than there was for Christianity.

January 26, 661

Muhammad the prophet, the founder of Islam, died in 632, and there was immediate fuckery following his death that eventually led to the Sunni-Shia split within the religion, based around an argument over which Muslim sect should be in charge.

Abu Bakr was the first caliph (head theocrat). His followers later became known as Sunnis, and he was popular. And that's partly why today 85 percent of Muslims are Sunni. After he died a couple years into his caliphate, there were two more Sunni caliphs and their reigns lasted over a decade apiece but were both ended via assassination. The first three caliphs are viewed as "nah forget those guys" by Shia Muslims. The fourth caliph, beginning in 656, was Ali, who had also begun the Shia branch back when Muhammad died in 632. Yeah, I know. It's confusing. Anyway, he reigned as caliph for five years, during which time there was a civil war within Islam between Sunni and Shia. Ali too was assassinated, on January 26, 661. That killing is what is known in history as a Big Fucking Deal, as it furthered the animosity between Sunni and Shia, contributing to an irrevocable schism. Iran and Iraq had a war 1,300 years later that killed a million people due in part to this division.

Technical clarification: Ali was stabbed with a poisoned sword on January 26 while at prayer but didn't actually die until a couple of days later. Ali is considered a martyr by Shia Muslims. See the aforementioned Big Fucking Deal.

After the assassination, the followers of Ali proclaimed his son Hasan the new caliph, but after six months Hasan decided he'd rather not die the way the previous three caliphs did, so he signed a peace treaty and abdicated, getting a nice cash settlement for doing so. Hasan then went off to be head Imam of the Shia. He still got assassinated though, by his wife. She poisoned him nine years later, allegedly after receiving a healthy bribe from Sunni leader Mu'awiyah, the guy Hasan abdicated to in 661. It's believed Mu'awiyah ordered the assassination because he was getting old and worried Hasan might prevent Mu'awiyah's son from becoming the next caliph.

If actuaries existed in the seventh century, I expect they'd proclaim caliph a high-risk occupation.

> **Hasan then went off to be head Imam of the Shia. He still got assassinated though, by his wife.**

Did Covid make it feel like your life was under siege? You don't know siege. Leningrad in World War II was a fucking siege. It was the deadliest siege the world has ever known, and if you were there, you were in what historians refer to as the "wrong fucking place at the wrong fucking time."

It began on September 8, 1941, and ended 872 days later on January 27, 1944. The in-between time could teach things that suck how to suck. It was the Eastern Front of WWII, Germany vs. Soviets.

There have been longer sieges, but not more brutal ones. At the beginning of the siege there were 2.5 million people living in Leningrad, but by the time it was over, more than a million of them would be dead, mostly due to starvation. It was no picnic for the German attackers either, as they suffered more than half a million casualties.

Some historians classify the siege as a purposeful genocide, which we know Nazis had no problem with, as starvation was weaponized by Germany to take as many civilian lives as possible. It wasn't just starvation that killed civilians; the Germans also used artillery and aerial bombardment. This indirectly contributed to the starvation, as early in the siege bombardments hit food warehouses (with incendiary bombs, because of course), and the subsequent fires burned up most of the stored food.

January 27, 1944

Food rationing was strict, money was irrelevant. People ate their pets and the animals in the zoo. Old leather was boiled and eaten. Fellow human beings were eaten. But it could have been worse. Leningrad has the Baltic Sea on the west side, and Lake Ladoga on the east. During the winter, the Soviet Red Army was able to keep supplies flowing into Leningrad across the frozen lake, and via boats in the warmer months. They called it the Road of Life. It wasn't enough, but it was something.

The almost two-and-a-half-year-long Siege of Leningrad finally ended when Soviet forces broke the German containment. It was the single largest loss of life in a modern city. It wasn't just those living in the city that died. Over a million people were evacuated early in the siege, mostly women and children, and many of them died from bombardment and starvation as they fled.

So maybe don't complain so much about how your social life took a hit due to Covid.

The Siege of Leningrad, 1942

In times of horror, when others lose their humanity, some people hold on to decency and compassion like a lifeline, even though it may cost them their own lives. Such is the case of Roddie Edmonds, an American prisoner of war who refused to identify the Jews imprisoned with him during World War II. With a Nazi officer holding a gun to his head and demanding he single out Jewish POWs, Edmonds said, "We are all Jews here."

January 28, 1945

Edmonds enlisted early in 1941, several months before the United States was even at war. And by late December 1944 he was a master sergeant leading green troops into Germany right when the bad guys launched their massive counterattack, the Battle of the Bulge. His troops had no chance and were quickly overwhelmed and taken captive.

Edmonds was the highest-ranking non-commissioned officer in the POW camp Stalag IX-A, and the German commandant told him that the next morning he was to order only the Jewish prisoners among them to go outside for the morning's assembly. The war was nearing its end and the Germans knew they were going to lose, but these Nazi crapnapkins still wanted to murder as many Jews as they could before it was done.

Rather than comply, Edmonds decided to say eat shit, you assbasket Nazi latrine of a person. On the morning of January 28, 1945, Edmonds ordered all of the camp's 1,275 prisoners to assembly. The commandant was pissed. Despite being threatened with immediate execution if he didn't identify the Jewish soldiers, Edmonds would not relent. The commandant then threatened to execute everyone, and Edmonds told him dude, if you do that, you're gonna be in major deep poo after the war. The commandant backed down in the face of Edmonds's defiance.

There were about two hundred Jewish prisoners in the camp whose lives Roddie Edmonds saved that day, and he told no one.

He fought again in Korea, and lived an otherwise unassuming life, dying in 1985 at the age of sixty-five. Many years later, his son Chris Edmonds began to dig into his father's history. He discovered witness statements given to Yad Vashem, Israel's memorial to victims of the Holocaust, telling of his father's heroism. Through Chris's efforts, in 2015 Roddie Edmonds was declared Righteous Among the Nations, Israel's top honor for non-Jews who saved Jewish people from the Holocaust. In 2016, President Obama lauded Edmonds in a speech in Israel.

"I think he just had a good sense of right and wrong," Chris Edmonds said of his father. Goddamn right he did.

It's true. Coca-Cola *did* have cocaine in it. Sort of.

Created and named in 1886 by John Pemberton, the recipe for Coke was sold for $2,300 to American business tycoon Asa Candler, who incorporated the Coca-Cola Company on January 29, 1892. And if you thought merely putting cocaine in the product was bad, I got news for you. A lot of people have died from the cocaine business, but also because of the Coke business, and not just from obesity.

The product took its name from two of its "medicinal" ingredients: extracts of coca leaves and kola nuts; coca leaves for the cocaine + kola nuts for the caffeine = bounce you off the goddamn walls. Although, even at its peak, it didn't contain a lot of cocaine: about a fifth of a line that you'd snort, if you're into that sort of thing. In 1903 the amount of cocaine in the drink dropped to a "mere trace," and it was eliminated completely in 1929.

The company line is that the product *never* contained cocaine, which is technically true. It had an *ingredient*—the coca leaves—that just happened to contain cocaine. So . . . semantics.

The addition of coca leaves is just a drop in the central-nervous-system stimulant bucket. In the 1990s, a Coca-Cola bottling plant in Colombia allegedly hired death squads to kill its own employees for trying to unionize. The same thing (allegedly) happened at a Coke plant in Guatemala, which has a long (alleged) history of company violence against its employees, with incidents as recent as 2010. There are also accusations of worker rights violations in Turkey and Russia. These are independently owned bottling plants, but you gotta take some responsibility for what's done in your name to sell your product.

January 29, 1892

There are regions in Mexico that have almost no running water because the local Coca-Cola plant is using up most of it. With no water, the inhabitants drink Coke, and their rates of obesity and diabetes have skyrocketed. It takes three gallons of water to make one gallon of Coke. The company has been accused of sucking up water supplies internationally, having a negative impact on communities and farms the world over.

This is the tip of the sugar-water iceberg. There is a rabbit hole you can go down that's full of accusations of anti-competition practices, shady advertising, complicity with South Africa's apartheid, racial discrimination against employees, and providing financial support to a fascist political party in Israel.

Oh, and they are the #1 plastic polluter in the world.

1968 was a fucked-up year. Dr. Martin Luther King Jr. was assassinated. Robert Kennedy was assassinated. I was born. And the Viet Cong and North Vietnamese Army launched a massive offensive against American troops that took them totally by surprise and had *CBS Evening News* anchor Walter Cronkite saying on live television that the war was unwinnable.

January 30, 1968

You want to know why the United States lost in Vietnam? Because the Vietnamese were willing to die, and Americans weren't. Sure, 58,000 Americans *did* die in the war, but over a million North Vietnamese and Viet Cong (communist rebels who lived in the South but were allied with the North) soldiers got snuffed. It was a twenty-to-one kill ratio for the United States even before you consider the hundreds of thousands of dead Vietnamese civilians.

Except body counts don't win wars. Making the other side give up does. The Tet Offensive was so named because it took place during the Vietnamese New Year, aka *Tết*. There was supposed to be a holiday truce, but the NVA and VC used their enemy's

complacency to launch a surprise attack on January 30, 1968. It was the biggest offensive of the war, encompassing locations across South Vietnam. There were three different phases that lasted eight months. By the time it was over, about 5,000 Americans (and a similar number of South Vietnamese soldiers) were dead, but the NVA and VC lost close to ten times that number.

The attackers imagined the offensive would lead to a popular uprising in the South that would collapse the government, but it didn't materialize. Rather, the Viet Cong was devastated and ceased to be a serious military threat. The Americans, who were always good at killing, fucked their shit up good, because this was their kind of fight. Not running around the jungle in small groups, but a stand-up contest of firepower.

So why did Cronkite say they couldn't win?

Until that time, the American public got a sanitized version of the war from the media. Most reporters hung around Saigon and had to go looking for the war, but this time it came to them. While there were already plenty of Americans against the war, many others believed the North was all but defeated. Then there was this massive attack and their boys were dying by the thousands, and people started saying the fuck are we doing over there?

Militarily, *Tết* was a failure for the North, but it was a PR win. Cronkite traveled to Vietnam to witness the tenacity of the enemy, reporting on February 27 that "we are mired in a stalemate." President Johnson said, "If I've lost Cronkite, I've lost Middle America." It spelled the end of his administration and led to the presidency of Richard Nixon. Ugh.

South Vietnamese soldiers defending Saigon

Chemical warfare in a relationship can result from eating too much broccoli or beans; a stenchy spouse may make you feel like you're gonna die. But in World War I people actually did die from gas attacks. Although, not the first time the method was used. That was a clusterfuck.

A big part of the twentieth century was Germans killing Russians and Russians killing Germans. Many forget that World War I also had an Eastern Front, possibly because it came to an end with Russia saying fuck this shit in 1917 and just walking away so they could make war among themselves over whether their flag should be white or red, or something. Anyway, I can't think of too many WWI Eastern Front movies, but it happened, and people died.

On January 31, 1915, the German forces made the first large-scale use of gas as a weapon of war, launching 18,000 canisters of xylyl bromide, an early type of tear gas, toward the Russian lines. I guess some dumbass didn't check the weather report though, because it was cold as fuck and the liquid that was supposed to vaporize didn't cuz brrrr. There are no known casualties. From the gas. The battle sucked though, and a shit-ton of people died. It was called the Battle of Bolimów.

> **I guess some dumbass didn't check the weather report though, because it was cold as fuck and the liquid that was supposed to vaporize didn't cuz brrrr.**

You'll notice I said "large-scale" use of gas. The previous year, the French had tossed some tear-gas hand grenades at the Germans, and a bit later the Germans tried shooting a few thousand canisters of a lung irritant at the British—but the explosive charge that launched the canisters also incinerated the gas, so that was a total nothing.

January 31, 1915

But they learned from their fuckups and a few months after Bolimów the Germans tried it on their western front and hit the Brits with chlorine gas and it worked, killing over 1,000 and wounding 5,000 more. And then commanders on both sides said oh this shit is awesome we need to do that too, and so they did, killing about 100,000 people via various gas attacks during the war.

Ten years after the war ended, the Geneva folks said hey, don't do that shit anymore, banning the use of asphyxiating, poisonous, or other gases for making war. Six decades later Saddam Hussein said you're not the boss of me and used that shit on Kurds and Iranians.

February

In 2017, I rode the "Vomit Comet," a converted 727 aircraft that had the chairs removed and the walls padded. The plane was flown in multiple parabolic maneuvers (climbs and dives) to give thirty seconds of weightlessness each time to a couple dozen passengers. And it was way fucking cool. I got to do it for free because I wrote an article about it. My son is still pissed I didn't pay the five grand to bring him along.

Anyway, space travel is awesome. And also hella fucking dangerous. But just like sailors dropping like flies from scurvy or drowning in storms while exploring the world, exploding spacecraft won't stop humanity's efforts to slip the surly bonds of Earth.

It had been seventeen years and three days since the *Challenger* blew up seventy-three seconds after liftoff when *Columbia* came apart on its return to Earth on February 1, 2003. They knew something was up, because the damage that caused the disaster took place upon liftoff; a piece of foam insulation from one of the external booster tanks flew off and hit the left wing of the shuttle. That sort of thing had happened on previous shuttle missions, causing minor damage, but for the crew of *Columbia* it proved fatal.

February 1, 2003

Engineers knew there was damage and were concerned it was worse than the other times, but NASA management limited the investigation because, well, there was fuck all that could be done; there was no way for them to fix it in space. So they relied on thoughts and prayers, which panned out as well as they usually do. After two weeks in space, as the ship flew just shy of Mach 20 at 200,000 feet above Earth, the heat shield was penetrated through the damaged wing and prompted the death spiral that ripped the spacecraft apart over the course of a minute and a half.

All seven crew members died, but several weeks later aluminum canisters were found among the debris that contained millimeter-long worms in petri dishes that were on the shuttle for biological research purposes.

The worms had survived.

NASA management limited the investigation because, well, there was fuck all that could be done; there was no way for them to fix it in space. So they relied on thoughts and prayers, which panned out as well as they usually do.

See this fuzzy boy? His name was Balto and he was a Siberian Husky who led a team of sled dogs through horrific winter conditions into the remote town of Nome, Alaska, carrying life-saving medicine to halt a diphtheria outbreak in what became known as the 1925 Serum Run.

I'm Canadian and have done 10-kilometer (6.2 mile) runs in –30° Celsius (–22° Fahrenheit). It's cold as fuck and frosts up the eyelashes so you can't see for shit. For this tale it was –46°C (–50°F), because it was way the hell north at the edge of the Arctic Circle and the temperatures were at a twenty-year low. Add in brutal winds, deep snow, and nonexistent visibility and you really just want to stay home and drink whiskey.

But in 1925 children were dying, the disease spreading.

The outbreak of the bacterial infection began in January, and the small town's sole doctor sent a desperate telegram calling for aid. Diphtheria is a toxin, and a life-saving antitoxin was needed. The nearest place that had serum that could halt the outbreak was located in Anchorage, but the engine on the only airplane that could fly it to Nome was frozen solid. Officials brainstormed and decided to send the serum north to the city of Nenana via train, where relays of mushers driving sled-dog teams would take it 674 frozen-as-fuck miles west to Nome.

One hundred and fifty dogs participated in the relay. Some of them died so children could live. Of more than twenty mushers, most of them Alaskan Natives, several suffered frostbite. The trip was made in a record-breaking five and a half days.

Norwegian musher Gunnar Kaasen and his Balto-led team made the final leg of the perilous journey. He was supposed to be the penultimate musher, but when he arrived at Point Safety at 2:00 A.M. he discovered his replacement was asleep, so he pressed on an additional twenty-five miles to Nome, arriving at 5:30 in the morning on February 2, 1925.

The serum was thawed and administered, and there were no further deaths. Kaasen and Balto became heroes. There is even a statue of Balto, who lived to be fourteen, in New York's Central Park. Balto was indeed a good boy, but his public status was achieved via being the one to lead the final leg. The *best* boy on the perilous journey was Togo. Balto traveled fifty-five miles, but Togo, also a Siberian Husky, led a team for almost five times that distance. He ran a whopping 260 miles, almost 40 percent of the entire relay. And he was twelve years old!

Balto with Gunnar Kaasen

Togo lived to be sixteen and sired many puppies. One of his direct descendants, Diesel, starred as his multiple-great-grandfather in a 2019 film titled *Togo,* alongside bipedal actor Willem Dafoe. It's an excellent movie. Have tissues ready.

A long, long time ago, when their plane went down on February 3, 1959, Buddy Holly was only twenty-two, the "Big Bopper" J. P. Richardson was twenty-eight, and Ritchie Valens was a mere seventeen years old. All music didn't die that day, but it was still a tragedy that took the lives of three rock-and-roll greats.

Officially, their tour was called the Winter Dance Party. Holly called it the "Tour from Hell." They drove around in shitty reconditioned school buses that kept breaking down. People were getting sick and even got frostbite as they traveled through the wintry Midwest.

The tour began on January 23 in Milwaukee and was scheduled to play twenty-four cities in as many days. But the dipshits at General Artists Corporation who organized the tour never looked at a fucking map. Rather than logically hopping from venue to nearest venue to minimize travel, the musicians meandered across the countryside back and forth and froze their asses off for several hours each day, then had to play at night, then do it all again. "It was like they threw darts at a map," Holly said.

On February 2 they played Clear Lake, Iowa, and Holly said fuck this I'm hiring a plane to take us to Moorhead, Minnesota. Two of his band members, Waylon Jennings and Tommy Allsup, were going to join him, but Waylon was saved via altruism, and Tommy by a coin toss.

February 3, 1959

Richardson had the flu. Jennings, being a good guy, gave up his seat on the small Beechcraft Bonanza aircraft. Allsup flipped a coin against Valens and lost his seat, but won a long life.

The flight departed at 12:55 A.M. Unbeknownst to the 21-year-old pilot, Roger Peterson, the weather was going to shit, and he was not yet rated to fly solely by instruments when visibility was nonexistent. He suffered spatial disorientation and the plane crashed only a few minutes after takeoff, killing him and his three passengers.

Holly's pregnant wife learned of his death via a news broadcast, and suffered a miscarriage shortly afterward, reportedly from the trauma. The events were immortalized in the 1971 Don McLean song "American Pie," and since that time the crash has been referred to as "the day the music died."

Sentenced to suicide seems the same to me as sentenced to execution. You're just as dead if you hold the blade as if someone else does. But, honor or some shit, which the samurai were awfully uptight about. Except these guys were no longer samurai. They were *rōnin* (wandering samurai with no lord or master). Forty-seven of them. And forty-six were made to take their own lives for their act of vengeance.

February 4, 1703

The story has been glamorized since then, including in a god-awful movie with Keanu Reeves, so who the fuck knows what's actually true. Here is my best shot. Below the head honcho, called a *shōgun,* were the *daimyōs.* In 1701 a *daimyō* named Asano was coming to visit the *shōgun* and needed to be instructed in court etiquette by a powerful official named Kira. As the story goes, Kira was an arrogant cockwipe and behaved like a total dick to Asano. Asano had enough and said fuck this guy and drew his dagger and stabbed Kira in his stupid face. It wasn't much of a wound, but drawing a weapon in the *shōgun*'s residence was a big-time "you gotta die" no-no.

Asano was ordered by the *shōgun,* Toku-

> As the story goes, Kira was an arrogant cockwipe and behaved like a total dick to Asano. Asano had enough and said fuck this guy and drew his dagger and stabbed Kira in his stupid face.

gowa, to do ritual suicide called *seppuku;* the *daimyo*'s property was confiscated, his family ruined, his subjects left without a lord. Forty-seven of his samurai, who were now suddenly *rōnin,* decided they needed to get some good old sharpened-steel revenge on Kira, even though the *shōgun* said listen I know the guy is a douche but NO revenge, k?

Kira knew he was in danger and made sure he was always well protected. The *rōnin* plotted for almost two years, then went all revenge-as-shit on Kira's ass. Late in 1702 they attacked Kira's palace, killing and wounding many while Kira hid like a little chickenshit. But they finally found him, chopped off his head, and laid the head before the tomb of their dead master as a tribute.

Terasaka, the lowest-ranked among the *rōnin,* was sent off as a messenger to say their revenge was complete, while the other forty-six turned themselves in to the authorities. The people considered them heroes and pleaded for them to be spared, but the *shōgun* said nope they defied me so they gotta die. On February 4, 1703, the forty-six *rōnin* were made to engage in *seppuku.* Terasaka was spared on account of his youth, and lived to be eighty-seven. Upon his death he was buried with his forty-six comrades.

There were three wars between Carthage and Rome, called the Punic Wars, that took place between 264 and 146 B.C.E. There were only three because after the third there was nothing left to fight over. I mean, the city of Carthage was gone. The Romans destroyed it. So that ended that. Except not really. Not for another two millennia.

During the period of the Punic Wars, Rome was the dominant empire of the region, kicking all sorts of ass o'er the Mediterranean. Carthage was a powerful Phoenician city-state residing in present-day Tunisia. They did *not* like each other, hence: war. Times three. The first one lasted twenty-three years, the second was seventeen years, and the third the Romans were tired of fucking around and got all their killing done in four short years.

The Romans won the first two wars as well, but not devastatingly so. The second is noteworthy because that was when Hannibal won a bunch of battlefield victories against the Romans using elephants. Not that the elephants made much difference. It just gets mentioned a lot because holy fucking shit he had elephants we should mention that in the history books. Despite Hannibal winning battles, the Carthaginians still lost that war.

By the time of the Third Punic War, Carthage wasn't much of a military threat to Rome, but they decided to fuck its shit up anyway. Why? Probably greed. Carthage was prosperous and posed something of an economic threat, and if Rome conquered it, they could do some looting and enslaving while they were at it. Not to mention that having an enemy to point to distracts the peasantry from the corruption of their own government.

So, Rome invaded, killed about three-quarters of a million people, enslaved the 50,000 survivors, destroyed the city, and turned the region into a Roman province. Nice. But the war didn't end. Not officially, at least. Because there was no one to make peace with. They were all dead or enslaved.

Realizing that they were still technically at war, 2,130 years later, the mayor of modern Carthage and the mayor of Rome signed a symbolic peace treaty between the two cities on February 5, 1985.

She only became queen because her uncle, Edward VIII, wanted to marry a divorced American woman so he abdicated in favor of his younger brother, Albert, who took the name George VI upon becoming king. When George died, his daughter Elizabeth became queen; she was the second-longest-reigning monarch in world history.

February 6, 1952

Louis XIV of France holds the crown—heh—as all-time champ for longest-serving head of a shitty system of governance at 72 years, 110 days. Born in 1926, Liz was #2 at 70 years, 214 days. Except she didn't govern. She never came close to Louis in terms of ability to wield power, because he reigned when people believed in that "divine right of kings" bullshit. Elizabeth's was largely a ceremonial role, one that still has a surprising amount of support in Britain.

Elizabeth was married in 1947 and wasted no time creating an heir, with Charles being born six days shy of her first wedding anniversary. Her dad's sickness had her standing in for him at public events and tours. Her private secretary knew her father was not far from the Great Kingly Beyond, and carried a draft accession declaration with him while Elizabeth was on tour. Good thing too, because

Queen Elizabeth II on her Coronation Day

Liz was in the middle of nowhere in Kenya when her father died at age fifty-six on February 6, 1952.

Elizabeth and her husband, Philip Mountbatten, were in the Treetops Hotel in Kenya's Aberdare National Park when her daddy, King George VI, died. They didn't have cell phones back then, and considering the romantic surroundings she probably would have had it on DO NOT DISTURB anyway, so she did not immediately learn that she had ascended to reigning monarch of the United Kingdom and Commonwealth Realms while playing hide the royal sausage with her third cousin, who was also her second cousin once removed. I don't know if we can blame Charles's massive ears on that or not.

It wasn't until they returned to Sagana Lodge, about fifteen miles away, that Elizabeth learned her father had died and she was queen. Her coronation took place in June of the following year, and to her husband's patriarchal chagrin the decision was made to have Elizabeth's family name used, retaining the House of Windsor rather than changing it to the House of Mountbatten. Feeling emasculated, Elizabeth's husband visited a dreary place I like to call "Crimea River," proclaiming, "I am the only man in the country not allowed to give his name to his own children."

The Bonfire of the Vanities was a mega-bestselling book and a really shitty movie. But the term did not originate in New York in the 1980s. It came from an actual bonfire in fifteenth-century Italy where religious wingnuts set fire to "sinful" objects such as art, cosmetics, and even books.

De jure is Latin to describe something legally recognized. *De facto* is also Latin, meaning what happens in reality, regardless of law. Dominican friar Girolamo Savonarola didn't have legal authority, but he was the de facto ruler of the Italian city of Florence from 1494 to 1498. And he was a fucking dick.

Perhaps not a complete dick. He did rail against corruption in the Church, despotic rule, and exploitation of the poor, but he was way uptight about anything that wasn't fiercely Christian. He prophesized Armageddon, which is something zealots often do, and when France invaded in 1494 and Florence was threatened, a bunch of people said, "Holy fucking shit, the end is near!" So, at Savonarola's urging, the local citizenry punted out the ruling Medici family and put him in charge by popular acclaim.

He proclaimed that Florence was gonna be the new Jerusalem, and more glorious and powerful and awesome than ever! And he went all puritanical more than sixty years before Puritans became a thing. New laws were passed cracking down on bum sex (even between husband and wife), adultery, and drinking. He also had his zealous youth followers patrol the streets to harass and beat people who dressed in ways the friar considered immodest.

February 7, 1497

The bonfire of the vanities wasn't just the burning of books, art, and cosmetics. It was targeting anything that might tempt one to "sin." This included mirrors, musical instruments, playing cards, certain types of clothing, or anything considered secular in nature. Because if it wasn't about the glory of Jesus, it had to go. Set that shit on fire. And so the mobs did on February 7, 1497.

The reigning pope wanted Florence to join his "Holy League" army to repel the French invaders. Giro said, "Nah you're on your own there, Pope." So the pope said, "Well fuck you. I'm excommunicating your ass." That happened a few months after the bonfire, but the Florentines continued to harbor Savonarola, who started preaching even crazier shit about how he could perform miracles. He also did some writing that inspired Protestant reformer Martin Luther. Eventually, however, people started to question his fuckery, and in 1498 he was arrested and tortured into saying no I really can't do miracles and I made up those prophecies. His captors decided to go karmic justice on his ass and set him on fire and he died.

In the West, most movies about the European theater of World War II involve Americans fighting Germans, but that was a relative walk in the park compared to Russians fighting Germans. Those two hated each other so much that if you became a prisoner of war, it was the definition of suck.

February 8, 1945

Mikhail Devyatayev was a Soviet fighter pilot who got his first kill on a German dive bomber only two days after Hitler attacked the Soviet Union. He shot down many more German planes and got fancy medals and shit. But on July 13, 1944, his luck took a temporary dip when he was shot down and became a prisoner of war.

He knew pilots were treated harshly, because people didn't like having bombs dropped on them (although he wasn't a bomber). He took the identity of a dead Soviet infantryman and eventually ended up in a Nazi concentration camp on an island in the Baltic Sea called Usedom. While there, he was forced to labor on the German missile program, making V-1 and V-2 rockets.

Conditions in the camp were brutal, and Devyatayev figured he'd never make it out alive. Despite security being tight, he decided to attempt an escape and convinced several of his fellow prisoners he could fly them out of that frozen hellscape back to their homeland frozen hellscape. On Febru-

ary 8, 1945, Mikhail and nine other Soviet prisoners were hard at work repairing the island's runway. Then prisoner Ivan Krivonogov bashed their Nazi guard's brains out with a crowbar, stole his clothes, and led the work gang as their "guard" to the camp commandant's Heinkel He 111 bomber aircraft. Then Devyatayev flew them out of that shithole.

German aircraft gave chase, but the Soviets had been advancing steadily westward and the escapees only had to fly about a hundred miles until they crossed into Soviet territory. Of course, seeing a German bomber coming at them and not knowing it carried their own soldiers, the Soviets tried to shoot it down and damaged the plane. But Devyatayev still managed to safely land in Soviet territory. Seven of the ten escapees were assigned to a rifle unit and sent back into the fight, and five of them died gloriously for the motherland. The three officers were held for investigation for having worked on behalf of the German war effort, albeit forced.

Devyatayev was branded a criminal and struggled to find work after the war. But in 1957 the head of the Soviet space program said Mikhail and the others had provided valuable information about the German rocket program and they should cut the guy some fucking slack. His name was cleared, and he was made a Hero of the Soviet Union.

What is it about people needing to prove that their religion is the right one by setting those who practice the "wrong" one on fire? "Ha! Look at him cry for mercy as he burns to death. We sure taught him a lesson about praying wrong." That's what happened to Bishop John Hooper when Queen Mary I decided all that Protestant Reformation stuff needed to be purged from England. With fire.

Mary I was the less-famous daughter of Henry VIII, Elizabeth I being the more famous "Cate Blanchett is gonna play me in two movies" one. Liz got the moniker "Virgin Queen" because she never married, although she probably did play some couch rugby. Conversely, her older half-sister was known as "Bloody Mary" because she bathed in it. Figuratively. Because how much blood is there when someone is burned at the stake? Doesn't it boil away?

John Hooper was a bishop and Protestant reformer. Just like poor people voting for Trump, he was actually *against* the plot to make Mary *not* queen despite it being light-years away from his best interests. Didn't help him much, though. Hooper espoused prudish Calvinist teachings and was seen as a highly visible representation of the more radical aspects of the Protestant Reformation in England, so of course the new Catholic regime had to make an example of him. With fire.

February 9, 1555

Since we were talking about nicknames, I hereby dub the poor fellow John "Sucks to Be Him" Hooper, because on February 9, 1555, he was burned at the stake for being a heretic, which I'm certain taught him a valuable lesson about the right and wrong ways to pray.

After Bloody Mary died, Elizabeth the Protestant became queen and Hooper was declared to be a martyr to the cause. His views were embraced by this new group of zealots that sprang up under Elizabeth's reign called Puritans, a bunch of whom later fucked off to America and made the country so fucking uptight about sex that you can't post a female nipple on Facebook without catching a ban.

> Liz got the moniker "Virgin Queen" because she never married, although she probably did play some couch rugby. Conversely, her older half-sister was known as "Bloody Mary" because she bathed in it.

It's probably not right to refer to Genghis Khan as a "motherfucker," considering many of the women he made into mothers were unwilling. It's believed almost half a percent of all men alive today, about 16 million dudes, are descended from his rampant raping (and probably an equal number of women, but the Y chromosome is easier to trace across time). That's some horrific legacy. Another legacy is that the empire he spawned brought the Islamic Golden Age to an abrupt end.

February 10, 1258

The Mongols were the greatest cavalrymen alive; they could control their horses with their legs to run circles around their enemy while they shot them full of arrows with their short bows. They boast the largest contiguous land empire in history, and in 1258, it was Baghdad's turn to fall to it.

Baghdad was the center of the Abbasid Caliphate's Golden Age, which began late in the eighth century and lasted almost half a millennium. At its peak the city's population exceeded a million people, which was a shitload of folks for back then. It was a center of learning, with Islamic scholars from around the world visiting to share their knowledge in areas of law, education, philosophy, physics, math, astronomy, geography, biology, and a bunch of other subjects I wasn't much good at. The list of inventions spawned is so long, a sample wouldn't do it justice. Google it.

The siege began in late January. This was more than three decades after Genghis died. His grandson Hulagu, brother of Kublai, who you may have heard of, pressed the siege. The defense had been hastily organized and lacked proper equipment and training. The reigning caliph, Al-Musta'sim, had stepped on his dick by not better preparing for a MONGOL FUCKING HORDE coming his way. Like, had he not heard about what happens when a MONGOL FUCKING HORDE arrives in your neighborhood?

The siege ended after thirteen days on February 10, 1258, with a Mongol victory. Duh. Halfway through the siege Al-Musta'sim had tried to negotiate but Hulagu said *bite me*. A few thousand nobles tried the same tack because the wealthy really don't like having their stuff taken almost as much as they don't like dying, and Hulagu had them all killed because fuck rich people.

Anyway, the Mongols entered the defeated city and it was . . . not nice. They did the kind of things conquering Mongols were known for, and Al-Musta'sim was rolled up in a rug and trampled to death by horses. Why a rug? Because they feared spilling royal blood on the ground would be an affront. The trampling part was deemed okay though.

Oh, and if you're pissed about the loss of the Library of Alexandria, there was another immeasurable loss in the destruction of Baghdad's House of Wisdom library. Thus ended both the Abbasid Caliphate and the Golden Age of Islam.

Why are there so many shitty people in politics? Simple: It takes a shitty person to be willing to do anything, no matter how shitty, to win. And when you're the type of shitty person willing to do all sorts of shitty things to win, you often do. What kinds of shitty things? How about gerrymandering a political district? Know who authorized that? A shitty guy named Gerry.

Congress in the United States is two different houses: the Senate, and the House of Representatives (aka the House). The Senate has its own fuckery, what with Wyoming's 586,000 people getting two senators and California's more than 39 million people also getting only two senators. But you can't use gerrymandering to win a Senate seat, unless it's to win a *state* senate race, which is how this bullshit began. At the federal level, it's about winning a seat in the House.

What the fuck is gerrymandering? Imagine this. You want to win an election. The

district you're fighting for has this small city just outside it that you know is full of people who like you (or, more likely, prefer the party you're running for). And if that city becomes part of your district the race will swing in your favor. What do you do? Your party engages in legal fuckery to redraw those district lines to include that little city and you win!

February 11, 1812

Said fuckery was the responsibility of Elbridge Gerry, who was such a dick he pronounced his last name with a hard *G*, like Gary instead of Jerry.

He'd been a Congress critter two decades previous, and more recently governor of Massachusetts. It was his party (called Democratic-Republicans) that pushed for the redrawing of districts for the state senate race, and he was opposed, yet also a wimp. He gave in to the pressure, and as governor signed the legislation on February 11, 1812. And it worked like a motherfucker, with the next election netting the Dem-Reps twenty-nine state senate seats and the Federalist Party only eleven, even though the Dem-Reps got fewer total votes than the Federalists. *Haha, you got pwned.*

The editor of *The Boston Gazette* looked at one of the new districts and said *that looks like some kind of fucked-up salamander* and created the portmanteau "gerrymander," publishing the word for the first time on March 26, 1812.

Gerry went on to become the fifth vice president of the United States.

"The Gerry-Mander" political cartoon

There is more than one *The Scream,* and the fucking things have been stolen more than once, too.

There are four versions of Edvard Munch's masterpiece: two in paint, two in pastel, with the first being painted in 1893, potentially influenced by the glowing skies created by the mega-explodey *kaboom* of the Krakatoa volcano a decade previous.

February 12, 1994

The original 1893 version was stolen first on February 12, 1994, during the Winter Olympic Games in Norway. And it was a clusterfuck.

Because of the Olympics, Norway's National Museum moved *The Scream* from its usual secure location to a gallery on the ground floor, in order to showcase Norwegian culture; they wanted to brag about their artist who died half a century earlier. From a security standpoint, this was a bad move, because ground floors are easy to escape from. But the museum was all nah we got cameras and alarms and shit it will be fine. It was not fine.

Thieves broke in at 6:30 A.M. and set off the alarm. The guard on duty called the cops and they arrived in minutes, but the perpetrators were already gone, having left behind a note that read, "Thousand thanks for the poor security." They'd completed the heist in under a minute.

The painting is worth a stupid amount, if sold legitimately. But even the most avaricious billionaire with a stolen collection would be a fool to purchase it. These dumbfucks didn't plan in advance, and obviously had no buyer lined up, because a month later the gallery received a ransom note for US$1 million. For comparison, in 2012 the *second* pastel version of *The Scream* sold for US$120 million. Fuck knows what the original painting is worth.

Anyway, the museum said feast upon our testicles and so the thieves cut the price even further and went looking for a dumbass buyer. Instead, they found themselves ensnared in a sting operation involving both Norwegian and British police. The painting was returned undamaged that spring, and the four thieves convicted. However, the British police had entered Norway using false identities, so three of the thieves were acquitted on appeal.

In an M. Night Shyamalan–level twist, back when he was good at that kind of thing, it was discovered they'd been hired to steal it by a gang of bank robbers who didn't want the painting. They wanted the police losing their shit over the theft so they could rob a bunch of banks unhindered. Their plan worked.

> **The painting is worth a stupid amount, if sold legitimately. But even the most avaricious billionaire with a stolen collection would be a fool to purchase it.**

In the spring of 2020 a lot of people figured North Korean despot Kim Jong-un was dead. Turns out he wasn't, but his older brother was, and it was his little brother who had it done. All because the guy wanted to visit Disneyland.

Eleven years older than Kim Jong-un, Kim Jong-nam had a different mother and was considered the heir apparent to the North Korean "throne" until 2001, when he answered the call of Mickey. Because North Korea sucks, Jong-nam made several clandestine visits to Japan, which does not suck (at least in its more recent history). In 2001 he wanted to go to Tokyo Disneyland, but the jig was up. He was arrested at the Tokyo airport for traveling under a Chinese alias and using a forged Dominican Republic passport. He was deported to China, and his dad, Kim Jong-il, who wasn't exactly known for being an understanding sort of fellow, was all embarrassed and shit, and ended up canceling a state visit to China.

This led to a loss of favor for Jong-nam, but according to Jong-nam the loss of favor was due to him advocating for reform, which was probably a crock of shit because he was a dick just like his dad and his younger brother, so don't go feeling sorry for him.

No longer wanted at home, by 2003 Jong-nam was living in exile in Macao. He had two wives and a mistress and half a dozen kids. He became an occasional critic of his homeland, and after his younger brother Jong-un took power upon the death of their father in 2011, Jong-nam met with a Japanese journalist to tell his story, which was published in a book. In it, he said Jong-un was too inexperienced and predicted that the North Korean regime was doomed to collapse.

February 13, 2017

South Korean intelligence proclaimed that Jong-un had put in place a standing order to assassinate Jong-nam, and there had been failed attempts. On February 13, 2017, the attempts to snuff Jong-nam failed no more. You know that nasty VX nerve-agent stuff from the 1996 Nic Cage movie *The Rock*? The movie representation of VX was of course bullshit, but it does kill motherfuckers, and that's what they used on Jong-nam. North Korean agents convinced a couple of innocent women in an airport in Malaysia to spray Jong-nam in the face with a spray bottle and then cover his mouth with a handkerchief. They had no idea the bottle was full of VX. The two women were told it was all part of a "TV prank." Doubtful Jong-nam found it funny.

In 2019 both *The Washington Post* and *The Wall Street Journal* reported that Jong-nam had been an informant for the CIA.

Madonna. **Bono. Sting.** Cher. Seal. Shakira. Sade. Akbar.

Akbar? He wasn't a singer, but he was just . . . Akbar. Aka "Akbar the Great," and he earned it and became known as *the* Akbar, Mughal emperor for almost half a century and doer of deeds both great and terrible that transformed the world.

February 14, 1556

Akbar ascended the throne of the South Asian empire of Mughal on February 14, 1556, at the age of thirteen, while his empire was in the middle of a war. A direct descendant of Genghis Khan—not that there was any shortage of such descendants—the lad decided to do some conquering. The Mughal Empire, which would come to cover much of the Indian subcontinent, had begun under Akbar's grandfather. But his father was overthrown, and Akbar was born in exile. Dad had only partially reclaimed the throne a few months previous when he died and Akbar ascended, inheriting a frail alliance of fiefdoms and having to fight to consolidate his power or be killed, because that's what usually happens to rival claimants to a throne: They get dead.

Motivated to not die, in the early years Akbar relied upon his regent, Bairam Khan, to whip the nobles into line to go on the offensive against the Afghans and Hindus,

> After forty-nine years of rule he met an ignoble end via dysentery, shitting himself to death in 1605.

where they kicked some ass. When he turned eighteen, Akbar came into his full power and kept up the imperial expansion, but he wasn't stupid about it. Akbar was a brilliant general who embraced the relatively new firearms technology, creating what was referred to as a "gunpowder empire" by unleashing such weaponry upon his foes to devastating effect.

Throughout history, conquerors often demanded heavy tribute taxes of their subjects, but otherwise left them to run their own affairs unsupervised. Akbar was different. The emperor created a centralized system of government and integrated conquered leaders into it. He rewarded talent and loyalty, regardless of race or religion. The state was secular, liberal (relatively speaking), and focused on cultural integration. He also used marriage as a tool to strengthen alliances.

Akbar took many princesses as wives and made their families part of his court. Just like Genghis, he was not a one-woman kind of ruler. This marrying of daughters to rulers had previously been viewed as an indignity, but Akbar changed the plot by elevating their families, transforming it into an honor, thereby forging strong bonds of loyalty and strengthening his empire further.

After forty-nine years of rule he met an ignoble end via dysentery, shitting himself to death in 1605. The empire he built, however, would last long after he was gone.

People think Canadians are nice, but sometimes we're just fucking not. In the early 1960s we were at each other's throats. It was over some serious shit: what our nation's flag would look like. We almost fucked it up, too, because the prime minister wanted something ugly. Good thing someone with a sense of style prevailed.

Canada officially became a thing in 1867, but we didn't get our current flag until almost a century later. We still used either the Union Jack or something called the Canadian Red Ensign, which had the Union Jack in the canton and the Canadian coat-of-arms shield on the fly side. Blarf.

Others agreed the situation was blarf, because in 1960 opposition leader Lester B. Pearson proclaimed a need "for finding a solution to the flag problem." The conservative prime minister, John Diefenbaker, did what many Canadian politicians do, which was consider even good ideas from the opposition to be stupid, and said get fucked Pearson.

Pearson headed the Liberal Party and made promising a new flag a platform issue. It helped them win power in 1963, but it was a minority government, which makes it more difficult to pass legislation because it involves consensus building rather than simply saying we're doing this shit. Good thing, because the design that was called the "Pearson Pennant" was butt-ugly. Blue stripes on either side to represent "From Sea to Sea," Canada's national motto, and the middle had a branch with three small maple leaves attached, same as on the nation's coat of arms. Google that hideousness.

There were loyalists to Mother England who wanted to retain the Union Jack, of course, but Pearson wanted to get rid of that imperialist bullshit. Diefenbaker, who was now a member of the opposition, wanted to keep the Red Ensign. There was a filibuster and the debate raged with no end in sight, so a "special flag committee" was formed with representatives from all five federal parties. Over six weeks and thirty-five lengthy meetings the committee considered 3,541 entries, the majority of which contained maple leaves. Three hundred eighty-nine contained beavers.

February 15, 1965

There was another entry, however, designed by historian George Stanley and slid in at the last minute by Member of Parliament John Matheson. With a single red maple leaf in the middle and red bars on either side, it was beautiful in its simplicity and also fulfilled the need of not including symbols "of a divisive nature." The conservatives on the flag committee figured liberals would prefer Pearson's ugly design and voted for Stanley's design as a fuck-you. Imagine their surprise when support for Stanley's flag was unanimous.

Diefenbaker was still a dick about it, but Stanley's design passed in the House of Commons 163 to 78. Queen Elizabeth said "Fuckin' Eh" and approved it via royal proclamation. It was inaugurated on February 15, 1965.

> *"Be a Don Cheadle not a Dave Chappelle."*
> —IMANI GANDY

Why? Because Chappelle believes one of the most marginalized groups on the planet should be made fun of. Conversely, on February 16, 2019, Don Cheadle hosted *Saturday Night Live* wearing a T-shirt that read PROTECT TRANS KIDS.

February 16, 2019

Don didn't say anything about the issue; he just wore the shirt for a bit. The media said lots the next day, and so did social media. Much of the commentary was positive, but much was . . . not, because some folks love to hate trans people. They even build an identity around it, make it a cornerstone of their "comedy" act or put silly descriptors like "gender critical" in their online bios, because they imagine that what is between a person's legs is all that matters. Fuck those bigots, and enough about recent history. Let's look way back, because trans people have existed for as long as people have existed.

The term "transgender" is new, but they are not. Records from ancient Mesopotamia, going back about five thousand years, refer to priests of the goddess Inanna called *gala,* who may have been trans. Graves from a few thousand years ago in Northern Iraq reveal burial rites that show they considered gender to be a spectrum. Archaeologists discovered different funerary artifacts for men than for women, and also different offerings for a "third gender."

In 2011 archeologists discovered a 5,000-year-old grave near Prague of a biological male buried with the funerary rites of a woman. In fifth-century Lebanon a person assigned female at birth masculinized their name from Marina to "Marinos" and joined a monastery as a child, living the rest of his life as a man, not even revealing his sex (sex, not gender) after being falsely accused of fathering a child, but rather accepting three years of exile as punishment. His sex was revealed only upon his death. The Sanskrit epic Mahābhārata, written in India 2,300 years ago, tells the story of a trans man named Shikhandi.

Elagabalus served as Roman emperor under the name Antoninus from 218 to 222 and was certainly trans. Contemporary Roman historian and statesman Cassius Dio referred to Elagabalus with female pronouns. Legally, Hierocles was the wife of Elagabalus, but Dio wrote that the "husband of this woman [meaning Elagabalus] was Hierocles." Dio wrote that Elagabalus preferred to be referred to as a wife and a queen, not a lord. She dressed and adorned herself as a woman of the time, and reportedly offered a fortune to any surgeon who could give her a vagina.

These stories are barely a sample. Across areas and eras, trans and nonbinary people have lived and loved and been both accepted and maligned. The prevalence of hate is nonsensical. In 2018, Dr. Joshua Safer, executive director of the Center for Transgender Medicine and Surgery at Mt. Sinai Hospital, said, "Being transgender is not a matter of choice. It is not a fad . . . it is generally an overwhelming sense that their gender is not the one on their birth certificate."

Private **Robert Preston** wanted to be an army helicopter pilot, but he flunked out. Nevertheless, he was required to serve four years, and the army made him a helicopter mechanic instead and stationed him at Fort Meade in Maryland. Preston wanted more out of his service; he'd done Junior Reserve Officers' Training Corps in high school and had obtained a private pilot's license while studying aviation management in community college. He enlisted in 1972 and had dreams of flying choppers in Vietnam.

His dreams crushed, and mourning a recent breakup with his girlfriend, he returned to Fort Meade after a night out in the early morning hours of February 17, 1974. On a whim, Preston decided to take one of the Bell UH-1 Hueys out for a spin. The base air controller, seeing a helicopter being stolen, called the Maryland State Police.

He flew around a bit then went to visit D.C., and local police took note because he was zooming around in mega-fucking-restricted airspace near the Lincoln Memorial. He then went over to buzz the White House, landing on the South Lawn for a moment.

This was long before 9/11 made the Secret Service trigger-happy as fuck. They didn't have surface-to-air missiles yet and had no firm policies about where and when to shoot at aerial intruders. Preston decided to go

back to Fort Meade but en route he was intercepted by two Maryland State Police helicopters. He did some fancy flying and evaded one, then caused a cop car to crash when he buzzed it. The other police helicopter continued the chase and Preston returned to the White House with the intent to surrender personally to President Nixon, who was actually in Florida visiting his sick daughter.

February 17, 1974

Seeing him return, the Secret Service said okay fuck this guy and opened fire with automatic weapons and shotguns. Preston was wounded in the foot and landed the Huey on the South Lawn. The Secret Service, who must have trained at the *Star Wars* Stormtrooper Academy of How to Shoot Good, fired about three hundred rounds and he was hit five more times, but they were all minor injuries. Preston jumped out of the Huey and ran toward the mansion. His adventure ended with him being tackled by agents.

> **Seeing him return, the Secret Service said okay fuck this guy and opened fire with automatic weapons and shotguns.**

They took him to the hospital, and he was reported to be "laughing like hell."

Preston was court-martialed and sentenced to a year in prison, as well as given a general discharge from the army.

Goddammit, Neil deGrasse Tyson. Pluto *is* a fucking planet.

Poor lonely, cold, distant Pluto. It was imagined decades before it was discovered. In 1840, via the use of Newtonian mechanics that I'm certain my engineer son understands and I don't, French astronomer Urbain Le Verrier saw that Uranus was perturbed; perhaps lay off the spicy chicken wings and draft beer. The perturbations of Uranus's orbit led to the discovery of Neptune, and about fifty years later math nerds determined Neptune couldn't account for all of it, and they surmised a ninth planet. That math turned out to be wrong, but never mind that. They began to search in earnest for what they referred to as "Planet X."

February 18, 1930

A wealthy Bostonian, Percival Lowell, who built the Lowell Observatory in Arizona in 1894, launched a project in 1906 to find the little fucker. And they did, in 1915, taking two images of it—but they didn't realize it. Lowell died the following year and there was inheritance bullshit over the observatory, and the project was sidelined for over a dozen years. Then, in 1929, some 23-year-old astronomy hobbyist named Clyde Tombaugh, who, despite not yet being formally educated, impressed the Lowell Observatory with his knowledge. So they gave him a job and said hey find this planet we've been looking for. And that's what he did.

It took him less than a year of searching, but on February 18, 1930, Tombaugh proclaimed, "There is the icy little asshole." Paraphrased. The discovery made international headlines and suggestions for a name poured in from around the globe, with the winning suggestion coming from an eleven-year-old English girl named Venetia Burney.

Clyde Tombaugh died in 1997, and nine years later the International Astronomical Union (IAU) pissed on his grave. They said Pluto meets only two of the three necessary criterions to be a planet: It orbits the sun and it's round. (Being round means it has the requisite mass to achieve such a shape.) But Pluto didn't meet the third criteria they established: having cleared its orbit of other objects. It's not the dominant gravitational object in its orbit the way the other eight planets are. It needs to either fling them away or merge with them.

So the IAU demoted the poor thing to dwarf planet, and since then Neil has been kind of a dick about it—even though he wasn't involved in the decision—insisting it was the right call. In 2015 he tweeted: "Dear Pluto, Lookin' good. But you're still a Dwarf Planet—get over it."

In 2015 he tweeted: "Dear Pluto, Lookin' good. But you're still a Dwarf Planet—get over it."

Dolly Parton frequently extols the need to believe in yourself, and in 1974 she epitomized this when she walked away from a popular TV show to go it alone.

Porter Wagoner sounds like quite the country and western name, doesn't it? Known as "Mr. Grand Ole Opry," he was country and western royalty with a syndicated TV program called *The Porter Wagoner Show* that began in 1961 and ran for two decades. His female star was a popular singer named Norma Jean, but she left in 1967 and the then-unknown Parton replaced her. People were not happy.

The audience liked Norma Jean, and suddenly there was this new woman and they automatically didn't like her because change

is bad. Some would chant "Norma Jean!" from the audience, which is a shitty way to treat anyone, but especially Dolly, dammit. However, because she's amazing, she won the crowd over and became beloved. She'd promised to be with the show for five years, and stayed for seven. It was during that time the world came to love Dolly Parton as she produced hit after hit, including several duets with Porter.

February 19, 1974

But the pair fought because "we were both stubborn," Dolly said. Porter thought he knew what was best for Dolly, and Dolly said *she* knew what was best for Dolly. She wrote "I Will Always Love You" about her professional breakup with Porter, which was announced on February 19, 1974. The song hit #1 on the *Billboard* Hot Country Songs chart. In 1982 she re-recorded it for a musical comedy she starred in alongside Burt Reynolds titled *The Best Little Whorehouse in Texas,* and it hit #1 a second time.

Dolly was right to believe in herself. Through hard work and talent her career reached all-new levels of superstardom, including a successful acting career. In addition to entertaining people for decades, Dolly is a generous philanthropist, especially in the area of literacy. In 2020 she donated a million dollars to help fund development of Moderna's Covid vaccine.

Dolly Parton and Porter Wagoner in 1969

If you allow capitalism to run amok, it will; money has no conscience. One example of avarice trouncing decency was the "secret meeting" Hitler had in 1933 with two dozen industrialists to fund his seizure of power.

February 20, 1933

This kind of history often repeats. Just like when several corporations supported Hitler for financial gain, many wealthy Trump supporters didn't embrace Eric's dad for his bigotry, but because of the tax cut he gave to the super-rich. They funded Danger Yam's campaign because they were paid back with a shit-ton of interest taken from the pockets of people sitting in rusty Dodge Rams wearing wraparound sunglasses making ranting videos about buttery males.

Okay, that went off into the rhubarb for a bit but my point is that money often gets people to not give a fuck about morality. Despite spending many years proving to the citizens of Germany that he was the fucking worst, Hitler had no problem raising money from a group of morally bankrupt capitalist fuckpuddles to aid his rise, because they saw him as the best financial choice for protecting their personal fortunes. Guess they didn't envision the country getting obliterated in a war.

The meeting took place on February 20, 1933, at the Reichstag, which would be set on fire a week later. In attendance were heads of many companies that still exist today, and you'd likely recognize the names of a few of them, such as automation giant Siemens, manufacturing company Krupp, and automotive company Opel.

Hitler wanted money to win enough seats in the upcoming election to pass the Enabling Act, giving him dictatorial powers. During the meeting, Hitler gave a lengthy speech about how dirty commies were coming for them all. He actually said democracy was to blame because it was enabling communism. He told them he needed to be a dictator to save their capitalistic asses, and they were all "Take my money!"

Hitler convinced them of a catastrophic scenario, saying the choice was "either Marxism in its purest form, or the other side." They chose the other side. He said he needed to "gain complete power" and they opened their checkbooks. He asked for three million reichsmarks and they coughed up a little over two, which is the equivalent of about US$14 million these days.

The murderous shithead got his Enabling Act passed, and one of the first things he did was make opposition to the fucking Nazi Party illegal. The industrialists got what they wanted: The Communist Party was outlawed, and they were free to get as rich as they possibly could.

Brazil has a long history of fascist governments, with recent years being no exception. During World War II it was ruled by a vicious military dictator, but the nation still knew that the fucking Nazis were bad, so Brazil sent an expeditionary force to side with the Allies to help defeat Hitler—the only independent South American nation to do so.

It was over 25,000 men and some women, and they were badasses. Referred to as the Smoking Cobras, they made a significant naval contribution to the Battle of the Atlantic and fought fiercely on land in the Mediterranean theater of the war under U.S. command. This is the story of their role in the Battle of Monte Castello.

Part of the Italian campaign, the fighting began in late November of 1944, and was the first time the Brazilian Expeditionary Force (FEB) entered combat on land. They were attacking a hill thirty miles north of Tuscany, where the Germans were dug in deep. It was critical that the hill be taken, because the Nazi ballsacks had ample artillery emplacements that halted the Allies from being able to push farther north toward Bologna and then continue their northward advance to retake all of Italy from the Axis powers.

The Brazilian soldiers were inexperienced and forced to learn on the job. Aka in combat. Fighting in coordination with American forces, the FEB helped capture Monte Castello in only two days. But then there was a massive German counterattack, and they lost the position. The winter sucked, the roads became a quagmire, and it was just generally not a fun place to be when you're trying to charge uphill through the mud while some Nazi shitbag is trying to kill you.

February 21, 1945

In this battle and the many that followed, the Smoking Cobras developed a reputation for courage and determination, lauded by their allies and feared by their enemies. Monte Castello was finally taken on February 21, 1945, at a significant cost due to the entrenched and elevated positions held by the enemy. A German captain said to a captured Brazilian lieutenant, "You Brazilians are either crazy or very brave. I never saw anyone advance against machine-guns and well-defended positions with such disregard for life. . . . You are devils."

Regarding the nickname, that was a fuck-you to their own government. The Brazilian government was trying to play both sides during the war, maintaining economic relations with Axis and Allies alike. It was only when Brazilian merchant ships suffered massive losses from Axis submarines that the FEB was sent. Prior to that, there was a saying that went "It's more likely for a snake to smoke a pipe than for the FEB to go to the front and fight." When they deployed, the FEB proudly wore badges depicting a snake smoking a pipe. The FEB also often wrote on their mortars (in Portuguese), "The snake is smoking."

To be "notorious" is to be well known, but for the wrong reason. A notoriously terrible Broadway play earned that moniker by having its opening and closing on the same night. Titled *Moose Murders,* it became the gold standard for sucking in the theater community.

This was 1978 *Star Wars Holiday Special* level of bad idea, and like that interstellar atrocity, I expect this play also involved significant amounts of cocaine. It was billed as a "mystery farce" and was the Broadway debut by playwright Arthur "I don't have a Wikipedia page for a reason" Bicknell. On February 22, 1983, its premiere stunk up the Eugene O'Neill Theatre so bad that that single night was the extent of its run.

What's it about? Some family buys the Wild Moose Lodge in the Adirondacks and on their first night they're trapped there with some other people because of a storm and they entertain themselves with a murder mystery game and some guy tries to fuck his mom and people die. Apparently, there is ableism in it too, because making fun of people with disabilities is fucking hilarious. Just ask Donald Trump.

The director was a no-name and gave top billing to his not-an-actress wife, who inherited boatloads of Texas oil money to fund the lighted-stage shitfuckery. The only recognizable performer, Holland Taylor, later played the mom on *Two and a Half Men.* Enthusiasm was so low they pulled people off the street to fill seats, one of whom was covered in his own vomit. Perhaps he knew how bad it was going to be and blew his groceries in advance.

So, yeah. They play a murder mystery game and people mysteriously die, so it's murder mystery inception and *additionally* there is a moose that . . . eats people? Right. A vegetarian animal that eats people. The audience was stunned with how horrible it was. June Gable was the only other actor of any note (she played Joey's agent on *Friends*), and said, "I don't think there ever was a show in the history of Broadway where you took a bow to silence."

The reviews fucking *eviscerated* it. The critics were so merciless that a bunch of people showed up the next night just to witness how god-fucking-awful it was, only to discover it was shuttered. A critic for *The New York Times* later proclaimed *Moose Murders* to be "a show so preposterous that it made minor celebrities out of everyone who witnessed it." Fifteen years later it was referenced in a review of the terrible TV show *Encore! Encore!* when the critic referred to it as "The 'Moose Murders' of sitcoms."

Like I said: Gold standard of sucking.

> **Enthusiasm was so low they pulled people off the street to fill seats, one of whom was covered in his own vomit. Perhaps he knew how bad it was going to be and blew his groceries in advance.**

ON THIS DAY IN HISTORY

Once upon a time, the television channel A&E, which stands for Arts & Entertainment, was not a steaming pile of fly-covered feces. It had great investigative and history programming before they realized that producing "reality" TV was cheap and easy and therefore more profitable. One program I remember had a countdown of the one hundred most influential people of the millenium, and #1 on that list was Johannes Gutenberg.

My wife and I watched the show. We were able to predict several of the top ten. When it came to "who is number 1?" we were mystified, but as soon as they said his name we went "Ooooh yeeeeaaaahhh." Gutenberg was born around 1400 in the city of Mainz in present-day Germany. Little is known of his early life, but when he was around thirty-seven his name was mentioned in court documents regarding a broken marriage promise. Knowing what I do of the time, perhaps he slept with a woman while engaged to her, then decided to break it off, which was considered practically criminal.

You're reading this in a book. Books are cool. Books are transformative. The mass availability of books is what caused literacy rates to skyrocket, changing the world. The first step in this shift began around 1440, when Gutenberg perfected the movable-type printing press. But it would be another ten years before it was put into operation. It is likely that the first thing to be mass-printed was a German poem. He raised investment funds and on February 23, 1455, printed what became known as the Gutenberg Bible, making a mere 180 copies.

February 23, 1455

The importance of creating the world's first printing press cannot be overstated. Prior to this, books needed to be copied by hand, which was slow, expensive, and prone to error. Gutenberg's technology is what gradually brought reading to the masses, and played a pivotal role in the Protestant Reformation, the Renaissance, the Age of Enlightenment, and the Scientific Revolution.

Except, Gutenberg wasn't actually first. A form of movable-type printing press was first created in Korea two centuries earlier by Choe Yun-ui, but for a number of reasons the invention didn't catch on in Asia. Gutenberg's version is the one that changed the world.

Prior to Gutenberg's invention, literacy and education were for the elite. This was a turning point that transformed society and led to our rapid growth in learning. It was a critical step in bringing an end to the so-called Dark Ages and accelerating progress toward a more enlightened time.

Looking at recent fuckery, there is still much work to be done, but trust me that things are better now, even with the growth of fascist websites spreading misinformation, than they were during a time when 99 percent of the population was doomed to a life of ignorance.

In the months following the December 7, 1941, surprise attack by the Japanese on Pearl Harbor, Americans were freaked right the fuck out. I mean, the Japanese telegraphed that Hawai'i shit, basically shouting that they were gonna do it. And yet, in one of the most epic intelligence failures in history, the United States was caught with its bathing suits down. But they weren't going to miss the next one. Everyone in the country was on high alert, especially those on the West Coast.

February 24, 1942

The United States declared war on Japan the day after Pearl Harbor and began installing anti-aircraft guns and bunkers all up and down the coast. Regular air-raid drills were conducted. Cities were blacked out and when merchant ships off the coast began getting sunk by Japanese submarines, everyone west of the Rockies was blowing blood vessels in anticipation of being blown to poop by a Japanese aerial attack.

In the early evening of February 24, 1942, U.S. intelligence services announced shit is gonna go down, Los Angeles, so be ready. They predicted an imminent attack by the Japanese. Later that night, air-raid sirens sounded and a blackout was ordered. Nerves got the best of the guys with their fingers on the triggers, and everything went to H-E-double hockey sticks.

In this incredibly stupid Battle of Los Angeles, thousands of .50-caliber machine-gun rounds were fired into the night sky at Japanese aircraft that weren't fucking there. Not only that, but for an hour in the middle of the night 1,400 rounds of 12.8-pound anti-aircraft shells gave every seagull for miles an anxiety attack as they exploded above the city. The cacophony probably sent all the stray cats in Southern California packing for the Mexican border.

Buildings and vehicles were damaged from falling shell fragments, and five deaths resulted from indirect causes. The chaos caused three people to die in car accidents, and two more kicked the bucket from *Holy fucking shit it's the Apocalypse!*–induced heart attacks.

Conspiracy theories as to the cause of the false alarm ran rampant. Over four decades later the U.S. Air Force *finally* came up with the explanation that weather balloons caused the panic. Fucking weather balloons. Those things get blamed for lots of stuff.

f the Catholics were coming for my pagan ass, I'd be tempted to do myself in too. That's what 4,000 Lithuanians did in 1336 when a large force of Teutonic Knights was headed their way to murder and/or enslave them for daring to not be followers of Jesus.

The campaign of Christian colonization was called the Lithuanian Crusade, and it had already lasted decades, because converting and massacring infidels is difficult, time-consuming work. And if they didn't convert, well, Saint Bernard of Clairvaux said in the twelfth century that "Killing an infidel makes an honor to a Christian, because it glorifies the Christ." Meanwhile, Jesus is all "You-fucking-what-when?"

After the held-at-sword-point "Pray to our god, dammit!" act had been going on for half a century, the people in Pilénai, a hill fort in Lithuania, had a pretty good idea that they were going to be in for a bad day when they saw 6,000 bloodthirsty Teutonic Knights come knocking on February 25, 1336. And you thought Jehovah's Witnesses waking your hungover ass up early on a Saturday was bad.

The details of what happened are limited, because everyone fucking died, and stories of a "valiant defense" have grown in the telling.

But these defenders weren't soldiers. They were mostly regular non-Christian folks who just wanted to be left the fuck alone.

February 25, 1336

The Teutons were looking for prisoners to enslave as well as to loot the city, and the Lithuanians denied them both, setting all their property aflame and engaging in mass self-slaughter after their hasty efforts at a defense of the fort proved futile. One story is that an old woman killed a hundred (willing) people with an axe before taking her own life. The resident duke also killed many (also willing) people with his sword, including his wife, before killing himself.

In an effort to be balanced, it's not like the Lithuanians never did anything bad. They'd been known to raid and pillage the Holy Roman Empire and weren't exactly nice to the captives they took. It's basically another example about how humans have always been fucking horrible to each other since way back when some hairy, smelly buff dude bashed the brains out of his rivals with a wildebeest femur, declaring himself Penis Numero Uno of the cave and getting all the Daryl Hannah he desired.

> **The details of what happened are limited, because everyone fucking died, and stories of a "valiant defense" have grown in the telling.**

John, **Robert, Stephen,** Bill, Wilfredo, and a pregnant Monica. These are the first names of the six people who died when the World Trade Center was first attacked by terrorists eight years before 9/11. Rather than highjacked aircraft, this attack involved a truck bomb parked underneath the North Tower.

February 26, 1993

The attack was planned and executed by terrorists from countries across the Middle East and Pakistan, with financing from Khalid Sheikh Mohammed, a Pakistani member of Osama bin Laden's al-Qaeda terrorist organization. Mohammed was also the principal architect behind 9/11. He's currently rotting in Guantánamo and never getting out. So, fuck that guy.

The bomb weighed over 1,300 pounds and was made from various chemicals I won't bother listing. The intention was for the attack to be much more horrific than it ended up being. They figured the bomb would cause the North Tower to topple and fall into the South Tower, killing tens of thousands of innocent people, because terrorists are diabolical dickbags. It's possible that might have happened had the truck been parked nearer the structure's poured-concrete foundation. But it wasn't. So, when

the bomb was detonated just after noon on February 26, 1993, only the six mentioned earlier lost their lives. More than a thousand others were wounded, mostly during the mass evacuation that followed the blast.

The motivation for the attack was to punish the United States for its support of Israel. One of the main perpetrators, a Pakistani named Ramzi Yousef who was also the nephew of the attack's financier, had sent letters to various media before the bombing calling for America to end its aid to Israel and cease interference in the Middle East. He did not include any religious proclamations regarding his motivation for the bombing.

The bomb had a twenty-foot fuse that gave the perpetrators twelve minutes to make their escape. Yousef fled to Pakistan shortly after the bombing, but Pakistani authorities caught the fucker two years later and extradited him to the United States, where he will remain incarcerated until he breathes his last.

All the perpetrators were caught but one. Google Abdul Rahman Yasin and memorize the photo. He's of Iraqi descent but was born in fucking Indiana. He was raised in Iraq and may have acid burns on his right thigh from bomb-making chemicals. If you see him, call the police. The reward for his capture is five million dollars.

All the perpetrators were caught but one. Google Abdul Rahman Yasin and memorize the photo. He's of Iraqi descent but was born in fucking Indiana.

Imagine this. You're facing a firing squad. You've declined a blindfold. You hear the word "Ready!" followed by "Aim!" and in the moment before the bullets fly you yell at those holding the rifles, "Shoot straight, you bastards! Don't make a mess of it!" It seems pretty badass, and it might be cool to glorify the man who went out that way, but Harry "Breaker" Morant was a murderous piece of shit who got what he deserved.

In the 1980 film *Breaker Morant,* Edward Woodward stars as the title character, and delivers that same final line for the screen. It tells the tale of events during the Second Boer War in South Africa, which was typical colonialism fuckery with the British Empire fighting against mostly Dutch descendants called Boers in a land that belonged to neither of them. The war wasn't going well for the Brits, but rather than give up they adopted a policy of scorched earth and putting women and children in concentration camps (more than 27,000 of whom died) to convince the Boers to give up. The British also killed a shit-ton of Native Africans, FYI.

Compared to all that sanctioned fuckery, it seems odd that Harry Morant was singled out as a war criminal, but he *was* still guilty of heinous crimes. Born in England in 1864, he moved to Australia when he was nineteen and worked a variety of jobs, including breaking horses, the origin of his nickname. He joined an Australian mounted infantry unit and headed off to South Africa to serve Queen and Country and all that imperialist dogshit. While there, he did some killing that he wasn't supposed to do.

February 27, 1902

During an ambush in the summer of 1901, the enemy killed the captain of Morant's patrol. The Australians were forced to flee, and when they returned they found the captain's body mutilated (allegedly). Well, Harry was pissed, and he ordered and engaged in a series of revenge killings against both prisoners of war and civilians. Several members of his regiment were aghast, and fifteen signed a letter a few months later detailing the crimes, sending it secretly to a commanding officer.

A court-martial of several soldiers with a variety of charges followed. The story of Morant only stands out among those tried because, even though it was not the director's intent, the film *Breaker Morant* raised him to the status of an icon, even a martyr, who was supposedly railroaded by British authorities. In 2010 a petition was sent to Queen Elizabeth to have Morant posthumously pardoned, even though the film clearly shows Morant was guilty as fuck. I suppose it's just that people are stupid and were probably captivated by those badass last words, which were spoken on the early morning of February 27, 1902, immediately before several high-caliber rifle rounds entered Morant's chest.

The actual fire was the day before, but the real shit-assery happened on this day, almost like those Nazi fucks set the Reichstag on fire themselves and blamed communists so they could issue a decree giving them dictatorial powers. Well, maybe.

February 28, 1933

Four weeks after that Nazi cockblanket Adolf Hitler was sworn in as Chancellor of Germany, the country's parliament building, called the Reichstag, went up in arsonist flames. It was blamed on a Dutch communist named Marinus van der Lubbe. He might have been guilty, but some historians consider him a pawn, and suggest that the fire was actually set by Nazis to further their fucktacular aims. Either way, they tried Marinus and executed him via guillotine the following year, three days before he turned twenty-five.

The day after the fire, on February 28, 1933, shit got real. Real shitty. Unless, of course, you were a fucking Nazi. The real shit was called the Reichstag Fire Decree, and it was some dastardly political maneuvering. See, Hitler was leader of a coalition government, meaning he had to cooperate with others to get anything done, which, if you know anything about Hitler, was totally not his style. So, he told German president Hindenburg to dissolve Parliament and call an election. The fire happened just a week before that election was scheduled.

The fire wasn't just blamed on Van der Lubbe, but was proclaimed to be a communist plot. The Nazi crudbuckets said a commie uprising was imminent and they were gonna eat your babies or some shit. They said the fire was a "signal for a bloody uprising and civil war." They used words like "pillage" and "terrorism" and plenty of Germans freaked entirely the fuck out. And when people are freaked out, they're less likely to notice the loss of their freedoms in the name of security.

The government threw a bunch of communists in jail, suspended the constitution, and abolished civil rights. All those freedoms around speech, press, assembly, not being thrown in prison for no good fucking reason? Gone. You got a warrant to search my house? Here's your fucking warrant [clubs homeowner over the head]. The night of the decree, more than 4,000 people were arrested, imprisoned, tortured. Hitler had the power to do this because just six days earlier he'd enrolled 50,000 Nazi Stormtroopers as auxiliary police. Almost like he'd been planning something like this all along.

In the election that followed a few days later, the German Communist Party won eighty-one seats, but weren't able to take them because all those who won were quickly arrested and treated like traitors. Being a communist in Germany had become de facto illegal. The decree remained in place during the remainder of the Third Reich, giving Hitler absolute power to do whatever the fuck he pleased.

And the world suffered for it.

Remember when Oprah picked James Frey's "memoir" of addiction titled *A Million Little Pieces* for her book club and it turned out to be full of shit and then Oprah lost her shit? That was nothing.

First published in 1997, *Misha: A Mémoire of the Holocaust* was later reclassified as a literary hoax. The author's real name is Monique de Wael, and she was born to Catholic parents in Belgium in 1937. During World War II her parents were murdered by those fucking Nazi fucks not for their religion, but for fighting in the Resistance. Sounds like her parents were cool, because resisting Nazis is awesome. Except her dad gave up the names of his fellow Resistance fighters after a nice bit of torture and everyone started calling Monique "the Traitor's Daughter."

Her parents were sent to a concentration camp where they later died, and Monique was raised by family members. It's not a happy story, but nothing like the whopper she fabricated for *Misha*.

Decades after the war ended, while in her forties, Monique changed her name to "Misha Defonseca" and began relaying a fantastical story that she was a Jewish survivor of the Holocaust, even using her bullshit tale of woe to solicit donations from the Jewish community. She said her "Jewish" parents gave her to a Catholic family to be raised during the war and changed her name to her actual real fucking birth name to hide her identity. In the story—I mean outrageous fucking lie—she said she left the family at the age of only six to wander across Europe in search of her parents. In the middle of a world war.

According to the tale, she walked almost two thousand miles, stealing food and clothing to survive. This is where she decided "Fuck it; if I'm going to lie, I'm going to lie big." She said when she was starving, she was adopted by a pack of wolves who protected her and let her eat the organs from their kills to survive. She wrote that. Holy shit. The fictional character of Misha makes it all the way to Poland, sneaks in and out of the Warsaw Ghetto, and kills a Nazi with a pocketknife when he tries to rape her. Sure.

The book was published by a small press in the United States and sold poorly there but did a lot better in Europe. What did Monique do then? She sued her publisher for poor marketing and for screwing her on overseas royalties, and the fucking judge awarded her $22.5 million. People had been saying the story was bullshit even before it was published, when those asked to provide endorsements said it was a crock. But with the judgment against them, the publisher worked to actively expose de Wael as being a liar.

It took time to unravel, but when Monique's Catholic baptism and school records surfaced, she admitted on February 29, 2008, that she'd made it up. Six years later a court ordered de Wael to repay her publisher the full judgment amount.

March

've been to the Smithsonian and seen the *Spirit of St. Louis* hanging from the ceiling. It's tiny. Charles Lindbergh became the first person to fly solo nonstop across the Atlantic in that wee thing when he was only twenty-five. And while Charles turned out to be not such a good guy (his antisemitism being one aspect), no one deserves to have their young son kidnapped and murdered.

Five years after the flight that brought international fame to his father, on the morning of March 1, 1932, it was discovered that twenty-month-old Charles Jr. was missing from the family's New Jersey home. Stuck into the windowsill was an envelope containing a poorly written ransom note demanding $50,000. At some point during the night a kidnapper had used a ladder to enter the child's room.

A mass investigation coupled with a media shitstorm ensued. A second note arrived via mail on March 6; the ransom was upped to $70,000. Shortly thereafter was a third note, and a fourth, to arrange a go-between to hand over the cash. More notes followed and eventually $50,000 was handed over to a stranger in early April who said the child could be found on a boat named *Nellie* at Martha's Vineyard. But the child was not there, because Charles Jr. had been dead since the day after he was taken.

On May 12, a truck driver pulled over to piss and found the decomposed body of Charles Jr. less than five miles from the Lindbergh home. His skull was badly fractured. A servant at the home was ruthlessly interrogated and ended up taking her own life the following month, only to have her alibi check out.

The ransom bills had the serial numbers recorded, and in an investigation lasting over two years police tracked many of them, spent along the subway route between the Bronx and Manhattan. Part of the ransom was also gold certificates, and an observant gas station attendant coupled with an alert bank teller handling the certificates helped point toward a German immigrant with a criminal record named Richard Hauptmann. The evidence found in his home was overwhelming and he was tried, convicted, and executed via electric chair in 1936.

Hauptmann maintained his innocence, which murderers often do. Conspiracy theories ran rampant, but the evidence is convincing he did it. Charles Lindbergh went on to have five more children with his wife, as well as seven children with three other women (while remaining married) in secret while stationed as a brigadier general in Germany in the 1950s and '60s. None of the secret children knew who the occasional visitor of a father was until one of them read an article about Lindbergh in the mid-1980s, ten years after Charles's death, and the story of the secret Lindbergh children slowly unraveled.

Like I said, he wasn't a great guy.

If you had a lot of product that was about to be made illegal, you'd unload it, right? Sell it fast and get some cash while you still can. Two years before the U.S. Civil War, Pierce Mease Butler didn't know chattel slavery was coming to an end. He was just a gambling addict with massive debts, so he hosted the single largest auction of enslaved people in U.S. history to pay them off.

March 2, 1859

Butler was a piece of fucking shit. You know how when you're driving, and some asshole cuts you off, and you call them a piece of shit? Not even close. He didn't even live on either of the plantations that made his family one of the wealthiest in the nation. He resided mostly in Philadelphia while enslaved people toiled and died over rice and cotton crops in Georgia so he could spend his inheritance like a spoiled idiot with lots of granddaddy money.

Pierce was dumb as an oversized bucket of dumbfuck. He tried all sorts of investment schemes and lost a bunch of money because he was stupid, spent lavishly on things he couldn't afford, and was the shittiest gambler ever, burning through the family fortune in no time. Creditors sold his man-

sion in Philadelphia but that wasn't enough. The only thing he had of value in racist slavery-nation America was the human beings working his two Georgia plantations, and so on March 2, 1859, the "Great Slave Auction" began in the city of Savannah. And it was "great" in the same way some people wanted to "Make America Great Again."

What I mean is, it was a fucking horror; 436 men, women, and children were auctioned off like farm animals. It became known as "the weeping time," because they were taken from the only home many of them knew as they were forcibly relocated. More awful was that, despite the auction having terms against separating families, little consideration was given to this. Sorry kid, I only want to buy you. I don't need your mom and dad. Stop crying.

Who am I kidding? They would never say sorry.

One 23-year-old man named Jeffrey begged his new owner to also buy his wife, Dorcas, but the piece of shit basically said nah fuck you Jeff shut up and get in the wagon.

Butler was flush again after the sale, blew through much of his ill-gotten payday, and died in 1867 from malaria. If you want to piss on Pierce Butler's grave, it's in the Christ Church Burial Ground in Philadelphia.

n 2016, actor Will Smith was on Stephen Colbert and said, "Racism is not getting worse; it's getting filmed." Yet despite the video evidence of the 1991 police beating of Rodney King, justice was nowhere to be found, and a city burned.

Early in the morning on March 3, 1991, Rodney King was with friends and speeding along a Los Angeles highway. He'd been drinking and tried to outrun police, later saying he fled because driving drunk violated his parole for a previous robbery charge, and he didn't want to go back to jail. We get it. He wasn't a saint. But what followed was a brutal beating that was caught on video and incensed the public. He had broken bones in his face and ankle, plus several bruises and cuts. Nurses at the hospital the police took King to reported that the officers laughed and joked about how many times they had hit him.

Four cops were charged with assault and excessive use of force; three were acquitted and one given a mistrial by a jury made up of ten whites, one Latino, and one Asian. The trial received significant public attention, and people were pissed. The city's Black mayor, Tom Bradley, said those police did "not deserve to wear the uniform of the LAPD." President Bush said he was "stunned" by the verdict, unable to reconcile it with what he saw on the video.

March 3, 1991

Almost immediately after the verdict was read, riots broke out in L.A. among a population sick of the regular police brutality experienced by their communities. The riots lasted six days, resulting in thousands of fires, over a billion dollars in damages, over 2,000 injuries, and 63 deaths. Smaller riots occurred in other cities, including San Francisco, Las Vegas, New York, Atlanta, and Seattle.

King appeared on television pleading for it to stop, asking, "Can we all get along?" But with rampant injustice and inequality that shows no signs of diminishing in the three decades since then, it seems the answer remains "No."

He wasn't a saint. But what followed was a brutal beating that was caught on video and incensed the public. He had broken bones in his face and ankle, plus several bruises and cuts.

Technically the Italians weren't Nazis, but in World War II they were allied with Nazis, so . . . fucking Nazis. Not much attention is paid to Greece during that war, but shit did go down there, too. They were occupied by the Axis (the bad guys), and because people didn't like Nazis, Greece had a resistance. In fact, the Greek Resistance was one of the strongest of all such groups fighting Nazis in the entire war.

March 4, 1943

The Battle of Fardykambos began on March 4, 1943, and some badass Greeks fucked some infected-testicle Nazi shit up. It's important to note that the Greek Resistance was not a monolith, but rather comprised several different groups with myriad political alignments. They were, however, united in their opinion that Nazis suck and needed to die. The main movement was the communist-aligned National Liberation Front, but their acronym is EAM because Greek, and the battle began with the ambushing of an Italian transport column. The nearby Italian garrison sent reinforcements to effect a rescue, and a full-on fight broke out between Italian forces and the EAM.

Guess what happened then? Fucking way cool shit is what happened. The sounds of the battle were heard by the local populace, and people said, "Hey! They're killing fucking Nazis. I want to kill some fucking Nazis too! Let's go help them kill fucking Nazis!" Okay yeah, they weren't for-real Nazis, but they fought in alliance with Hitler, so close enough. Fuck them up.

And fuck them up they did. Even the rival Resistance groups from the right-wing end of the political spectrum got in on the fun. The battle grew from the location of the ambush into a general uprising, with the larger fight taking place at Fardykambos against the Italian garrison lasting another two days. By the end of it, people from across the land flocked toward the battle, wanting to get in on the killing of the oppressors who'd brutally occupied their land for the previous two years.

In the battles, only four Greeks lost their lives, but close to a hundred Italians were killed and over five hundred screamed "Please stop killing us!" and were taken prisoner. The victory created a critical liberation zone for Greece that initiated a steady withdrawal of the invading fascists from the peninsula.

Members of the Greek Resistance, 1944

Joseph Stalin was a murderous piece of shit, and after he finally went off to Godless Communist Hell, his successor, Nikita Khrushchev, began a process called "de-Stalinization."

A kind estimate is that Stalin's three-decade rule of the Soviet Union was responsible for 10 million deaths. There were massive purges of people who he didn't like, people who he didn't like dying in Gulags, intentional famines killing people who he didn't like . . . you get the idea. But when he died of a cerebral hemorrhage on March 5, 1953, many mourned.

One thing we've seen throughout history is that the cult of personality is bad, and Stalin definitely had that. If people are beholden to a leader rather than a system of government, not only does it allow leaders to get away with whatever the fuck they want, it makes transition to new leadership all the more challenging. There was a reason many wanted Rome to remain a republic rather than transform into an empire under Julius Caesar, because it places a nation under the whim of a very mortal ruler. They may be great, they may be horrible, but either way they eventually die. Strong systems of government, however, can survive no matter who is in charge.

Stalin's image was everywhere, with him presented as the all-powerful and all-knowing leader. Kind of like what they have going on in North Korea. MAGA hats were a similar idea, embodying that twice-impeached, peach-colored pus bucket. Despite Comrade Joseph being made of ass,

love for Stalin was so great that Khrushchev needed to engage in "silent de-Stalinization" so people didn't get their knickers twisted over disrespect for the memory of their lauded leader.

March 5, 1953

Khrushchev created a more collective leadership and eased Stalin's one-party totalitarian system of government. The Gulags were mostly emptied. Stalin's image was gradually purged from public view; cities, landmarks, and facilities bearing his name reverted to their former names. The State Anthem of the USSR and anthems of various republics were changed to get rid of any mention of the mustachioed motherfucker.

On February 25, 1956, Khrushchev finally called Stalin out in a "secret speech" made to the Communist Party. Titled "On the Cult of Personality and Its Consequences," the speech outlined Stalin's abuse of power and use of mass terror against innocents to maintain control. The speech leaked, and even though it had been three years since Stalin died, people were fucking pissed. There were riots. In the United States, the speech decimated the American left by revealing communism as shitty, resulting in a rapid exodus of 30,000 members from the U.S. Communist Party.

This time of relaxed repression and censorship became known as the Khrushchev Thaw.

Sometimes a person accomplishes so much in their life that when it comes to writing about them you think—holy shit, where to start? Let's begin with Grace Hopper's appearance on *60 Minutes* in 1983, when a member of Congress saw her on TV and said holy shit she is way too awesome we need to recognize that.

March 6, 1983

Born in New York in 1906, Hopper became a computer scientist, and was awarded a PhD in mathematics from Yale in 1934. She attempted to enlist in the navy during World War II but was denied because apparently the age of thirty-four was too old. So, she joined the Naval Reserve instead, and had to get an exemption because she weighed fifteen pounds less than the minimum 120-pound requirement. She graduated top of her class from the Naval Reserve school and was assigned to Harvard's Computation Project in 1944.

Hopper was part of creating UNIVAC I, one of the earliest commercial computers, and her work with programming languages led to the development of COBOL. Her later efforts transformed the way Defense Department computer systems went from centralized toward more distributed networks.

Grace Hopper proved so invaluable that

Grace Hopper

the navy couldn't get enough of her. Regulations forced her to retire in 1966 at age sixty with the rank of commander. The following year the navy called her and said yeah we really need you back for six months. That six months turned into an "indefinite assignment." She retired again in 1971 at age sixty-five and a year later they said, uh, Grace? Can you please come back again and she said fine and returned and they promoted her to captain. Then, on March 6, 1983, at the age of seventy-six, she was interviewed by broadcast journalist Morley Safer about being the oldest woman still serving in the entire U.S. Armed Forces. Congressman Philip Crane was watching and said why is she only a captain? He sponsored a joint resolution in Congress that led to her being promoted to commodore later that year via special presidential appointment. Two years later the rank of commodore was renamed, and she officially became Rear Admiral Grace Hopper.

Hopper finally retired in 1986, a few months shy of her eightieth birthday. At the time, she was the oldest active-duty commissioned officer in the navy of any gender. But she didn't stop working, taking a consultancy position with Digital Equipment Corporation shortly afterward.

Grace Hopper died in 1992 at the age of eighty-five and is buried in Arlington National Cemetery.

Electing assholes to senior political positions is nothing new. Edward Wakefield was a member of Parliament for both Canada (when it was still a British colony, not a country) and New Zealand, helping found the latter as a nation. He was also a pile of poo who kidnapped a young girl and forced her to marry him in an effort to steal her inheritance. And it wasn't the first time he'd done something like that.

This fucking guy. Born in London in 1796, when Wakefield was twenty he set his sights on seventeen-year-old Eliza Pattle, a wealthy heiress, and convinced her to elope because he wanted her family's money. The parents, faced with the marriage being a done deal, said well fuck fine I guess and gave him the modern equivalent of seven million dollars because that's how shit often worked back then. Eliza died a few years later giving birth to their second child, and Ed pawned the two kids off on his sister and went in search of more cash, because seven million bucks wasn't enough for this douche.

On March 7, 1827, when Wakefield was a few weeks shy of thirty, he abducted fifteen-year-old Ellen Turner, the only daughter of a wealthy English politician. Wakefield took her to Scotland, which had weak marriage laws, and forced her to marry him in what I'm certain was a very romantic ceremony conducted by a blacksmith. Ed figured the same thing would happen as last time: The parents would say fine and give him money. But Ellen's dad said no way fuck that guy. And by that he meant he didn't want his sweet daughter Ellen to be fucking that guy.

March 7, 1827

Ed had taken Ellen to Paris, and her dad got the authorities involved. Ellen's uncle, a police officer, and a lawyer traveled to Paris and said we're taking her home. Ed said no you can't we're married. Ellen said he stole me I don't want to be married to this jackass. So, they took her home and that Wakefield dickthrob got his ass thrown in prison for three years, the marriage annulled. Hooray!

Once out of prison he was a changed man. Kidding! He got big into the land thievery in the name of colonialism in Canada, Australia, and New Zealand and became a politician known for engaging in a number of sleazy schemes. To this day, there is a river, a port, and a street named after him in Adelaide, Australia.

Two years after her abduction, Ellen Turner married a wealthy neighbor and lived to the ripe old age of . . . [checks notes] . . . died in childbirth at nineteen.

On **March 8, 2014,** Malaysia Airlines Flight 370 disappeared along with its 227 passengers and a dozen crew. Years later, the evidence points to the flight captain intentionally crashing the plane in a mass murder-suicide.

March 8, 2014

The fuck happened? The Boeing 777 was flown by a first officer doing his final training flight prior to full certification, and the captain was one of the airline's senior pilots. It departed from Kuala Lumpur for Beijing; air traffic control had final communication thirty-eight minutes after takeoff. Military radar tracked it for another hour as it deviated west of its intended flight path. It then turned south over the Indian Ocean and remained aloft for another six hours. Satellite data revealed a steep descent that obliterated the plane, approximately eight hours after taking off from Malaysia.

It crashed somewhere in the southern Indian Ocean. Dozens of ships and aircraft participated in the search, but it would be more than a year before any debris floated ashore. Massive investigations followed. The Malaysian government is corrupt as fuck and was the opposite of helpful. Conspiracy theories abounded, but all that can be deduced from the evidence is that the loss of Flight 370 was intentional. Someone on board made it happen. It can't be explained by mechanical failure or naturally occurring phenomena. The flight path is too bizarre, yet controlled.

What's more, it happened from within the cockpit. There is no other way to control the plane. Being that the course diversion took place only two minutes after the captain's final conversation with ATC, and the cockpit was secured against forced entry, it's most unlikely this was a hijacking. Considering the limited possibilities, it seems either the captain or first officer purposely caused the crash. Such a thing has happened several times before, where a pilot decided to murder crew and passengers in taking their own life.

The background of the first officer sends up no alarms, but an investigation into Captain Zaharie Ahmad Shah is full of red flags. He was described as lonely and sad after the breakup of his marriage. Records show he conducted a flight simulation roughly matching the final path of Flight 370. It would've been easy for the captain to order the first officer to check something outside the cockpit, lock him out, then depressurize the cabin, causing everyone aboard to lose consciousness and eventually die via hypoxia. Added to this, a longtime friend of Zaharie's, also a captain, reluctantly proclaimed that his friend probably was the guilty party, describing it as "the necessary conclusion." In 2020, Tony Abbott, the former prime minister of Australia, shared a rumor that top Malaysian officials had come to the same conclusion mere days after the crash.

The original Barbie doll, and those that followed for decades, had impossible proportions. Still, over a billion of them have been sold. Barbie's creator, Ruth Handler, had a radical mastectomy due to breast cancer in 1970. Not satisfied with the prostheses available and knowing a thing or two about designing artificial breasts, she made her own.

Ruth married her high school sweetheart Elliot, who went into business with Harold "Matt" Matson to make picture frames. The guys portmanteau'd their names to create Mattel in 1945. They turned the scraps left over from manufacturing frames into dollhouse furniture, which sold better than the picture frames, and a toy giant was born. Matson got sick and sold his share to the Handlers in the late 1940s and Ruth became company president.

Seeing her daughter Barbara play with paper dolls, Ruth said, I know, I'll give her a plastic Marilyn Monroe, if Marilyn ate a dozen ~~amphetamines~~ diet pills a day instead of food. People were like, little girls don't want to play with voluptuous women and Ruth said you don't know shit about little girls. On March 9, 1959, the first-ever Barbie doll debuted at the American International Toy Fair in New York.

Problem was, Ruth kind of stole her design from a German doll called "Bild Lilli" that was based on a comic strip and sold to adults as a gag. And yeah, Mattel got sued and settled out of court and, in 1964, bought the copyright and patent rights for Bild Lilli.

March 9, 1959

Parents weren't real thrilled with those two rockets attached to Barbie's chest, but you know how kids are. "Mommy, I WANT it!" Like I said, over a billion sold, helped by an aggressive TV advertising campaign. Barbie was one of the first toys to be marketed that way, and it worked so well that other toy manufacturers said holy fucking shit we need to buy up ad space during all those kid shows too!

The company has listened to feedback about the doll, at least some of the time. For the first dozen years Barbie's eyes were demurely cast off to the side in a "hey big fella I'm just a girly girl and you're such a manly man and the patriarchy is awesome" kind of way. But since 1971 her eyes have looked forward in more of an "I am woman don't fuck with me" way.

Barbie has been one helluva career woman, because accessories sell. She's been a veterinarian, doctor, marine biologist, park ranger, astronaut, judge, cop, firefighter, and presidential candidate. As a testament to such evolution, flight attendant Barbie was released in 1961, but it wasn't until 1990 that airline pilot Barbie finally hit the scene.

> **Barbie has been one helluva career woman, because accessories sell. She's been a veterinarian, doctor, marine biologist, park ranger, astronaut, judge, cop, firefighter, and presidential candidate.**

There are shitty ways to die, and then there is the way Jean Calas died. Picture this. You find your son has taken his own life. Distraught, you make it look like a murder, because eighteenth-century Catholicism wasn't tolerant for shit. And then the government blames you for the "murder" and tortures you to death. Yeah, that sucks.

March 10, 1762

In sixteenth-century France there was plenty o' killin' of Protestants because Catholics didn't like that Reformation stuff. Two centuries later things had chilled out, but France still wasn't a great place to be Protestant. Catholicism was the official state religion and there was no legal right to practice any other form of invisible sky fairy. Reaction to Protestantism had evolved from "Let's kill those motherfuckers" to "We shall just barely tolerate those motherfuckers."

Jean Calas was a Protestant merchant who lived in Toulouse. In 1756 his son Louis converted to Catholicism, possibly because it involved less suffering, even though Catholicism kind of digs the whole suffering thing. Anyway, five years later the family discovered that their other son, Marc-Antoine,

had hanged himself in the family home. Suicide was considered a terrible crime against the self, and to teach the dead a lesson the practice was to defile the corpse. So, the family said he'd been murdered. The authorities saw a chance to fuck over a dirty Protestant and said, well looks like that Marc-Antoine was going to convert to Catholicism just like your other son did, Jean, and you didn't like that, so you killed him. Come with us for some torturing, please.

Calas then said no really he took his own life and the judge said ha ha no backsies, you're guilty, time for some agonizing pain. For two days they publicly tortured Calas on "the wheel." His arms and legs were dislocated, their bones broken. He had gallons of water poured down his throat. All the while, he proclaimed his innocence, right up until his death on March 10, 1762.

The philosopher Voltaire said now that was some fucking bullshit. No fan of the Catholic Church, Voltaire launched a successful campaign to prove that Marc-Antoine had killed himself over gambling debts and saw that Jean Calas was posthumously exonerated and the family awarded financial compensation by the king as a "yeah sorry we killed your dad/husband in the most horrible way possible" gesture.

In sixteenth-century France there was plenty o' killin' of Protestants because Catholics didn't like that Reformation stuff.

"Bring me Muhammad Ali" is not something you expect as part of a list of terrorist demands during a hostage-taking negotiation. During the 1977 Hanafi Siege, 149 hostages were held at gunpoint for two days at three locations across Washington, D.C., by orthodox Sunni Muslim militants. Future Washington mayor Marion Barry was wounded by gunfire during the crisis. The episode revealed deep divisions within America's Black Muslim community.

Hamaas Abdul Khaalis, born a Roman Catholic as Ernest McGhee, had been national secretary for the Nation of Islam, a Black political and religious movement in the United States with a dark history. But he split with them in 1958 and became highly critical of the organization, referring to its leader Elijah Muhammad as a "lying deceiver." In turn, the Nation of Islam accused Khaalis of being a "white man's tool." Khaalis then worked to convert people to Hanafi Islam on his own. One such convert was basketball great Kareem Abdul-Jabbar. In reprisal for his criticisms, a Nation of Islam–affiliated crime group called Black Mafia brutally murdered Khaalis's family, including a nine-day-old baby, in 1973. Fucking hell. Hamaas was not home during the murders.

It was a desire by Khaalis to bring national attention to the murder of his family that prompted the siege, which began on March 9, 1977. The primary siege was of the Jewish organization B'nai B'rith in downtown Washington, where more than a hundred hostages were taken by Khaalis and six members of his group. An hour later three men took eleven hostages at the Islamic Center of Washington. Two more Hanafis attacked the District Building, which holds the office of the mayor and is just a few blocks from the White House. When an elevator door opened at the District Building, the pair of attackers were startled and shot a radio reporter to death. They also injured a police officer during the raid; he later died of a heart attack. During the shooting at the District Building, Marion Barry, who was then a city councilman, was hit by a ricochet that lodged near his heart.

March 11, 1977

During the siege, the attackers criticized the Jewish judge who'd presided over the trial of the murderers of Khaalis's family, saying, "Jews control the courts and the press." They demanded the killers be handed over. They also wanted the Nation of Islam members who had assassinated Malcolm X, who had been a close friend of Khaalis's. It's presumed their intent was to execute these killers for their crimes. Yet another demand was to have boxer Muhammad Ali, who at the time was a supporter of the Nation of Islam, visit them.

The crisis was resolved by the actions of three Muslim ambassadors from Egypt, Pakistan, and Iran. They entered the three siege locations, read the Quran with the attackers, and pleaded with them, including Khaalis, to end things peacefully. Their efforts were successful, and the siege ended without further bloodshed on March 11, 1977. Hamaas Khaalis was convicted for leading the siege and died in prison in 2003.

Anschluss is German for "unification." Many refer to the joining of Austria with Germany prior to World War II as an annexation—the forcible acquisition of a state—but judging how Austrians filled the streets on March 12, 1938, to cheerfully welcome the fucking Nazis marching into their country, the word "annexation" doesn't quite fit.

March 12, 1938

And it wasn't just the fascist-lovers cheering the Nazis on, but people from across the political spectrum. The reasoning is that Austria in the 1930s was the shattered remains of a once-great empire that was devastated by World War I. The treaties following that war said hey Austria, no joining up with Germany, because we don't want to have to go through this world-war bullshit again. Two decades later, the country wasn't doing so hot and saw big Germany as a potential savior.

Late in the 1930s, Austria was still suffering from the Great Depression and had a lot of skilled people sitting around doing fuck

Crowds greeting (fucking) Nazis in Vienna

all because there was no work. Germany had gone through a rapid rearmament in a fuck-you to the 1919 Treaty of Versailles and looked south at all those potential soldiers and weapons-manufacturing workers, plus all of Austria's natural resources, and said "Hmmm . . ."

The German Nazis launched a propaganda campaign in Austria, promoting slogans like "One People, One Empire, One Leader." And like a bitch in heat Austria said, "Take me." Well, there was a bit more to it than that. Austrian Nazis launched terror attacks against their government and killed the Austrian Chancellor. Hitler put continued pressure on Austria to join Germany. Finally, in 1938, Austria said fine we'll vote on it. How does March 13 sound?

Hitler said fuck your vote and invaded Austria on March 12, 1938, unopposed by the Austrian military. The cheering crowds welcomed the Germans with Nazi salutes, Nazi flags, and flowers. Most Austrians were thrilled with this idea of a "Greater Germany" and besides, Hitler was born in Austria so he's one of us and we also don't like Jews so come on in.

Hitler's popularity in Austria was massive, and anyone who spoke out against him got the brutal Nazi oppression those fuckers are well known for. A referendum on the "annexation" was held on April 10. The "Yes" on the ballot was in large font, and the "No" was in small font in a "You better fucking vote the way we want" not-so-subtle hint. The vote was 99.71 percent in favor of annexation, so, yeah, there was probably a bit of vote rigging too. Classic Nazi.

The Dutch are confusing. The country is called the Netherlands, but some also call it Holland. The people are Dutch and they speak Dutch but there is also a dialect called Flemish. Jesus Christ. If I were Spain, I'd want to kick their asses too.

History has many examples of the [pick a number] Years' War. "Hundred" had Joan of Arc. "Seven" was about colonial rivalries. "Thirty" had up to 8 million dead in the name of the right way to pray to Jesus. The Eighty Years' War, however, is often overlooked. It's also known as the Dutch War of Independence. So fucking what? Did they fight over windmills? The fucking what is that it saw the decline of one powerful empire and the rise of another that embraced the shit out of capitalism to screw over a big chunk of the world, creating negative ripples of colonial fuckery across the centuries. It all began in a town called Oosterweel.

In the sixteenth century, the area known as the Netherlands-Holland-Clogland was ruled by Spain. The Dutch were getting pissy about the lack of self-rule, the taxes imposed by the Spanish, and the fact that they preferred that new Protestant thing and the Spaniards were all we'd really prefer if you did the Catholicism thing.

To display their anger, Protestant mobs across the Netherlands began to destroy Catholic art. Sixteenth-century Spanish Catholics weren't so tolerant of that sort of thing and launched a surprise attack on the rebels on March 13, 1567, at Oosterweel in the Antwerp province. And they kicked Dutch ass. It was a fucking slaughter, with the Spanish killing over 2,000 rebels.

But the Dutch wouldn't give up. The secret to their victory? Fuckin' finance it. Capitalism was becoming more of a thing, so the Dutch got loans to hire mercenary armies and build fleets. And they were real good customers. Their credit-purchased ships got control of valuable trade routes, so they had the money to pay back those loans, get more credit, build more fleets, hire more mercenaries, and kick some Spanish ass.

March 13, 1567

The Spanish failed to contain the rebellion because they sucked at paying back loans, so guess where the money flowed? To the rebels. It didn't end there. The Dutch Empire that followed wasn't built by the state, but by the merchant class looking to make money. The British had their evil East India Company colonizing swaths of Asia; the Dutch version of that was just as shitty. The Dutch East India Company ruled Indonesia for two centuries, and then the Dutch state took over and ruled it for another 150 years. The company also conquered to the west.

As an example, you know how Wall Street is the center of the financial world for the West? Before it was called New York, it was called New Amsterdam. The Dutch taught humanity a lot about how to exploit people and resources for profit, and the world continues to suffer for it.

Jack Ruby was innocent. Yeah, I know he said, "Hey, Oswald!" and then *Blam!* and Oswald was all "Oh fucking shit that hurts!" [paraphrased] and 80 million people saw it on TV, but . . . Ruby wasn't guilty. For real.

March 14, 1964

This takes some explaining.

Who killed John F. Kennedy? According to Lee Harvey Oswald, not him. "I'm just a patsy!" he proclaimed. And we should believe Oswald, because in the history of murder no killer ever proclaimed they didn't do it. Oh, wait.

There are allegations the mob had JFK killed because he hadn't done anything about Cuba going commie, which cost the mob a shit-ton of money. And his little brother was attorney general and was going after the mob, so they (figuratively) pulled

Jack Ruby shooting Lee Harvey Oswald

RFK's teeth by snuffing his president brother. Jack Ruby was tied to the mob, and allegedly Ruby killed Oswald on the orders of said mob to silence said patsy.

Live TV is an awfully public way of silencing someone though.

What's a more likely motivation is what Ruby proclaimed: He was a huge fan of JFK. Fucking adored the guy. And he was overwhelmingly pissed at the murder and saw an opportunity for revenge and so he shot Oswald. It was a single shot to the guts from a .38 revolver that killed him almost by luck, because it tore through his aorta. Or maybe it was fucking space aliens. I don't know.

Ruby shot Oswald, but he was still not guilty, legally speaking. On March 14, 1964, Jack Ruby was convicted of the murder of Lee Harvey Oswald and sentenced to death via that uncomfortable chair that plugs into the wall. But he never got electrococksuckered. Rather, in the final appeal before the execution was carried out, the sentence was overturned, because it was decided the judge in his original trial was a total knob and had committed numerous legal errors. And so, a new trial was ordered.

However, before the new trial, Jack Ruby died of a pulmonary embolism caused by his lung cancer. At the time, he was in a legal limbo where his previous conviction was vacated but he hadn't yet been convicted in the newly ordered trial. And so, technically speaking, he was innocent until proven guilty in a court of law. The second time, I mean.

Some called it the Anti-Extradition Law Amendment Bill Movement. You probably know it as the 2019–20 Hong Kong protests. The former doesn't sound terribly exciting, but it does give more insight into what kicked things off, capturing the world's attention.

In terms of places to live, China is . . . not the best. It's a wonderful land with wonderful people, but the government sucks. People keep complaining about there being only two viable political parties in the United States. Try living in a one-party state. That, boys and girls, is called a dictatorship, and it's the opposite of fun.

But Hong Kong had its fun. Yeah, it's got those colonial roots because the British said this shit is ours now and we're gonna use it as a base of operations to flood enough opium into China to mindfuck your population by the millions. But as a silver lining, over a century of being under colonial control allowed Hong Kong to avoid the upheavals that took place in mainland China during that time. It wasn't British "spreading democracy" idealistic bullshit, but the imperialism *did* indirectly result in Hong Kong becoming a much freer bastion of democracy, huddled next to the overbearing giant of Do What We Fucking Say.

Hong Kong was transferred from the United Kingdom back to China in 1997 and became a "special administrative region" of China, operating under a concept of "one country, two systems." But a new bill amending extradition to allow accused crim-inals to be handed over from Hong Kong to China threatened the independence of Hong Kong's legal system. And so, on March 15, 2019, a sit-in at the government headquarters in Hong Kong began to protest said amendment.

March 15, 2019

That initiated a chain reaction, and a few months later hundreds of thousands were protesting, and on June 15 the Hong Kong government said fuck it, fine, we'll suspend the bill. And all the protestors said okay that's good and they went home. Ha! Nope. They protested way fucking harder the next day saying fuck your bill. We don't want it suspended. Cancel that bitch!

It wasn't just that. The protesters wanted an investigation into the police brutality at previous protests, the arrested protestors to be released, the government to retract references to the protests as "riots," and universal voting rights. Oh, and there was this politician named Carrie Lam running Hong Kong. They wanted her gone.

They did not get what they asked for. The bill was formally withdrawn in October, but that's it. And so the protests continued, with other cities around the world joining the Hong Kong protestors in solidarity. In 2020, the outbreak of Covid largely silenced them, however.

Fight the motherfucking power.

On March 16, 1968, American soldiers did their best to exterminate a village filled with Vietnamese women and children in the Mỹ Lai massacre. Approximately five hundred unarmed people were murdered by U.S. troops, but helicopter pilot Hugh Thompson risked his own life, defying orders, to save as many as he could from his rampaging fellow soldiers. And he paid the price for his heroism.

March 16, 1968

It was a horror. Green troops expecting to find enemy Viet Cong decided that instead of leaving this peaceful village alone, they'd kill everyone. Then they realized, oh, wait, we can do some raping first. Yeah, that happened. While the boys in Company C were displaying the worst of humanity, Thompson was flying a small observation helicopter with two other crewmen. He witnessed the massacre taking place and rather than say "None of my business," he made it his fucking business.

Thompson landed his craft and confronted the heavily armed American soldiers who were in the process of raping and murdering the civilians. He confronted the lieutenant, who said he was "just following orders." Thompson replied with "Whose orders?" and the lieutenant said, "It ain't your concern" and told Thompson to get in his chopper and fuck off. At that point, one soldier began to open fire on wounded civilians lying in a ditch to kill anyone still moving.

In disbelief at what he was witnessing, Thompson went to look for any civilians he could save. He found eleven people and called in a gunship to transport them out. He and his two crew members stood guard over the terrorized civilians until evacuation arrived. He told his crew that if any Americans tried to shoot the civilians they were protecting, that they were to open fire on their fellow Americans. As a small mercy, the evacuation was successful.

When they returned to base, Thompson saved many more lives by reporting the massacre to his superiors. The operation–turned–mass murder was to include forays into many more hamlets that likely would have suffered a similar fate, but a halt was commanded.

Thompson was awarded the Distinguished Flying Cross for his actions, and he threw it away because the commendation said it was for rescuing a child caught in crossfire, with no mention of the massacre. When the story broke the following year, Thompson was summoned to appear before Congress where they ripped him apart, saying he was the one who should be court-martialed, for pointing his weapon at fellow soldiers.

Thompson became an outcast, saying people thought "I was a traitor. I was a communist. I was a sympathizer . . . that went on for about thirty years." There were death threats and dead animals left on his porch. In terms of "justice," the man leading the massacre, Lieutenant William Calley, was the only one punished. He was sentenced to life in prison, but President Nixon intervened, and he only served three and a half years' house arrest.

The photo was dubbed "Burst of Joy" and won a Pulitzer Prize. It portrays a man seeing his family for the first time in over five years after being a prisoner of war in North Vietnam. A teenage girl runs toward her father, arms wide in an anticipated embrace, her three siblings and mother following close behind. Everyone is smiling. But there is a story behind the photo that sucks.

Conflicting emotions on this one. Lieutenant Colonel Robert Stirm was a fighter pilot leading a bombing run over Hanoi in 1967. Many civilians died in those bombing runs. He was shot down and spent five and a half years in hell, suffering torture, mock executions, starvation, and sickness.

War isn't "complicated." It's fucked-up. The photo elicits an emotional response, but put this alternative image in your brain: A burned North Vietnamese child, lying in a hospital bed, learning their entire family has been incinerated by American bombs. Who do *they* think are the "good guys" in all this? On the other side, we have a man who answered the call of duty from corrupt politicians. He did his job and suffered greatly for it. As I said, war is fucked-up.

While a POW in horrific conditions, the only thing that kept Stirm alive was hope he would one day see his family again. Then, three days before he was scheduled to arrive home, he was given a "Dear John" letter

from his wife. Within a year of him being captured, she'd begun seeing other men, hiding it from her children. Three of those men had proposed marriage to her.

The emotions of Robert Stirm in the photo were bittersweet. He'd finally escaped hell, and his children were overjoyed to see him, but he also knew that the woman he loved wanted a divorce.

Yet there is an important fact that must be considered. Robert's family didn't know if he was alive or dead. When his wife wrote the letter, she'd begun a new relationship and, not knowing her husband had been taken prisoner, sent it as a form of closure. She never imagined he'd read it. When her husband did return, she broke off her new relationship and tried to make things work with Robert, but they divorced a year later.

The divorce court ordered that Loretta be awarded 43 percent of Robert's military retirement pay; it's not like she could be left destitute to raise their two youngest children (the two oldest went to live with their father). It all just sucks.

All four of the children have a copy of the photo hanging in their homes, but not Robert. When asked why, he referred to his ex-wife and said, "Because of her."

> **Then, three days before he was scheduled to arrive home, he was given a "Dear John" letter from his wife.**

People like to hold up FDR as one of the good presidents, but like all presidents, he made his share of dick moves. One such move was the establishment of the War Relocation Authority just a few months after the attack on Pearl Harbor, which allowed the U.S. government to take Japanese Americans into custody.

March 18, 1942

These were the American concentration camps. People weren't sent there to die, but to be "secured," just in case they might pose a threat to national security, without any intent to file charges or have trials. Canada did it too, because we were all paranoid fucking dicks in those days.

It began on March 18, 1942. At first, the WRA was under the direction of General Eisenhower's younger brother Milton, who wanted to round up Japanese men only, and to leave women and children out of it. He also proposed to instead send Japanese people to farms that were struggling to find workers, what with all the men going off to war. But he was not heard, and resigned after only ninety days in the role.

There were 127,000 Japanese people forcibly relocated and incarcerated during World War II. Eighty thousand of them had been born in the United States and had full citizenship. The incarceration was seen to be more about racism than any actual security

threat, and in California anyone with even 1/16th Japanese ancestry could be incarcerated. Colonel Karl Bendetsen, who created the program, proclaimed that even if someone had only "one drop of Japanese blood," they qualified for internment. Douche. By comparison, only about 10,000 Germans and Italians were placed in the American concentration camps, even though the United States was at war with those countries as well.

While not on par with life in a German concentration camp, life in the American camps was far from pleasant. They were hastily constructed and crowded. In many cases, twenty-five people lived in a space designed for only four. Privacy was nonexistent. The camps were mostly located in remote and desolate areas and surrounded by armed guards. These people were incarcerated for years, having committed no crime other than possessing what their government deemed to be a threatening ancestry.

In 1980, President Carter began an investigation into the legality of the mass incarceration, and eight years later President Reagan signed into law the Civil Liberties Act of 1988, which said hey we're real sorry about that, so here is twenty grand for anyone still alive who we forced into one of these camps. It was a paltry sum compared to the losses and damages, both physical and psychological, that were experienced by those unjustly incarcerated.

When one of my kids would come home from school all sneezy and snot-nosed from licking playground equipment, then that sickness would rip through the entire family, I'd refer to them as "Typhoid [kid's name]." The real Typhoid Mary, however, was the epitome of "Sucks to be you," because she was forced to spend her life in quarantine even though she felt fine.

Born in Ireland in 1869, Mary Mallon is believed to have come into the world with typhoid because her mother was infected with it during pregnancy. When she was fifteen she immigrated to New York and worked as a maid, and by the time she was in her thirties she was working as a cook for a series of wealthy families.

When an outbreak of the bacterial infection typhoid fever hit a Long Island family in 1906, the source became a mystery in need of solving. An investigator, George Soper, focused on the family's new cook, Mary. What he learned was that for the past seven years she'd worked for eight different families, and seven of them had contracted the disease. Mary was the first person in the United States shown to be an asymptomatic carrier of typhoid.

Mary was arrested for being a threat to public health on March 19, 1907, and sentenced to quarantine on a small island on the East River. Soper wrote an article about her in the *Journal of the American Medical Association* and the news of her story spread, leading to the "Typhoid Mary" nickname, which she despised.

March 19, 1907

After almost three years of incarceration, she was released on the condition that she no longer work as a cook, and would take special hygienic care to prevent spreading the disease, but as we learned more than a century later with Covid, plenty of people don't give a fuck about spreading deadly diseases.

Mary was now working as a laundress, but the pay was shit compared to cooking, so she violated the conditions of her release and began cooking again under a fake name for a variety of restaurants and hotels and a hospital. And guess what? More people got sick and more people died. In all, Mary Mallon was shown to have infected fifty-three people. Three of them died, but some believe Mary's death toll to be far higher.

Soper was called in again in 1915 to trace the outbreak and was all Jesus fuck Mary not you again. She fled, but the police tracked her down and she was sentenced back to the wee island to quarantine for the rest of her life, another twenty-three years. They didn't treat her like total shit though. She got a private cottage, was allowed day trips to Manhattan, and was given work in a laboratory.

The ethics of her incarceration remain a subject of debate.

Sir Walter Raleigh had quite a résumé. He was an author, soldier, explorer, politician, and spy. Yet he just couldn't help but keep pissing off the English royalty and getting his ass thrown in the Tower of London.

Queen Elizabeth, the first one, liked the guy. Hell, she gave him a royal charter to pillage those "heathen and barbarous lands" across the Atlantic, saying he could have 20 percent of the gold and silver they ~~thieved~~ found.

The problems began with his penis.

You know Virginia? The state, I mean. The name of the colony he founded was possibly Raleigh's paying homage to the "Virgin Queen" Elizabeth. Maybe. But he pissed her off when he secretly married one of Liz's ladies-in-waiting in 1591 without asking permission, because he'd already put his penis in there, and a baby was gonna happen. The queen found out and said, "Those motherfuckers!" and put both Walt and his bride in the Tower of London because they weren't supposed to be fucking without permission.

She let him out a few months later and said, "Take these ships and go fuck up the Spanish." And so he did and took a richly laden merchant ship as prize. He came back and Queen Liz said, "Niiiicccce." Then she threw his ass back in the Tower. A year later he was a member of Parliament because doing crime is often a road to political success.

He did more exploring and shit for a decade, but then the queen died in 1603. James I was now in charge and there was a plot to overthrow him. Someone said hey Walter Raleigh was part of that plot and even though he totally wasn't they put him back in the Tower. At least they let him have conjugal visits, because his son was conceived and born while Walt was in stir.

On March 20, 1616, after having been in lockup for thirteen years, the king let him out and gave him a pardon then said hey go to Venezuela and look for that El Dorado place. I want that fuckin' gold. While he was there a detachment of his men went against orders and attacked a Spanish outpost. At the time, the English were trying *not* to piss off the Spanish, so that was bad. When Sir Walter returned home the king said sorry dude rules are rules off with your head and that's what they did.

And because people are weird, they embalmed his head and gave it to his wife. She was like oh cool, thanks, and kept it.

> **She let him out a few months later and said, "Take these ships and go fuck up the Spanish."**

Virginia Hall shot herself in the foot, literally, and lost the bottom half of her left leg. But she later learned caution for a career where the smallest mistake was lethal—being a Resistance leader in France during World War II. The Nazis called her "the most dangerous of all Allied spies." She barely escaped their grasp in 1942, fleeing to Spain by walking fifty miles through the mountains on an artificial leg. Then, with D-Day looming and the French Resistance needing her once again, she went back.

Hall was born in Baltimore, Maryland, in 1906. In 1933, when she was twenty-seven, she worked at the American embassy in Turkey. While bird-hunting there, she tripped and *Kerblam!* She named her new leg "Cuthbert." She wanted to be a diplomat, but the Department of State said sorry you need two legs for that. President Roosevelt, the guy in the wheelchair, said come on let her. But they said nope and she said fuck you I quit and went to drive an ambulance in France while the Germans were in the process of conquering it.

Having to flee the Blitzkrieg, she met James Bond, or some other British spy, and Hall said fucking hire me and the Brits said spies don't need two legs so okay. Based in Vichy France—the part the Germans hadn't yet occupied—she was the first female spy in France for the U.K.'s Special Operations Executive (SOE). For more than a year she worked to organize resistance movements, supply them with

Virginia Hall

weapons and cash and medical assistance, and help downed Allied airmen escape.

March 21, 1944

She was uptight about security, and when SOE sent her a supervisor named Georges Duboudin she said no fuck this guy he sucks and will get us killed. She refused to introduce him to her contacts. She was right, because Georges's lack of caution saw him die in a Nazi concentration camp in 1945.

In late summer of 1942, she helped a dozen Resistance agents break out of prison and the fucking Nazis were pissed and cracked down. She said oh fuck gotta nope outta here, and she and Cuthbert fled across the Pyrenees.

Upon her return to England, Hall was made an honorary Member of the Order of the British Empire and she said that's nice send me back to France. They said no and she said goddammit but then the precursor to the CIA said hey, and on March 21, 1944, she arrived back in France to fuck some more Nazi shit up. She had to go by boat, because Cuthbert didn't appreciate jumping out of airplanes.

She played a critical support role for D-Day, and after the war joined the CIA. The world has only recently learned of her, because Hall didn't discuss her wartime exploits, explaining, "Many of my friends were killed for talking too much."

Do you remember being young and as nervous as a chihuahua on a meth bender while buying condoms for the first time? Imagine it being in Massachusetts before 1972, when making that purchase could land your ass in prison. For real. If you weren't married, buying contraceptives of any kind was against the law of the state. Until nineteen-seventy-fucking-two. Jesus Christ. Speaking of which, followers of Jesus did have a lot to do with such laws.

March 22, 1972

In 1963, Bill Baird was working as the clinical director for a birth control manufacturer named EMKO. He was doing research at Harlem Hospital when an unmarried mother of nine staggered into the hallway in front of him. From the waist down she was covered in her own blood. The woman had attempted to give herself an abortion using a coat hanger. She died.

The experience was a transformative moment for Baird. He began giving away free samples of contraceptive foam at malls. Religious wingnuts hassled him. Police threatened to arrest him. He drove around in a delivery truck nicknamed the "Plan Van" giving away free birth control. He was arrested numerous times for distributing literature about contraception and abortion, because fuck his First Amendment rights. Feminists flocked to his defense.

In 1967, Baird delivered a lecture at Boston University about birth control, once again giving away free contraceptives. He was arrested, charged with a felony, and convicted of "crimes against chastity." Christ-on-a-pile-of-contraceptive-foam that is some draconian dumbfuckery.

So he appealed, and that shit went all the way to the United States Supreme Court. It took five years from the time of his arrest, but on March 22, 1972, the Court ruled 6–1 (two justices were not sworn in) that you didn't actually have to be married to possess contraceptives. Chief Justice Warren Burger, a Nixon-appointed conservative who I expect never once found the clitoris, was the only dissenting vote.

The judgment was still kind of fucky, saying states retained the right to prohibit the rubbing of slippery bits outside of marriage, but they slid in some language that said the right to privacy means the government has no business intervening in the consensual no-pants dance between adults, regardless of marital status, and that did make it better.

The judgment became a foundation for *Roe v. Wade* the following year, as well as the gay rights victory of *Lawrence v. Texas* in 2003. Baird had two additional victories in the Supreme Court, in 1976 and 1979, allowing for minors to have access to abortions without getting parental consent. He has often been referred to as the "father" of both abortion and contraceptive rights.

Alas, it wouldn't last. In 2022, Trump's Supreme Court decided to take away that right to choose.

On **March 23, 1775,** future U.S. presidents George Washington and Thomas Jefferson were at a meeting of the Patriot legislature in a church in Richmond, Virginia. Attorney, politician, and orator Patrick Henry took the stage and gave an impassioned speech about how much the Brits sucked, shouting, "Give me liberty, or give me death!" So a Brit said "death" and shot him. I jest. His speech inflamed the crowd, leading to the American Revolution.

During his speech, Henry proclaimed war with Britain was inevitable, saying, "Gentlemen may cry, Peace! Peace! But there is no peace. The war is actually begun! . . . Our brethren are already in the field! Why stand we here idle?" He said that peace should not be purchased at the price of chains and slavery, which was hypocritical as fuck considering how many enslavers were in the room.

He closed with the liberty-or-death part, being all dramatic and shit by pretending to plunge a letter opener into his chest. The room was stunned to silence. But his speech moved them to vote for what he was calling for: A resolution to declare the colonies independent from Britain. Remember, this was more than a year away from the Declaration of Independence. It wasn't yet a big public fuck you Britain, but rather a quieter precursor fuck you Britain.

Henry was named chair of a committee to raise a militia and begin preparations for war, even though he was a bit of a plagiarist. The 1713 play *Cato, a Tragedy,* written by Joseph Addison, has the line "chains or conquest, liberty or death." The play was popular in the colonies and it is a near certainty Henry was familiar with it. Going back even further is the opera *Artemisia,* written by Nicolò Minato in 1657, which contains an aria called "Give me death or freedom." The context is different in the opera, however, as it's not about political freedom but freedom from love because some poor lass got her heart broken and she couldn't bear it.

March 23, 1775

At any rate, Lord Dunmore, who was the British dude in charge of the Virginia colony, got wind of this treason and a month later said I'll teach those militaristic mofos and took all the gunpowder from Williamsburg and put it on a Royal Navy ship. Patrick Henry led a militia to the city to get it back, and Dunmore said oh fuk they gon' kill me, and he fled, ending British control of Virginia. After the Declaration of Independence the following year, Patrick Henry became the first governor of Virginia.

He closed with the liberty-or-death part, being all dramatic and shit by pretending to plunge a letter opener into his chest.

When it comes to Best Actress, only one Black woman has ever claimed it: Halle Berry for the 2001 film *Monster's Ball.* The Oscars are like the sun: blindingly white.

March 24, 2002

The first Oscar ever won by a Black person, and the first Black person to even be nominated, came in 1940 when Hattie McDaniel won Best Supporting Actress for playing "Mammy" in *Gone with the Wind.* She couldn't attend the premiere of the film in Atlanta because the theater was for whites only. When it came to the Oscars ceremony, the whites-only Ambassador Hotel in Los Angeles said okay I *guess* we can let her in, but she needs to sit at a segregated table off to the side of the room.

A total of five Black men have won Best Actor, beginning with Sidney Poitier in 1964. Since the award's inception, only twenty-two times has a Black person won an Oscar for their acting. Often the award was for a role that reinforced stereotypes about Black people, like being a maid or a football player. Denzel was passed over for *Malcolm X,* but won for being a corrupt cop. Whoopi didn't win for *The Color Purple,* but did for playing a con artist in *Ghost.* Other Oscar categories are woefully underrepresented as well. With over three thousand Oscars

awarded since 1929, only fifty-four have gone to Black people (as of 2023). Also of note: There have been six nominations of Black people for Best Director, but no wins.

In *Monster's Ball,* Halle Berry starred as the wife of a man executed for murder. It was a controversial role, with Berry playing a tragic and complicated woman who has sex with the racist prison guard who oversaw the execution of her husband, although at the time her character did not know he had been a corrections officer. The sex scene is graphic.

When she won the Best Actress Oscar on March 24, 2002, Berry was congratulated by the NAACP, but *Ebony* magazine reported that many in the Black community were critical of the role she played, especially the sex scene. Fifteen years later Halle Berry said in an interview regarding her Oscar win, "That moment really meant nothing." She repeated, "I thought it meant something, but I think it meant nothing."

Berry was reacting to how her win failed to open doors for Black people in film, and how many years later she remains the only Black woman with a Best Actress win. Halle was also showing support for a movement begun by Black activist April Reign on Twitter two years earlier.

The tweet, posted on January 15, 2015, read: "#OscarsSoWhite they asked to touch my hair."

> **With over three thousand Oscars awarded since 1929, only fifty-four have gone to Black people (as of 2023).**

"The free market will regulate itself!"
—SOME LIBERTARIAN DOUCHE

Rights come from fighting for them, not asking nicely. Advancements in society are made because people are pissed about not being treated with a modicum of decency, and they're willing to reveal just how pissed they are. Those with power will ignore anyone petitioning for change that doesn't serve the interests of the powerful. They must be forced to change by making it more costly to ignore demands than accede to them. Across areas and eras, it has repeatedly been shown that this is how the world works.

On March 25, 1911, a terrible fire broke out in the Asch Building in the Greenwich Village neighborhood of Manhattan. The factory manufactured women's blouses called "shirtwaists." In making such shirts, many lives were wasted.

It was mostly immigrant women who worked in the factory, many as young as fourteen. They worked nine hours a day Monday to Friday, and an additional seven hours on Saturday. For their 52-hour workweek of hard, hot labor, they were paid between $7 and $12 a week. In current value, that translates to about $200 to $350 a week.

The fire began in a bin filled with scrap cloth on the eighth floor, possibly due to someone carelessly tossing a cigarette butt into it because they couldn't go outside for a smoke break because the fucking owners locked the fucking doors of the factory. Flames raced up the building; the workers were trapped by the locked doors. The asshole foreman who held the key had fucked off via one of the few open exits to save his own worthless ass and took the goddamn keys with him. I just want to pause for a moment to say fuck that guy with a cactus.

March 25, 1911

In all, 123 women and 23 men, most of them very young, lost their lives that day. Some jumped to their deaths. In one tragic scene, a man and a woman were seen to kiss each other before they leaped to their doom. Fucking hell.

The owners were put on trial for manslaughter and acquitted. A civil trial followed, and they had to pay $75 per life lost, but the insurance payout on the fire worked out to $400 per victim. Again: Fucking hell.

In the aftermath, legislation for worker safety was improved, and the power of the International Ladies' Garment Workers' Union led to it becoming one of the largest and most powerful labor unions in America.

Those with power will ignore anyone petitioning for change that doesn't serve the interests of the powerful.

Rebellions by native peoples against colonist conquerors don't often succeed, and the Riel Rebellions were little different. In fighting for their survival as a distinct people, the rebel forces were crushed by an overwhelming force of Canadian militia and, despite national cries for clemency, executed the leader, transforming him into a martyr.

March 26, 1885

The Métis are descendants of both First Nations and European settlers (mostly French). As political leader of the Métis, Louis Riel launched his first rebellion against the new federal government of Canada in 1869, just two years after the nation was granted independence from Britain. It became known as the Red River Rebellion and was largely a successful one in that a number of rebel terms were accommodated, resulting in the Red River Colony becoming part of the Canadian Confederation as the province of Manitoba. Other victories for the rebellion included separate French schools for Métis children and protection of their Catholic faith.

Louis Riel (center) and the Provisional Métis Government, ~1870

However, Riel had executed the pro-Canadian Thomas Scott for threatening to murder him, and after the agreement he was forced to flee to the United States to avoid prosecution. During his exile, Riel was elected to Canada's parliament three times but could never assume his seat.

By 1884, Métis leaders in Saskatchewan were pleading with Riel to return because, big surprise, the Canadian government was fucking them over. This eventually led to the second Riel-led uprising, called the North-West Rebellion, beginning on March 26, 1885. It was far larger and more violent than the first.

What began as a movement became something of a holy war under Riel. He gave the rebellion a fiercely religious tone, and the Catholic clergy were not impressed because I guess they weren't into that whole Crusades thing any longer. The white population of the region wasn't enthusiastic about joining either, but Riel mustered about two hundred Métis and a smaller number of Cree warriors to launch their attacks against Canadian Militia and North-West Mounted Police forces in a fight for their survival as a distinct people. They were successful at first, but the Canadian government had trains to bring in a seemingly endless supply of troops.

By mid-May the rebellion was crushed at the four-day-long Battle of Batoche, resulting in Riel's surrender. He was put on trial and hanged on November 16, 1885. The legacy was that the prairie provinces came to be controlled by Anglophones rather than Francophones, and lasting animosity was created nationwide between English and French in the bilingual nation.

Historical opinions on Riel are divided, with some viewing him as a religious nutjob and traitor, and others seeing the man as a hero fighting against an oppressive state.

There are many heroes in this story; one of them a quadruped.

In 1952 in Seoul during the Korean War, a boy, tears in his eyes, sold his beloved racehorse "Flame" to the U.S. Marines so he could afford to buy an artificial leg for his monoped sister.

The 5th Marine Regiment trained Flame as a packhorse to carry ammunition as well as wounded marines. She was allowed to wander freely and developed a reputation for consuming anything in sight, including Coke, beer, and poker chips.

They renamed her Reckless as a contraction of "Recoilless" because her primary task was to pack 24-pound shells for the recoilless rifles. And also because the guys who manned those guns were crazy motherfuckers. Reckless was one smart fucking horse. They trained her to avoid getting tangled in barbwire, to lie down under fire, and even to run for a bunker when she heard the word "Incoming!" She also learned how to travel her pack routes unguided after being led only a few times.

On March 27, 1953, during the brutal Battle for Outpost Vegas, Reckless became a hero.

The battle lasted three days, and in the middle of it she made fifty-one solo trips between the front and the rear in a single day, packing up over 9,000 pounds of ammunition, and carrying several wounded men to safety. She was wounded twice during the action but kept up her duties. For her heroic actions, she was promoted to corporal.

March 27, 1953

Later, she was given a battlefield promotion to sergeant, with a full ceremony and everything. Shipped to Camp Pendleton in California after the war, in 1959 Reckless was again promoted, to the rank of staff sergeant.

Sergeant Reckless and U.S. Marine Sergeant Joseph Latham

For her actions during the war, she received two Purple Hearts for the wounds suffered during Outpost Vegas, as well as a Marine Corps Good Conduct Medal, a Presidential Unit Citation with bronze star, and a shit-ton of other medals, all of which were worn on her horse blanket.

Staff Sergeant Reckless continued to serve at Camp Pendleton, birthing four foals in that time, until her retirement in late 1960. In lieu of a pension she was provided food and shelter for the remainder of her life, which was another eight years. In 1997 *Life* magazine recognized her as one of the top 100 all-time American heroes.

The name "Agreement for the Peaceful Liberation of Tibet" contains three lies. It wasn't an agreement, it wasn't peaceful, and it was the opposite of a liberation. And it resulted in a series of guerrilla conflicts that culminated in a mass uprising that led to the killing of tens of thousands of Tibetans by Chinese forces during a horrifically bloody two-week period in 1959.

Tibet, which is the highest elevation region on the planet, had previously been under Chinese rule for a couple of centuries. But in 1912, with the fall of the last Chinese dynasty (the Qing) in the Xinhai Revolution, Tibet declared its independence. Four decades later China decided they wanted to take it back.

The seventeen-part "agreement" was signed in 1951 under duress. But not according to China, which considers it totes legal, even though it was done after its massive army invaded and had kicked the Tibetans' asses then said, "Here. Sign this." The "or else" was implied.

Many Tibetans weren't thrilled with their new Chinese overlords and began an insurgency campaign. The reprisals by China's People's Liberation Army (there is another lie for you) grew increasingly vicious. In 1956 the United Nations said hey China cut that

shit out and China said haha fuck you come and make me. And being that this was the UN, they did not make anyone do shit. Since they didn't like commies all that much, the CIA began to give covert support to the Tibetan rebels in the form of commie-killing guns, commie-killing bullets, and commie-killing training.

By early 1959, the situation was a powder keg. On March 10, the sporadic guerrilla movement transformed into a mass rebellion with attacks on Chinese government officials and troops. The Chinese said wow these people really don't like us perhaps we should leave. Well, maybe one guy said that, and he probably got shot in the fucking head. The rest of the occupying forces laid down the pain.

Over the next two weeks the "Liberation Army," which was both real large and real good at killin', took the lives of about 87,000 Tibetans at a cost of only 2,000 of its own soldiers. Another 100,000 refugees fled to India, Nepal, and Bhutan.

On March 28, 1959, the Tibetan government, which was headed by the Dalai Lama, was dissolved by the occupying Chinese; the Dalai Lama began his permanent exile in India three days later. Afterward, China began to close Tibetan monasteries and impose Chinese law and customs across the land. Over the next two years another 340,000 Tibetans died in famines caused by the economic reforms thrust upon them.

Four years after the United States flattened a couple of Japanese cities with atomic weapons and the Soviets said holy fucking ass crackers we need those things too, they got those things too. Part of the reason they got them was American treachery, with the U.S.-born Rosenbergs giving them secret plans on how to build such fission-explode toys.

Lawyer Roy Cohn was a steaming pile of hematochezia. Don't google that. He was a McCarthyism (neurotic-level anti-communism) lackey who also targeted homosexuals as being threats to national security while himself being a closeted gay man. He first made his name in the prosecution of Julius and Ethel Rosenberg, who were on trial for giving atomic weapon secrets to the commies. Cohn wanted them to die.

Cohn wasn't lead prosecutor but played a key role when he examined Ethel's brother, David Greenglass, getting him to testify that he took plans stolen by Manhattan Project scientist (and spy) Klaus Fuchs and gave them to Julius, also saying that Ethel typed up notes about the plans. It was clear Julius, who loved that communism stuff, was fucking guilty, but the whole question of his wife, Ethel, was in some doubt. Especially

Julius and Ethel Rosenberg, 1951

considering Greenglass later said he lied on the stand to protect himself and his wife, and that the prosecution urged him to do so.

March 29, 1951

On March 29, 1951, both Julius and Ethel Rosenberg were found guilty of espionage, and a week later, quite possibly due to the urgings of Roy Cohn, they were sentenced to the hot squat on Old Sparky. Two years later they both rode the lightning on the same day, June 19, 1953, at Sing Sing Correctional Facility. Their two sons, only young boys at the time, later launched a campaign proclaiming their parents' innocence.

Cold War paranoia contributed to the convictions and sentences, but that doesn't mean they didn't do it. Evidence was slowly declassified and trickled out over the years that proved Julius was indeed involved, which his sons acquiesced to, but they then said the information their father provided was superficial and didn't help the Soviets much. Further evidence, including 2009 documentation from the KGB, showed Ethel was also almost certainly guilty, but that didn't stop the sons from entreating President Obama to give her a posthumous pardon.

Senator Elizabeth Warren supported pardoning Ethel, but no government action was taken. Most historians consider her guilty, but a question remains as to whether a death sentence was appropriate for either Rosenberg. Cohn, bastard that he was, considered the executions a significant career accomplishment. Later, he became a lawyer for Donald Trump.

Told you he was a dick.

Apparently, Siberia wasn't big enough or far away from everything enough, so in 1732 Russian fur trappers said, "Hey, across that freezing fucking cold ocean is even more frozen-as-fuck land. Let's go kill some critters there, too." There is a reason it had the nickname "Siberia's Siberia." The Russians set up business on the other side of the Bering Strait without the benefit of a land bridge, and the Russian Orthodox Church sent some missionaries over because Christians just *love* to try and convert heathens, but they never set up a colony. They basically laid claim to a place twice the size of Texas with only seven hundred Russians in residence, saying, "We own this shit." They called it Russian America, which reminds me of that 1984 *Red Dawn* movie with Patrick Swayze where they pretended that high schoolers were more than a match for trained soldiers.

March 30, 1867

By the middle of the nineteenth century Russia completed its sea-otter holocaust in the Americas and were like, well, fuck, what do we kill now? Speaking of killing, around the same time Russia got killed in the Crimean War by Britain and France, and wars cost money so they were looking for shit to sell. They were also facing the reality that if gold was discovered in Alaska then Canadians and Americans would come pouring in and say get the fuck out Russians we want those yellow rocks and we'll kill you to take them. So, they decided to unload the place.

Canada was still part of Britain and they'd just gotten beat up by Britain, so the Russians said fuck Canada and fuck Britain too; hey 'Murica you wanna buy it? America said, "Kinda busy with a civil war right now. Call back later."

Okay, phones weren't invented yet, but later they did "call back." On March 30, 1867, Alaska was sold to the United States for $7.2 million, which is about $130 million today. Helluva deal! Except perhaps not. Modern-day economist David Barker asserts the cost of purchasing and administering Alaska is greater than the revenue generated via taxes and royalties on the exploitation of natural resources.

Speaking of exploitation, no one ever consulted Native Alaskans on any of this.

> ## America said, "Kinda busy with a civil war right now. Call back later."

He's just a skinny little my-daddy-was-prime-minister-of-Canada boy. He gon' get his ass whooped by that other dude. Except that's not what happened.

Justin Trudeau, who at the time was a Liberal member of Parliament, was challenged to a charity boxing match against Conservative senator Patrick Brazeau, and Justin wrecked his shit in just three rounds.

At the time, Justin wasn't taken seriously as a politician; he was just a famous name. And Patrick Brazeau, a black belt in karate, said he didn't think Justin could take a punch. One conservative commentator said Brazeau had probably been in more fights in a month than Trudeau had been in his entire life.

The bout was staged for a good cause, raising money for cancer research, and the stakes were high: The loser would get their hair cut off and have to wear a hockey jersey with the winner's party logo on it for a full week. Everyone thought Justin was going to get destroyed. Patrick was a buff bad boy from a tough neighborhood with lots of tattoos, so people who don't know shit about boxing favored him to win 3–1.

But karate is not boxing, and not only did Justin have a significant height and reach advantage, he had the right training and much better endurance. Brazeau charged out in the first round and gave Trudeau a num-

ber of good shots, which Trudeau handily absorbed, but by the end of the round you could tell the tide was about to turn in the future prime minister's favor.

March 31, 2012

In the second round, Brazeau was gasping for breath, and Trudeau landed punch after punch as the senator struggled to defend himself, barely surviving the round. In the third, Justin showed no mercy, charging out right at the bell and crushing the conservative with an impressive pugilistic performance that punished Patrick's proboscis. A series of successful left-right combos staggered Brazeau and led to a second standing eight count, after which the ref called the fight for Trudeau.

> **The victory did wonders for Trudeau's reputation, and a year later he won the leadership of the federal Liberal Party.**

The victory did wonders for Trudeau's reputation, and a year later he won the leadership of the federal Liberal Party. Two and a half years after that, he kicked Conservative ass again, this time at the ballot box, beating the shit out of incumbent prime minister Stephen Harper to win a majority government for his party.

The year following the fight, Patrick Brazeau faced numerous criminal charges for assault, sexual assault, cocaine possession, and fraud. He was kicked out of the Senate and managed a strip club for a while, but was later allowed to return as a senator.

April

In the 1970s, in North America alone, AMC sold almost a million of the ugliest car you ever saw. I shit you not, the design chief for AMC sketched their internal combustion catastrophe on an airline barf bag. Really.

At the time, AMC was not one of the motor vehicle behemoths but it still wanted to compete with the foreign compact cars flooding the American market. So, they came up with a godawful mess and released it on April 1, 1970, but it was not intended as an April Fool's joke. Just to fuck with people, they called it the Gremlin.

The designer said people would see the car as either "cute or controversial, depending on one's viewpoint." I think he meant depending on how many drugs they'd taken. He referenced it being "perfect for the freethinking early 1970s." There is freethinking, and then there is overdosing on LSD.

Even the name was fucked. Merriam-Webster defines a gremlin as "a cause of error or equipment malfunction." Equipment malfunction? This is a fucking car! That's a *bad thing*. But young people are stu-pid and don't use dictionaries, and the "cute and different" marketing strategy worked, with the under-35 crowd buying a shitload of the ugly cars. I mean, people bought pet rocks and shag carpets back then too, so I suppose it makes sense.

April 1, 1970

Despite its glitchy name, the car was actually pretty reliable and considered a good value for the money. What's more, in a decade where most other cars blurred together for their style aesthetic, the Gremlin stood out for its hideousness. I guess in this case there really was no such thing as bad publicity.

The car was discontinued in 1978, and in 2007 *Time* magazine put the Gremlin on their list of "The 50 Worst Cars of All Time," describing the back end as looking like "the tail snapped off a salamander." But the fucker still sold. Hell, Presidents Bill Clinton and George W. Bush both drove Gremlins.

The 1974 AMC Gremlin

Some call the event the "biological Chernobyl," although it occurred seven years before that reactor went boom.

April 2, 1979

Sverdlovsk, now Yekaterinburg, was a "closed city" during the Cold War, meaning you couldn't visit it without special permission because of all the secret military shit going on there. It was a city known for its toxic fuckery, because in 1957 a nuclear waste facility blew up there. We don't know how many died as a result because the commies didn't want to tell anyone, but the number is believed to be somewhere between "a lot" and "a shitload."

Anyway, fucking anthrax. In the dying days of World War II, the Soviets happened upon some biological warfare plans during their invasion of Manchuria, where the Japanese had been experimenting with that nasty shit on the Chinese. And the Soviets said hey fuckin' cool we can put this into ballistic missiles and point it at the Americans, which was a mega violation of the Biological Weapons Convention.

Decades after the war, the anthrax produced in Sverdlovsk was some seriously toxic shit, and it's downright diabolical in how it came to be. In 1953 there was a *different* anthrax leak, in the city of Kirov—Jesus fucking Christ, Russia, get your shit together—and it went into the sewers and fucked up the resident rat population. Three years later some mad scientist found that the Kirov rats were carrying an even *more* virulent strain of anthrax, so they cultured that shit, called it "Anthrax 836," and started mass-producing it. You know, just in case.

The biological agent had to be dried out to be weaponized. Some flunky removed a clogged filter on the drying machines and left a note saying, "Replace the filter before you turn that thing back on." His boss was probably up to his eyeballs in vodka and ignored the note, and during the next shift, on April 2, 1979, he turned the machine on sans filter and oops fucking anthrax everywhere.

At least a hundred people died, and probably a lot more, but we don't know exact numbers because the KGB immediately started burning hospital records in a fire big enough to roast a thousand kolbasa. Remember that drunk-ass Yeltsin guy who was President of Russia when Soviet leader Gorbachev let the USSR go bye bye? He was First Secretary of the city at the time and led the cover-up. The deaths were blamed on contamination in a meatpacking plant.

It could have been a lot worse, but the winds blew the anthrax away from the city instead of toward it, snuffing out a shit-ton of livestock. To this day, the facility is under lockdown, surrounded by hundreds of heavily armed soldiers with lots of big dogs who have big teeth and who probably haven't been fed in a while.

> **To this day, the facility is under lockdown, surrounded by hundreds of heavily armed soldiers with lots of big dogs.**

The man who shot the man who shot the man who shot Jesse James was a cop. Let's do this in reverse and see if we can keep it straight.

Edward O'Kelley died by gunshot on January 13, 1904, in Oklahoma City, at age forty-six. He was a criminal and a drunk. That night, he'd been arrested and released and was all fuck da police! He said the cops better leave him alone, and he went out walking again. An officer, Joe Burnett, was walking his beat and said a friendly hello to O'Kelley, and in response O'Kelley punched him and drew his pistol. The cop grabbed the gun and a struggle ensued, with O'Kelley firing all his rounds while swearing his head off. All the shots missed, however, and Burnett only suffered powder burns on his ear and probably some deafness. Out of ammo, O'Kelley started to bite Officer Burnett. At that point a bystander grabbed O'Kelley, and the cop was able to get his gun free and he shot O'Kelley twice and he died.

Robert Ford died by gunshot on June 8, 1892, in Creede, Colorado, at age thirty. He'd been operating a saloon in Creede for only a month, opening it because silver had been discovered and miners like to drink. It might have been for the fame of killing the man who killed James, but it's unknown why O'Kelley walked into Ford's saloon with a shotgun, said "Hello, Bob," and gave him both barrels in the neck. Ouch. Anyway, O'Kelley got life in prison but was released after nine years because of a 7,000-name petition asking for his release, because killing Ford wasn't seen as a bad thing by many, and also because O'Kelley had a medical condition.

April 3, 1882

Jesse James died by gunshot on April 3, 1882, in St. Joseph, Missouri, at age thirty-four. He was a well-known outlaw, a gang leader, and a robber of trains and banks. His enslaving family fought as guerrillas on the Confederate side in Missouri during the Civil War, and Jesse and his brother, Frank, were known to have committed war crimes. After the war, he had a lengthy criminal career, but the romanticized version of him being a modern-day Robin Hood who stole from the rich and gave to the poor is bullshit. He was a thieving murderer and he sucked.

In spring 1882 a young Robert Ford joined what was left of Jesse's mostly annihilated gang, pretending to be Jesse's friend but intending to kill him for the reward, which he did by shooting the unarmed James in the back of the head. Rather than being lauded as heroes, Robert Ford and his brother Charley were indicted, sentenced to hang, and pardoned all on the same day. They were given a small portion of the bounty on James upon their release.

A **racist piece of shit** inspired another racist piece of shit to murder a great man. James Earl Ray, who was a convicted felon and escaped fugitive, assassinated civil rights leader Dr. Martin Luther King Jr. The motivations for him doing so can be traced to the presidential campaign of Alabama governor George Wallace.

April 4, 1968

Fucking Alabama. Between 1963 and 1987, Wallace spent sixteen years as governor. And make no mistake, he was a garbage human who had gone head-to-head against Dr. King numerous times. Alas, there are plenty of people who dropped out of middle school to pursue a career in competitive cousin-fucking who love to vote for such garbage.

James Earl Ray was a career criminal eight years into a twenty-year sentence at Missouri State Prison when, in 1967, he escaped by hiding in a bakery truck. Ray moved around a lot, and later that year landed in Los Angeles and became enamored with Wallace, who was running a third-party presidential campaign for the 1968 election. Ray, who was racist as fuck and a fan of Hitler, embraced Wallace's segregationist platform and spent a lot of time volunteering at the candidate's campaign headquarters. As a third-party candidate Wallace never had a chance, but he did win five Southern states and took forty-six Electoral College votes.

Dr. Martin Luther King Jr. in 1964

Seven months before the election Ray traveled to Birmingham, where he bought a hunting rifle. He then went to Memphis and rented a room across from the Lorraine Motel, where King was staying during his visit to support a sanitation workers' strike. On April 4, 1968, Ray fired a single shot, hitting King in the face and killing him. He then fled the scene.

Ray was seen running from the rooming house and his prints were found on the rifle. He made it to England and was arrested at Heathrow Airport the following June while attempting to travel to Rhodesia (now Zimbabwe), a known haven for white supremacists. Questions were raised about whether there was a greater conspiracy at play in the murder of King.

It was well known that the FBI was targeting King to discredit the civil rights movement. After his arrest, Ray's story changed multiple times. He pleaded guilty, then recanted three days later and kept saying he was innocent. Other times, he said he was part of a larger conspiracy and that "Raoul" told him to do it. The year before Ray's death, Ray met King's son Dexter and told him he didn't do it. The King family believed him and appealed for a new trial. And yet, multiple investigations into King's death proclaimed no need for a new trial. A third inquiry into the assassination, made a month before Ray died, said "the evidence against [Ray] is overwhelming" and there was no evidence of a larger conspiracy. Some remain unconvinced.

There is so much myth surrounding Pocahontas, starting with her name, which was actually Amonute. She also had a more private name, Matoaka. "Pocahontas" was a nickname that referenced her being a disobedient child. As the Pulitzer Prize–winning American history professor Laurel Ulrich said, "Well-behaved women seldom make history."

You might have thought that quote was from Eleanor Roosevelt, but powerful quotes are often attributed to more famous mouths. Ulrich wrote it as a student in 1976.

Anyway, Pocahontas was the daughter of the leader of almost three dozen Algonquin tribes near what is now Jamestown, Virginia. The story goes that English settler John Smith was about to be executed by her father, and the young Pocahontas stepped in and rescued him from certain death. But that is probably not how shit went down. It's believed Smith embellished the truth significantly years later to garner Pocahontas an audience with the Queen of England.

John Smith's self-congratulatory version is that Pocahontas was smitten with him, because those smelly Europeans were just so dashing, how could she resist? It reveals a tale of the "savage" who sees white culture, people, and religion as "superior" and embraces it. To many Native Americans, this story of Pocahontas seems terribly unrealistic.

More in-depth research reveals someone even more brave and resolute than the Disney portrayal: a woman who, when her people were faced with a powerful and more technologically advanced invader, used her courage and cleverness to learn their language and transform them from potential enemies into allies.

April 5, 1614

In 1609, Smith was injured and returned to England for medical care. That same year, a war broke out between the colonists and Natives, leading to Pocahontas being captured in 1613. Not everyone agrees, but it seems she was treated well during her captivity, improving her English and learning about—or perhaps being indoctrinated into—Christianity. During that time, she converted and took the name Rebecca. She then met colonist John Rolfe, a hardcore Bible thumper who proclaimed to love her dearly, but worried over marrying a heathen, even though she'd been baptized. He finally decided that he, a lifelong Christian, would be saving her newly Christian soul and they were married on April 5, 1614, when Pocahontas was about eighteen. The marriage between them served to create peace between Jamestown and her father's tribes.

She gave birth to a son the following year, and a year after that they traveled to London to present her to English society, saying, "Hey! Check out this savage we civilized. Isn't that awesome? We can convert the whole lot of them to Jesus if you just give us money." Pocahontas became a celebrity in England.

As the family was preparing to return to the Americas, she took ill with a mysterious disease and died in March of 1617, at approximately twenty-one years old.

The hatred fueling the Rwandan genocide wasn't based on differences of religion or culture, but wealth. In simple terms: rich vs. poor, exacerbated by colonialism. The land was dry grass just awaiting a spark; the match struck when the plane carrying Rwanda's president was shot down.

April 6, 1994

Hutu arrived in the Great Lakes region of Central Africa a few thousand years ago; they were mostly farmers. About four hundred years ago, the more nomadic Tutsi arrived, and settled among the Hutu. Before long, however, economic differences arose. The Tutsi mostly herded cattle, while Hutu tilled soil. Cattle were more profitable, and over time the minority Tutsi attained positions of power over the Hutu. It was much more about class division than ethnic differences.

Then the Belgians, who have much to atone for regarding how they fucked over large regions of Africa, showed up and made things worse. Although it should be noted Germans invaded the region first in 1884, and the Belgians took it from them in 1917. Anyway, the Belgians separated the two groups further, making them carry identification cards, and permitted only the Tutsi access to higher education and positions of power. Classic divide-and-conquer dick move.

Independence from Belgium came in 1962, and the region was split into new nations. Subsequently there was much fighting for control between the two groups in Burundi, Uganda, and Rwanda. In Rwanda, the Hutu were a significant majority and won power handily. Violence existed between the Hutu and Tutsi in the region for the subsequent three decades, but it was the events of April 6, 1994, that transformed it into genocide.

On that day, a plane carrying Rwandan president Habyarimana, a Hutu, was shot down. (The plane also carried the Hutu president of Burundi.) Violence had been escalating in the three years leading up to this, with the Hutu government fighting a group of Tutsi rebels called the Rwandan Patriotic Front. President Habyarimana had agreed to a peace agreement with the RPF, but then he got blown out of the sky, taking the peace along with him. It's uncertain who shot down the aircraft, but what is not debated is who got the blame and what resulted.

Rwandan Hutu extremists saw this as a green light to commit the genocide against Tutsi they'd been longing for. The killings began the next day. It was brutal in its organization and efficiency, and in a mere three months more than half a million Tutsi were murdered. With Hutu forces focused on massacres, by mid-July the Tutsi-led RPF seized control of the government, and the revenge killing of approximately 100,000 Hutu followed. Canadian general Roméo Dallaire, commander of a small UN observer force in Rwanda, saw the genocide coming months earlier and warned his superiors, but was told to stand down. The international community could have intervened and saved many, but instead did nothing.

They called her crazy, but shooting fascist chucklefuck Benito Mussolini in the face could be perceived as the act of a sane person. That's what Violet Gibson did, and she gave no explanation for it. Because, really, what explanation is needed?

Mussolini came to power in Italy in 1922 via a fascist coup d'état. And being fascist, he sucked, using his secret police to eliminate all opposition to his dictatorial reign. His douchey example inspired other fascist fucksticks such as Hitler in Germany, Franco in Spain, and Salazar in Portugal.

Violet Gibson was an Irish aristocrat, the daughter of Baron Ashbourne, who lived a life of privilege. She was also a sickly child at a time when medicine had few clues on how to deal with that shit. People said she was kind of an asshole, too, prone to fits of violence. As an adult she suffered even more health issues that caused chronic pain, and in 1922 she had a breakdown and was admitted to a mental hospital. She was released after two years, and in 1925, while living in Rome, she attempted to take her own life by shooting herself in the chest, but she survived.

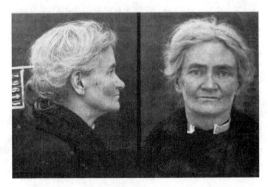

Violet Gibson mug shot

The following year, the target of her ire switched from herself to Mussolini. On April 7, 1926, Mussolini was walking among the crowd in Rome. Gibson, who was fifty years old at the time, walked up to him and fired a shot directly at his face, but his head moved at that precise moment and the bullet only grazed his nose. She pulled the trigger a second time, but the gun misfired, and she was tackled by the crowd.

April 7, 1926

The mob almost lynched her, but the police arrived and saved her life because they wanted to beat her up themselves back at the jailhouse. Fascist cops just like doing that kind of thing.

Her powerful family begged for her release, saying hey she's crazy send her home and we'll lock her up in the bin for good. Mussolini said yeah sure why not, get the crazy bitch outta my country. The British government said swell thanks Benito you're an all-right guy.

And that's what happened. She spent twenty-nine years, the remainder of her life, locked up in a mental hospital in Northampton, England. You'd think that after they saw the shit Mussolini pulled in subsequent years they might have reconsidered and released Gibson and pinned a bunch of medals on her, but nope. They instead adopted the attitude of "Bitches be crazy. Lock 'em up." Good thing times have changed since then and we've learned to respect women. Wait. Fuck.

People of any age can walk up close to the Venus de Milo in the Louvre in Paris and see a two-millennia-old carving of a woman's nipples, and you just know that *someone* is gonna get the vapors over that because think of the children!

The marble statue is dated to around 100 B.C.E., and presumed to have been carved by Alexandros of Antioch. Many scholars believe it depicts Aphrodite, the Greek goddess of love. Others proclaim she is a representation of Amphitrite, a goddess of the sea who was venerated on the Greek island of Milos. The name is fucked either way, because "Venus" is the *Roman* goddess of love.

Anyway, Milos is a small volcanic island in the Aegean Sea with a current population of about 5,000 people. On April 8, 1820, almost two thousand years after she was carved, Venus was unearthed. Who discovered her is a subject of some debate. It might have been a peasant named Theodoros Kendrotas, or it might have been his son Giorgios. Or maybe someone else entirely. Anyway, *someone* was digging around some ancient ruins a couple hundred years ago and discovered a small cave that had been carefully concealed with a heavy slab of rock.

The rock was moved, and her torso was poking out and she said hi, 'bout fucking time. Venus was found in two pieces, upper

and lower. Fragments of both arms were also found, the left hand holding an apple. While there is no doubt that it's a priceless statue, she became famous because of a marketing campaign. Napoleon had plundered a shit-ton of art, but after he got his ass kicked at Waterloo other countries were all hey give that shit back, so the French gave that shit back and the Louvre was looking mighty fucking empty. Venus was quickly "acquired" by some French diplomats in Greece in a controversial sale and made a gift to King Louis Bunch of Numbers and he handed it over to the Louvre and they were all fuck yeah *this* is *way better* than that Venus de' Medici we had to give back to Florence in 1815. Come visit! Try the veal.

But it was not better than the other Venus. One of the ways the French promoted the Venus de Milo was by lying about when she was carved, saying she came from Greece's classical age rather than being carved half a century later (roughly 100 B.C.E.) during the artistically "inferior" Hellenistic period.

If you can anthropomorphize a statue, I expect she was sick of being hidden away. Alas, Venus had to suffer the indignity a second time when the fucking Nazis invaded in World War II. Venus, along with several other priceless works of art, spent the war in the French countryside until the fascist bastards were kicked out.

The island of Milos, by the way, would really like their statue back.

Sacagawea was a Lemhi Shoshone woman and famed explorer who was born in 1788 and died in 1812 at the age of twenty-four. Or, possibly, she lived a whole lot longer, and didn't die until she was ninety-five.

Lewis and Clark would have been turned into cougar poop if not for her. She did not have an easy life. When she was twelve, she and several other girls were kidnapped from their home in present-day Idaho by Hidatsa Sioux and taken to what is now North Dakota. A year later she was sold to a Quebecois trapper named Charbonneau for a nonconsensual marriage. Or he may have won her gambling. Either way, she was basically sold into sexual enslavement by a colonist. Three years later, in 1804, Lewis and Clark, who were part of the Corps of Discovery, showed up and were looking for someone who spoke Shoshone to help them find their way west. When they learned Charbonneau's "wife" Sacagawea, who was pregnant, spoke it, they hired them both.

During the journey to the Pacific, Sacagawea served in multiple roles, all while caring for an infant son. She was an occasional guide; she helped prevent starvation by knowing what was edible and what was not; she served as interpreter; and perhaps most important, her very presence in the expedition demonstrated to Natives they encountered that they came in peace. All-out war against Native Americans would come later, when the colonists had numbers on their side.

It is generally believed that Sacagawea died in 1812 from an unknown illness. But record-keeping at the time wasn't much of a thing, and Charbonneau had more than one wife. So, when the death of his unnamed wife was mentioned, there is no guarantee it was Sacagawea.

April 9, 1884

Her son, Jean-Baptiste, had been entrusted to Clark for his education, as the explorer had become fond of the boy and felt like a second father to him. Sacagawea gave birth to a girl in 1810, but no later mention of her was made so it is believed she died in infancy. Potentially having no dependents and married against her will, there are other possibilities regarding the fate of Sacagawea.

Stories persist that she did not die, but rather fled Charbonneau and married into a Comanche tribe in Oklahoma, staying with them for several decades. Then, in 1860, at the age of seventy-two, she finally returned to her native Shoshone in Wyoming. It is in that state, in the cemetery of the Wind River Indian Reservation, that a large granite tombstone proclaims the final resting spot of Sacagawea, the date of her death inscribed as April 9, 1884.

Who is truly buried there? We likely will never know.

> **All-out war against Native Americans would come later, when the colonists had numbers on their side.**

A **scientist** named Dr. Katie Bouman did some science stuff and we got to see a picture of a giant space anus. Dr. Bouman was not the only scientist involved in capturing the first-ever image of a black hole, generated on April 10, 2019; it was a team of over three dozen people from around the globe working in concert for many years to achieve such an amazing feat. But Bouman was personally thrust into the spotlight because at the moment the first image of the hole was produced, a colleague snapped a photo of the delighted young scientist and that pic went interstellar across the interwebs. When a *woman* became the public face of the project, the manbaby mob got big mad.

April 10, 2019

Bouman, an expert in computer imagery with a PhD from MIT, wrote a dissertation with the words "Imaging Black Holes" in the title. She'd been part of the Event Horizon Telescope team since 2013, leading the development of an algorithm that made capturing the image possible. She deserves much credit for the discovery, but in her own words, "No one algorithm or person made this image. It required the amazing talent of a team of scientists from around the globe and years of hard work to develop the instruments, data processing, imaging methods, and analysis techniques that were necessary to pull off this seemingly impossible feat."

Why near-impossible? Because the gravi-tational pull of a black hole is so great, even light is like oh fuck guess I'm stuck here too. So, you can't actually see the fucker. But how did we see the fucker? We saw *around* the fucker. The appropriately termed "supermassive" black hole is 6.5 billion times the mass of our sun, and it casts a shadow. The shadow is what an international team using various computer programs and a network of eight ground-based radio telescopes saw.

The black hole was found in the center of a galaxy far, far away, about 55 million light-years, called Messier 87. And like *Star Wars* has its toxic fandom, so, apparently, does the search for intergalactic space oddities. Bouman never tried to claim responsibility for the discovery, making her comments about it being a team effort in a viral Facebook post the same day it was imaged; her post included a photo of most of her imaging colleagues. Nevertheless, the misogynistic attacks against her were instantaneous and relentless. Outraged, the incel army found an ovary-absent hero in Bouman's team member Dr. Andrew Chael, creating a meme proclaiming HE was the real genius behind imaging the black hole, and Bouman's celebrity was just feminist media wanting to hold up an undeserving woman as responsible.

But then Chael was all the fuck you talking about? He explained that the meme making him the hero was bullshit, decrying the "awful and sexist attacks on my colleague and friend Katie Bouman." He added: "if you are congratulating me because you have a sexist vendetta against Katie, please go away and reconsider your priorities in life."

You will never convince me there wasn't alcohol involved in this caper. It was the theft of a big fucking rock. But it's an important rock. A rock that was used for centuries in coronations of Scottish monarchs.

The rock is called the Stone of Scone, and it got its name because it was housed at the monastery of Scone, not because it looked like a baked good. It was an important Scottish artifact, so naturally those English fucks took it. In 1291 some English cock named Edward I said, "Spoils of war, muthafuckas!" and stole that rock and put it in Westminster Abbey where it was used for crowning *their* monarchs because fuck you Scotland, I guess. The stone was integrated into an English coronation chair; even though the rock sort of looks like an "off with their heads" chopping block, you don't place your head across it; you sit on it. Well, not *you*, ya fuckin' peasant.

Some six and a half centuries after the

The Stone of Scone in the Coronation Chair at Westminster Abbey

limeys took the fuckin' thing, four brave young Scots, three men and a woman, decided they were going to take it back. On Christmas Day 1950 the four students from Glasgow broke into the abbey, took the rock, then fucking dropped it and it broke in two. It also broke two toes on one of the thieves. Told you they were drunk.

April 11, 1951

Not realizing how heavy a big fucking rock can be, they had to drag the bigger piece down the hall on top of a coat to a waiting car. The smaller piece was put in a separate car by two of the thieves, and they were almost busted by a cop, but one of them was the woman in the crew so they started making kissy-face, because it was five in the morning so why else would two young people be in a car at that time?

After making their getaway, they took the two parts of the stone to a mason to have it fixed. During the repair, the mason placed a brass rod with a note inside it within the stone. *And no one knows what it says.* The man who wrote the note took that secret to his grave. Probably something like "Fuck you, England. Scotland rules!" Anyway, after three months the police were closing in on the thieves, so on April 11, 1951, they left it at the Arbroath Abbey in Scotland, and told the cops where to find it. The stone was taken back to Westminster; Elizabeth II was crowned on it the following year. Forty-three years later she said fine have your fucking rock back and returned it to Scotland. It now resides in Edinburgh Castle, but England borrowed it for a bit in 2023 for Charles III's coronation.

That **"We choose** to go to the moon" speech JFK gave in 1962? That was the public proclamation. Its proposal before Congress happened more than a year previous. It was motivated by those damn Soviets beating America into space a month earlier.

Cosmonaut Yuri Gagarin was born in 1934, and when he was seven, during the fucking Nazi invasion of the Soviet Union, those fuckers went right through his village. A German officer said hey I'm taking your house, but I will be generous and give you permission to build a small mud hut in the yard. Also, we burned down the school.

Yuri lived in that mud hut for almost two years. During that time, he sabotaged German tanks. When the Germans fled his homeland, he showed the Red Army where the Germans had buried mines. Later he worked in a steel plant and joined the air cadets. In 1955 he joined the air force flight school and almost flunked out because he was so damn short, he couldn't see to land the plane. His instructor said hey sit on this pillow and Yuri said thanks that's way better and he graduated in 1957 as Lieutenant Gagarin.

Yuri Gagarin in 1961

In 1959 the Soviets launched Luna 3, the first-ever mission to photograph the far side of the moon, and Yuri said that's fuckin' cool I wanna be a cosmonaut. His superiors said yeah sure and he was off to space school. They tested the shit out of him both physically and mentally, and the fact that he was only five-foot-two was a bonus because small cosmonauts = less fuel. It wasn't just command that preferred him; almost all his fellow cosmonaut candidates thought Gagarin the best choice for the mission.

The first manned launch into space happened on April 12, 1961. Gagarin learned he would be the pilot only four days before. The Vostok 1 spacecraft launched at 6:07 A.M. "Off we go!" Yuri exclaimed at liftoff, which became a popular expression in the USSR afterward. It was a short mission: one lap around Earth taking 108 minutes, then landing in Borat-land. Except he didn't "land," he ejected from the capsule at 23,000 feet and parachuted. Jesus.

The flight was a triumph and made Gagarin a hero who got all the medals. It was his only space flight. He was on backup for the 1967 Soyuz 1 mission that killed his friend, and the Soviets couldn't have the first man in space die, so they said no more space for you. Back to flying plane. Is much safer. Alas, a year later the MiG-15 he was piloting crashed and Gagarin died.

Danuta Danielsson hated Swedish Nazis. And fucking Nazis are a problem in Sweden. Sweden is actually racist as fuck, with a terribly segregated labor market, the worst in Europe for people with a foreign background. Anyway, Danuta had enough of their shit, and gave some Nazi snot-goblin a smack upside the head.

On April 13, 1985, there was a speech by the leader of the "Left Party–the Communists" in the small city of Växjö, Sweden. Following the speech was a government-approved rally of fucking Nazis. Even before the rally began, lefties and fucking Nazis were beating the shit out of each other.

"Danielsson" was Danuta's married name. She'd been born in Poland two years after World War II ended and moved to Sweden only a few years previous to this event. She was of Jewish descent, her mother an Auschwitz survivor. In the war, Poland suffered more per-capita casualties than any other country, most of them Jewish. Danuta was rightfully pissed when she saw some Nazi oxygen thieves marching through her new homeland. So, she whacked that feculent Nazi wank-stain in the face with her purse.

I guess others thought fucking up some Nazi shit was a great idea and proceeded to attack them after the rally. They were pelted with eggs, and one was kicked unconscious. The Nazis fled and, being pieces of shit, appropriately hid their smelly asses in the bathrooms of the train station until police arrived and escorted them to safety.

April 13, 1985

Photojournalist Hans Runesson snapped a pic of Danielsson at exactly the right moment, just as her handbag was about to connect with a Nazi skull. The photograph was published in Sweden's national newspaper the following day, as well as in *The Times* of London. Danielsson shunned attention, however, fearing prosecution for assault as well as reprisals from those Nazi cocktoboggans. Although some locals likely recognized her, she was not publicly identified as "The Woman with the Handbag" until 2014, when there was a debate over erecting a statue depicting her righteous attack. Her son came forward saying she wouldn't have liked that, and that she hated the photograph. The statue was erected anyway.

Danuta Danielsson suffered mental health issues, but her son said she knew exactly what she was doing when she hit that Nazi pisswhistle. Alas, the attention that photo garnered weighed on her, and she took her life in 1988. The piece of shit on the receiving end of the handbag was Seppo Seluska. Later that year he tortured and murdered a gay Jewish man and was sent to prison. Too bad Danuta's handbag didn't have bricks in it.

In Nuremberg on the early morning of April 14, 1561, there was a big-ass sighting of unknown shit in the sky. It was about three centuries before the first weather balloon, so we can't be blaming the mass UFO sighting on that. People didn't think it was little green men from Mars. They figured God was up to something.

The celestial event began around 4:00 A.M., and here is part of the written description of what went down: "a dreadful apparition occurred on the sun . . . two blood-red semicircular arcs . . . other balls in large number . . . three in a line and four in a square . . . blood-red crosses . . . blood-red strips." The phrase "blood-red" got used a lot. They talked about rods and globes and how these things "all started to fight among themselves" and then they "fell from the sun down upon the earth," and "wasted away on the earth with immense smoke," so they probably thought some serious battle between good and evil was going on and maybe we should pray or kiss our asses goodbye or something. The latter part of the description makes reference to "God" seven times, because it's not like these folks knew fuck all about astrophysics.

Carl Jung wrote about the event in 1958 in a book titled *Flying Saucers: A Modern Myth of Things Seen in the Skies,* but he was all about the psychoanalysis of those who viewed the phenomenon. Jung's work doesn't hold up well under modern examination, so forget that part. Jung did say it was probably a natural phenomenon and not "God did it."

Many others, the types who would love to storm Area 51, consider it a massive space battle that just happened to take place over a German city. But *something* did happen, and what was seen was immortalized in a woodcut by Hans Glaser, who was a real person living at that time and was known for doing woodcuts. So yeah, they saw crazy shit, but probably not Martians and Venusians meeting at the halfway point to make war upon each other. Far more likely it was a "sun dog" (known also by its more scientific name, "parhelion"), which is an "atmospheric optical phenomenon" that is created by a bunch of ice crystals suspended in the atmosphere. And science types say Nuremberg had the right conditions for this to occur at that time. No E.T. No gods. Just ice.

So yeah, they saw crazy shit, but probably not Martians and Venusians meeting at the halfway point to make war upon each other.

In 2013, I was writing a fitness column for the *Los Angeles Times* and regularly covered the subject of running. I never considered trying to qualify for the Boston Marathon, however, as it's exceptionally challenging. But then some assholes blew it up.

I won't say their names. Their names are Asshole 1 and Asshole 2. Asshole 1 was born in the Soviet Union in 1986. His brother, Asshole 2, was born in Kyrgyzstan in 1993. Asshole 2 came to the United States in 2002 with his parents, and Asshole 1 followed two years later.

The father of the two assholes is Muslim and raised them as Muslims, but not to be extreme. The two assholes found extremism on their own. The supposed motivation of the two terrorist assholes to blow up innocent people, including a little boy, was the American military presence in Afghanistan and Iraq.

On April 15, 2013, at 2:49 P.M., two homemade bombs set by Asshole 1 and Asshole 2 exploded seconds apart near the finish line of the Boston Marathon. At the time of the first explosion, the race clock read 4:09:43, which is when the bulk of finishers were crossing. The timing of the explosion had been planned for maximum carnage. Three people died. Their names were Martin Richard, age eight; Lü Lingze, age twenty-three; and Krystle Campbell, age twenty-nine. Almost three hundred others suffered injuries, seventeen of them losing limbs.

A massive manhunt followed, during which the assholes shot and killed a member of the MIT Police Department, Sean Collier. Four days after the bombing the two assholes had a shootout with police. Asshole 1 was shot, and Asshole 2 ran his asshole brother over with their stolen vehicle while trying to escape, and Asshole 1 died. Two police officers were seriously injured in the gunfight. One, Dennis Simmonds, died a year later. Fifteen other officers were also injured.

April 15, 2013

Asshole 2 drove a short distance from the gunfight, then fled on foot. A resident found Asshole 2 hiding in his boat and told the cops. Asshole 2 was shot then arrested. He was tried and sentenced to death, but that sentence was later overturned pending resentencing. In March of 2022 the sentence of death was reinstated by the U.S. Supreme Court.

I did manage to qualify for Boston, barely, and was there on Patriots' Day of 2014 to help with reclaiming the finish line as a triumphant experience rather than a terrifying one. More than double the usual number of spectators were present on that beautiful April day, cheering us on.

Rosalind Franklin, who made a vital contribution to understanding the structure of DNA, missed out on not just one Nobel Prize, but two. Was it unethical, or outright thievery? Throughout history—and the present—men take credit for the work of women, and Watson and Crick were no exception.

April 16, 1958

Scientists James Watson and Francis Crick were at the University of Cambridge. Scientists Rosalind Franklin and Maurice Wilkins were at King's College. Wilkins was shy and Franklin forceful. They did *not* get along. Watson and Crick tried to crack DNA in 1952 and it was a colossal fuckup. Meanwhile, Franklin was mostly working on her own because Wilkins couldn't handle her. Wilkins started hanging out with Watson and Crick, becoming pals.

The decoding of DNA happened because of an X-ray, taken by Franklin's PhD student Raymond Gosling under her guidance, called "Photo 51." Franklin was a chemist and X-ray crystallographer, and I don't know what that is. Photo 51 is an X-ray diffraction picture of a paracrystalline gel made of DNA fibers. Lost me on that, too. What's important is that in January 1953, when no one else was around, Watson, who was still fucking lost on modeling DNA, was visiting Wilkins at Kings, and Wilkins said hey check out this Photo 51 shit. Cool, right? It's important to note this was done without Franklin's permission; that was definitely unethical.

In Watson's own words on seeing the photo, "My mouth fell open and my pulse began to race." He said it gave him a critical understanding of the double helix structure. But he needed more. To understand the exact chemical organization of the molecule, he required the precise observations from the X-ray, which Franklin unwittingly provided the following month in an informal report to a molecular biologist at Cambridge; those numbers eventually found their way to Watson and Crick. The report wasn't confidential, but they came about it dishonestly and didn't ask Franklin's permission to interpret her data.

Watson and Crick cracked the code a month later, and almost immediately afterward Franklin abandoned her work on DNA and moved to Birkbeck, University of London, to work on the molecular structure of viruses. Alas, she died from ovarian cancer on April 16, 1958, aged thirty-seven. She never learned how much Watson and Crick relied on her work, and in 1962 the pair, along with Wilkins, won the Nobel Prize in Physiology or Medicine for the discovery. Watson said that had she lived, Franklin likely would have won the Nobel Prize in Chemistry, but posthumously awarded Nobel Prizes are rare.

Regarding the second Nobel, her team member at Birkbeck, Aaron Klug, continued Franklin's pioneering work after her death, winning the Nobel Prize in Chemistry in 1982.

"**H**ey there,** you handsome Nazi fella," the beautiful young woman said. "Wanna ditch this place and go somewhere more private?" Off into the Dutch forest they went, and then *Blam!* She shot that Nazi assbucket right in his fucking face.

They were three young, attractive women who were members of the Dutch Resistance. Their names were Hannie Schaft and sisters Freddie and Truus Oversteegen. Together they would kill a lot of Nazis; only two of them would survive the war. And they were fucking heroes who used their beauty to lead Nazis by their sickly Nazi dicks to their well-deserved deaths.

Germany invaded the Netherlands in May 1940, conquering it in four days, but many Dutch remained in the fight. At the time, Freddie was only fourteen, Truus was sixteen, and Hannie nineteen. Freddie was the first to kill, in 1942, shooting a Nazi in a drive-by on her bicycle.

Their efforts in battling fucking Nazis included sabotage of bridges and railroads using dynamite, and smuggling Jewish children out of the country. The Oversteegen family hid a Jewish couple in their home for the entirety of the war.

The girls would also go into bars to meet Nazis and ask them to "go for a stroll." *Hint, hint.* And then, thinking he was gonna get lucky, he instead got a high-velocity metal projectile to the brain.

April 17, 1945

Hannie learned to speak German fluently to aid in her Nazi-killing efforts. She also had no mercy for collaborators or traitors. However, she drew the line at harming children. When the Resistance asked her to kidnap the children of a Nazi official, she said no. Her exploits became so well known that she made the top of the Nazis' most-wanted list as "the girl with the red hair." So, she dyed her hair black.

Hannie Schaft

The Oversteegen sisters survived the war and received numerous awards for their heroic actions. Both lived to be ninety-two. Hannie, however, was arrested for carrying anti-Nazi propaganda through a military checkpoint in March 1945. She was repeatedly tortured but would not confess. Eventually, it was the red roots of her hair growing in that gave her away.

On April 17, 1945, with the end of World War II only a few weeks away, she was executed by a pair of Dutch Nazi traitor asshole fuckfaces. One shot her at close range, only wounding her. She spat at him, "I shoot better!" The other Nazi fucknugget shot her a second time, killing her.

The Diet of Worms was not nearly as disgusting as it sounds, although that may depend on your perspective.

It was an "imperial diet"—the "diet" actually means "assembly," called by the Holy Roman Emperor Charles V and held in the German city of Worms, because the emperor was mega pissed at Martin Luther. Three years earlier ol' Marty, a theology professor and priest, had (allegedly) nailed his 95 Theses to the door of the All Saints' Church in Wittenberg, Germany. More importantly, he used whatever the sixteenth-century version of the post office was to send his tirade to the Archbishop of Mainz. The basic message was that the Church was wrong to say people could buy their way into heaven, or something. Oh, and the date was October 31. Trick or treat, motherfucker.

April 18, 1521

That was the start of the Protestant Reformation, and three and a half years later Emperor Chuckie called his worm diet, telling Luther to take back his words. Back then, heresy could get you into some deep, deep poo. But on April 18, 1521, Luther was all nah, dude, saying, "If I now recant these, then I would be doing nothing but strengthening tyranny." Burn.

Speaking of burning, Charles was not impressed, and these folks were fond of setting heretics on actual fire. Charles ordered Luther to be named an outlaw, made it illegal for anyone to give him aid, banned his teachings, and basically said that if someone wanted to off him, it was cool. Totes legal. Kill away.

So Luther fucked off to Wartburg Castle in Eisenach, where he was protected by folks who liked his ideas. After some of the heat died down he returned to Wittenberg in secret the following year and managed to live another quarter century. During his exile Luther translated the Bible from Latin to German, making it accessible to the people rather than having to trust some priest's interpretation, and that shook shit up. He also said Jews should die. Not such a nice guy after all.

For quite some time the people who liked what Luther had to say didn't get along so well with those who were into the old ways (meaning Catholics). Nobody expects the Spanish Inquisition to add Protestants to their shit list.

But yeah, the whole Protestantism thing really took off, there were thirty years of war with 8 million dead, then a bunch of them hauled ass to America. Over the next five hundred years, some became chill and started ordaining gays, and others did fucked-up shit like playing with snakes and getting Trump elected.

Your mom had sex, and so did Mae West. Mae was even in a play about sex. It was called *Sex.* And she went to jail for it. Because 1927. And Puritans.

Most people like fucking. Even Puritans liked sex, but only in ways their god said was okay. They got their multiple layers of panties in a bunch if anyone hosted a bedroom rodeo in a way the sky fairy didn't approve of.

Puritanism began in the 1530s in England when King Henry VIII (who definitely liked fucking) told the Catholic Church to suck dicks (let's not go there) and started the Church of England. The Puritans thought this new church was not "fully reformed," and they said fuck it, figuratively, and did their own thing.

The name "Puritan" was actually an insult that emerged in the 1560s because they slavishly followed the Bible as a guide to daily life. Then a bunch of them fucked off to America and, along with folks from several other religions based in the teachings of that uptight motherfucker John Calvin, spent the next several centuries expending a lot of energy trying to dictate what other people could do with those fun things between their legs.

Enter Mae West, figuratively speaking.

West's first Broadway role was in the play called *Sex,* which she not only starred in, but also wrote, produced, and directed. One of the things Puritans and other Calvinist-based religions were fond of was lobbying the government to enforce moral standards. The play was popular, which certain religious groups could not abide, because women were supposed to be humble and obedient and not enjoy making their own decisions, especially if such a decision involved fucking someone other than their husband.

These religious groups complained to city officials, who had police raid the theater and arrest the entire cast. On April 19, 1927, West was sentenced to ten days in jail for "corrupting the morals of youth." She could have paid a fine but took the jail term like a champ to make a statement about the levels of bullshit it all was. Go Mae.

The jail term stirred up great publicity, and she was crowned the darling "bad girl" of the era. Not one to back down, her next play was about homosexuality.

> **Puritanism began in the 1530s in England when King Henry VIII (who definitely liked fucking) told the Catholic Church to suck dicks (let's not go there) and started the Church of England.**

We've all read profound, insightful quotations with the attribution "Anonymous." You know that's because a woman probably said it, right? Insecure penis-possessors couldn't handle something smart being said or done by a woman; throughout history they either ignored their work, stole it, or made them invisible. If the penisers weren't such sexist ass-wagons always putting women's ideas down, we'd probably have colonies throughout the solar system by now. Instead, we have just one shitty little space station.

Sigh.

Born Maria Skłodowska in Poland in 1867, Marie Curie was the first woman to win the Nobel Prize, and the only woman ever to win it twice. She's also the only person to win Nobels for two different scientific fields—physics and chemistry.

She shared her first Nobel with her husband, Pierre. This was not an example of "we need a dude's name on this." He actually knew his shit and they had a loving marriage. In fact, the Nobel committee wanted to give it to *only* him, but Pierre was all you better include my wife or you can shove that Nobel up your alimentary canal. Good husband, that Pierre. Alas, he got his head fatally squished by a horse-drawn cart in 1906. Gross.

Marie and Pierre Curie in their lab

> **She shared her first Nobel with her husband, Pierre. This was not an example of "we need a dude's name on this." He actually knew his shit and they had a loving marriage.**

April 20, 1902, was the day Marie and Pierre successfully isolated radioactive radium salts in their Paris laboratory.

The term "radioactivity," aka "invisible cancer air," was coined by Marie. She'd been studying a mineral called pitchblende, of which uranium is the primary element. She figured it contained additional radioactive stuff. Pierre joined in her research and in 1898 they discovered polonium, so named after Marie's home country. Polonium, FYI, is the shit the Russian government (allegedly) used to poison former KGB agent Alexander Litvinenko in 2006, after he blabbed about their corruption.

Anyway, radium does not freely occur in nature, and they painstakingly refined tons of pitchblende to isolate one-tenth of a gram of pure radium chloride.

Because capitalism, radium would come to be used in many products, such as to make watch dials glow, and in toothpaste. It also has medical and industrial uses, despite being radioactive as fuck. Actually, because it's radioactive as fuck. Curie died in 1934 at the age of sixty-six from aplastic anemia, believed to be caused by her exposure. Drag. Many other people died working with the stuff. Google "Radium Girls." Nasty stuff.

By the way, Marie and Pierre's older daughter, Irène, followed in her parents' footsteps, winning a Nobel Prize in Chemistry in 1935 for the discovery of artificial radiation.

On **April 21, 1918,** the German fighter pilot and "ace of aces" of World War I—"Red" Baron Manfred von Richthofen—was shot down, but not in flames, although these planes were as motherfucking flammable as newspaper dipped in napalm. They were constructed with dry wood and covered in fabric coated in a doping agent so combustible it could catch fire if you ate a jalapeño pepper then farted on it. And American commanders, who didn't fly and had no understanding of the courage of those who did, refused to issue parachutes because they worried pilots would jump at the first sign of danger. If your plane caught fire it was either jump to your death, shoot yourself in the head, or ride it all the way to the ground while screaming "I'm on fire!"

April 21, 1918

Germans began using parachutes in the final weeks of the war—one even saved the

The remains of Richthofen's plane after it was looted for souvenirs

life of German ace Ernst Udet—but a parachute wouldn't have done Richthofen any good even if he had one.

Holding the rank of captain at twenty-five, Manfred was credited with eighty combat victories. His brother Lothar had forty victories and was considered the better pilot, but he was also a risk-taker, whereas Manfred was more tactical, leading his squadron in coordinated attacks.

Nine months prior to his death, Manfred received a head wound that temporarily blinded him, but he was able to recover and land his plane. It took several surgeries to remove bone splinters, but he was back on active service, against doctor's orders, three weeks later. The wound caused lasting damage, and many believe it contributed to his death by affecting his judgment. Richthofen had been a cautious warrior, but on that fateful day he fixated on his target and flew too low to the ground across enemy lines, failing to appreciate the surrounding dangers.

Canadian air ace Captain Arthur Brown was first credited with the kill, but historians now agree the single .303-caliber bullet that entered Richthofen's chest was almost certainly fired from the ground, possibly by Sergeant Cedric Popkin, an Australian.

The Red Baron used the final moments of his life to execute a rough landing in enemy territory. His body was treated with respect and given a military burial. His mostly intact aircraft, however, was taken apart by souvenir seekers.

Asshole alert! Pedro Álvares Cabral was the impetus to fucking over half a continent. He's the reason Brazilians speak Portuguese, and also why most of the Indigenous population got wiped out.

A minor Portuguese nobleman, Cabral was tasked with leading a spice-buying expeditionary fleet to India, traveling via the newly discovered Cape of Good Hope in South Africa.

Pedro took the scenic route.

For reasons unknown, Cabral was like that station-wagon-driving dad who refuses to ask for directions. He went way wide of the intended route through the Atlantic, and on April 22, 1500, the fleet made landfall on the coast of what would later be named Brazil. They immediately encountered Indigenous inhabitants and had friendly first contacts, presenting them with gifts.

Then he left them in peace. Haha, jk.

Cabral spent about ten days in Brazil, during which time he reprovisioned his fleet and introduced the locals to Jesus. He also claimed the land for Portugal, DESPITE THE FACT THAT THERE WERE ALREADY A BUNCH OF PEOPLE LIVING THERE.

Before continuing on to India, Cabral dispatched one of his ships back home to inform King Manuel I of the righteous find, ripe for exploiting.

Three decades later, Portuguese colonization of Brazil began in earnest, and with colonization comes genocide. If the Portuguese hadn't done it, it's a certainty the Spaniards would have genocided the fuck out of the locals instead. And if not the Spaniards, the English or French would have been happy to. Homo sapiens excel at genocide; we've been wiping other hominids from the face of the Earth for several dozen millennia.

April 22, 1500

You know how if you say a word a bunch of times it begins to sound weird? Not so with "genocide." It's a motherfucker every single time. Genocide. Genocide. Genocide.

In the century following Cabral's first contact, of approximately 2.5 million Indigenous people living in the region at the time, a staggering 90 percent were wiped out, mostly due to the spread of European diseases such as smallpox, for which they had no immunity, but also from constant war with European colonizers, enslavement, and starvation. Oh, and there was plenty of rape, too.

It's not all ancient history, either. After Brazil won its independence in 1822, the slaughter didn't stop. Encroachment into the Amazon continues unabated, and the Indigenous population now represents a mere 0.4 percent of the country's total.

> **If the Portuguese hadn't done it, it's a certainty the Spaniards would have genocided the fuck out of the locals instead.**

Gesundheit. *Schadenfreude. Rein-heitsgebot.*

German is rarely referred to as a beautiful language, but many consider that last word to be a wonderful thing. It's the Bavarian "Purity Law," enacted on April 23, 1516.

April 23, 1516

Since we're talking about Germans and purity, I must mention this has nothing to do with ethnicity. It's about beer. Specifically, the allowable ingredients for brewing it.

Issued by Duke Wilhelm IV, the law decreed their beer would have no ingredients other than barley, hops, and water. The omission of yeast is a subject of debate. It occurs naturally via the brewing process, and some believe its existence was not yet known. Others contend brewers were well aware of it, because they harvested the fluffy layer at the bottom of the fermenter that was left over at the end of the brewing process and used it for the next batch. They referred to it as *zeug*, which means "stuff."

"Hey Reinhold, you drunk-ass motherfucker! Don't forget to put the *zeug* in the next batch."

It must be noted that this law was initially for brewing lagers, a more complicated process than making ales. At that time, Bavaria was the only place in the world making lagers.

FYI, the rest of "Germany," which wasn't really Germany yet, was not impressed. Fucking lager-makers, shitting on our ale-making ways. Fuck those guys. You've seen guys drink beer and get into fights? These dudes fought about how to make that beer in the first place.

But then, there was unification.

In 1871 the loose collection of German states became a German empire, but Bavaria said if they didn't adopt their brewing laws then the rest of Germany could just eat a box of snake cocks. Who knew people could be so uptight about getting fucked-up?

It took some time, but by 1906 the law was being applied across Germany, although the name *Reinheitsgebot* didn't become a thing until the Weimar Republic began in 1918. Since then, the law has spread and evolved and been used as a marketing gimmick. Coors Light uses cans that turn blue to sell beer; others use a concept of purity. There is even a brewery in British Columbia that makes a "1516 Lager."

Please get fucked-up responsibly.

Since we're talking about Germans and purity, I must mention this has nothing to do with ethnicity. It's about beer.

Imagine loving and trusting someone so much you let them shoot cigarettes out of your mouth in a crowded theater.

Born Phoebe Ann Mosey in Ohio in 1860, Annie Oakley had a shitty childhood. Annie was the sixth of nine children, and seven of those children actually lived, which wasn't bad for an impoverished nineteenth-century family. Her dad died of pneumonia when Annie was five, transforming poverty into near destitution.

To help the family, young Annie began trapping and hunting, selling the game to local shopkeepers. But there was a two-year period from ages nine to eleven where she was "bound out" in near slavery to some horribly abusive motherfuckers on the broken promise of payment and an education. She didn't shoot them, but she did run away, eventually returning home. She used her hunting skills to sell game and paid off the mortgage on the family farm by the time she was fifteen.

That same year, Annie made her public shooting debut.

In 1875 in Cincinnati, traveling-show marksman Frank Butler made a bet with a hotelier that he could beat any local shooter. Annie's skill had become well known, so the hotelier set up a competition between the two.

Annie won, but Frank was not bothered over being beaten by a young woman. Rather, he fell in love.

Ten years later, on April 24, 1885, the couple joined Buffalo Bill's Wild West show, cementing her fame. Annie stood only five feet tall. Fellow performer Sitting Bull named Annie "Little Sure Shot." Before long, Annie was the highest-paid performer in the show; other than Buffalo Bill Cody, that is, because it was his show.

April 24, 1885

Annie could cut in half a playing card held edge-on at thirty paces. She shot dimes out of the air. She could riddle a playing card flipped into the air with several holes before it hit the ground. Frank let her shoot cigarettes out of his mouth. The crowd loved her almost as much as Frank did.

Annie performed for kings, queens, and presidents. An advocate for equal rights, she taught thousands of women to shoot and donated most of her fortune to charities for women's rights.

Annie died from pernicious anemia in 1926, aged sixty-six. Husband Frank was so distraught at losing the woman he'd loved for over half a century that he stopped eating and died eighteen days later.

Annie Oakley

Despite being invented by a Canadian, basketball has a terribly racist history. Just kidding; Canadians can be some racist-ass motherfuckers too.

John McLendon, a Black man, was a student of James Naismith, the game's inventor. Later becoming a high school and college coach, McLendon pioneered fast-break basketball and the full-court press, yet received little credit at the time because his accomplishments were at Black colleges during segregation.

April 25, 1950

In 1944, McLendon organized a secret game between his team of all-Black players at what is now North Carolina Central University and a team of white players formerly of Duke University. The match was run like an undercover operation, hidden from the public and played on a Sunday morning while most were in church. There were no spectators.

Coach McLendon's team won 88–44. Can you imagine a crowd of melanin-deficient North Carolina folks in 1944 watching their side getting destroyed by a team of Black players? There would have been fucking riots. Twenty years later President Johnson

made a comment about how the "lowest white man" desires to consider himself "better than the best Black man." And he was right.

A massive barrier for Black players was broken by Chuck Cooper six years after the secret game. Chuck was a high school basketball star in Pittsburgh and was drafted to serve in the U.S. Navy during World War II. After the war he attended Duquesne University, where he was an All-American and set a school record with 990 points scored in four seasons.

On April 25, 1950, Chuck Cooper was the first Black man to be drafted by the NBA. He played for the Boston Celtics, the Milwaukee Hawks, and the Fort Wayne Pistons. His NBA career totaled 409 games and 2,725 points.

A car crash ended his career and Cooper returned to school, attained a master's in social work, and was tireless in his efforts to improve the lives of the people of Pittsburgh.

Today, 75 percent of NBA players are Black. Despite that, racism flourishes. One sad example is that in 2017, LeBron James, one of the greatest men to ever play the game, had his Los Angeles home defiled, spray-painted with a racial slur.

April 26, 1986, was the day shit glowed in the dark at the Soviet-era power plant Chernobyl.

The explosion of Reactor #4 qualifies as a "colossal fuckup." Corruption in the Soviet system of government is largely to blame for the catastrophe. Despite what you might have seen on HBO, the explosion was no one person's fault, but rather owed to an organizational structure where overly compliant workers taught not to question authority and cutting corners were the norm.

Additionally, the death rate from the explosion may have been, uh, well, overblown. There is much debate on this subject. The official death toll is in the dozens, but a 2005–06 report by the United Nations attested that as many as 4,000 may die over the long term, due to radiation exposure. Others say the death toll was and is far higher.

The truth is that we can't know for certain how many died from the Chernobyl explosion. It was a monumental tragedy that qualifies as probably the single largest anthropogenic disaster in human history.

If you saw the HBO special, you will recall that three engineers volunteered to drain millions of gallons of water from beneath the burning reactor in the days immediately following the meltdown. They had to wade through highly contaminated water to do so, donning only light protection from the radiation. One of those three men lived for another nineteen years, and the other two are still alive today.

April 26, 1986

I repeat that the Chernobyl disaster was a colossal fuckup that happened due to what can perhaps best be described as ingrained fuckery in the Soviet system of government. But its legacy, along with the negative portrayal of nuclear power in *The Simpsons* (really—there are research studies about this), has served to taint international opinion on what is one of the safest and cleanest methods of power-generation humans have ever created.

The truth is that we can't know for certain how many died from the Chernobyl explosion. It was a monumental tragedy that qualifies as probably the single largest anthropogenic disaster in human history.

No Kum-Sok was a North Korean fight pilot who said fuck this place and pointed his plane southward in search of freer pastures.

Kum-Sok defected, flying his Soviet-made MiG-15 into South Korea. The United States was all hey awesome thanks for taking us up on our offer here is your $100,000. And Kum-Sok said what offer I just wanted to get the fuck outta that place.

April 27, 1953

It was called Operation Moolah and launched on April 27, 1953, during the Korean War. Communicated via radio and leaflet drops, it began: "To all brave pilots who wish to free themselves from the communist yoke . . ." The Americans offered $50,000 (double for the first one to defect) to any pilot bringing them a MiG-15, because USAF pilots said it was a better plane than theirs.

The MiG-15 showed up early in the war and American pilots were kinda freaked out, saying the plane had numerous advantages over their F-86 Sabres. But they weren't exactly correct about that, and Moolah ended up being something of a successful failure. The Korean War ended in an armistice three months after the operation began, with no takers, but what did happen was that MiGs were grounded for several days right after the public bribe campaign began, possibly for the North to do a psychological evaluation of their pilots to weed out any who might be tempted to defect.

And when the MiGs started flying again, Americans began blowing them out of the sky at an unprecedented rate. Not only that,

but North Korean MiG-15 pilots often just noped right the fuck out of their aircraft, pulling the ejection cord at the first sign of American fighter planes. The reason was that the Soviet pilots—the ones who weren't supposed to be involved in the war in the first place—had been grounded because the USSR was fearful one of their own might take up the Americans on their offer, which would be a PR catastrophe.

Two months after the war ended, Kum-Sok showed up in his MiG at Kimpo Air Base in South Korea, having no knowledge of the financial reward for doing so. He said he'd heard rumors his loyalty was being investigated and in North Korea that is a *bad thing,* so he said fuck you guys and boogied for the South.

Famed test pilot Chuck Yeager flew the captured MiG and said it was "the most demanding situation I ever faced." The North's aerial victories were not due to the plane being amazing, he said, but that the Soviet pilots were well trained in dogfight tactics.

Kum-Sok immigrated to the United States, changed his name to Ken Rowe, went to school, and worked as an aeronautical engineer for companies such as Boeing, Gruman, Pan Am, and Lockheed. He lived a long life, but his best friend didn't. North Korea executed his friend and four of his fellow pilots as punishment for his defection.

No Kum-Sok meeting Vice-president Nixon

He could hit you so hard, your grandchildren would be born dizzy. But Muhammad Ali's most important fight was for the liberation of his people.

"I ain't got no quarrel with them Viet Cong," Ali said upon learning he was subject to be drafted into the U.S. Army. He was opposed to the war on numerous grounds, including religious ones, and refused to "go ten thousand miles from home and drop bombs and bullets on brown people" when people of color at home were fighting for basic human rights.

It was on April 28, 1967, that the 25-year-old Ali presented himself in Houston for his scheduled induction into the army, but when his name was called, he refused to step forward. Three times he was called, and three times he refused. An officer then warned Ali he risked five years in prison, but the boxer would not budge.

Ali was arrested, stripped of his title as heavyweight champion, and lost his boxing license. At his trial two months later, he was found guilty of draft evasion after only twenty-one minutes of jury deliberation. Years of appeals ensued, until the conviction was unanimously overturned by the Supreme Court in 1971.

The conviction prevented him from boxing for over three years. His trainer Angelo Dundee said, "He was robbed of his best years, his prime years." But for Ali the sacrifice was worth it, and he became a popular public speaker and civil rights champion, energizing the movement. In 1970, Ali was presented with the Dr. Martin Luther King, Jr., Memorial Award for his efforts.

April 28, 1967

Despite the lengthy, government-enforced hiatus, Ali's return to boxing would be triumphant, and he would eventually regain the heavyweight championship title in the "Rumble in the Jungle" bout against George Foreman in 1974.

Ali's refusal to be drafted, to be cowed into submission by an oppressive system, had a profound effect both in terms of turning public opinion against the war in Vietnam, and in promoting racial justice. He was a persistent thorn in the side of the American government; both the NSA and FBI illegally spied on him.

"It's not bragging if you can back it up," Ali once said. And he could.

> **Ali's refusal to be drafted, to be cowed into submission by an oppressive system, had a profound effect both in terms of turning public opinion against the war in Vietnam, and in promoting racial justice.**

When I was seventeen, I was attending Iron Maiden concerts and counting the days until high school was over. When Joan of Arc was seventeen, the iron-encased maiden was leading French troops to victory against the English.

April 29, 1429

In the early fifteenth century, France was in deep *merde*. The Hundred Years' War with England for control of the French crown had been going for, well, almost a hundred years, and they were getting their derrières kicked. Fourteen years after English monarch Henry V revealed the awesome power of the longbow against armored cavalry at the Battle of Agincourt, a critical turning point in the war was about to take place during the Siege of Orléans.

All because of an illiterate peasant girl.

Joan experienced her first vision at the age of thirteen while in her father's garden, she would later testify, asserting Saints Michael, Catherine, and Margaret commanded her to drive the English from her homeland.

Her visions were so powerful she convinced a series of French soldiers to get her an audience with Dauphin Charles, eldest son of the incapacitatingly bugshit-crazy King Charles VI. Her saintly apparitions instructed her to cut her hair and wear men's clothing to meet the dauphin. Doing the *Mulan* pretend-to-be-a-boy thing, Joan said to him, "Hey, Charlie. I'm just a girl but I'm gonna lead your army, cuz angels said so." (Not her exact words.)

"BAHAHAHAHAHA!!!" Chuck said, followed by, "Oh, wait. You're serious. Let me laugh even harder."

Except no, because for a generation the French had been getting fucked by the English in ways even Europeans find freaky. The French regime was near collapse, the entire country demoralized, defeated. And in comes this convincing young woman saying God is on her side and Charles must have been like ah fuck it what have we got to lose?

She arrived at Orléans with the French army at her back on April 29, 1429. She wasn't a soldier, but an inspiration. She waved a banner, not a sword. Before her arrival, the defenders of Orléans had been doing only that: defending. Joan's encouragement prompted a powerful counteroffensive that saw the siege lifted nine days later.

The quick victory was taken as a sign, and Joan became the French army's good luck charm, although her strategic recommendations were also given weight by military leaders. A series of victories led to Dauphin Charles finally being anointed king at Reims in July 1429, crowned Charles VII. Five months later Joan and her family were ennobled for her actions.

The following spring Joan was captured by the Burgundians—French who were allied with the English—then handed over to the latter. The French whose kingdom she'd helped save were all yeah she's outlived her usefulness so whatever. They put her on trial for both heresy and . . . cross-dressing? Yeah, fucking cross-dressing. Anyway, it took a full year for the invaders to run their kangaroo court, and she was burned at the stake on May 30, 1431. She was nineteen.

Today happens to be the anniversary of a murderous Nazi assmunch shooting himself in the head in a Berlin bunker. But fuck that guy. Let's talk about a Jewish super genius instead.

Unlike me, Albert Einstein was actually good at math. He was a gifted student, but not a well-behaved nor attentive one. He considered himself "a pariah" among academics who was misunderstood for his nonconformity. And it is the nonconformist who looks at the genius work of Newtonian mechanics and says it's not good enough.

Many refer to 1905 as Einstein's "miracle year." While working at the Swiss Patent Office, he published four groundbreaking papers in his spare time, one of which was that $E=mc^2$ stuff. But overlooked from the same year is that on April 30, at the age of twenty-six, he finished his doctoral thesis, titled *A New Determination of Molecular Dimensions,* and was awarded his PhD by the University of Zurich.

It is worth noting there is significant historical debate as to how much contribution Einstein's first wife, Mileva Marić, a mathematician and physicist, made to her husband's theories. Some historians say it was considerable, others say not at all. Albert dumped her in 1913 and married his cousin.

Einstein had only taken the job at the patent office because he'd spent two fruitless years attempting to find a teaching position, but his miracle year was a harbinger of change, launching his academic career in earnest. He held teaching positions at universities in Bern, Prague, his alma mater in Zurich, and the Humboldt University of Berlin. It was during his tenure at the latter that he developed the theory of general relativity in 1915 and won the Nobel Prize in Physics in 1921.

April 30, 1905

In 1933, Einstein was visiting the United States when a certain genocidal assdouche came to power in Germany. Among many, many other atrocities, one was a new law that barred Jews from holding any official position, including teaching at universities. Einstein said that the fucking Nazis can inhale a bag of dog farts and decided to stay in America, which, as history shows, was a wise decision.

Albert Einstein, age 25

Berlin's loss was Princeton's gain, with Einstein taking a position at the Institute for Advanced Study, where he was an intermittent lecturer until his death in 1955. It is often said that those who can't do, teach. In the case of Einstein, the reverse was true. He was an outstanding researcher, but his biographer Walter Isaacson said, "Einstein was never an inspired teacher, and his lectures tended to be regarded as disorganized." Kinda like his hair.

And FYI, before you share a meme with a "quote" by Einstein, google that shit first. He is one of the most popular figures to whom quotes are misattributed.

May

The name "Illuminati" is regularly associated with conspiracy theories about a "New World Order" run by a secretive power elite determined to replace sovereign nation-states with an authoritarian world government. But the actual Illuminati was a real thing, and it had no such designs. Quite the opposite.

The Bavarian Illuminati was indeed a secret society, founded on May 1, 1776. But the group's ambitions were more in line with the promotion of science over superstition. The organization began because some dude was too poor to join the Freemasons.

The pope had disbanded the Jesuits three years earlier, but they were still mostly running the show at the University of Ingolstadt (in Bavaria) and they were total dicks to anyone at the school who was non-clerical. They were the "Let's own some libtards" of the day.

Adam Weishaupt, the only nonclerical professor at Ingolstadt, was on the Jesuits' shit list. He despised the control religion had over people's lives and embraced the teachings of the Enlightenment. Adam was all about reason and science and liberalism.

Since Adam couldn't afford the Freemason fee, he said screw you guys I'll start my own club. The Illuminati began with Adam and four students and grew slowly from there. Eventually it expanded to include several hundred direct members, and perhaps thousands of affiliated members, many holding influential positions in society.

May 1, 1776

Things were looking good for the society when Charles Theodore became Duke of Bavaria in 1777 and initiated a series of liberal reforms. Except he was a total jam tart, and the clergy strong-armed the weak-willed monarch into reversing those reforms. D'oh!

Unfortunately for the Illuminati, not everyone was good at keeping the secret order a secret. They became boastful and openly critical of the monarchy, which caused the Duke to ban all such secret societies in 1785, and two years later he passed another edict making being a member of such an order punishable by death. Harsh.

And that was pretty much it for the Illuminati except in the dreams of conspiracy-minded morons who probably think the group is still in league with our reptilian overlords to harvest organs from people wearing Q SENT ME T-shirts to sell as a delicacy on the intergalactic hors d'oeuvres market.

Unfortunately for the Illuminati, not everyone was good at keeping the secret order a secret.

M
A
Y

129

A piece-of-shit terrorist was killed by U.S. troops on this day, and did that fucker ever have it coming. Yet this history isn't much about the hunting and killing of Osama bin Laden, but rather the role that torture did *not* play in ultimately tracking him down.

May 2, 2011

George W. Bush was not a strong-willed president, and many of the War on Terror policies his administration enacted were put in place due to the machinations of his piece-of-shit vice president, Dick Cheney. One such policy was "enhanced interrogation techniques," which is a euphemism for good old-fashioned torturing the fuck out of your enemies, but you don't call it "torture" because you want to pretend that you're better than your foes.

Anyway, yeah, the United States tortured people. A lot. And the resulting intelligence gathered through this fucked-up effort amounted to the square root of fuck all. Not according

> **George W. Bush was not a strong-willed president, and many of the War on Terror policies his administration enacted were put in place due to the machinations of his piece-of-shit vice president, Dick Cheney.**

to that *Zero Dark Thirty* movie, though. That movie made it seem torture was totes legit and a big reason Osama was located. FYI, even Republican senator John McCain, who was tortured as a POW of North Vietnam, criticized the film, saying it made him feel sick.

In reality, the torture program was more likely to generate false or misleading information, and numerous insiders confirmed it played no role whatsoever in the locating of bin Laden's compound.

After bin Laden's death, a bipartisan intelligence committee completed a 6,700-page "torture report" on the enhanced interrogation program. Its findings asserted the program was not effective in gaining either intelligence or cooperation from detainees, the claims made by the CIA about its effectiveness were bullshit, and the techniques used by the CIA were way worse than what they'd said they were, plus a bunch of other stuff revealing it to be a total shitshow. Again, the report was 6,700 PAGES.

One thing the program did accomplish was to inspire a lot more terrorists. Funny how that works.

"**Grow your dick** with all-natural Viagra from a Nigerian prince who has you on video!" No matter how tempting the subject line, do NOT click the link in that email.

But really, where does the term "spam" come from?

Originally, it's a disgusting (or perhaps you consider it yummy, in which case, go you) canned meat product first made by Hormel Foods in 1937 that gained popularity during World War II. Stylized as SPAM, popular belief is it's an abbreviation of "spiced ham," but according to Hormel, the name's origin "is known by only a small circle of former Hormel Foods executives."

So there's your first mystery . . . meat.

The second mystery refers to the email variety of spam. If you're wondering whom to curse for all the shit in your inbox, his name is Gary Thuerk. Gary was a marketing manager for a now-defunct company called Digital Equipment Corporation, and on May 3, 1978, he had an assistant send out a mass advertising email to 393 recipients on a precursor to the internet called ARPANET.

People were pissed. But . . . sales! And because the message made money, an annoying-as-fuck advertising medium was born.

It would be another sixteen years before it really caught on, and, big surprise, it was a couple of goddamn lawyers who did it, to advertise their immigration services. Again, mega backlash, but the pair told their critics to eat electronic feces cuz free speech. They even wrote a book titled *How to Make a Fortune on the Information Superhighway.* Assholes.

May 3, 1978

But what about that spam name?

There are a few hypotheses, with the most appealing one (therefore I'm gonna say it must be true) coming from a Monty Python sketch. In a popular skit from the comedy troupe's *Flying Circus* show, a group of Vikings sing "Spam!" over and over, drowning out all other communication. Kind of like what happens in your inbox. Others allege it is an acronym that stands for "simultaneously posted advertising message" or possibly "single post to all mailboxes."

Wherever the name originates, most of us can agree it fucking sucks.

If you're wondering whom to curse for all the shit in your inbox, his name is Gary Thuerk.

When it comes to remembering the Kent State Massacre, two things stand out: the song "Ohio" by Crosby, Stills, Nash & Young, and the photograph of a despairing Mary Ann Vecchio kneeling over the body of a slain protestor.

May 4, 1970

On May 4, 1970, students at Kent State University in Ohio were protesting the expansion of the Vietnam War, with U.S. forces bombing neutral Cambodia. Two thousand people showed up. So did the National Guard.

They tried to disperse the crowd with tear gas, which was thrown back at them by the protestors. Despite the protesters being at least seventy feet away and unarmed, dozens of Guardsmen proclaimed to fear for their lives and opened fire on the crowd. A presidential commission later asserted the slaughter was "unnecessary, unwarranted, and inexcusable." No shit.

The body Vecchio cried over was that of Jeffrey Miller. The photograph seems to convey an image of a young woman crying over the death of a friend, but she didn't know the man. Mary Ann was a fourteen-year-old runaway from Florida who was only on campus that day because it was where hitch-hiking had taken her. "I didn't know what to do," she said of that moment. "I was screaming because I couldn't help him."

The image ran on the front page of almost every newspaper in the United States and many other publications internationally. For novice photographer John Filo, it won him a Pulitzer and launched his career. For Mary Ann, she said it ruined her life.

The governor of Florida said Vecchio was part of a communist conspiracy. When she returned home to her parents, neighborhood children and classmates shunned her. She received tens of thousands of pieces of hate mail saying things that would make any YouTube comment section seem tame by comparison.

Vecchio would struggle for years, eventually marrying and settling in Las Vegas. On the twenty-fifth anniversary of the massacre, she finally met the man who made her famous. John Filo approached her with sadness in his eyes, and she burst into tears and embraced him. Filo, who also suffered much backlash over the photo, said of the meeting, "I'm just glad she doesn't hate me."

And the song? Many radio stations banned it because of its criticism of President Nixon, but it was inducted into the Grammy Hall of Fame in 2009.

"**O**kay."—Me

It's not.

There. Job done. Not quite.

Mexico did indeed fight for self-rule; the country's Independence Day is September 16, marking the outbreak of the rebellion against its Spanish overlords in 1810, a war that would last for eleven years and result in almost half a million lives lost.

Cinco de Mayo is about a different war in Mexico, one that happened half a century later. It commemorates a single battle in Puebla, which is now a city of over 3 million, but back then it was just a small town in east-central Mexico.

At the time, Mexico had experienced years of internal strife, which is never good for the economy. It was in deep debt to Britain, France, and Spain. Back then, when you couldn't pay your debts, you didn't get harassing phone calls from some soulless douche at a collection agency; you got warships.

Late in 1861, the pissed-off Europeans landed at the port of Veracruz in the Gulf of Mexico. The Mexican government was able to come to an understanding with the British and Spaniards, who withdrew their fleets.

But the French decided to be dicks. I mean, they were being ruled by a guy named Napoleon III at the time, if that tells you anything. Guys with that name do tend toward dick behavior.

May 5, 1862

France wanted to carve a chunk out of Mexico and claim it for its own. Six thousand French troops marched inland to attack Puebla. On May 5, 1862, a meager 2,000 poorly armed defenders launched a counterassault against the French and kicked some Euro ass. By the time the French withdrew, they had lost almost 500 soldiers, but the Mexicans lost fewer than 100.

Strategically, it wasn't a major victory in the war, which had the descriptive name of "The Second French Intervention in Mexico," but symbolically it energized the resistance to the invaders. Eventually the United States got involved on the side of Mexico, and the French withdrew in 1867.

In modern Mexico, they don't care much about Cinco de Mayo except in the state of Puebla. North of the border, however, plenty of melanin-deficient folks use the date as a reason to scarf pathetic honky tacos made from an Old El Paso kit. Note: No one needs an excuse to eat tacos. Now I want tacos. Real tacos. Not pretend ones.

Here is a story that should surprise no one. In 1868, the U.S. government made a treaty with the Sioux called the Fort Laramie Treaty to establish the Great Sioux Reservation, a sizable section of land west of the Missouri River, promising to preserve Sioux sovereignty and their way of life as well as protect them from incursions by white settlers. The treaty also proclaimed the Black Hills as "unceded Indian Territory." But then shiny yellow rocks were discovered on those Sioux lands, and the government was all like, "Treaty? What treaty?" The United States redrew the boundaries and said yeah no more hunting grounds for you, gotta be farmers now.

May 6, 1877

Prior to the treaty, in 1866, General William Sherman began to build military forts in Sioux territory because of the discovery of gold on the Bozeman Trail in Montana. A young Sioux warrior named Crazy Horse had already distinguished himself in battle the previous year against the U.S. Army and had earned the title of "Shirt Wearer," a war leader. Late that year, Crazy Horse led a small band of warriors toward the forts to act as a decoy to draw the forces into a trap.

The trap worked, the U.S. soldiers were surrounded and all eighty of them killed, their bodies hacked apart to send a message to Sherman. The following year, Sherman sought peace and withdrew the disputed forts, yielding the region to the Sioux in the aforementioned treaty that they fucking

broke cuz gold in them thar Black Hills. Needless to say, the Sioux were unimpressed.

As railroads moved west, tensions rose again. In June of 1876, during what would be called the Great Sioux War, Crazy Horse led a group of 1,500 Lakota and Cheyenne against the forces of General George Crook at the Battle of the Rosebud. It was not a bloody battle, but it served an important purpose: It delayed Crook from joining General George Custer at the Battle of the Little Bighorn, contributing to Custer's defeat.

A week later that fateful battle took place, and while Crook wasn't there, Crazy Horse was. He was a major participant in what would also come to be known as Custer's Last Stand. Several of his fellow warriors attested to Crazy Horse's courage and prowess, saying "The greatest fighter in the whole battle was Crazy Horse" and that he "was the bravest man I ever saw." If you are a *Star Trek* fan, you know how Lieutenant Worf often said, "Today is a good day to die." Guess who he got that from.

The American people were outraged at the defeat of Custer and demanded revenge. A winter campaign was launched against the Sioux. The following spring Crazy Horse and his fighters were outnumbered, low on ammunition, sick, and starving. Realizing they faced extermination, Crazy Horse and 1,100 others surrendered on May 6, 1877.

Five months later, Crazy Horse was fatally stabbed while in Fort Robinson, Nebraska, by a guard for allegedly resisting imprisonment.

A century ago, crossing the Atlantic was no picnic. If it wasn't the icebergs, it was the damn torpedoes.

Well, if you were rich it could be pretty nice. The *Lusitania* was a helluva ship with all sorts of fancy shit for those who weren't down in steerage with Leonardo DiCa—Oh, shit. Wrong boat. Anyway, for a time the *Lusitania* was the world's largest passenger ship and held the record for fastest commercial Atlantic crossing.

On May 7, 1915, the ship was nearing the end of its New York–Liverpool crossing when a German U-boat attacked. Because, World War I. Except they called it the Great War back then; they didn't know some German corporal was gonna go full fucking murder-psycho and try to rule the world two decades later. The war to end all wars my ass.

The ship had 1,266 passengers and 696 crew aboard. It also had a shit-ton of munitions for the Allied war effort, so the Germans figured fair game and launched a torpedo, which struck her starboard bow while the ship was eleven miles from the coast of Ireland. A second, internal explosion sank her in just eighteen minutes, and 1,198 passengers and crew died.

May 7, 1915

As they are often wont to be, Americans, who had 128 citizens die in the sinking, were ever so pissed. Prior to the sinking, there had been plenty of pro-German voices in the United States, but the torpedoing mostly shut them right the fuck up. President Badass Wilson (sarcasm) sent some stern letters to Germany, which were mostly ignored.

But the sinking did start a trend, turning American public opinion against the Germans. It took a couple more years, but then this thing called the "Zimmermann Telegram" was intercepted by British Intelligence in January 1917. It was a secret message from Germany to Mexico, proposing an alliance against the United States, and promising Mexico they'd get Arizona, Texas, and New Mexico out of the deal.

That did not go over well in the United States at all, and they entered the war on the side of the Allies on April 6 of that year.

The *Lusitania* in New York on her maiden voyage, 1907

M
A
Y

135

Once upon a time, there was a prevailing belief that Nazis were bad. People embraced the idea so vehemently, much of the world went to war to stop them. Those were the fuckin' days. Well, those days were hell, but they got the job done, and on May 8, 1945, Germany surrendered. They called it VE Day: Victory in Europe.

May 8, 1945

By the way, when I say "they," I mostly mean Russia. Russia led the way in getting the job done. If I were being fair, I'd say VE Day was May 9, because that's when Russians celebrate it; the German surrender came after midnight, Russia time. But Stalin was a dick, so May 8 it is.

Russia takes VE Day—they just call it Victory Day—very seriously. It's a national holiday. The sixtieth and seventieth anniversaries in 2005 and 2015 were the largest holi-

Londoners celebrate the end of the war in Europe

day celebrations—complete with the big-ass military parade—in Russia since the demise of the Soviet Union.

How come America doesn't get a day off for VE Day? Well, maybe it's because they didn't lose in the neighborhood of 26 million people fighting the fucking Nazis. About 95 percent of Allied deaths dealt by Germans were Soviets. Likewise, three-quarters of the German losses in World War II came at the hands of Soviet soldiers. They weren't nice to the Germans after the war either.

The Russians don't call it World War II. They call it the Great Patriotic War. And these soldiers *were* patriots. The opening scene of the 2001 movie *Enemy at the Gates,* showing only one rifle for every two Soviet soldiers, and depicting fleeing Soviets being gunned down by their officers, is about as faithful as Jude Law when a hot young nanny walks into the room.

Fleeing soldiers were more likely to be court-martialed and put in "penal battalions," and those guys *were* used as cannon fodder. But the Soviets weren't actively trying to lose the war by needlessly throwing lives away. It's just that Hitler was dedicated to depopulating the East to make room for the expanding German Empire, and therefore dedicated far more military resources to the Eastern Front.

Americans certainly helped win the war in Europe, but the next time someone tells you it was the United States who beat the fucking Nazis, give them a solid eye-roll.

Contraceptives allow people to put off being elbow-deep in diarrhea until they're ready, or just forgo procreation altogether.

Prior to the FDA approving oral contraceptives—"The Pill"—on May 9, 1960, women didn't have a lot of great options for controlling their own reproduction. If they wanted to fuck, it was mostly about setting up some kind of barricade and saying to the incoming ejaculate, "You shall not pass!" Problem is, there are a couple hundred million swimmers in each load, so like the storming of Helm's Deep, some of those fuckers might get through.

Prior to the 1960s, the most popular method of preventing pregnancy was the condom. But that's mostly controlled by the dude, and we know how men can be about that with their "Oh, I'm too big for condoms" bullshit. The Pill gave women the control to separate sex from procreation.

As the '60s progressed, the radical idea that single women were allowed to enjoy sex began to take hold. Feminism asserted that women had needs and should have the same sexual freedoms as men. Conservatives didn't like that, and many blamed the Pill. They figured that the fear and "shame" of having a child outside of marriage was enough to prevent single women from having sex, or married women from having affairs. The Pill, they thought, created a massive spreading of legs and oh god won't someone think of the unconceived children?

May 9, 1960

It was a double standard. Single men were allowed to blast semen all over creation, but women weren't allowed to say yeah, I want some of that. The Pill was seen as sexual anarchy, the downfall of society, and as dangerous as the nuclear bomb. While the Pill is neither a perfect preventative nor perfectly safe, it's generally considered safer than pregnancy and birth.

Studies have shown that prior to the Pill, plenty of single women were having sex, but just using less-effective methods of birth control. The Pill helped make this reality more public so that existing sexual mores could be more openly discussed and continue to evolve.

Prior to the 1960s, the most popular method of preventing pregnancy was the condom. But that's mostly controlled by the dude, and we know how men can be about that with their "Oh, I'm too big for condoms" bullshit.

So many criminals who have never served a day in prison become world leaders. This is the story of a political prisoner who spent almost three decades behind bars, won the Nobel Peace Prize, and led a country out of apartheid.

May 10, 1994

Born in South Africa in 1918, Nelson Mandela was politically active from a young age. For almost twenty years he battled the institutionalized racist and segregationist policies of the ruling whites under apartheid, and was determined to overthrow them. Although he had been committed to nonviolence, that changed in 1960 with the Sharpeville Massacre when South African police opened fire on a crowd protesting segregation, killing sixty-nine. Twenty-nine of them were children; many were shot in the back while attempting to flee.

The massacre prompted Mandela to cofound the armed wing of the African National Congress the following year. Called uMkhonto we Sizwe, meaning "Spear of the Nation," the organization was dedicated to acts of sabotage against the white-ruled government. Upon its formation, Mandela gave his famous "I Am Prepared to Die" speech, saying, "It would be unrealistic and wrong for African leaders to continue preaching peace and nonviolence at a time when the government met our peaceful demands with force."

The organization blew up government machinery and power stations and was classified as a terrorist organization. The following year (1962), Mandela, who had been repeatedly arrested and even unsuccessfully prosecuted for sedition in the past, was again arrested and sentenced to life in prison for attempting to overthrow the government. He would serve twenty-seven years, finally released in 1990 by President de Klerk amid growing domestic and international pressure.

Mandela used his newfound freedom to negotiate an end to apartheid, winning the Nobel Peace Prize in 1993. Due largely to his efforts, South Africa held a multiracial general election in April of 1994, which saw Mandela lead the ANC to victory.

On May 10, 1994, Nelson Mandela was inaugurated as South Africa's first Black president, serving a five-year term. He declined a second term and dedicated the rest of his life to combating poverty and HIV/AIDS. He died in 2013 at the age of ninety-five.

Nelson Mandela, age 19

This motherfucker. I'm not a fan of the death penalty, but Adolf Eichmann was a piece of shit who absolutely deserved to die.

For a couple hundred years in Europe there was this horrifyingly antisemitic thing called "The Jewish Question." It was a debate about what should be done regarding the status and treatment of Jews. Considering them human beings with equal rights wasn't given much consideration.

In Nazi Germany, the belief that Jews posed a problem for the state prompted the development of a "Final Solution" to this question. Adolf Eichmann was the primary organizer of said solution: the Holocaust.

After World War II, Eichmann was captured by U.S. forces but escaped before they learned of his true identity. Afterward, false documents and assistance provided by Nazi-sympathizing Catholic clergy enabled him to escape detection and eventually flee Europe. He relocated to Argentina in 1950, later getting a job with Mercedes-Benz.

There were plenty of other Nazis for Eichmann to hang with in Argentina, so he didn't lay that low. American intelligence got tips about Eichmann but didn't consider Nazi-hunting one of their jobs. They also feared Nazi testimonies would bring embarrassing things about certain West German allies into the light. Holocaust survivors, however, were determined to track these fuckers down and bring them to justice for their crimes against humanity.

A seven-year intelligence operation by Nazi hunters and Israeli intelligence culminated in the Mossad, Israel's intelligence agency, sending an eight-man team to capture Eichmann and put him on trial.

On the night of May 11, 1960, the team stopped Eichmann after he got off the bus he'd taken from work and was walking the final steps to his home. They wrestled him to the ground and shoved him into a waiting car, driving him to a Mossad safe house. They held him there for nine days while his identity was confirmed, then drugged him and flew him to Israel in secret. When the Argentinians found out, they were *pissed.*

The televised trial lasted fifty-six days and saw 112 witnesses, many of them survivors of the Holocaust, testify. It received prominent media coverage and served to substantially raise international awareness of the Nazi acts of genocide.

Despite using the "just following orders" excuse, Eichmann was found guilty and executed by hanging on June 1, 1962. He was immediately cremated, and his ashes scattered in the Mediterranean outside of Israeli territorial waters by the Israeli Navy.

There was no singular event that defined the amazing career of Florence Nightingale, so let's acknowledge her birth on May 12, 1820.

May 12, 1820

In the mid-nineteenth century, there was a thing called the Crimean War because Russia and rights of Christians in the Holy Land blah fucking blah. Okay, briefly, the Russian Empire was expanding and the Ottoman Empire was declining and Russia wanted to take some Ottoman shit in what is now Romania, and the stuff about Christian rights was more of an excuse for Russia to be a dick. Britain and France saw that going on and sided with the Ottomans cuz "balance of power" bullshit. Anyfuckingway, the important thing about the war was that it came to represent a more modernized type of warfare that involved things like railways and telegraphs. There was also that whole Charge of the Light Brigade fuckery (really, it was a major leadership fuckup where the British force got obliterated) that had the Brits demanding there be *less* fuckery and more professionalism in how they made war.

Florence Nightingale came to epitomize that professionalism.

Nightingale was born to a wealthy and influential British family, which in the nineteenth century meant she was destined to marry and start popping out aristocratic babies. In 1844 she said whatever the patrician

Florence Nightingale in 1858

version of "fuck that" is and entered nursing studies instead, much to her family's chagrin.

In 1854, reports from the war in Crimea revealed to the British the horrific conditions for their wounded soldiers. Being wounded in battle and sent to a field hospital sucks. Being wounded in battle and sent to a field hospital prior to the twentieth century super sucked.

Nightingale took a staff of thirty-eight volunteers that she had trained—all women—plus fifteen Catholic nuns, and deployed toward the Black Sea.

The place was a fucking mess. That's why so many were dying: horrific sanitation. She cleaned shit up, literally. There were overflowing sewers and a lack of ventilation, resulting in far more men dying from cholera, dysentery, typhoid, and typhus than from wounds sustained in battle. Her direct work and influence led to greatly improved cleanliness and conditions in healthcare settings, and the death rate plummeted. She became a national hero.

The Nightingale Fund was established for the training of nurses, and there was no shortage of generous donations. After the war, Florence used the money to establish the Nightingale Training School at St. Thomas' Hospital in London. It still exists today, as the Florence Nightingale Faculty of Nursing.

There is a reason why her birthday is celebrated as International Nurses Day. If you are a nurse, have an awesome day!

'm not Catholic, but in Spring 1981 I clearly remember thinking, *Why the fuck would someone want to shoot the pope?* Turns out, that's a question without a clear answer.

On May 13, 1981, Pope John Paul II was making an appearance in Saint Peter's Square in Vatican City to a crowd of adoring fans. Except for Mehmet Ali Ağca. He was not a fan. He was armed with a 9mm pistol and shot at the pope four times, hitting him with all four rounds, two of which passed through him and hit bystanders. People in the crowd jumped on Ağca, preventing him from firing more shots. The pope survived.

The motivation behind the attempted assassination remains a mystery.

A popular hypothesis perpetuated by right-wing media in the United States was that the Soviet Union was behind it, because back then American right-wingers liked blaming things on Russians. Anyway, they alleged that John Paul II, who was Polish and was supporting the Polish Solidarity movement, threatened Soviet control over the Eastern Bloc, so they wanted to snuff him. The accusation was so prominent that Tom Clancy wrote a boring novel about it titled *Red Rabbit;* it was certainly no *The Hunt for Red October.* Anyway, others assert there is no evidence to support the claim of Soviet involvement.

May 13, 1981

A counterhypothesis involves Ağca's time as part of a far-right terrorist group in Turkey called the Grey Wolves. It was alleged that Ağca acted as an assassin for hire on behalf of the Grey Wolves, who were paid three million deutsche marks by West German intelligence to assassinate the pope and then blame it on the Soviets.

Ağca, for his part, told an endless stream of lies after his capture. Fascinated with end times, he even said he was the second coming of Christ and had co-conspirators highly placed within the Vatican who saw John Paul II as the devil.

The pope used his influence to see Ağca pardoned in 2000. He was then deported to Turkey to serve a term for murdering a left-wing journalist in 1979. Prior to his release in 2010, he converted to Roman Catholicism, which is yet another fucked-up part of this whole story.

The lasting result was the pope getting a sweet new bulletproof ride they called the popemobile.

> **The lasting result was the pope getting a sweet new bulletproof ride they called the popemobile.**

For most of history, a smallpox infection had a fatality rate of 30 percent, even higher in babies. Survivors were often left horribly scarred and even blind. People were motivated to find a way to prevent the spread of one of the most lethal diseases in history.

May 14, 1796

Because humans are fucking horrible, there are multiple examples of smallpox being used for biological warfare. In one case, top brass in the British Army sanctioned its deliberate spread among North American Natives in the eighteenth century.

Prior to the vaccines, people were also purposely given smallpox as a way to *save* their lives. The process was called "variolation." It dates back to fifteenth-century China, where they took powdered smallpox scabs and rubbed them into superficial scratches on the skin of an uninfected person—usually during a time of outbreak—to protect them against infection by giving them a milder form of smallpox. Still, mild smallpox isn't fun, and people *did* die from this method—between 1 and 2 percent of those variolated got too sick and kicked off—but it was way better odds than full-on smallpox.

In 1752, when Edward Jenner was thirteen, he was apprenticed to an apothecary in Berkeley, England. At that young age, he noticed cattle workers who caught cowpox

didn't get smallpox, but being thirteen, didn't give it much additional thought. Later, when he became a practicing physician, there was an outbreak of smallpox and he advised the local cattle workers to get variolated. But they were like nah, dude. We're good. They'd had cowpox and knew it would keep them safe.

This confirmed his childhood suspicions, and his research on creating a smallpox vaccine began in earnest. In 1796 milkmaid Sarah Nelmes came to him for treatment of cowpox, and on May 14, 1796, Jenner used the opportunity to take material from one of her lesions and inoculate his gardener's son, James Phipps, because the FDA was not yet a thing. The boy got a mild fever and a local lesion but was fine a few days later. Then Jenner tested smallpox on the boy via variolation, and he had no reaction; he was immune. The world's first vaccination was born. Or so the story goes. Jenner wasn't the first to use cowpox for inoculating against smallpox, and the whole milkmaid story might not even be true. What is true is that he was a master of promotion, so Jenner did *popularize* the first vaccination.

Anti-vaccine fucknuts are nothing new; it would take almost two centuries to eradicate smallpox due in part to people being resistant to getting vaccinated. Smallpox still managed to kill 300 million people in the twentieth century. Almost a third of a billion, dead. In the twentieth century. And the last case was in 1977. Fucking hell.

Vaccinate your goddamn crotch goblins.

Antisemitism is not only a right-wing phenomenon. Plenty of lefties who believe themselves ever-so-progressive have no problem being antisemitic as fuck, with the existence of the State of Israel as their primary target.

After 6 million Jews were systematically murdered by fucking Nazis, the Jews' desire for a safe haven reached a tipping point. Back in 1917 the British government made the Balfour Declaration, supporting a "national home for the Jewish people" in Palestine, which was under control of the Ottoman Empire at the time. Britain got control of the region in 1920, and a quarter century later lotsa Jews wanted to nope the fuck out of Europe, for obvious reasons, and Britain said feel free to go to Palestine. Many of the Jewish people arriving in the Israeli cities of Tel Aviv and Haifa were survivors of the Holocaust, having lost their entire families. They were handed rifles by their fellow Jews who'd already settled in the region and told to defend their new homes.

From the Palestinian perspective, what had been a gradual influx of Jewish immigrants over several decades was suddenly a flood of people they saw as invaders of their homeland. The founder of the State of Israel, David Ben-Gurion, empathized, saying were he an Arab leader he would wage perpetual war against Israel. Ben-Gurion understood that Palestinians were not at fault for the Holocaust, and that from the Palestinian perspective, "We have come here and stolen their country."

The British mandate for administering Palestine ended on May 14, 1948, and the region was partitioned, with a little over half the area going to Jews. The Jewish people accepted the terms, immediately declaring independence as the State of Israel. The United States quickly acknowledged the new nation as legitimate, followed by many others. But Arab countries viewed it as an affront, and Egypt, Transjordan, Iraq, and Syria attacked Jewish settlements the following day, May 15.

May 15, 1948

Although outnumbered and geographically disadvantaged, Israel was better equipped, financed, trained, and motivated than its adversaries. Within six months, the Arab alliance was crushed.

Atrocities were committed on both sides, civilians massacred, homes burned. Israel used its military success to grow beyond the original partition to attain more defensible borders via the destruction of Palestinian villages.

Palestinians mark May 15 as the *Nakba,* or "catastrophe." The initial partition allotted Jews 55 percent of historic Palestine, but after the war this expanded to 78 percent being under Israeli control. For their part, Jews had faced centuries of exile, persecution, and annihilation, and had long sought self-determination through a national home they could defend against future attempts at genocide. The situation led to a state of frequent war and permanent siege. Jewish Israelis are surrounded by enemies who call for their utter destruction, whereas Palestinians are oppressed and discriminated against by the Israeli government, with some human rights groups accusing the nation of being an apartheid state. Late in 2022, Israel elected a far-right government, with numerous cabinet positions given to ultranationalists.

Animosity runs deep in the region, and peace remains elusive.

Just like those professing to "Make America Great Again" didn't, the "Great Leap Forward" in China wasn't. That's because cults of personality rarely end well, and Mao Zedong was one of the biggest cult leaders in history.

In 1958, Chairman Mao, Communist ruler and founder of the People's Republic of China, launched his plan to transform China into a modern industrialized state, the Great Leap Forward. And for some fucked-up reason he thought establishing "people's communes" in the countryside, focused mostly on producing steel, would be a good way to go about it. Yeah, let's take a bunch of folks who only know farming and get them to leave their fields to become steelworkers. That will work out well and 30 million people totally won't starve to death.

Oops.

And some in government learned that lesson. Moderates reversed the dumbfuckery of the Great Leap Forward in the early '60s, cutting Mao out of economic decision-making. And, being Mao, he seethed, because he saw his political prestige declining, and so he began planning his resurgence/revenge with even more dumbfuckery.

It began with Mao purging those of questionable loyalty from powerful positions, replacing them with sycophants, which is also reminiscent of MAGA bullshit.

Then, on May 16, 1966, there was a "notification." A tremendous, beautiful, HUGE notification. Mao declared the beginning of the "Cultural Revolution." He said the not-totally-bugshit moderate approaches that followed the catastrophe of the Great Leap Forward were bad, and that the Communist Party of China had to re-impose Maoism. Bigly.

He called on his cult followers to rise up in violent class struggle, proclaiming "to rebel is justified." Jesus Muppet-Fucking Christ, this shit sounds familiar. Anyway, instead of Twitter, he had a "Little Red Book," a collection of his sayings for his followers to fawn over.

Once again, Mao's big plan was a big failure. Countless people were persecuted, massacres were abundant, and millions more died. Oh, and because you need lots of stupid people to power such a cult following, intellectuals were maligned, and schools were closed. They went so far as to forcefully transport 17 million young, urban intellectuals to the countryside to be made to work as farmers as punishment for their pro-bourgeois thinking. All in all, it was another massive setback for the country.

In the early twentieth century Spanish philosopher George Santayana wrote, "Those who cannot remember the past are condemned to repeat it."

Yeah. That.

> **Once again, Mao's big plan was a big failure. Countless people were persecuted, massacres were abundant, and millions more died.**

"Separate but Equal." Now there is a bullshit claim if ever there was one. That's what the Supreme Court called their 1896 ruling on *Plessy v. Ferguson* that upheld segregation as totally peachy. And it would last another fifty-eight years, until May 17, 1954, when racial segregation in public schools was unanimously ruled unconstitutional in the landmark *Brown v. Board of Education* case.

The case was a culmination of a multi-year campaign conceived two decades prior by Charles Houston, a Black Harvard Law graduate and Dean of Howard University Law School. He was known as "The Man Who Killed Jim Crow" for his dismantling of Jim Crow laws across the country, which had enforced racial segregation after the Civil War. His star pupil was Thurgood Marshall, who enacted his mentor's vision of school desegregation.

The *Brown v. Board of Education* case began in 1951 in Topeka, Kansas, when an all-white public school refused to enroll Oliver Brown's daughter, even though it was close to her home, claiming she could take the bus to a Black elementary school farther away. The Browns, along with a dozen other local families, said screw that and banded together in a class-action lawsuit in federal court.

But they lost. The court pointed to the *Plessy v. Ferguson* case from more than half a century before and said, "These dead white dudes said segregation is okay." That's when Marshall, who at the time was chief counsel for the NAACP, entered the picture. He appealed the case to the Supreme Court.

When *Plessy v. Ferguson* took place, the Fourteenth Amendment had already been around for almost thirty years. Since most people only know about the first two amendments because of the endless shrieking about them on social media, I'll elaborate. The Fourteenth Amendment is one of the Reconstruction Amendments after the Civil War and is actually pretty damn important. It concerns the granting of citizenship, and for the first time declared that formerly enslaved people are full citizens. The amendment contains the Equal Protection Clause, saying no state could deny people equal protection under the law.

May 17, 1954

Marshall argued segregation violated that clause, and he won the landmark *Brown v. Board of Education* decision, not only opening the door for school integration, but serving as a model for future cases designed to affect societal change. One fact that helped sway opinion is that the Soviets were getting a lot of propaganda mileage from exposing American segregation laws, and Yanks didn't like being laughed at by commies. Alas, changing the law didn't change the practice, and for several decades many states refused to integrate all of their schools.

Thurgood Marshall would go on to become the first Black man appointed Justice of the Supreme Court of the United States, serving from 1967 to 1991.

You know how America has no shortage of TV evangelists preaching from their megachurch while also being a total hypocrite regarding what they're preaching? Aimee Semple McPherson taught them how to do that before TV even existed, using radio.

May 18, 1926

Aimee popularized using modern media to transform Jesus into home entertainment. Born in Canada in 1890 to a Methodist family, she was taught evolution in high school and didn't like that one bit. She wrote a letter to the editor of a newspaper asking why taxes were being spent to teach heathen science. People from across the country replied to that letter. She got her first taste of fame and liked it.

At seventeen she married a Pentecostal missionary and converted. He died of dysentery two years later. She remarried soon after (twice, and divorced twice) and started her ministry, ending up in Los Angeles in 1918, because she wanted to be in show business: fundamentalist Christian show business, with faith healing and speaking in tongues and all that.

She started the Foursquare Church, which now has more than 350,000 members, using radio evangelizing to raise funds to build one of the first megachurches: Angelus Temple, which still packs 'em in. Aimee

Aimee Semple McPherson preaching at Angelus Temple in 1923

used her massive radio reach to fight against teaching Darwinism in schools during the time of the 1925 Scopes Trial.

But she wasn't all bad. She desegregated her churches. The KKK attended services in full garb in response, but the story goes they were so touched by the service that hoods and robes were found on the ground afterward. Aimee was also dedicated to charity work.

She was also involved in scandals. On May 18, 1926, Aimee was "kidnapped" from a beach in Santa Monica. More than a month later she showed up in Arizona with a fantastic tale. She said she'd been abducted and hidden in a shack in the Mexican desert, but eventually escaped and walked twenty miles to the border. Tens of thousands greeted her return to Los Angeles. Prosecutors investigated her claim and came to the conclusion she'd actually spent several weeks shacking up with a former employee in a resort town.

Aimee and others were charged with criminal conspiracy and obstruction of justice, and the case was set for trial, but eventually dismissed for lack of evidence. There were claims of numerous other affairs and financial improprieties, and several lawsuits were brought against her. She also fell from grace with the press. None of this deterred her faithful followers.

She died of an unprescribed barbiturate overdose at the age of fifty-three, which was ruled accidental.

How is it that women kept agreeing to marry Henry VIII? Oh, right. It was the sixteenth century. And he was king. They didn't have much say.

Happy anniversary, Harry and Meghan. Hope your marriage, celebrated on this day in 2018, works out better than Henry and Anne Boleyn's did. Because May 19 is also the day Henry had his second wife beheaded.

Oh, Henry.

He was king for thirty-eight years and kicked off the English Reformation because the pope wouldn't let him annul his first marriage. Power mad, he was a fan of executing people for treason without trial if they looked at him sideways. Treason was one of the things Anne was falsely charged with that led to her execution, but it was really about miscarriages and mistresses.

Henry had been playing hide the royal sausage with Anne's sister, Mary, while he was married to his first wife, Catherine. But then he decided he liked Anne better. And Catherine was a positively ancient forty years old and only one of her six children lived, and it was a girl, dammit. (Spoiler: That girl, Mary, would eventually reign as queen for five years and be nicknamed "Bloody Mary" for her prosecution of Protestants.) Hank sent love letters to Anne saying he would be loyal to her, and by that he meant he'd fire all his other mistresses and she'd be the only mistress. Anne said no. Queen or GTFO.

Henry agreed. Catherine was out, Anne was in. But the honeymoon was short-lived. They married in secret because the whole annulment thing with Catherine wasn't settled; they were in a rush because Anne was preggers with another damn daughter.

Two (or possibly three) miscarriages followed, and by this time Henry was eyeing Jane Seymour, and not the *Dr. Quinn, Medicine Woman* one. Anyway, being Henry, the king had bullshit charges of treason, adultery, and incest drummed up against Anne followed by a quick trial then off with her head. Sucks to be Anne. Especially when you consider how she's been portrayed as a scheming temptress. Her reputation suffered due to the people liking her predecessor, Catherine, and seeing Anne's marriage to Henry as a scandalous usurpation.

Perhaps Anne would have taken solace in knowing her daughter, Elizabeth I, would ascend to the throne after the death of her older half-sister Mary, reign for forty-four years, and be hailed as one of England's greatest monarchs.

Many consider the Bible to be the word of God. History indicates it's the word of man. Several men. A group project. A bunch of dudes who got together in the early days of Christianity to decide what unifying beliefs they were gonna sell to the masses at mass.

May 20, 325

Constantine I, or "Constantine the Great," the reigning Western Roman Emperor, convened the Council of Nicaea on May 20, 325, to chat about God, man, and whether a certain man was also God.

Christianity had been around for a few centuries, and despite all the persecution it still managed to spread like a virus. The religion gained such a following that at a certain point it became politically expedient to say, "Fine. We'll stop allegedly feeding you to lions." That was Constantine's doing in 313 with the Edict of Milan, giving Christianity legal status within the empire.

A dozen years later shit got more serious. Constantine called together a few hundred bishops in pointy white hats to figure this Christianity stuff out, and they came up

> **Christianity had been around for a few centuries, and despite all the persecution it still managed to spread like a virus.**

with the Nicene Creed to define their faith and tell their growing flock what they were supposed to believe. It's heavy shit. Behold:

"We believe in one God, the Father, the Almighty, maker of heaven and earth, of all that is, seen and unseen. We believe in one Lord, Jesus Christ, the only son of God, eternally begotten of the Father, God from God, Light from Light . . ." plus a bunch of other stuff about Holy Spirits and virgins and going zombie on the third day plus coming back another day to judge people.

So, yeah. Big day. I mean, the council lasted a few months. But May 20 was when it began.

Constantine, for his part, wasn't even Christian. At least not yet. Twelve years and two days later he died, but he knew death was imminent and asked to be baptized just beforehand. It's believed he put it off because he had a metric shit-ton of sins he wanted to be absolved of and he wanted to keep on sinning right to the last minute.

A little more than half a century after the First Council of Nicaea, in 380, Christianity would be named the official state religion of the Roman Empire under Emperor Theodosius I.

Today is the anniversary of when a dude with fucked-up ideas about racial purity, who also cheated on his wife a whole bunch, first flew the Atlantic solo in 1927. Five years later to the day a much cooler person did it. Let's focus on her.

Amelia Earhart didn't like being told what she couldn't do because of her gender. As a child, she kept a scrapbook of newspaper clippings of women doing jobs traditionally reserved for men, such as law, mechanics, and film directing. In 1920 her father took her to an airshow, and three days later she was taken for her first flight. She was hooked. A week later Amelia began flying lessons.

Although intelligent and enthusiastic, Earhart was reportedly not a natural pilot and struggled to learn the skill. But she was determined to persevere. She set a women's altitude record of 14,000 feet in 1922, and by 1925 was gaining notoriety as a female flyer. The year after Charles Lindbergh's transatlantic flight, George Putnam (who was the publisher for a popular book about said flight) approached Earhart to be the first woman to accompany a transatlantic flight.

There were other female pilots, but George preferred Amelia because she was educated and attractive and therefore "the right sort of girl" [insert barf noises]. Although essentially a passenger on a flight made by men, it made her a celebrity. Some newspapers nicknamed her "Lady Lindy," comparing her to Lindbergh. Others more respectfully called her "Queen of the Air."

Years of flying, breaking more records, and speaking on the subject of women in flight would follow. During that time, after his sixth proposal, she agreed to marry Putnam. She told him they'd have an open marriage, and she wouldn't be taking his last name.

May 21, 1932

No one had made a solo transatlantic flight since Lindbergh in 1927. Earhart intended to follow the same route from New York to Paris on May 21, 1932, but harsh weather forced her to land in a field in Northern Ireland. A farmhand asked her, "Have you flown far?" She replied, "From America."

The flight saw her fame grow exponentially, but she would not rest. After numerous other flying accomplishments, Amelia Earhart disappeared on July 2, 1937, while attempting to be the first aviator to complete an equatorial circumnavigation of Earth.

Amelia Earhart in 1936

May 22, 1947, marks the unofficial beginning of the Cold War, when President Truman signed the Truman Doctrine into law. The gist? Commies bad. Contain that shit.

May 22, 1947

Unlike modern times, where having them interfere in U.S. elections is seen as no big deal, back then Russians freaked Americans right the fuck out. Sure, they'd been on the same side in World War II and the Western Allies even let the Soviets do most of the dying in beating the fucking Nazis, but that was a whole two years earlier, and capitalists couldn't abide the geopolitical spread of that heathen pinko bullshit.

After WWII, the Soviets were actively trying to spread communist revolution throughout the world to get it to turn red, so they'd have more allies. They figured the United States was tired of fighting. They were wrong. 'Muricans love a good scrap.

The Soviets already controlled most of Eastern Europe and were looking to the Mediterranean, which was still reeling from the war. The Truman Doctrine committed almost half a billion Real American Dollars to stabilize Greek and Turkish governments, so they'd be *their* allies instead. That opened the door to America spending another $17 billion (almost $200 billion in today's dollars) in rebuilding Western European economies to contain the threat of them embracing communism. (This was the Marshall Plan, named after U.S. secretary of state George Marshall.) During the late 1940s and early '50s the money went to rebuilding cities, industries, and transportation networks across Western Europe, which had recently gone through several years of getting the everloving fuck blown out of it. During that time period, the United States dedicated a whopping 5 percent of its GDP to helping their allies, and it made them awfully grateful and willing to act as a bulwark against the spread of communism. It's like that CeeLo Green song: Why go Atari when you can get a Ferrari?

Then, of course, there were the wars. The Soviets and the United States had plenty of thermonuclear kaboom toys, and were reluctant to confront each other directly lest they make the planet glow in the fucking dark. And so, America went after numerous smaller countries that dared to elect governments that had a whiff of communism, to prevent the ideology from spreading.

Oh, Guatemala toppled its military dictator and had its first-ever democratic election, then started giving land to peasants? Sounds commie to us. Send in the CIA and topple that motherfucker.

Dammit, now there are commies running Indonesia. No problem, we'll just help a murderous far-right psycho genocide the hell out of a million people and problem solved.

Well, shit. Now we need to bomb Vietnam back to the Stone Age because they didn't do democracy the way we wanted.

There wasn't a peace treaty that ended the Cold War in 1991. The Soviets just ran out of money and imploded. The good guys outspent them. Hooray for capitalism! Want to buy some blue jeans?

"**ncel**" is a portmanteau of "involuntary celibate." This fuckless—I mean feckless—group comprises almost exclusively young men, usually white, who lament their inability to get laid. It's a toxic online subculture that despises women while also wanting to use them for sex. But it's not really about the sex. Rather, incels are a hate group that cannot abide having their sense of entitlement thwarted. They want to conquer the bodies of beautiful women to gain status in the male hierarchy, or some dumbfuck bullshit idea like that.

The Isla Vista, California, massacre on May 23, 2014, brought the word "incel" into the common vernacular. The term was actually coined by a woman in the '90s as a way to help people. But like many things it was co-opted and warped by men like Elliot Rodger.

Rodger, a 22-year-old virgin, couldn't find a girl-friend, and to him that was enough to justify mass murder. But not before writing a 107,000-word hate-filled manifesto about how much he despised women for "starving him of sex." Using a combination of stabbing, shooting, and his car as a weapon, he murdered six people and wounded fourteen others during his rampage before putting his gun to his own head.

I wish people bent on murder-suicide would do it in the reverse order.

May 23, 2014

To give you an idea of how fucked-up the incel community is, they anointed Rodger "Saint Elliot" because he "martyred" himself to the cause. Incels number in the tens of thousands online, and several mass murders have been committed by them in North America, resulting in dozens of deaths. A shift in how these killings are treated came as a result of a February 24, 2020, stabbing attack in Toronto that killed one woman and injured another. A minor-aged male incel was charged. Police later labeled it an act of terrorism.

And that is an accurate determination. Incels are as radicalized as any terror group. They have their own lexicon to slot people into various groups. They are nihilists who feel their lives are doomed due to not being considered conventionally attractive, so burn the world down. But they are not all beyond hope. There are many former incels. Learn the terminology and seek to intervene if you know someone who is at risk of being sucked into this terrorist organization.

> **Rodger, a 22-year-old virgin, couldn't find a girlfriend, and to him that was enough to justify mass murder.**

Half a dozen years before the U.S. Civil War, the Kansas Territory—it wasn't a state yet—was a harbinger of things to come. That's why they called it "Bleeding Kansas," a regional civil war over the subject of, you guessed it, slavery.

May 24, 1856

There was some other shit people were disagreeing over too, but slavery was the big one. Just like the Civil War was largely about treating humans like things and not what those coal-rolling Confederate flag–waving fuckwipes claim was "a war of Northern Aggression" where the South was fighting for "states' rights."

Anyfuckingway, Kansas was bleeding, and John Brown—a white man—was ready to go all massacre on some slavery-supporter shitburgers.

This dress rehearsal for the Civil War saw several dozen killed in clashes between those who believed enslaving people was just peachy and others who said yeah no that's some evil-ass shit. The massacre in question was in reaction to two events. Lawrence, Kansas, was an anti-slavery town, and on May 21, 1856, three hundred pro-slavery cockbags sacked the place, burning and looting as they went. That pissed off those in Kansas who wished to abolish slavery.

The abolitionists were further vexed by the events of the following day. Senator Charles Sumner had recently given a fiery speech to a full Senate called "The Crime Against Kansas." In it, he called out some pro-slavery senators for sucking. One of those senators targeted in Sumner's speech was Andrew Butler. Butler's nephew Preston Brooks couldn't abide the truth being told about his assbutt of an uncle, and attacked Sumner on the Senate floor with a cane, beating him near to death.

That's when radical abolitionist leader John Brown decided fuck this, we need to start wasting these assholes. On May 24, 1856—two days after the attack on Sumner—Brown, along with five of his sons and three others, committed what would be called the Pottawatomie Massacre. Late at night, the nine men attacked three separate pro-slavery settlements near the banks of Pottawatomie Creek. The men in the settlements were taken from their homes and murdered via a combination of shooting and sword hacking by Brown and his crew. Five men were killed in the massacre. As you might imagine, the massacre did not improve relations between pro- and anti-slavery groups in the Kansas Territory. Rather, it led to months of retaliatory raids and battles.

Three years later, Brown led a raid on a Virginia armory to gain weapons to support an uprising of enslaved people in the South. The attack failed and Brown was captured and tried for treason. Found guilty, he was hanged on December 2, 1859, the first person to be executed for treason in America.

The U.S. Civil War erupted sixteen months later, resulting in approximately 650,000 lives lost, the deadliest war in the nation's history.

Toward the end of the nineteenth century, Oscar Wilde was the talk of the theater scene in London for writing plays such as *The Importance of Being Earnest.* It was during that play's run that Oscar ran afoul of England's stodgy sex laws, and was sent to prison for the crime of being gay.

Despite homosexuality being a criminal offense, Wilde was not overly discreet. Where he got into trouble was owing to his tempestuous gay relationship with Lord Alfred Douglas. Regardless of the risks, Douglas flaunted his sexual orientation like it was San Francisco in June. Douglas introduced Wilde, who was known for saying "I can resist everything except temptation," to the underground world of gay prostitution, where he began to solicit a series of impoverished boys as young as sixteen.

The story broke because Douglas's dad was one of those manly men (sarcasm font) who didn't like that gay stuff. He held the title of Marquess of Queensberry and is credited with sponsoring the development of

Oscar Wilde (left) and Alfred Douglas

the modern rules of boxing (called Queensbury Rules). The Marquess preferred to punch men's faces rather than kiss them, and he threatened to "thrash" Wilde for his relationship with his son.

May 25, 1895

When the Marquess made a public accusation of sodomy against Wilde, the writer made the ill-advised decision to prosecute his accuser for criminal libel. Of course, truth is a defense against libel, so the Marquess hired private investigators to find evidence of Wilde's homosexual acts. And find them they did. The libel charge was dropped, and instead Wilde found himself facing prosecution for "gross indecency."

Now, while the criminalization and persecution of homosexuality has long been a blight upon human history, in modern times Wilde could be charged under U.K. law with "paying for the sexual service of a child" for the hiring of underage prostitutes. As Wilde said, "The truth is never pure and rarely simple." While homosexuality should not be punished, his predations upon underage prostitutes are another matter. Under modern morals of fucking we'd proclaim Wilde was prosecuted for the wrong fucking thing.

Friends advised Wilde to flee to France, but he would not. The first trial was a mistrial. But in the second he was found guilty on May 25, 1895, and sentenced to two years of hard labor.

He served his time, which wore on his fragile health, then fled to France the day of his release, where he died three years later at the age of forty-six.

On May 26, 1987, a radio announcer was excited about how "It was twenty years ago today" that the Beatles album *Sgt. Pepper's Lonely Hearts Club Band* was released. I was nineteen and asked my father what the big deal was. "It just really blew people away," he said.

May 26, 1967

You know how some bands have a great debut, or perhaps even a few good albums, then rapidly begin sucking? Not so with the Beatles. *Sgt. Pepper's* was their eighth studio album, and it stayed at #1 on the U.K. Albums Chart for twenty-seven weeks. Released June 2 in the United States, it also spent fifteen weeks in top spot on the *Billboard* Top LPs chart.

It was an early "concept album," where the Beatles created an alter ego in the form of the Sgt. Pepper band. The album is considered a progenitor to progressive rock, which sought to elevate rock music to a higher level of respectability by using classical influences to focus more on composition and displays of musicianship rather than just singing about how some woman loves you followed by the word "yeah" over and over. It also had an incredibly cool album cover.

Sgt. Pepper's opens with a bang on the title track and includes many songs that remain popular over half a century later, including "Getting Better," "Lucy in the Sky with Diamonds," and "With a Little Help from My Friends." Then, the album ends with what has been described as "one of the most harrowing songs ever written," "A Day in the Life." The record won four Grammys, including Album of the Year.

It has sold over thirty million copies and *Rolling Stone* didn't say it was one of the best albums of all time. They left the "one of" part out. Rather, they ranked it simply as "the greatest album of all time." The magazine later updated the list (more than once) after repeated criticisms of it being dominated by white dudes, and the album slipped in the rankings.

Rankings by music critics are fucking stupid anyway. The fact is that *Sgt. Pepper's* still slaps more than half a century after its release. You go listen now.

> **Then, the album ends with what has been described as "one of the most harrowing songs ever written," "A Day in the Life." The record won four Grammys, including Album of the Year.**

While everyone in Mother England was freaking out over *Sgt. Pepper's* dropping the day before, Australia was taking steps toward atoning for colonialist sins. Words tend to matter when they're written into a constitution, and the will of the people can change those words.

When people are segregated it becomes easier to marginalize and oppress them. Prior to 1967, Aboriginal populations in Australia had a separate census. It was separate because there were separate laws for governing them, as per Section 51 of the country's constitution, which said Federal Parliament could make laws for: "The people of any race, other than the aboriginal race in any State, for whom it is deemed necessary to make special laws."

The referendum was to get rid of the "other than the aboriginal race in any State" part so that Federal Parliament had the power to make laws for all races, rather than leaving the issues of laws specifically for Aboriginal peoples in state hands.

The referendum was also to completely delete Section 127, which read: ". . . reckoning the numbers of the people of the Commonwealth, or of a state or other part of the Commonwealth, Aboriginal natives shall not be counted."

These amendments were the culmination of a lengthy struggle for equal rights supported by both the Aboriginal community and its allies. Many think it had to do with voting rights, but that is a separate and complicated history in Australia. It was not until 1983 that total equality was achieved regarding voting, making it mandatory for Aboriginals, as it was for other Australians.

May 27, 1967

What the 1967 Referendum accomplished was to unify the country as one people, with Aboriginal people included as members of the national community. And that is how the "Yes" campaign was run. Rather than focusing on boring constitutional legalese, campaigners made the event about inclusion, friendship, and atoning for past injustice and inhumanity.

Interestingly, there was almost no opposition campaign to the "Yes" vote, and on May 27, 1967, the referendum passed with over 90 percent of the vote. But it was largely a symbolic victory. It showed that Australians considered the Aboriginal people to be part of the same country. While it had little legal power in itself, the move opened the way for more specific legal changes in the granting of equal rights to Australia's Aboriginal people.

The odds were one in fifty-seven million. No fertility treatments. Just a married couple living in a farmhouse in central Ontario, Canada, who did what married couples do and happened to make five identical girls. Then the government took the babies away and put them on display. Because, money.

May 28, 1934

The Dionne Quintuplets, born on May 28, 1934, were two months premature. Delivered by obstetrician Dr. Allan Dafoe and two midwives, they became the first quintuplets to survive to adulthood, but their childhood was totally fucked-up.

News of the unusual birth spread, and everyone wanted a peek. The Chicago World's Fair, with pressure from Dr. Dafoe and the family pastor, convinced the parents to sign a contract saying they could display the quints. But Mom and Dad realized

Ontario premier Mitchell Hepburn with the Dionne Quintuplets

their mistake and decided to sign them over to the Red Cross to get out of the state fair contract.

Instead, the *parents* went to Chicago to make stage appearances as the mother and father of the famous babies, and—hypocrisy alert!—the premier of Ontario, Mitchell Hepburn, said, "Oh, they're bad parents who will exploit them, so let's ram through the 'Dionne Quintuplets Act' so the government will be their guardians (and we can exploit them instead)." Paraphrased.

Three thousand tourists a day flocked to the government-built nursery and controlled compound to watch them play. The kids had minimal contact with their parents, despite Dad setting up a souvenir shop across the street. The attraction was called "Quintland" and was the province's biggest tourist trap of the time, netting more visitors than Niagara Falls.

The five girls appeared in three feature films, and were used to hawk products such as soap, toothpaste, and chocolate bars. And guess who was chief overseer of the girls? The same doc who delivered them. Dafoe made the modern equivalent of close to three million dollars off them as the celebrity doc of the day.

The quints were returned to their parents when they were nine, but it wasn't a happy reunion. Their parents, also made wealthy by their children's labor, had since had three more kids, and treated the returning girls poorly. In 1995 the three surviving sisters accused their father of having sexually abused them as teens. Two years later they wrote an open letter to the parents of the newly born McCaughey Septuplets cautioning them to not put the babies' lives on display, because their lives had "been ruined by the exploitation we suffered."

Say the words "Roman Empire" and what comes to mind? Caesars and gladiators and coliseums and *et tu, Brute?* Say "Constantinople" and many get an earworm of an old novelty song about how Istanbul used to be Constantinople but now it's—*AAAAUUUGGGGHHH GET IT OUT OF MY FUCKING HEAD!!!!*

The Roman Republic began about half a millennium before Jesus. It took until about 300 B.C.E. before it began to expand beyond the Italian peninsula, making it a de facto empire if not a de jure one. Julius Caesar was dictator for a brief time in 44 B.C.E. before being assassinated, but it was his adopted son Octavian who was declared "first citizen"—basically emperor—in 27 B.C.E. That's when the transition from republic to empire was complete.

That empire ended in 465 C.E., but that was the *Western* Roman Empire. The *Eastern* Roman Empire would survive another thousand years. Because, you see, in 285 C.E. it was decided the empire had grown too large to manage, and it was split in two, with the eastern capital in Constantinople—*THERE'S THAT FUCKING SONG AGAIN!*

May 29, 1453, marks the end of the Eastern Roman Empire, which had also come to be known as the Byzantine Empire, with the fall of Constantinople to another empire: the Ottoman.

Led by 21-year-old Sultan Mehmed II, the Ottomans besieged the fortress of Constantinople with overwhelming force for fifty-three days. The taking of the city marks a number of turning points in history. Many historians consider it to be a symbol of the end of the medieval period, which had begun with the fall of the Western Roman Empire.

May 29, 1453

It also revealed the power of gunpowder, as prior to this time substantial fortifications such as Constantinople's were effective at repelling invaders, but large cannons proved to be an effective counter to such defensive boundaries.

Finally, Constantinople represented a barrier between Asia Minor and Europe. With its fall, the Ottoman Empire was better positioned to invade mainland Europe, leading to its control of much of the Balkan peninsula.

By the way, the original version of the song "Istanbul (Not Constantinople)" was released in 1953, on the 500th anniversary of the fall of Constantinople, by a Canadian group called the Four Lads. It was certified gold and has been covered a number of times since.

Few know much about the Nigerian Civil War. Even many Nigerians prefer to forget it. While the world was focused on Vietnam, a region of Eastern Nigeria seceded, launching a war that lasted almost three years and led to millions of deaths, most of whom were children.

May 30, 1967

Tensions in Nigeria were plentiful for many years leading up to secession. The Igbo people, one of the largest ethnic groups on the African continent, felt that the political, cultural, religious, ethnic, and economic divides between them and the leadership centered in Northern Nigeria were too vast to be mended. Nigeria had only decolonized from Britain a few years earlier; imperialism had exacerbated the divisions by separating Nigeria into three regions. It led to political parties being formed along regional and tribal lines.

The Igbo were persecuted. Nigeria being an oil-rich country, there were fights over control of its production. Prior to secession, there was a military coup followed by a countercoup. Afterward, approximately one million Igbo relocated to southeast Nigeria, and on May 30, 1967, the Republic of Biafra was declared as an independent state. Four African states, as well as Haiti, recognized the new nation, and several European countries offered support.

After a period of blockade, the Nigerian military advanced into Biafra beginning on July 6, 1967. Resistance was fierce, but by 1968 the Nigerian army had surrounded Biafra, cutting off port access. The war then became a stalemate.

Battle casualties numbered approximately 100,000 dead. The surrounding of Biafra led to mass starvation, with estimates of as many as 3 million dead, three-quarters of them children. Despite international relief efforts, hunger was an effective, deliberate weapon used by Nigerians for winning the war. But using starvation as a tool of genocide was far from the only atrocity committed.

The Igbo were largely Catholic, whereas the Northern Nigerians were primarily Muslim. A PR campaign highlighting this generated much sympathy for Biafrans in the United States. It also popularized the trope of using images of starving children to represent Africa. With the assistance of Britain, which got involved because it wanted to keep the cheap oil flowing, the Nigerians launched a final offensive at the end of 1969 and brought the war to a swift end.

No perpetrators were held accountable for the genocide. Rather, the government chose to sweep it under the rug by embracing the words of Nigerian head of state General Yakubu Gowon, who proclaimed, "No victor, no vanquished." To this day, Nigeria struggles with ethnic unity, which is why many in the nation's government wish to forget this travesty. The country's leaders don't wish to remind their citizens it could happen again.

n 2016, Donald Trump campaigned for president of the United States by giving a series of speeches that were a lot of euphemisms for "Brown people scare me." He was seen as a joke for most of the campaign, but there was little to laugh about on election night. Many wondered how he could have been elected; they didn't realize just how deep racism runs in America.

On May 31, 1921, what is considered the single worst incident of racial violence in American history took place in Tulsa, Oklahoma. Time for another euphemism-o-rama so as not to offend the fragile-ass #AllLivesMatter Casper Americans.

Some milky motherfuckers dropped bombs on a Black neighborhood using goddamn airplanes. Of course, it all began because of a false accusation of assault. A nineteen-year-old Black man named Dick Rowland tripped getting into an elevator, prompting the frost-faced seventeen-year-old female operator to scream.

Rowland was arrested and an infuriated creamy crowd of approximately two thousand massed outside the courthouse. Fearing Rowland would be lynched, several members of the Black community came to the courthouse to protect him. Some of them were armed. It's unsure if it was accidental or meant as a warning, but a Black man fired a single shot, hitting no one. The snowmen returned fire with intent to kill, and a gun battle ensued.

The pasty people weren't the greatest of shots though, based on the numbers. Two Black men and ten lotion-colored lads died in the exchange. And of course that could not stand. The town went completely bugshit, exploding into vanilla violence against what was, at the time, the richest Black community in the entire United States—Tulsa's Greenwood District.

May 31, 1921

Throughout the night and the next day there were gunfights between drywall dudes and Black people. Then the baking-powder bastards began to set fires. And, as mentioned, the alabaster attackers dropped incendiary bombs from private airplanes onto the neighborhood, and also fired rifles at people on the ground. It should be noted that the dropping of bombs and shooting from planes is based on several eyewitness accounts but remains "unconfirmed." There definitely were several planes circling above.

The National Guard was brought in and established martial law to end the violence. The death toll remains uncertain, but it's approximated at two hundred, mostly Black people. Hundreds more were injured, and thousands of Black families were left homeless.

Nab Negro for Attacking Girl In an Elevator

A negro delivery boy who gave his name to the police as "Diamond Dick" but who has been identified as Dick Rowland, was arrested on South Greenwood avenue this morning by Officers Carmichael and Pack, charged with attempting to assault the 17-year-old white elevator girl in the Drexel building early yesterday.

He will be tried in municipal court this afternoon on a state charge.

The girl said she noticed the negro a few minutes before the attempted assault looking up and down the hallway on the third floor of the Drexel building as if to see if there was anyone in sight but thought nothing of it at the time.

A few minutes later he entered the elevator she claimed, and attacked her, scratching her hands and face and tearing her clothes. Her screams brought a clerk from Renberg's store to her assistance and the negro fled. He was captured and identified this morning both by the girl and clerk, police say.

Rowland denied that he tried to harm the girl, but admitted he put his hand on her arm in the elevator when she was alone.

Tenants of the Drexel building

A newspaper clipping that contributed to the Tulsa Race Massacre

June

"**f it's not Scottish,** it's crap!" Not true though, as there are plenty of good whiskies out there, and they're all capable of giving you one of the worst hangovers you ever had. Let me hear you say *uisge-beatha na h-Alba* after you've had a few drams. That's Scottish Gaelic for "Scotch whisky."

The first day of June 1495 was a great day. A great, great day. Although some would come to curse the name of John Cor, it was on that day the Tironensian monk stationed at Lindores Abbey in Fife had his name mentioned on the Exchequer Rolls of King James IV for making batches of what some say tastes like turpentine, and others are willing to spend stupid amounts of money on. To give you an idea of how seriously the Scottish took this new invention, on said Exchequer Rolls it was referred to as *aqua vitae:* water of life. Well, they'd been making whisky for a while before then, but that date is the first time someone finally crawled out of a drunken haze long enough to write shit down.

You know how all thumbs are fingers but not all fingers are thumbs? Same with Scotch. It's all whisky, but not all whisky—or whiskey—is Scotch. Regarding spelling, Americans and Irish write it as "whiskey," and most everyone else, including my fellow Canadians, term the liquid gold as "whisky." For a long time, *The New York Times* took an ethnocentric approach and used the American/Irish spelling regardless of whose potent potable they referred to. But, after a raft of presumably drunken complaints, in 2009 they switched to the preferred spelling of the country of origin when discussing whisky. Or whiskey.

The stuff was originally made from malted barley, but then people got creative in coming up with new and interesting ways to kill brain cells. "Aye, Angus! Dinnae be puttin' any o' da corn shite in me Scotch or I'll jam a caber up yer arse!"

June 1, 1495

The Scottish are pretty uptight about the definitions and labeling for Scotch.

Oh, and if Henry VIII wasn't enough of an asswipe already, what with all the tyranny and wife murdering, after he defeated James IV of Scotland in battle, he dissolved the monasteries where it was made and proclaimed the making of Scotch illegal. *Ye bastard!* Yeah, that worked about as well as the Eighteenth Amendment—the not-drinking one—to the U.S. Constitution did. Later on, the English figured out they could tax the stuff, and all of a sudden the gubmint approved.

The Irish had been in the whiskey game for a while already, having beaten the Scots to it by about ninety years, but it's still not Scotch. Scotch is from Scotland, obviously, but in the centuries since its creation the Scots have experimented with and refined their approach to making it. Americans often like putting corn in theirs and calling it bourbon whiskey. Canadians are known for their rye whisky. There are a small number of whisky distilleries in England, which I expect many Scots consider a crime against humanity.

Finns, Germans, Mexicans, Danes, and many others make the stuff now. If you ever get a chance to try Yamazaki whisky, do it. In Japan they sell it at 7-Eleven.

She turned me into a newt! Rich trials have a witch history. Wait, what? Hey, there's an idea. Putting rich people on trial. All in favor say, "Burn the rich!"

In the late seventeenth century the practice of burning witches was fading in Europe, but those crazy 'Muricans weren't yet ready to let go of their killing of audacious women. I mean, we're talking about Puritans here. And since dudes were always having "sinful" thoughts about what was under all those many layers of women's clothing, then it must be the women who were the sinners, right? That's why 80 percent of witchcraft accusations were against women, specifically targeting those who didn't comply with ideas of gender norms.

Seventeen-year-old Elizabeth Hubbard was part of the Massachusetts Bay Colony, and she internalized misogyny like a fucking champion. She was the main instigator of the trials, faking "supernatural fits" and saying they were caused by witchcraft. During the year of witch trial hysteria, she would file forty legal complaints of witchcraft, and testify thirty-two times.

Anything could trigger an accusation, including just being plain old pissed off at someone. Neighbor's dog won't shut the fuck up? It's because Snoopy is telling you its owner is a witch. Burn her! Actually, in Salem they were hanged. But dead is dead.

Bridget Bishop was accused of using witchcraft against five young women, including the aforementioned Elizabeth Hubbard. The women testified Bishop's specter would appear and pinch, choke, or bite them. So obviously the witch had to die. Others jumped on the bandwagon with additional accusations, and they inspected her body and found a third nipple, which is totally a witch thing. Then, later, they couldn't find the additional nipple, which was even more proof of her guilt because she obviously used witchcraft as a form of seventeenth-century plastic surgery to remove it.

On June 2, 1692, Bridget Bishop was the first person condemned to death for practicing witchcraft during the Salem Witch Trials. She was hanged on June 10 that year.

All told, twenty women and men were executed for witchcraft during the trials, and five more died in prison.

Witch hunts may not happen in Massachusetts anymore, but they are not a thing of the past in the rest of the world by any stretch. Rather, they are far more prevalent now in regions such as India, South America, and Africa, with a much higher death toll than previous centuries.

> **Neighbor's dog won't shut the fuck up? It's because Snoopy is telling you its owner is a witch. Burn her! Actually, in Salem they were hanged. But dead is dead.**

It's good to be king. Perhaps it's better to be happily married.

After the way Henry VIII treated his wives, Edward VIII may have felt the need to redeem the English monarchs with eights after their names, at least regarding having a lasting marriage. He would do anything for love, even abdicate.

On January 20, 1936, at the age of forty-one, Edward ascended the throne upon the death of his father, King George V. And while his reign wouldn't last, his marriage would. Although there's debate regarding how happy that marriage was.

Edward served in the British Army during World War I and had a penchant for putting his royal penis in places his father did not approve of. He had an affair with a Parisian courtesan during the war, then with a married textile heiress. His womanizing ways would not change during the 1920s and '30s. He seemed to like the married women. I believe the British term for his behavior is "cad."

The king preferred Edward's younger brother Albert and Albert's daughter Elizabeth as heirs to the throne, saying, "I pray to God that my eldest son will never marry and have children, and that nothing will come between Bertie and Lilibet and the throne."

Unsurprisingly, Edward didn't like being king, and didn't take his role seriously. A few months into his reign he caused a constitutional crisis by proposing marriage to a soon-to-be-twice-divorced American woman, Wallis Simpson. Oh goodness gracious me no. A twice-divorced Yank as queen consort of England. Perish the thought!

June 3, 1937

The outcry was religiously motivated, because the Church of England didn't approve of remarrying after divorce if the former spouse still lived. The actual crisis was that the current democratically elected government, headed by Prime Minister Stanley Baldwin, stated it would resign if Edward married Wallis, forcing a general election and violating the rules of the monarchy being politically neutral.

But Eddie was all fuck you guys. Take this crown and shove it where the bangers and mash come out. He abdicated on December 10, reigning for less than a year. He was demoted to Duke of Windsor, and on June 3, 1937, after her second divorce was finalized, Wallis and Edward married.

In the early days of World War II, Edward and Wallis were stationed with the British Expeditionary Force in France. But Eddie and Wallis were a bit too cozy with those Nazis fellas, and when this became public, he was special-projected into irrelevance as governor of the Bahamas. After the war, the couple retired to France to be party people. They remained married until Edward's death in 1972, six days shy of their thirty-fifth wedding anniversary.

Having the name "Dick Best" is a lot to live up to; the man did have a set of aircraft-carrier-sized gonads. Speaking of, he was one of only two pilots in history to score direct hits on multiple aircraft carriers in a single day. The other pilot to hold that distinction was Norman Kleiss, in the same battle: Midway.

June 4, 1942

The Japanese were doomed the day they decided to attack the United States, and many in their military leadership knew it. The bombing of Pearl Harbor was a gamble. The idea was for the Japanese to deliver such a devastating blow to the U.S. Navy that the Americans would say, "Oh, wow. You guys are total badasses. We give up. Please do continue on with your imperial expansions. We shall bother you no further. Just don't hurt us anymore."

Yeah, right. All you had to do was look at American history to see these folks weren't afraid of a fight. Rather than terrify the United States into peace, it galvanized them for war. And from that moment on, Japan was fucked with a capital firetruck.

The Battle of Midway, on June 4, 1942, is seen as a major turning point in the Pacific theater of World War II. And there was a lot of luck involved in the American victory. That luck began with the fact that the U.S. Navy's aircraft carriers were out on training maneuvers during the attack on Pearl Harbor and therefore avoided destruction and were available to fight at Midway six months later.

It was more than luck, of course. Pearl Harbor had been an intelligence catastrophe for the United States, whereas Midway was an intelligence coup, allowing the Americans to lay a trap for the Japanese fleet and kick some serious buttocks. But there was luck in the American planes finding that enemy fleet in order to attack them in the first place, because the Pacific is a big fucking ocean. And when you consider that dive-bomber pilots Best, Kleiss, and others had to fly their planes through an unimaginable onslaught of anti-aircraft and enemy fighter fire to destroy four Japanese aircraft carriers that day, there was probably a bit of luck mixed in with the skill and bravery there too. About 150 U.S. aircraft and their crews were lost in the battle, roughly half the American air force that saw battle that day.

But luck or no, intelligence victory or not, the Japanese never stood a chance in the grander scheme of the war once America decided it was game on. The reasons being that the Americans had twice the population of Japan, oil coming out their asses, and a far greater manufacturing capability. Add to this that Japan had already been fighting for years as part of its imperialist expansion, which took a toll on their resources and manpower, whereas the United States was fresh and ready to rumble. The Japanese could have destroyed every ship in the U.S. Navy and the Americans would have built more, bounced back, and still fucked Japan's shit up.

Victories such as Midway were important in hastening Japan's defeat, but the reality is the war was lost for Japan the day they attacked Pearl Harbor.

There has been ample media coverage, including social media, of the Black Lives Matter movement. And there are many a brainless fuckpuddle who don't like that one bit. They proclaim that any white person who writes about the oppression of Black people in American society is "virtue signaling," an insulting way of silencing people by accusing them of being insincere and just jumping on an anti-racist bandwagon to "signal" to the world that they're a good person.

They also say that such writings accomplish the square root of fuck all; it doesn't affect real societal change. And yet, there is compelling evidence the fuckpuddles are wrong. Case in point: the publication of *Uncle Tom's Cabin* as a forty-week serial in the abolitionist publication *The National Era* beginning June 5, 1851.

It's the story of a white farmer's decision to sell two of those he enslaved to pay his debts. One enslaved person is a middle-aged man named Uncle Tom, who has a wife and children. The other is Harry, the only surviving child of the farmer's maid, Eliza. It is about families being ripped apart, humans sold like consumer goods because a farmer needs the money, and the heartache that ensues. Telling that story changed history.

Considering the glacial pace of evolution via natural selection, we Homo sapiens plowed our way to top of the food chain with lightning speed, and we were able to do that because we're fucking smart. We rule the planet. I mean, we've been total dicks about it and I'm not saying humanity is awesome, but there is no question our massive brainpower is what made us dominant. We used that brainpower to communicate and to organize, to share common beliefs and

values and goals. Might often makes "right," and ideas can generate a mighty following. Such was the case with Harriet Beecher Stowe's writings.

June 5, 1851

The series was so popular the *Era* got complaints if the next installment didn't appear in the latest issue. It was published as a novel in 1852 and sold 300,000 copies its first year in the U.S., and 200,000 in the U.K. Selling that many copies of a book in 1852 qualifies as "a metric shit-ton."

Stowe, a white woman, had a Christian savior complex and failed to present Black people as humans worthy of the same rights as their white counterparts, but she did get an important message across: Chattel slavery is wrong.

Of course the pro-slavery shitnuggets blew their poop so hard their outhouses overflowed. They called the book fake news. The next year Stowe was all "References, motherfuckers!" with the publication of *A Key to Uncle Tom's Cabin,* a nonfiction book citing numerous real-life equivalents to people in the novel. It too became a bestseller.

The stories *reached people.* It made them rethink the plots of their own lives and the society they were a part of, supplying rocket fuel to the abolitionist movement. The readings were so influential that in 1862, a year into the American Civil War, President Abraham Lincoln met with Stowe and is believed to have said, "So this is the little lady who started this great war."

Keep telling those stories, and be ready to reference a motherfucker.

Sometimes, punching Nazis isn't enough. You need to bomb, shoot, and stab those motherfuckers. Kick their asses so hard their vertebrae pop out of their mouths like a goddamn PEZ dispenser. (I stole that line from Reddit.) They are not very fine people. They never were. So let's celebrate the anniversary of the biggest amphibious invasion in history when nations banded together to fuck some Nazi shit up.

June 6, 1944

To give you an idea of how determined the Allies were to defeat the fucking Nazis on the Western Front, on June 6, 1944—also known as D-Day—there were 287,000 personnel aboard ships crossing the English Channel. This doesn't include the 24,000 airborne troops who parachuted into France in the early morning hours.

Storming the five beaches that day were 73,000 British soldiers, 59,000 Americans, and 21,000 Canadians. The troops faced 40,000 Germans in bunkers in elevated positions. As we know, the Allies won the day and began the inexorable push into West Germany. But victory came at a terrible cost. The cost in lives could have been far higher, however, or the Allied landings a devastating failure, if not for one critical component of the campaign that made it successful: disinformation.

U.S. soldiers approaching Omaha Beach on D-Day

Storming the five beaches that day were 73,000 British soldiers, 59,000 Americans, and 21,000 Canadians. The troops faced 40,000 Germans in bunkers in elevated positions.

In *The Art of War* Sun Tzu wrote, "All warfare is based on deception . . . when we are near, we must make the enemy believe we are far away; when far away, we must make him believe we are near." The Allies took that advice.

The Allies had their shit wired tight when it came to the secrecy of the D-Day landing location. The British Isles were locked down, and German spies had no success in penetrating the counterintelligence veil of secrecy. Rather, spies were caught and told to be double agents or face execution.

There was fake radio traffic, controlled leaks, and even an entire fake army with inflatable tanks and fake paratrooper landings to make the Germans believe the attack was coming at Calais, France, which made sense due to it being by far the closest point to England. When Normandy was attacked, the deception continued to make the Germans believe the invasion was a feint to draw German troops away from Calais, where the "real attack" was imminent. But Normandy, 150 miles to the south of Calais, was the planned attack all along. The Allies were far away from Calais, and made the Germans think they were near.

By the time the Germans realized their folly—the military one, I mean, not the decision to be fucking Nazis in the first place—it was too late. Hitler was so well and truly fooled by the deception that it was *seven weeks* before he authorized releasing reinforcements from Calais to head to Normandy. But by then a solid beachhead was established by the Allies, and the fascists' days were numbered.

In 2016, President Barack Obama said, "Every great religion promises a pathway to love and peace and righteousness, and yet no religion has been spared from believers who have claimed their faith as a license to kill." Christians, you listening? Your faith is no exception.

June 7, 1099

Jerusalem is one of the oldest cities in the world, and its ancient stones are soaked with rivers of blood. The place holds special significance for the three major Abrahamic religions: Judaism, Christianity, and Islam. Over millennia, Jerusalem has been attacked more than fifty times, captured and recaptured forty-four times, under siege almost two dozen times, and twice destroyed. It was on June 7, 1099, that one of the most historically significant sieges of Jerusalem began.

In 1095, Pope Urban II basically said to the faithful Christians, "I want the Holy Land back. Get it for me and all your sins are washed away. Killing infidels is fine, by the way." And kill they did.

The siege lasted thirty-eight days and represented the climax of the First Crusade. It had all the trappings of what you might see in a movie about medieval warfare: siege towers, battering rams, and mangonels (a form of trebuchet—a rock-throwing thingy).

On July 15 the crusaders entered the city and started killing in earnest. And by that, I mean everyone. Muslims and Jews, who had fought side-by-side to defend the city, were massacred; approximately 40,000 people were killed. The atrocities committed were considered excessive even by medieval standards, like there was a perverse need to cleanse the city with blood spilled in the most egregious ways imaginable.

That's history for you. Brutality often pays off, at least for a while, and it's usually the meanest motherfuckers who get to rule. The Christian crusaders held Jerusalem for almost a century, but were expelled in 1187 by Saladin, the Sultan of Egypt and Syria. Saladin had already captured most of the other crusader cities, and he didn't want to wreck Jerusalem's shit via an extended and bloody siege, so he offered terms. Most of the Christian inhabitants were able to buy their freedom to escape the city, although several thousand were enslaved by the conquering Muslims.

Of course, the Christians were pissed at having lost Jerusalem, so another crusade immediately followed, led by King Richard the Lionheart. As did several other crusades after that one failed, all with decreasing degrees of success, because humans kinda suck at learning from history.

> Of course, the Christians were pissed at having lost Jerusalem, so another crusade immediately followed, led by King Richard the Lionheart.

When it comes to folks from long ago who became famous due to their deeds, like say starting a global religion that would one day have billions of followers, we rarely know their birthdays. That's because back then, when you were born a nobody, the day Mom squeezed your big head out of her small orifice wasn't worth marking on a calendar. That goes for you too, Jesus.

Muhammad, the prophet of Islam, was born a nobody. That is why we can only approximate that he arrived slimy and squalling—just like everyone else does—around the year 570 in Mecca.

Today, Christianity has 2.4 billion followers, and Islam 1.9 billion. Both achieved that because devotees actively sought converts; they wanted to spread the word. This was done via myriad methods, including dispatching missionaries *and* by the sword. If you're unaware, "by the sword" means telling a conquered people "You're gonna pray to our god now or [looks toward sharp implement of death with an unsubtle gesture]." Such a strategy was common for Christianity and Islam alike.

And that's not entirely bad. Hear me out.

I mean, it sucks for the people getting conquered, but from a long-term historical perspective, for all the fuckery committed, religion has been a binding force for humanity through the creation of shared mythology. It has the power to turn several small warring tribes into a cohesive nation capable of great things. Then those nations can fight other nations, but I'm getting away from the point.

The point is Muhammad unified a divided people. He began to have visions around the age of forty and proclaimed there was a single god that people must submit to. The polytheists were not fans, but Muhammad won converts. And as his following grew, so too did the threat he represented to the status quo. Eventually there was war, because my god is better than your gods, and vice versa.

June 8, 632

Muhammad died on June 8, 632, at the age of approximately sixty-two. The leadership succession did not go smoothly. Some favored Ali, Muhammad's cousin/son-in-law. Others preferred Muhammad's friend Abu, who ended up being confirmed as caliph—the chief Muslim religious and civil leader. But Ali's supporters didn't just accept that. Abu's much larger following would eventually be called Sunni Muslims, and Ali's followers Shia Muslims. War eventually followed, creating the Sunni-Shia split in the religion that has never been mended.

Today, Shia make up 10 to 15 percent of world Muslims, with most living in Iran. There have been extended times of peace between the two groups, but just like with Protestants vs. Catholics, there have been bloody conflicts. Most recently, Sunni-dominated Iraq warred with Shia Iran for most of the 1980s, resulting in approximately one million deaths.

You know how in the age of Trump, people on the right pointed fingers and shrieked "Antifa!," proclaiming it a terrorist group responsible for all types of fuckery, despite a dearth of evidence? That shit happened before. In the 1950s, "McCarthyism" was all about government repression by means of baseless accusations of communism.

June 9, 1954

Republican senator Joseph McCarthy was, among many things, a piece of shit. To his credit, he could have gotten a waiver for World War II because he was a judge, but he volunteered for the Pacific theater. He was an intelligence REMF (rear-echelon motherfucker) for a dive-bomber squadron but *did* volunteer for a dozen gunner/observer combat missions, followed by doing the uncool thing of giving himself the nickname "Tail-Gunner Joe." You're never supposed to give yourself a nickname. That's not how it works. Anyway, he later lied and said he flew thirty-two missions so he could qualify for a Distinguished Flying Cross, adding stolen valor to his list of douchebaggery.

After the war he was elected senator of Wisconsin and became an even bigger cocknocker by spreading fear of communism into every corner of American life.

It was a tense time. The Soviets tested their first nuke in 1949, and in 1950 Korea became a staging ground for war with Communist China. Then a senior official in the State Department was convicted in an espionage case, and McCarthy milked that for career advancement by saying he had a list of commies working in the State Department. Suddenly, he was thrust into the national spotlight as the Communism Inquisitor Numero Uno, saying they'd infiltrated the government, armed forces, universities, and film industry.

His unsubstantiated smears and accusations of treason became ever more ridiculous, and McCarthyism reached a tipping point on June 9, 1954. Joseph Welch, who was chief legal counsel for the U.S. Army while it was under investigation for alleged communist activities, clapped back against McCarthy's laughable accusations against one of his colleagues, calling McCarthy cruel and reckless. Then Welch directed these fateful words to McCarthy in front of a national TV audience.

"Have you no sense of decency, sir? At long last, have you left no sense of decency?"

McCarthy tried to continue his attack, but Welch shut him down and basically said, "We're fucking done here" and the crowd broke into applause. And that brief exchange transformed history right there. It was a sudden shift where people rapidly began to come to their senses, and McCarthy's witch hunt lost steam. Joe McCarthy died three years later at age forty-eight.

n 2017 comedian Eli Yudin wrote on Twitter, "Being an old-timey doctor would rule, just drunk as hell like 'yeah u got ghosts in your blood, you should do cocaine about it.'" When it comes to the man who co-founded Alcoholics Anonymous on June 10, 1935, there are similarities, specifically regarding the "drunk as hell" doctor part. The organization has an interesting beginning.

The previous year, Bill Wilson, who was not a doctor, was drunk as fuck. All the time. He tried to quit, to no avail. He staggered into Towns Hospital for substance abuse in New York City where they sedated him with chloral hydrate and paraldehyde to calm his agitation from detoxing, allowing him to sleep. He was regularly wakened to be administered a cocktail that included tincture of belladonna, a potentially toxic plant that can cause hallucinations.

On the second or third day of detox, Wilson's former drinking buddy, Ebby Thacher, visited him. Thacher had gotten clean by embracing Christianity and implored Wilson to turn to Jesus. The hallucinations belladonna triggers tend to be based on recent discussions, made fantastical. Wilson called out, "If there be a God, let him show himself!" He saw a blinding light, felt peace, and never drank again.

Enter Bob Smith, the drunk-as-hell doctor.

Like many people, Bob began drinking in college, and he was one of those assholes who didn't get hangovers. So he was drunk all the time and still managed to graduate. He then drank his way through med school and barely finished. Afterward, he became an ass surgeon—the kind that solves problems with the poop chute, not the Kardashian implant sort—and continued to drink his fucking face off.

June 10, 1935

He knew he had a problem, and tried to quit numerous times, even checking himself into hospitals. None of it worked.

But then in 1935 he met Bill Wilson, who kept his own sobriety up through helping others quit. Wilson was determined to help Smith. The first try didn't take, but the second began on June 9, when Wilson gave Smith a few drinks to avoid delirium tremens, which is when severe ethanol withdrawal causes you to see snakes and spiders and shit. The next morning Smith drank a single beer to calm his nerves so he could perform an operation. It would be the last drink he ever took and is celebrated as the beginning of AA.

Since then, the organization has helped many get sober. It has also been frequently criticized as unscientific, cult-like, and having a low rate of success.

In the early '60s most Americans couldn't find Vietnam on a map; many still can't, despite eight years of massive military intervention. But in 1963 the injustices taking place in the country where an American-puppet dictator ruled would become well known internationally, due to the self-sacrifice of one man.

June 11, 1963

On June 11, 1963, Thích Quảng Đức, a Buddhist monk, entered a busy intersection in downtown Saigon to engage in an act of protest that would hit the front page of newspapers around the world. A significant majority of the South Vietnamese population was Buddhist. South Vietnam president and U.S. lackey Ngô Đình Diệm, however, was part of the Catholic minority, and his government enacted numerous discriminatory policies against the Buddhist population.

Đức sat down on a cushion, assuming a meditative lotus position. Another monk poured a five-gallon can of gasoline over him. Đức rotated wooden prayer beads through his fingers and chanted; he struck a match.

Đức was engulfed in flames, but did not cry out, did not move.

Think of how much it hurts when you get the slightest burn. How long can you hold your hand to a flame? What would it take for you to not react to the pain? Thích Quảng Đức showed no sign of suffering as he burned alive.

Monks, nuns, passersby, even police, prostrated themselves before the burning monk. Cameras snapped photos. President John F. Kennedy said of one photo taken by American journalist Malcolm Browne, "No news picture in history has generated so much emotion around the world."

That photo later won a Pulitzer Prize. It also served to get Americans to question the support of Diệm's government. Via radio, President Diệm made noises of concern over the event and promised to renew the stalled negotiations with Buddhists, but as historian Seth Jacobs said, "No amount of pleading could retrieve Diệm's reputation." Jacobs also said of Đức's self-immolation that it "reduced America's Diệm experiment to ashes as well." The crisis deepened and on November 1, 1963, with assistance from the CIA, President Diệm was overthrown and assassinated.

Later, Communist China used the image for propaganda purposes, printing millions of copies and distributing them as an example of American imperialism.

Some guy on Twitter said racism doesn't exist anymore in America, and anyone who says otherwise is just a race-baiting social justice wanker. But to give you an idea as to just how fresh the egregious laws are that helped create institutionalized racism, interracial marriage didn't become legal in the United States until 1967. Nineteen-sixty-fucking-seven.

They were called "anti-miscegenation" laws and were enforced throughout numerous states, not just the southern ones. You couldn't marry or even have sex with someone of another race. It was all about keeping the white race "pure" and was mostly designed to prevent whites from having relationships with Black people, but also with other races. If two non-whites from different races decided to get it on, like an Asian and a Native American, no one gave much of a shit. Although the laws were often used as an extra level of punishment for Black people. In numerous states they were permitted to marry/have sex *only* within their own race.

Mildred Loving was a woman of color living in Virginia. Her exact ancestry is uncertain, but from a legal perspective what mattered was that she wasn't white and had the audacity to marry a white man, Richard Loving, and—gasp!—have children with him.

In 1958, Mildred was eighteen and pregnant with Richard's child, so they got married in neighboring Washington, D.C., where it was legal, and returned home. The marriage violated Virginia's "Racial Integrity Act," and some anonymous racist crudpuddle ratted them out to the 5-0. Being such hardened criminals, their house of evil was of course raided by police. Being sick bastards, the po-po wanted to catch them in the act of having sex, since interracial intercourse was also illegal in Virginia. But, like most married couples, they spent 99 percent of their mattress time asleep. Startled awake, Mildred pointed to the marriage certificate on the wall, and the cops were like, "Nope. Doesn't count. You're under arrest."

June 12, 1967

It was illegal for them to marry out of state and return to Virginia. They were convicted and sentenced to a year in prison each, which they avoided by agreeing to leave the state and not return for twenty-five years. They moved to D.C., but six years later were all "Fuck this. We want to visit our families." So, Mildred and Richard, with the help of the ACLU, took their case to the state supreme court and lost, then appealed to the Supreme Court of the United States.

> **On June 12, 1967, the Supreme Court ruled unanimously in favor of the Lovings, striking down all anti-miscegenation laws throughout the United States.**

On June 12, 1967, the Supreme Court ruled unanimously in favor of the Lovings, striking down all anti-miscegenation laws throughout the United States as a violation of the Equal Protection Clause under the Fourteenth Amendment.

Nineteen-sixty-fucking-seven.

n the 1983 film *Scarface* a drug dealer asks his henchman Omar what he thinks of this up-and-comer gangster Tony Montana and Omar replies, "I think he's a fucking peasant." For all of history, elites have looked down upon lower classes, seeing them as little more than a source of labor and tax revenue. But sometimes the peasantry gets tired of being seen as filthy and revolting and actually revolts, which happened in England in 1381 and led to a flowing of blue blood.

Fourteenth-century Europe was a fucked-up place, what with the Black Death wiping out almost one-third of the population. In the aftermath, there was a lot of socio-political upheaval, because that's what happens when all of a sudden there isn't a glut of labor to exploit and the peasants can start saying shit to the ruling classes like "You need us more than we need you." Now there was more land than peasants to work it, and wages went up while profits for the land-owners went down. You know, supply-and-demand kinda shit.

There was also this Hundred Years' War thing going on, and wars cost money and that means extra taxes and the peasants were all fuck your taxes. As the peasants grew not only in financial power but also in freedom to do things other than dig in the dirt all day, the elites became more fractious and divided.

There was a moral panic about these cheeky lower classes seeking to rise above the station God meant them to be in [sarcasm font], and there were years of turmoil preceding the 1381 Peasants' Revolt that began in late May in Essex when some royal fuck-truffle said hey where's our fucking taxes? Rather than say oh sorry here are your taxes, milord, shit got mean, and the violence spread o'er the land with grand rapidity. Before long, teenage king Richard Number Two was hiding in the Tower of London going number two in his pants because he rightfully believed they wanted to waste his ass and his troops were off fighting that hundred-year thing in France.

Shit got real on June 13, 1381, when the revolting peasants destroyed the Savoy Palace and went on a royal killing spree across London. The next day the hoards entered the Tower of London and killed the Lord Chancellor and the Lord High Treasurer, while at the same time King Richard was meeting with the rebels and saying okay I'll go along with these demands of yours. But it was all about buying time to get his forces mustered to crush the rebellion, which was complete by the following November, and Richard said fuck your demands and reneged.

In the aftermath the crown did decide to pull back from its war with France and didn't pursue the additional taxes or engage in reprisals against the peasantry, out of fear of another rebellion.

Today is a dark day in history. Barely a year after the fascists were defeated in World War II in Europe, a future "leader" was defeated into existence in the United States. A hateful, racist, incompetent, orange-tainted blithering blowhard son of a KKK member anal fissure of a fascist. A smegma stain on the Stars and Stripes. And since it would drive him bugshit, let's make this entry about the myriad accomplishments of the man Trump hates more than anyone else: President Barack Obama.

Barack Obama was the first U.S. president not born in North America. And no, it wasn't Kenya. That's a racist rumor spread by that callous cockwomble with an insectoid IQ. President Obama was born in Hawai'i, which IS part of the United States, just not North America, so fucking get over it.

In fact, celebrate. These are President Obama's words: "The opportunity that Hawai'i offered—to experience a variety of cultures in a climate of mutual respect—became an integral part of my world view, and a basis for the values that I hold most dear."

He didn't have daddy bucks or influence to get him into fancy schools; he went to a top-tier private school with the help of a scholarship, also taking a job at Baskin-Robbins. He succeeded via his intelligence and drive while simultaneously facing down centuries of systemic racism that threw roadblocks in front of him at every turn for no other reason than his skin contained more melanin than the ruling class's does.

A mere fifteen years after the assassination of Dr. Martin Luther King Jr., Barack Obama graduated from Columbia University with a degree in political science, specializing in international relations. In 1988 he began studying law at Harvard and was the first Black person to head the *Harvard Law Review.* Afterward, he worked as a civil rights attorney while teaching constitutional law at the University of Chicago for a dozen years. He served three terms in the Illinois state senate, then won his U.S. Senate seat in a landslide in 2004. In 2008, he became the first Black person to win the presidency, clearing the electoral college vote at 375 to 173 and nabbing the popular vote at 52.9 to 45.7 percent.

June 14, 1946

In 2009, he won the Nobel Peace Prize. Oh, and he knows words. President Obama is the actual author of four books, three of which hit #1 on *The New York Times* bestseller list. He served two terms as president, and while there are criticisms to be levied, most who aren't irradiated Oompa Loompa cultists would agree Obama did a decent job most of the time, especially when you consider that the GOP basically declared war against his administration. Alas, his successor had the personality of a toilet bowl owned by someone prepping for a colonoscopy. Rather than accept the results of the 2020 election, the corrupt motherfucker attempted a violent coup. Then in 2023, this man with an ability to transform any clitoris into a clitorisn't became the first American president to be indicted on criminal charges.

June 14, 1946, was a dark day in history indeed.

Worst. King. *Ever!*

That's the way many felt about King John of England in the thirteenth century. He'd lost his lands in France and wanted them back, which meant taxes. People don't like taxes, but fuck those people. I'm the king! He taxed his barons up the ass and if they didn't pay, he would punish them and seize their lands. Despite all the taxes to pay for his wars, he didn't get those lands in France back. D'oh!

June 15, 1215

He was known for being petty, spiteful, and cruel. When he returned from France in failure, he faced a rebellion among his barons because they'd had enough of his shit. King John basically said fuck you and the barons said no, fuck *you,* and they attacked and surrounded London and John said fine let's do this peace treaty thing.

That's what Magna Carta, signed on June 15, 1215, was: a peace treaty. The full name is *Magna Carta Libertatum,* which means "Great Charter of Freedoms." It had sixty-three clauses, most of which were to address how John was a total dick and that he needed to stop doing dickish, autocratic things. One of the most famous was the 39th clause, which gave "free men" the right to justice and a fair trial.

FYI, that "free men" stuff is kind of like the "all men are created equal" part of the Declaration of Independence. Just like how the 1776 document was written by dudes who enslaved hundreds of people and had a pretty narrow idea of what "men" meant, Magna Carta's "free men" didn't include the majority of the population, who were unfree peasants. It was an important historical document focused on improving the lives of already rich and powerful people.

Anyway, neither side abided by the accord, and the First Barons' War broke out within a few months. A year later King John assploded himself to death from dysentery.

But the treaty did end up having a lasting legacy, providing a framework for relations between king and subjects. It put forth the idea that everyone, including the king, was subject to the law. It was resurrected and revised a number of times—the majority of its clauses have been repealed—but many consider Magna Carta to be the foundation of English democracy.

Its most iconic and lasting legacy is asserting that when a leader is an evil and corrupt motherfucker, the people don't have to stand for that shit.

People don't like taxes, but fuck those people. I'm the king! He taxed his barons up the ass and if they didn't pay, he would punish them and seize their lands.

He wasn't executed. He was murdered. It was state-sanctioned murder.

In March of 1944, in the small town of Alcolu, South Carolina, two young white girls were found brutally murdered. Their names were Betty June Binnicker, age eleven, and Mary Emma Thames, age seven. Alcolu was a working-class mill town, with racial segregation marked by a set of railroad tracks. There was little interaction between Black and white.

The girls had been riding their bicycles, seeking flowers to pick. As they passed by the Stinney house, they asked fourteen-year-old George and his little sister Aimé where they could find maypops. The girls were later found dead in a ditch from blunt-force trauma to their heads. Aimé said George was with her at the time of the murders, but police were looking for someone to pin them on.

The police showed up to the Stinney house while the parents weren't home. Sister Aimé hid in the chicken coop as both George and his older brother Johnnie were hauled away in handcuffs.

Johnnie was later released, but George was questioned alone in a small room, without his parents or an attorney. Police claimed he confessed to the murders, but no evidence of a confession exists. He was kept prisoner for weeks without being permitted to see his parents. On April 24 there was a two-hour trial. George's court-appointed attorney had political ambitions and did not question the police, who proclaimed that George had confessed. Neither did he call George's sister as an alibi. After ten minutes of deliberation by an all-white jury, George Stinney was found guilty. George's piece-of-shit attorney didn't even bother to appeal.

June 16, 1944

On June 16, 1944, George Stinney was murdered by the state of South Carolina. The weapon used was the electric chair. He was only five feet tall and under a hundred pounds; the straps on the chair were too large for his small body, and prison officials used the Bible he was carrying as a booster seat. During electrocution, his bodily convulsions caused the mask to fall from his face, revealing a burned scalp and tears streaming from his eyes. Two additional jolts and eight minutes later, his teeth smoking, and one eye boiled away, he was finally pronounced dead. He wasn't just murdered; he was tortured to death.

Seventy years later a circuit court judge proclaimed that George Stinney had not received a fair trial and vacated his conviction.

George Stinney's mug shot

Ever since Nixon's resignation, people love to add "gate" to some form of wrongdoing, legitimate or not, to make it *more* scandalous. The only time it's been funny was in the comic strip *Calvin & Hobbes,* when Calvin informed his father of his dropping in the polls, citing "Bedtime-gate" and "Homeworkgate" as scandals plaguing Dad's administration.

June 17, 1972

Watergate was a real thing, a real place, a real scandal, and it led to the downfall of a corrupt president during a time when that was still possible because the GOP had something of a conscience.

Watergate is an office complex in Washington, D.C. In the early morning hours of June 17, 1972, five men broke into the Democratic National Convention offices in that building in an attempt to place listening devices so they could gather intelligence to help in President Nixon's reelection campaign.

But due to an observant security guard named Frank Wills, who found tape on door latches to prevent them from locking, the men were caught by police. Later that summer the five—along with break-in organizers G. Gordy Liddy, who was finance counsel for the Committee for the Reelection of the President (meaning Nixon), and former CIA officer Howard Hunt—were indicted on charges of conspiracy, burglary, and violation of federal wiretapping laws. They all were

eventually convicted (one pleaded guilty) and given a variety of sentences, with no one serving more than five years.

Almost immediately after the break-in and arrests, the cover-up began to try to save Nixon's ass. One of the crazier things that happened as part of the cover-up was that Martha Mitchell, wife of attorney general and CRP head John Mitchell, was "basically kidnapped" on orders of her husband and held incommunicado in a hotel room when the burglary story first broke, to prevent her from blowing the whistle about the White House connection to the break-in. Martha knew that one of those arrested, James W. McCord Jr., worked for her husband at the CRP, and could therefore tie John Mitchell to the crime.

Nixon did win reelection that year, in a landslide. It would take two years of investigations and additional cover-ups about Watergate that would destroy Nixon's support and lead to three articles of impeachment being approved against him, but he resigned before actual impeachment, on August 9, 1974.

Perhaps you're thinking: *That's it? So fucking what? That wouldn't even rate compared to Trump's scandals.* It probably wouldn't have made front-page news, let alone spawn a movie with the hottest movie stars of the day. Don't get me wrong. Nixon was a piece of shit. But comparatively speaking, the Trump bar was so low it must have had some bizarrely powerful magnetic attraction to Earth's molten core.

ABBA wrote a song proclaiming that Napoleon surrendered at Waterloo, but that's not true. He *lost* that battle, fled, and surrendered to a British Navy captain a month later.

The French Revolution began in 1789, and for ten years Napoleon was a skilled military leader who rose through the ranks, eventually seizing control of the government in a 1799 coup d'état. He declared himself emperor of France and looked beyond its borders to do some conquering. And he had the army to do it, because in 1793 the basis for a mega force was laid via *levée en masse,* which loosely translates to "You can hold a gun? You're in the army now." Conscription has long been an effective tool of those who wish to play war from a safe distance.

But Napoleon liked to be part of the fray. He waged war all over Europe for several years, then did a dumbass thing, invading Russia in winter in 1812. The fact that only 100,000 of his 600,000-strong invading forces made it out alive kind of soured the French people on him, so he was forced to abdicate two years later and exiled to the island of Elba.

Less than a year later, in early 1815, he was all like, "I'm back, motherfuckers!"

Napoleon escaped Elba and was welcomed back to France by cheering crowds. There's no record to tell us if the crowds had red hats proclaiming to "Make France Great Again." Then he began his "Hundred Days campaign," because other European nations were not thrilled to see Bonaparte back in power, and they were determined to do something about it. But Napoleon was not one to wait around to be attacked and decided to go on the offensive against this new coalition that was determined to fuck his shit up.

June 18, 1815

And fuck Napoleon up they did, on June 18, 1815, at the Battle of Waterloo in Belgium. "They," in this case, were mostly the British and Prussians (a German state). Bonaparte had kicked some Prussian ass at Ligny two days previous but hadn't destroyed their army. That turned out to be a mistake.

This is how Napoleon lost: Napoleon faced off his 72,000 French soldiers against a British-led coalition 68,000 strong, led by the Duke of Wellington, whom the beef is named after. Bonaparte was a talented tactician yet made a terrible blunder. The ground was wet, and he was like "Fuck it. We'll chill and wait for it to dry before we get to the killing." That gave the 30,000 Prussians who fled Ligny time to join the fracas—cool word, "fracas"—and turn the tide.

It was a rout. That's another cool word that means "flee in chaos." Napoleon's forces suffered approximately 42,000 casualties, almost 60 percent of his army.

Wellington went on to become British prime minister, and Napoleon was exiled to a new island and died a few years later, most likely from cancer.

A law is only as good as one's ability to enforce it. And when President Lincoln said okay enough of this slavery bullshit with an executive order known as the Emancipation Proclamation on September 22, 1862, it wasn't like the waving of a magic wand. Hell, the proclamation itself didn't go into effect until January 1, 1863, and the Southern slavers were nah fuck you make us free our enslaved people and that's exactly what the Union Army did. For another two and a half years.

June 19, 1865

"Juneteenth" is a portmanteau of June nineteenth. It is also referred to as "Freedom Day" and "Jubilee Day" because it marks an important turning point in the history of slavery. Texas, big surprise, was part of the Racist as Fuck Confederate States of America. But it was way south and didn't see a lot

Juneteenth celebration in 1900

of the fighting. As a result, it took a while after the Civil War ended for Union troops to move in.

Traitorous General Lee called the war quits on April 9, 1865. But there was no #LeeSurrenders or #LoserConfederacy hashtags to trend on Twitter. It took a while for some people to get the memo.

But finally, on June 19, 1865, more than two months after the racist traitors adopted solid white as their official flag with the yeah-okay-we-lost-we-give-up surrender at Appomattox, the Emancipation Proclamation was read in Texas. It was the last Confederate state to have the proclamation announced, and the document was read by Union general Gordan Granger in the city of Galveston, stating, "The people of Texas are informed that, in accordance with a proclamation from the Executive of the United States, all slaves are free. This involves an absolute equality of personal rights and rights of property between former masters and slaves . . ." That "absolute equality" stuff is definitely still a work in progress, but the Texas announcement became the basis for a holiday that was celebrated the following year and has seen a significant renewal of attention in recent decades.

The actual proclamation had taken place more than two years before, but Southern slavers weren't exactly willing to spread the word while the war was still on. The Thirteenth Amendment, abolishing slavery, was passed by the House on January 31, 1865, a few months before the war ended, and fully ratified and adopted six months after the first Juneteenth.

I **hate that fish.**

That fucking *Jaws* movie. I grew up in a small town with one movie screen. When I was seven, my parents dumped my sister and me off at the theater so they could have some 1970s-style adult fun time, or something. Assholes. That movie fucking traumatized me. Decades later I can't go snorkeling without hearing the music.

Duunnn dunnn . . . duuuunnnn duun . . . duuunnnnnnnn dun dun dun dun dun dun dun dun dun dun. On June 20, 1975, people were suddenly afraid to get in the water, me included. *Jaws* made Steven Spielberg a household name and, because it became the biggest-grossing movie to date, it also launched the concept of the "summer blockbuster."

The bestselling Peter Benchley book it was based on, published the previous year, had some fucked-up shit in it that the screenwriter wisely cut. Like, the whole mafia plotline, someone murdering a cat, and the fact that Roy Scheider's wife was having an affair with Richard Dreyfuss, and while Dreyfuss was being eaten by the shark Scheider shot him in the neck as an additional fuck-you for fucking his wife. Well, he *was* aiming for the shark. Supposedly.

Jaws was influenced by *Moby-Dick,* and the Quint character, a survivor of the sinking of the USS *Indianapolis* (google that—it's relevant), is totally like Captain Ahab on a mission to rid the world of those evil man-eaters. Quint even named his boat *Orca,* which is the only predator the great white has. Other than humans, I mean.

June 20, 1975

I wasn't the only one freaked out by the film. Beach attendance went down the summer it was released, and shark sightings went up. The movie did a terrible injustice to sharks as a species, perpetuating a stereotype of them as remorseless eating machines thirsting for the blood of middle-class white people.

> That movie fucking traumatized me. Decades later I can't go snorkeling without hearing the music.

Benchley, for his part, regretted the portrayal and its aftermath, which came to be called the "*Jaws* Effect," where fishermen went about killing sharks like it was a national pastime, believing they were doing some kind of community service. The author, after learning sharks were *not* hunting humans for sport, dedicated himself to rehabilitating the damage he'd done to their reputation.

Since then, many shark species have been added to the endangered list.

In the mid-twentieth century it came as a big surprise to many that smoking caused lung cancer. I mean, it's fucking *smoke*. Inhaled into the *lungs*. It's basically one step down from breathing in *fire*.

June 21, 1954

I guess when you have ads proclaiming "More doctors smoke Camels than any other cigarette," it helps those coughing up black shit every morning live in blissful denial for a while. But smokers don't live as long as nonsmokers do, which is what a turning-point study revealed in 1954.

Prior to 1900, lung cancer was uncommon, but then fancy new manufacturing technology coupled with runaway capitalism started cranking out the cancer sticks by the billions. The military gave smokes to soldiers for free in both World Wars, eventually killing more men with friendly cigarette fire than died in battle. In 1900, the average cigarette consumption per capita in the United States was 54 per year, just over one a week. In 1963 that number had climbed to 4,345 cigarettes per year. That's 84 per week, a dozen a day. Per person.

Beginning in 1952, two scientists working for the American Cancer Society, E. Cuyler Hammond, and Daniel Horn, did a cohort study of 188,000 men to analyze smoking habits, health, and mortality. They found a "considerably higher death rate" among smokers, mostly due to heart disease and cancer, with a specific spike in lung cancer. Duh.

Fun fact: they were both heavy smokers, and the study prompted them to switch to smoking pipes, because they imagined that might be better. Oops.

The study, which was presented on June 21, 1954, at an American Medical Association conference, launched a new wave of research that led to political pressure to do something about the health crisis smoking presented. A decade later there was a damnation of smoking's deleterious health effects in a Surgeon General's Report, which led to sweeping changes enacted in American tobacco policy. Since that time, rates of smoking in the United States have dropped to less than half of 1960s levels.

Oh, and big surprise, lung cancer rates have fallen as well.

The military gave smokes to soldiers for free in both World Wars, eventually killing more men with friendly cigarette fire than died in battle.

Italian astronomer Galileo Galilei had an inquisitive mind, and the Roman Catholic Church held an Inquisition into such inquisitiveness because Galileo's facts didn't care about the Church's feelings.

It began in 1610 when Galileo published a brief astronomical treatise titled *Starry Messenger* describing surprising observations made with a new telescope he'd constructed. In it he explained how the surface of the moon was ragged and not smooth, that the Milky Way was a collection of stars, and that Earth was not the only planet with a moon. There is a reason why four of Jupiter's moons—Europa, Callisto, Ganymede, and Io—are referred to as "Galilean satellites"; he discovered them, and they were the first moons humans observed that were orbiting a planet other than our own. A few years after publication, having made observations of the phases of Venus, Galileo began promoting a heliocentric model that Polish astronomer Nicolaus Copernicus had formulated the previous century.

"Heliocentric" refers to the sun being the center of the solar system, with the planets revolving around it. And it's true. That's the way it works. Really. Not the geocentric model, which is the idea that everything revolves around Earth. I'm spoon-feeding this because a 2012 survey found that 26 percent of Americans believe in the geocentric model, which calls for a hair-pulling *"What the fucking fuck?"* I mean, Catholic Church four centuries ago I understand, but Jesus Chocolate Christ on rubber crutches get your head out of Uranus. The Earth revolves around the sun, not the other way around.

Where was I?

So Galileo was spreading heretical ideas and such thinking was banned by the religious thought police and blah blah shut the fuck up Galileo or we'll Inquisition you and you won't like that. But he did not shut up, and twenty-three years of religious fuckery against science followed. In 1632, Galileo published *Dialogue Concerning the Two Chief World Systems,* once again promoting heliocentrism. It received great acclaim, but the Church was ever so pissed.

The book was banned by Pope Who Cares There Were a Lot of Them, and Galileo was put on trial for heresy. And although Galileo did have allies within the Catholic Church, the majority believed feelings > facts. The brilliant science guy was found guilty of "a strong suspicion of heresy" on June 22, 1633.

Galileo was sentenced to imprisonment, but it was commuted to house arrest, where he spent the remainder of his life, which was another nine years, although he did publish another book in 1638 covering much of his life's work in physics.

The Church finally dropped the ban against books promoting heliocentrism more than a century later, in 1758.

When the movie *Braveheart* came out in 1995, you couldn't grab your phone and look something up. I was watching it on VHS with my new bride and became curious about where things were going. I paused the tape, grabbed my *Dictionary of Wars* by George Kohn off the shelf, and flipped to the stuff about William Wallace. "Uh, sweetie," I said. "You need to prepare yourself for an unhappy ending to this movie."

June 23, 1314

The final scene—not Mel Gibson's guts getting ripped out, but rather the Battle of Bannockburn—began on June 23, 1314. If you were wondering what *Braveheart II: The Bravening* would reveal, here you go.

It was the First War of Scottish Independence. Considering that the word "First" is used and Scotland is united with England now, you can imagine that this war wouldn't

Robert the Bruce addressing his troops at the Battle of Bannockburn

be the final one between Brits. But that's another tale or five.

How do you get "the" included between your first and last name? "James the Fell" has a cool ring to it. It makes my name no longer a complete sentence. And I'm quarter Scottish. Anyway, Robert the Bruce was a guy. A Scottish guy. King of Scotland guy.

He'd been king for seven years but didn't have a firm grip on power. In 1313 he demanded that all those loyal to his predecessor, who had been ousted by invading English forces in 1296, had to be loyal to the Bruce or they'd lose their lands. The English King, Edward II, got wind of this and said, "Sounds like we have a badass over here" and decided to go fuck him up on the field of battle.

The Battle of Bannockburn was a "pitched battle." That means not a chance encounter, but a more or less agreed-upon time and place to engage in the manly pursuit of seeing what your enemy's insides look like when they're on the outside. Despite Edward II having a force two to three times the size of the Bruce's, things did not go well for Eddie.

Most medieval battles lasted a few hours, but this went on for two days. Fueled by haggis and righteous indignation, the Scots did a heap o' killin', including eviscerating many English nobles and capturing several others. Edward and the English fled the field in disarray. Afterward, the Scots kept up the pressure for fourteen more years, and in 1328 England recognized the independence of the Kingdom of Scotland, with the Bruce as its rightful king.

"The enemy of my enemy is my friend" is an ancient proverb that often holds true only as long as the common enemy remains, because after World War II the Western Allies and the Soviets didn't waste any time rattling their sabers across a conquered and divided Germany.

The term "Iron Curtain" was made famous during a speech by Sir Winston Churchill in 1946. It became a dividing line in Europe over four thousand miles long, running between east and west, populated by walls, fences, minefields, and watchtowers.

The city of Berlin was unique in that it was a hundred miles into the Soviet side of the Iron Curtain, yet had its own mini iron curtain within it, dividing the city between American, British, and French allies on one side, and Soviets on the other. Western Allies wanted to unify and build West Germany back up as a powerful ally against the Soviets. Russia had been invaded by Germany twice in living memory and didn't like this idea. Neither were they excited about a capitalist Berlin inside their zone of control.

In 1947, America and Britain unified their German territory into one. The Soviets were pissed. The French added their territory to that of the U.S. and U.K. in 1948. The Soviets were more pissed. Then the Western Allies created a new currency—the deutsche mark—on June 18, and Soviets were all fuck you guys, we're gonna starve Berlin.

June 24, 1948

For the previous three years the Western Allies had relied on Soviet "goodwill" to permit rail, road, and water access to West Berlin through Soviet-occupied East Germany. On June 24, 1948, that access came to an abrupt go fuck yourself. And the Western Allies went "No, fuck *you*. We got planes."

Using previously negotiated air corridors through Soviet territory, the "Berlin Airlift" began. You can turn around trucks and trains without violence, but the only way to stop a plane is to shoot it down, and the Soviets weren't prepared to blow up unarmed cargo planes using agreed-upon routes.

The scale of the airlift of supplies of food and fuel to sustain 2 million West Berliners was an unimaginable 5,000 tons a day, but the Allies kept it up. Life wasn't easy in West Berlin during this time, but the population saw this deprivation as preferable to going commie. The blockade was a massive failure for the Soviets; it actually made them look like dicks (hint: they were) and hastened the creation of West Germany to thwart Soviet expansion. The blockade ended eleven months after it began, in May 1949.

Jim **Parsons** is an openly gay man who played the character Sheldon Cooper on *The Big Bang Theory.* Sheldon had a web show within the show called *Fun with Flags* where he analyzed the history and symbolism of various flags, from Bavaria to Nebraska to *Star Trek*'s United Federation of Planets. But he did not cover the vexillology of the LGBTQ+ rainbow flag, so let's have some fun.

June 25, 1978

A symbol of pride and social movements, the rainbow flag originated in San Francisco, making its first appearance at the city's Gay Freedom Day Parade on June 25, 1978. It was designed by Gilbert Baker, a gay man and civil rights activist. He was tasked with making the flag by Harvey Milk, the first openly gay elected official in California.

Prior to 1978, the symbol for the LGBTQ+ movement was an inverted pink triangle, but this had significant negative connotations, what with it being designed by fucking Nazis to identify and persecute homosexuals. Although it had been reclaimed as a symbol of pride in the face of homophobia, Milk still wanted something uniquely their own.

One rumor proclaims Baker was inspired by Judy Garland singing "Over the Rainbow" in *The Wizard of Oz,* as Garland was one of the first gay icons. Another hypothesis states he borrowed from the World Peace Association's multicolored Brotherhood flag.

Baker's original design was eight-colored: hot pink, red, orange, yellow, green, turquoise, indigo, and violet. The colors represented, respectively: sex, life, healing, sunlight, nature, magic/art, serenity, spirit. Thirty volunteers hand-dyed and stitched two flags for the parade.

Five months later, Harvey Milk was assassinated; demand for the flag grew. Hot pink was dropped because of lack of availability of that fabric color. A year later, turquoise and indigo were merged into a single royal blue to make a six-stripe flag that remains most popular, although numerous other variations have sprung up over the years.

Thirty-seven years and one day later, the White House was illuminated in the colors of the rainbow flag to celebrate the federal legalization of gay marriage. And in June 2020, in a historic decision, the Supreme Court of the United States voted 6–3 asserting federal law prevents employers from discriminating against workers for being LGBTQ+.

History should take note that Justices Samuel Alito, Brett Kavanaugh, and Clarence Thomas voted on the side of bigotry.

History should take note that Justices Samuel Alito, Brett Kavanaugh, and Clarence Thomas voted on the side of bigotry.

You ever watch *Narcos* on Netflix or those *Sicario* movies and think about how evil the Latin American drug cartels are? Well, let me tell you a story about one of the largest and most nefarious drug dealers in history: the British Empire.

In the late eighteenth and early nineteenth centuries, Britain had a large trade deficit with China, and one way to balance that out was to take massive quantities of opium from its territories in India then turn around and sell it to the Chinese. But it was totally legit and not evil at all because it was done by the British East India Company, which was also referred to as the "Honorable East India Company," so of course they were on the right side of history, right?

Over the course of a century Chinese emperors issued several edicts making opium illegal, but that didn't stop the Brits drugging their people and profiting from it. In 1839, troubled by both the mind-fucking of its populace and the outflow of silver, the Chinese seized 3,000 tons of opium in the port city of Canton (now Guangzhou) and blockaded all foreign ships from entering.

The Brits went all Bugs Bunny: "Of course you realize this means war."

And war it was, the First Opium War (there was a second such war fourteen years after the first one, and the Chinese lost that one too). From 1840 to '42 the British Navy won a series of conclusive battles against the Chinese, resulting in the Treaty of Nanking going into effect on June 26, 1843. It was the first of what the Chinese would come to call "the unequal treaties," which isn't foreboding at all.

June 26, 1843

The terms of the treaty were "We're gonna import enough opium to fuck up half a continent and you're gonna buy it." The British also got an assload of financial reparations for the opium confiscated in 1839, and, most importantly, they got Hong Kong.

Hong Kong Island was made a crown colony, ceded to Queen Victoria "in perpetuity" to provide British traders their own harbor for their opium-loaded ships. In 1860 the territory was expanded to include the Kowloon peninsula, the mainland portion of Hong Kong. In 1898 the colony further expanded with a 99-year lease. The territories were transferred back to the People's Republic of China on July 1, 1997, finally bringing the last vestige of the British Empire to an end.

> **The terms of the treaty were "We're gonna import enough opium to fuck up half a continent and you're gonna buy it."**

You know the young fellas in short-sleeved white shirts and fancy ties who want to save your hungover soul early on a Saturday morning? The guy who started that religion died in a, shall we say, interesting way.

The founder of Mormonism, Joseph Smith Jr., wasn't raised in an overly religious family. As a teen he became concerned about eternity, and prayed on the matter. God and Jesus—the other third of the Trinity was busy, I guess—appeared to him and said, "Hey, pubescent American nobody. All these other churches? Totes wrong. YOU are gonna restore White Jesus Christianity right here in this land you stole from Natives."

A few years later he received additional visions from Angel Moron—Wait. Moroni. Joe said the angel's name was Moroni—and then it was all hidden golden plates and sister wives and magic underpants and Black people are cursed and blah fucking blah let's fast forward to interesting death.

In 1844, Smith was mayor of the town of Nauvoo, Illinois (fans of *The Expanse* are going "Oh!"). Non-Mormons began a newspaper called the *Nauvoo Expositor,* and in the first and only issue exposed Smith as corrupt as fuck. Smith said fuck the First Amendment and sent his cronies to destroy *Expositor*'s printing press and fuck up the building

housing it. Smith's opposition got a warrant for his arrest. Smith declared martial law and unleashed a city militia of 5,000 zealots. The Illinois governor got involved. Smith fled. A posse gave chase. Smith, his brother Hyrum, and several associates surrendered themselves in the town of Carthage where they were charged with treason, a capital offense.

But there was no trial. The region had no shortage of anti-Mormons who went way beyond "Get the fuck off my porch with that bullshit!" Protection of the Smiths was handled by an anti-Mormon militia: foxes guarding the henhouse. Knowing this, a Mormon church leader smuggled a small Second Amendment Freedom Blaster pistol into Joseph's cell.

On June 27, 1844, an angry mob of two hundred armed men approached the jail. Smith thought it was his pals from Nauvoo coming to rescue him, but they were like, "Ha-HA! Nope!" The "protective" detail was all "Oh, no. You can't come in. Please don't." But come in they did. Hyrum was shot in the face and died almost instantly. Joseph went down in a blaze of polygamous glory, possibly wounding three of his attackers before they returned fire, two of whom allegedly later died. Hit three times, Smith fell out of the second-story window of the jail. Not convinced he was *dead* dead, those on the ground shot him some more.

And so, Joseph Smith became a martyr to the Mormons, who proclaim he sealed his testimony with his own blood.

No one seems to remember that Sophie died too. That's Archduke Franz Ferdinand's wife. In the June 28, 1914, assassination by a member of the Serbian secret society "Black Hand" during a state visit to Bosnia, it wasn't just the heir presumptive to the Austro-Hungarian throne who went down in a hail of gunfire, but the Duchess of Hohenberg as well. And then, war. A big one. A "Great War."

In modern analysis, Germany shoulders much of the blame for the outbreak of World War I. That's because winners write history and also write things like the Treaty of Versailles that punished Germany after the war, contributing to a "Fuck you and fuck this treaty too" big-ass war two decades later. There was lots of militarism, imperialism, and ethnic nationalism involved in launching hostilities, but exactly how the assassination of one man and his wife triggered many millions more deaths is complicated.

The Black Hand is the more popular name, but the group was also known as "Unification or Death." Austria-Hungary had annexed Bosnia and Herzegovina six years earlier, pissing off Serbian nationalists who believed those territories belonged to them. Austria-Hungary blamed the Serbian government for the assassination and declared war on them.

I mean, imagine this: You're Austrian emperor Franz Joseph I. Your younger brother is dead. Your son is dead. And now your nephew, the heir to the fucking throne, and his wife, are gunned down in the street in Sarajevo cuz some dumbass motherfucker in Ferdie's motorcade took a wrong turn and stopped right in front of a nineteen-year-old Black Hand member who was basically "Holy shit! There he is." *Pow! Pow! Pow!* Note that this took place *after* the Black Hand had tried and failed to blow Ferdinand up earlier in the day.

June 28, 1914

Where was I? Oh, the Austrian emperor was pissed, so fuck you Serbia.

Russia said, "No, they're our friends. Fuck you."

Austria-Hungary looked to Germany and said, "Lil' help?"

Germany said, "We got you, fam."

France said, "Well, we don't actually like Russians, but they technically are our allies, so, well, fuck. War is fun. Game on, muthafuckas."

Germany ignored Russia and went after France via Belgium because fuck waffles. England was all "Not the waffles!" and joined the killing.

And then a bunch of other countries entered the fray on both sides, including the United States right at the tail end so they could say they saved Europe or some shit.

And that's basically it.

In 1996 Madonna was in a musical called *Evita,* about Eva Perón. It has a 64% rating on Rotten Tomatoes, so might be worth checking out if you're into that sort of thing. Anyway, this isn't about Eva Perón, because, spoiler alert: She died young. Eva was Argentine president Juan Perón's second wife. This is about wife #3.

June 29, 1974

Let's begin with Juan. He was president of Argentina from 1946 to 1955. Then there was a coup d'état and he was punted out of the country with a "Fuck you and don't come back." Eva died of cancer in 1952 at thirty-three. As an aside: If you'll note the timing, Juan was also totally into protecting fucking Nazi war criminals who fled Europe.

María Cartas dropped out of school after the fifth grade and later became a nightclub dancer, adopting the name Isabel. She met Juan in exile in Panama and he liked her a lot, possibly because she was thirty-five years younger than him, and rich and powerful men seem to be into that. In 1960 they moved to Spain together and after a while the local Catholics were getting huffy about him shacking up with a woman who wasn't his wife, so he was all fine I guess she'll be wife #3.

But Isabel became more than just a hot and much younger wife. Juan began to re-insert himself into Argentinian politics from across the pond, but he couldn't actually travel there because the Argentinian military said, "You better fucking not." So Isabel went in his stead, acting as a go-between.

In 1973 a Peronist won the Argentine presidency and welcomed Juan home. Then that president resigned a month later and Juan was back in with a snap election, naming Isabel as vice president. Thing is, Juan was seventy-eight, senile, and in ill health. Isabel was mostly running the show. On June 28, 1974, less than a year into his third term as president, Juan had a series of heart attacks. On June 29, Isabel was secretly sworn in as president, and although not elected to the position, she thus became the first woman in the world to attain the title of "President" (as opposed to Prime Minister or Queen or Tsarina or whatever). Juan died two days later.

Isabel would last as president for a tumultuous two years, before being overthrown in a military coup. After the coup there was a seven-year period of U.S.-backed terror and repression in Argentina referred to as the "Dirty War." Isabel spent five years under house arrest, then in 1981 was exiled to Spain, where she continues to live today.

Anyway, this isn't about Eva Perón, because, spoiler alert: She died young. Eva was Argentine president Juan Perón's second wife. This is about wife #3.

t was a very big explodey-pow. Cue the dinosaurs: "You call that a meteor? Well, when I was a kid . . ."

The Tunguska meteor is the largest impact event in Earth's *recorded* history, because the dinosaurs couldn't write shit down. And precise details for just how much of an Earth-shattering kaboom it made are not known, because it was June 30, 1908, in the middle of butt-ass nowhere Siberia, eastern Russia. The location is so remote it took nineteen years for a scientific expedition to assess the site. Since then, many estimates have been made about the impact, and at the low end the explosive force was akin to 200 Hiroshima bombs, but others think it might have been as powerful as 2,000 said war atrocities. And that's a helluva non-nuclear detonation for something that was only (guessing time again) between 160 to 620 feet in diameter.

But the meteor never actually hit the ground.

Just like our modern-day city-destroying intercontinental boomsticks are designed to devastate and irradiate via airbursts, the Tunguska meteor came screaming toward Earth at over 30,000 miles per hour, and that high speed coupled with entering the atmosphere superheated the chunk of rock to the point where it finally ended its interplanetary journey with a massive fuck-you-I'm-done, self-annihilating *kerblooey* at a height of just under what modern jetliners fly.

Then, shock wave.

The 1927 scientific expedition had trouble getting locals to talk about it, because they saw it as a religious event, a godly punishment for . . . something. Cuz God was like "Fuck you, trees." That's what mostly happened: 80 million trees were flattened over an area of about 830 square miles. Of course, a lot of critters died too. And it's alleged three people as well, but there is no proof of that.

> **Cuz God was like "Fuck you, trees." That's what mostly happened: 80 million trees were flattened over an area of about 830 square miles.**

One witness said of the event, "The whole northern part of the sky appeared covered with fire . . . The earth trembled." He was forty miles away and felt like his skin was burning. When the shockwave hit, he was thrown several feet. It broke windows hundreds of miles away and was measured via seismic instruments in Western Europe. Night skies across Asia and Europe glowed for days.

If you can anthropomorphize an asteroid, there may be one out there watching, waiting, and saying, "If you keep fucking things up, I'ma comin'."

July

Oh, Canada. It's your birthday. And things are pretty awesome here. So long as you don't mind the winters. And you're white.

Canada didn't fight for independence; it was granted. On July 1, 1867, Canada went from being three British colonies into a federation of four provinces called the Dominion of Canada. Since then, six provinces and three territories have been added.

There are myriad explanations for why Britain finally said, "We're out. Be a country." One reason is 'Murica. It'd just finished a big-ass civil war and had a lot of men who knew how to fight. There were Americans who did not like Britain and wanted to take Canada from them. But if Canada was independent, the international optics of conquering a sovereign nation of mostly white people were far less favorable than taking colonies from those limey imperialists.

When looking southward, it's hard not to be grateful for living in Canada, as I do. We've had universal healthcare for several decades. We also outrank the United States by a considerable margin on economic freedom, quality of life, test scores, and percentage of people with university degrees. Crime and suicide are lower. Lots of rural folks own firearms as tools, but we don't have any of that concealed or open carry bullshit. Owning a handgun in Canada is a restrictive bureaucratic nightmare and most of us prefer it that way. We live longer, have more money, less economic disparity, and few feel the need to send their kids to private school because the public system is pretty good. There is maternity leave and paid vacation, and we have more sex. We also legalized gay marriage a decade before our southern neighbor. We're not nearly so religious and there are no legal restrictions on abortion.

July 1, 1867

But there is much Canada has to be ashamed of.

We're good at sweeping racism under the rug. Treatment of Indigenous populations has been and remains horrific. We removed Indigenous children from their homes and put them in assimilation camps called "residential schools" in order "to kill the Indian in the child." The last such school didn't close until 1996. We had Japanese internment camps too. In 2017 a white man murdered six people and injured nineteen others in a mosque shooting. That same year, Quebec banned face coverings.

And our police can be racist. The Black population of Toronto, our largest city, is 8.8 percent, and yet Black people account for 61 percent of deaths from police use of force. It climbs to 70 percent if the cop used a gun.

As a white man, it's great to be Canadian, so long as I bury my head in the snow about how it's not so good for those with more melanin.

Happy birthday, Canada. Let's do better.

> There is maternity leave and paid vacation, and we have more sex. We also legalized gay marriage a decade before our southern neighbor.

The expression "blow off some steam" refers to getting rid of excess energy. And steam was an energy source that changed the world. The first steam-powered device was patented by a Spaniard in 1606, but an English dude also got a patent ninety-two years later, so of course he is the one everyone says invented the steam engine.

July 2, 1698

Jerónimo de Ayanz y Beaumont was a Spanish inventor and engineer. When he was thirty-four the Spanish monarchy put him in charge of their mining operations. The problem with mines is that when you dig deep, they flood with groundwater. And humans always be wanting more. I mean, there's coal and shit down there, and this fucking water bullshit needs to go. So, let's use water to get out the water.

Jerónimo's invention used steam pressure to pump out the water. WeLL aCtUaLLy it wasn't really a steam "engine" he created, but more of a "precursor."

It was first proven that steam could make things move at around the time Jesus was stirring up shit. Some Greek Math Hero did it. (His name was Hero, and he was into math.) Anyway, Thomas Savery was the aforementioned British inventor who, on July 2, 1698, patented the first commercial steam "engine" (it was actually a pump) to do the same stuff Ayanz y Beaumont's did: pump water out of mines.

And that created a ripple effect.

Once the literal power of steam became well known, further experimentation began. With the ability to do so much more than humans or horses alone, the steam engine became the most important aspect of the Industrial Revolution, which transformed humanity. It was critical in providing power for machines that significantly improved the speed, capacity, and efficiency of manufacturing, agriculture, and transportation, leading to massive growth in a variety of industries. It also freed up industrial geography by no longer requiring it to be located near a source of waterpower, such as a river.

In addition to polluting the fuck out of everything from burning all that coal, steam led to the growth and industrialization of cities, population explosion, and bigger and more deadly battles because of greater capacity to transport soldiers and materials to the front lines. Railways opened up continents to colonization and the genocide of native populations. Steam gave humanity an even greater thirst for power: the power to move people and earth, to build and destroy. Its adoption launched us toward the world where you can hop in your assembly-line manufactured Japanese vehicle to zoom down to the local store to buy Guatemalan bananas, New Zealand lamb, and Italian wine while wearing clothes made in Bangladesh.

When are politicians going to learn to stay the fuck out of Afghanistan? You can't win there. Don't try. Even if you think you're helping, you're not.

Between 1839 and 1919 the British fought three wars in Afghanistan and didn't learn. The Soviets didn't either. In 1978 they backed a communist coup d'état, and that dragged them into a war with anti-communist Islamic guerrillas called the "mujahideen," which is the plural word for Muslims engaged in jihad: a holy war against enemies of Islam.

In 1979 the United States was still big into the Truman Doctrine—the containment of communism—and it bought into that enemy-of-my-enemy-is-my-friend stuff, so they decided to help out the mujahideen because fuck the USSR, let's give them their

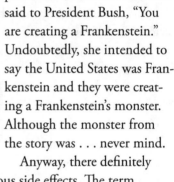
A mujahideen fighter with a surface-to-air missile launcher

own Vietnam. Stinger missiles for everyone!

It was called "Operation Cyclone" and it was signed by President Carter on July 3, 1979, as a secret CIA program to support the rebels and draw the Soviets into a war they couldn't win. (Britain's MI6 ran similar operations, and Saudi Arabia and Pakistan gave massive support as well.) The program started small under Carter, but Reagan had a Republican erection for killing commies and he expanded the shit out of the operation. During the '80s, Americans sent billions in aid, making it one of the most financially substantial and lengthy CIA operations in history. By 1989 the crumbling Soviet Union was sick of getting blown out of the sky by rebels on horseback using expensive American toys, and packed up its shit and left.

And so did the Americans. Having got what it wanted, the United States significantly reduced its funding to the rebels, and to the millions of Afghan refugees who fled to Pakistan.

July 3, 1979

The rebel Afghan groups supported by the Americans were pretty fucking hardcore. I'm not just talking good fighters, but militant mindsets. In the late '80s, Pakistani prime minister Benazir Bhutto said to President Bush, "You are creating a Frankenstein." Undoubtedly, she intended to say the United States was Frankenstein and they were creating a Frankenstein's monster. Although the monster from the story was . . . never mind.

Anyway, there definitely were monstrous side effects. The term "blowback" was coined by the American intelligence community to describe negative repercussions from covert operations, and that's what they got. Many critics assert the American support of the mujahideen created a region ripe for the growth of terrorism, playing a role in the 9/11 attacks in 2001 (bin Laden fought with the mujahideen), which led the United States back into Afghanistan to fight those they once assisted. And America remained there for two decades, finally withdrawing in August of 2021, having effected no real change in the nation, but rather inspiring more terrorists.

Oops.

Gerard Butler's chiseled abs instilled a belief that Spartans could not be defeated.

What? You thought I was gonna write about 'Murica for today? After the events of January 6, 2021, when Trump incited the storming of the Capitol Building, I decided I wanted to examine the death of a *different* democracy for a change.

July 4, 362 B.C.E.

In addition to being racist as fuck, the film *300* was only slightly more historically accurate than *Star Wars* with its "long time ago" stuff. One line that irks me most comes from narrator Dilios, who proclaims the Persians were "ready to snuff out the world's one hope for reason and justice." Like, if not for Greece, democracy would never exist.

The word "demos" referred to lower-class citizens, and FYI philosophers Socrates and Plato were not fans of this group's rise to power. But etymology is not destiny. Democracy has sprung up across an expanse of areas and eras. From 460 to 430 B.C.E., during the time of prominent Greek statesman Pericles, the aristocracy ruled Athens in a golden age of literature, drama, and art. But Pericles died and then Athens got her ass kicked during the Peloponnesian War, and people were like fuck these aristocrats and the demos took over. Athens wasn't the first democratic city-state in the region by far, but it did become the most famous one. Socrates, via Plato's *Republic,* referred to de-

The Death of Epaminondas

mocracy as a chaos of class violence, decadence, and degradation.

Myriad examples across the ages reveal a governmental pattern of monarchy → aristocracy → democracy → dictatorship. Most of humanity's governments have been oligarchies, where a minority rule via birthright (aristocracy), religion (theocracy), or wealth (democracy). Look at the United States and tell me that last one isn't true.

Where was I? Oh, on this fucking day, July 4, 362 B.C.E., there was a battle, another one of those historical turning points. It was the Battle of Mantinea, with Thebans and Arcadians and some others on one side, and Spartans, Athenians, etc., on the other. The Spartan/Athenian side lost, but the Theban leader (Epaminondas) was fatally wounded, so both alliances were debilitated.

Afterward, class war ran rampant. Debtors murdered creditors, poor massacred rich. Democracy was seen by upper and middle classes as empowered envy; the poor viewed it as a fraud, because wealth > voting.

In other words, things went to feces.

Meanwhile, this dude Philip II in a northern Greek kingdom called Macedon looked at the chaos to the south and said, "Gonna conquer that shit." And conquer he did, completing the circle back toward dictatorship in 338 B.C.E. Many wealthy Greeks welcomed him, seeing authoritarianism as preferable to revolution.

A while later, his son Alexander decided he wanted "the Great" added after his name, looked to Persia, and said, "Payback time, motherfuckers."

look at calculus and see Latin.

July 5, 1687, is when one of the most important math and physics books, Sir Isaac Newton's *Mathematical Principals of Natural Philosophy,* was published. In Latin.

So, what's in it and why does it matter? Here is the "guy who sucks at math" interpretation. (I should have had my son the engineer fact-check this before publishing.)

Newton's laws of motion: three physical laws forming the foundation of classical mechanics, which are not people who play Mozart and work on cars. There is the inertia one, but a lot of people don't realize it's not just about a body in motion staying in motion unless acted on by an outside force. It is also about staying at rest. Like, when Netflix asks, "Are you still watching?" Yes, I'm still fucking watching because I'm suffering from inertia and can't get off this goddamn couch unless acted upon by the outside force of that beer I drank needing to vacate the premises.

The two other laws I don't really understand, so look it up.

There was also some stuff about gravity and how it sucks. I guess this was important because he used "empirical observation" and "inductive reasoning" to develop a "physical law" of the universe about how when you're drunk some invisible force sucks your face toward the ground. Not a hypothesis or a theory; gravity is the fucking *law*! There was probably no apple.

The book also had some stuff about how planets move, with a hat tip to German astronomer Kepler.

Newton's book was presented to the Royal Society of London for Improving Natural Knowledge, but they'd just blown their publishing wad on a book titled *A History of Fishes,* which I'm sure is fascinating. And so, Edmond Halley—the comet guy—came up with the cash to publish Newton's book. Tragically, the fish book sold poorly; the Royal Society took a bath on it and ended up telling Halley they'd not be able to afford his salary as clerk of the society, so they paid him with excess copies of the fish book.

Newton's book was way more popular than the fish one; no other book is more seminal to the development of modern physics. And it stood up for more than two centuries until Einstein said, "Newton, I love ya, but shit is actually weirder than this." And then he wrote some shit about warping space and time and I don't know, ask my son.

And it stood up for more than two centuries until Einstein said, "Newton, I love ya, but shit is actually weirder than this."

Attenuate. *Verb.* /əˈten-yə-ˌwāt/ reduce the force, effect, or value of. An attenuated vaccine is one that has weakened the infecting agent enough to not get you sick, but still give your immune system schooling on how to fight it. The first ones were created by the guy whose name appears on your milk. Even that almond bullshit.

July 6, 1885

Three of Louis Pasteur's five kids died of typhoid; I expect he wasn't a fan of infectious diseases. Although the concept of germ theory had been around for centuries, Pasteur's work with milk gave it strong support and helped nail the coffin shut on the competing "miasma theory" of sickness, which is disease ghosts in the air or some shit.

While working on a cure for chicken cholera in 1878, Pasteur tried injecting fresh bacteria cultures into chickens to give them immunity, but it killed a lot of them; the vaccine was as bad as the disease. Then there was a happy accident. Pasteur said to his assistant, "Be sure to inject those chickens with fresh cultures before you go on vacation." The assistant said, "Sure thing, boss." But the assistant forgot and came back a month later and was all "Fucking hell I'm in so much trouble," and injected the chickens with the now significantly weakened cultures that had been sitting out for a month.

The chickens didn't die, and were also immune. Eureka.

Then Pasteur killed the wabbit. Many wabbits. Pasteur gave rabies to rabbits, then harvested their spinal cords and dried them out to weaken the virus. Joseph Meister was a nine-year-old boy who'd been badly mauled by a rabid dog and was certain to die. But on July 6, 1885, Pasteur injected him with the attenuated rabies vaccine he'd taken from the bunnies. It wasn't just a "Fuck it, let's see what happens." It had already been successfully tested on dozens of dogs. Over the next eleven days he gave the boy thirteen progressively stronger inoculations (made stronger by drying them for a shorter time). The boy lived. Good thing, too. Because Pasteur was not a doctor and would have been in deep shit if the kid died. Instead, he became a hero.

Later analysis of Pasteur's notebooks revealed that prior to Joseph, Pasteur had treated two others for rabies. One survived but might not have had rabies. The other died. Of rabies. Anyway, the successful treatment of young Joseph paved the way for the development of many other vaccines.

Louis Pasteur experimenting in his lab

Marco! Polo! Marco! Was that a gunshot? Fuck! Shoot back!

In tales of World War II, the Western world doesn't think too much about China, despite its having a similar death toll to that of the Soviet Union, which was roughly forty times the number of American deaths, about 20 million people.

In 1931 Japan invaded and occupied Manchuria, the northeast corner of China, and created a puppet state. Needless to say, the Chinese were displeased. An unsteady truce lasted the next six years, as Japan moved more and more soldiers into the occupied territory. Then, on July 7, 1937, a critical confrontation happened—what the Western world would come to call the "Marco Polo Bridge Incident." (The local name is Lugou Bridge.)

Many consider the start of WWII to be Germany's 1939 invasion of Poland, but the Chinese are inclined to disagree. As the story goes, on the evening of July 7 a Japanese soldier went missing while on maneuvers. His comrades demanded entry into a small town near the bridge to search for him. The local Chinese garrison told them to fuck off. A shot was heard, then both sides began blasting away like thirty to fifty feral hogs invaded a hillbilly barbecue.

Then everything rapidly went to excrement. Efforts made to defuse tensions were fruitless, and both sides rapidly began massing troops to square off against each other; the battle escalated. The Japanese used the incident as an excuse for a full-scale invasion of China. Referred to as the Second Sino-Japanese War, it merged with the overall Big Second Let's Kill a Bunch of Humanity Extravaganza when Japan attacked Pearl Harbor in 1941.

July 7, 1937

The Japanese captured Beijing, Shanghai, and Nanjing, which was then the capital. And there was this thing that happened called the "Rape of Nanjing," which was just as horrible as it sounds. The Japanese used poison gas on Chinese soldiers and civilians more than 2,000 times during the war. They also dropped bubonic-plague-infested fleas on Chinese cities, causing massive outbreaks of the disease. The invaders also used Chinese people as medical guinea pigs, performing horrible experiments. China would suffer until the Japanese surrender to American forces on August 15, 1945. With the millions of Chinese dead during the eight years of war, most of them civilians, it is accurately referred to as the "Asian holocaust."

Since the war, Japan has been parsimonious in the offering of apologies for these atrocities, and relations between the two countries remain strained.

Humans just can't let shit be. For all of history, when we saw a neighbor who had something we wanted, we went and took it, saying, "This is our land now. We're in charge." Empire building is just a thing we do. The first big land grab we know of was the Akkadian Empire of Sargon the Great during the twenty-third century B.C.E. A few thousand years later, explorer Vasco da Gama became the first European to reach India by sea, opening a new age of intercontinental imperialism.

July 8, 1497

We all know about Columbus, that dick. Fewer consider the role of da Gama in European conquest. Five years after Columbus tried to reach India by going the wrong fucking way and accidentally bumping into a whole other hemisphere, Vasco left for his first voyage to India on July 8, 1497.

Da Gama was Portuguese; they were renowned navigators. Prior to his voyage, the only way western Europeans reached India was through the Mediterranean, which was hostile territory, then a land crossing of the Arabian Peninsula, which was also hostile territory. Previous European efforts to reach India by sea had ended the lives of thousands of sailors, lost to shipwrecks and attacks.

So, da Gama went the long way, a *real* long fucking way, taking his four ships around the southern tip of Africa, called the Cape of Good Hope, then hugging the east African coast northward, making a final sailing across the Indian Ocean, landing in Calicut almost eleven months later. The entire round trip was by far the longest sea voyage ever completed, comprising a distance greater than Earth's circumference.

FYI, on the return trip he ignored the local advice about monsoon season, it took forever to get back to Africa, half the crews died, and the rest were scurvy as fuck and smelling like a goat orgy in a steam room. But they eventually returned to Portugal with spices 'n' shit. Da Gama was rewarded by the Portuguese crown with a lordship, an admiralty, and a shit-ton of cash.

Da Gama undertook a second such voyage in 1502, during which he did some nasty shit, including burning alive 400 Muslim pilgrims on their ship as they begged for mercy. That tanked his reputation, so he did fuck all for two decades. Then there was a new king who liked da Gama's style and he was back in and named viceroy of India. He made his third voyage in 1524, landed in India and said, "All right, motherfuckers, this is how shit is gonna be," contracted malaria, and died.

But his fuckery lived on. The Portuguese opened the Asian door for some good old European conquering, and various countries spent the next few centuries stampeding on through it.

> **It took forever to get back to Africa, half the crews died, and the rest were scurvy as fuck and smelling like a goat orgy in a steam room.**

"**The Great**" was added after Catherine's name because she did great and terrible things. But not with horses.

You've heard of Elizabethan and Victorian Eras as golden ages for Britain? Russia's golden age was the Catherinian Era. Born to Prussian royalty without much money, she had that "marriageable" quality of being a woman and a princess, which could be used to advance familial interests.

She met her second cousin Peter III, who would become emperor of Russia, when she was ten and was like "Ew, gross. He sucks." But her mom was all "Tough shit you gotta marry him so I can be rich and famous," and so much to her chagrin Catherine was forced to marry Peter at the age of sixteen.

Catherine made the most of it. She charmed Peter's aunt, the reigning Russian empress, and dove into learning the Russian language and culture. The people liked her. Oh, and they gave her the name "Catherine" when she converted to Russian Orthodox Christianity. She was actually born Sophie. Anyway, she never grew to like Peter, because he *was* a total knob, and she focused on educating herself and reading Enlightenment works rather than entertaining her alcoholic oaf of a husband.

Pete's aunt, Empress Elizabeth, died in January 1762, when Catherine was thirty-two. Peter ascended and immediately began pissing off powerful nobles who just happened to think Catherine was swell. Six months later they were all fuck this guy and coup d'état-ed his drunk ass on July 9, 1762. Peter was forced to abdicate in favor of Catherine, and he died eight days later under Jeffrey Epstein–like circumstances.

July 9, 1762

Catherine ruled for thirty-four years, the nation's longest-reigning female monarch. She expanded education and borders alike. She invested in the arts and embraced the ideals of the Enlightenment. And yeah, she had slippery naked fun time with a lot of dudes and gave them positions of power until they bored her then she pensioned them off. So fucking what? Like no powerful man ever did that.

Catherine was meant to be a pawn, but like the queen in chess, proved powerful. Lotta dudes didn't like that. After her death, critics slut-shamed her and said she died copulating with her favorite horse. That's bullshit. She Elvis'd her exit, stroking out on the toilet at the age of sixty-seven. Well, Elvis copied her. Whatever. They both died while pooping.

You know that U2 "Sunday Bloody Sunday" song about a day of violence in Northern Ireland in 1972? That day wasn't the first Bloody Sunday. Another one took place there over half a century earlier.

July 10, 1921

Early in the twentieth century Northern Ireland was one-third Catholic. It is far from absolute, but Irish Catholics tend to identify as Irish and saw the independent Republic of Ireland as their brethren. The majority Protestants in Northern Ireland, conversely, were more likely to consider themselves British and viewed independent Ireland as a foreign nation. The former are "nationalists," and the latter are "unionists" or "loyalists" because of their support for the British monarchy.

The Irish War of Independence involved the Irish Republic—an unrecognized revolutionary state comprising the entire island—declaring its independence from the U.K. The war began in 1919 as a guerrilla action by the Irish Republican Army (nationalists) against the British Army and the Royal Irish Constabulary (unionists). Over a two-year period, several hundred died in the violence. June 1921 proved particularly bloody, leading to efforts to curtail the killing via a truce agreement taking place on July 9 in neutral Dublin. Many of the unionists saw the truce as a sellout to the republicans, and they weren't going to stand for it.

And so, in the early morning hours of July 10, 1921, Bloody Sunday began when unionist forces launched an attack on the Catholic community of Lower Falls in Belfast. Scouts saw the raiding party approach and sounded the alarm; IRA volunteers counterattacked. The battle was a match to a powder keg, sparking fighting between Protestants and Catholics throughout west Belfast. Sixteen people died and almost two hundred homes were destroyed. Most of the death and destruction was borne by Catholics.

The violence continued for a few days, followed by a lull, and then it flared again in late August. A treaty was signed the following December establishing an Irish Free State in the region, now known as the Republic of Ireland (meaning the entire island excluding Northern Ireland, which opted out), as a dominion of the British Empire. Many IRA in the newly created Free State refused to accept the treaty, leading to the Irish Civil War breaking out in June of 1922 between pro-treaty and anti-treaty forces. The civil war lasted almost a year; the Irish Free State lasted fifteen years.

never saw *Hamilton,* but I imagine that while the events chronicled were taking place there was far less singing involved.

Aaron Burr Jr. was third vice president of the United States, serving during the term of President Thomas Jefferson, a man who owned and raped enslaved people. During Burr's fourth year as veep, he killed a man. And unlike what Trump said about blowing someone away on Fifth Avenue, there were consequences to his political career.

Alexander Hamilton was named a key Founding Father of the United States for his role in creating the country's new government. He was first secretary of the Treasury and authored President Washington's eco-nomic policies. Anyway, Burr and Hamilton hated each other. In 1791 Burr beat Hamil-ton's father-in-law in a senate race, and Hamilton was pissed.

July 11, 1804

Burr founded a bank in New York in 1799, breaking a banking monopoly of which Hamilton was part. Hamilton got more pissed at Burr. In 1800 Burr became VP and Hamilton didn't like that either be-cause he saw him as dangerous and corrupt. Hamilton was even more pissed. Jefferson didn't like Burr either and was gonna punt

The duel between Burr and Hamilton

him as veep, so Burr decided to run for governor of New York in 1804. Hamilton was all no fucking way and used his influence, trashing the shit out of him, to ensure Burr lost.

It was that smear campaign that led to the duel.

Burr was all "You say some shit about me?" and Hamilton went "Who, me?" and Burr said, "You better take that shit back" and Hamilton didn't wanna because he had already been disgraced by getting naked with someone he shouldn't have and didn't think his reputation could survive the additional shame of rescinding more than a decade of trash talk.

Rather than sacrifice his reputation, he atoned with his liver and spine.

That's where Burr's bullet hit him in the July 11, 1804, duel to satisfy matters of honor. Hamilton croaked the next day and Burr was charged with multiple crimes, prompting him to flee the jurisdiction. But the charges were quashed, and he returned to D.C. to complete his term as VP.

But people didn't take kindly to the killing; Burr's political career was as dead as Alexander Hamilton. And aside from a brief foray into treason, which is a whole 'nother story, Burr spent the rest of his life in obscurity.

Aaron Burr Jr. was third vice president of the United States, serving during the term of President Thomas Jefferson, a man who owned and raped enslaved people. During Burr's fourth year as veep, he killed a man.

Jimmy Carter is a swell guy. A champion of human rights and winner of the Nobel Peace Prize, he continued working with the non-profit housing organization Habitat for Humanity well into his 90s. But he didn't win reelection, getting obliterated in 1980 by Reagan.

Jimmy's VP was Walter Mondale, and in 1984 the sidekick decided to have another go at Reagan. It was even more of a blowout. Reagan was so damn popular the Democrats could have run white Jesus and they'd still have lost, but Mondale wasn't much of a candidate. What makes his candidacy noteworthy is that on July 12 of that year, Mondale chose a woman as his running mate.

And an exceptional woman she was. Geraldine Ferraro was a wife and mother who kept her birth name. She began her career as an elementary school teacher, but decided to attend law school at night because she wanted to do more with her life. The admissions officer for Fordham University Law School said to Ferraro that she better be serious because, "You're taking a man's place, you know." Afterward, she worked as a civil lawyer in her husband's real estate firm, then as a prosecutor in Queens County, New York, when the city had few women in that role. Within a year she was assigned to the Special Victims Bureau and two years after that she was the bureau's head. She then successfully ran for Congress in 1978.

Ferraro rose rapidly in the house, achieving numerous powerful committee positions, then became the first woman in U.S. history to run as VP on a major party ticket. Unlike the second woman to hold that distinction—the one who didn't actually say she could see Russia from her house, but we believed she did indeed say that because she *is* plenty stupid—Geraldine was qualified.

July 12, 1984

It was an exciting leap forward for women in American politics, and her nomination acceptance speech was an emotional affair. In it, she quoted Dr. Martin Luther King Jr., spoke of her dreams of creating a future for her children, and brought up how her father was an Italian immigrant who came to love his new country. She mentioned the need for fairness, for increasing opportunities for all Americans, rightfully excoriating Reagan's policies by saying "under this administration, the rules are rigged against too many of our people." *American Rhetoric*'s list of the Top 100 Speeches of the 20th Century puts Ferraro's at #56.

She faced ample sexism during the campaign, being repeatedly asked if she was tough enough for the job. There was also much ado about her husband's finances that damaged her. Additionally, she was attacked by the Catholic Church for being a pro-choice Catholic in a way that male pro-choice Catholic candidates did not experience.

Fast-forwarding a few decades, America wasn't ready for a woman president in 2016, and the country suffered horribly for it, but Americans finally did elect a female VP—a woman of color, no less—in 2020.

It seems **Rami Malek** was born to play Queen singer Freddie Mercury, and despite the lack of historical accuracy in *Bohemian Rhapsody*, I loved it. When it comes to ascertaining the film's veracity, however, you're likely to miss one important reality. It's to do with the Live Aid concert for famine relief in Ethiopia. It probably did more harm than good.

July 13, 1985

Road to Hell, good intentions, something something.

On July 13, 1985, Live Aid was held simultaneously in London before a crowd of 72,000, and in Philadelphia for 89,000. The main organizer was Bob Geldof of the Boomtown Rats, who also performed in London along with acts such as U2, Dire Straits, David Bowie, Sting, Elton John, the Who, and the aforementioned Queen. Charles and Diana attended. The United States show included Madonna, Tom Petty, Black Sabbath, the Beach Boys, Eric Clapton, Duran Duran, and what was left of Led Zeppelin. Almost two billion watched the show on TV.

Those impressive lineups, noticeably lacking in African performers because white savior complex, raised a couple hundred million

> **The money raised from Live Aid probably killed as many as it saved. Mengistu used the aid to add to the problem in Ethiopia rather than be part of the solution.**

dollars for famine relief in Ethiopia. Geldof bathed in adulation over his magnificent humanitarian accomplishment. Except it was more of a clusterfuck.

The Ethiopian famine wasn't a natural disaster so much as a genocide. Before the concert the legit aid organization Doctors Without Borders warned Geldof about Ethiopian leader Mengistu Haile Mariam, who had caused the fucking famine in the first place. Mengistu was involved in a civil war and used hunger as a weapon to starve the insurgents into submission. But Geldof refused to listen, allying himself to a ruthless dictator by providing funds for his ongoing butchery. Mengistu had been deadlocked in the war, but the influx of cash allowed him to continue his brutal reign and finance his resettlement campaign that killed about 100,000 people and displaced many more. And although the claims remain controversial, it is near certain a significant portion of the donations were diverted to buy arms to supply both sides in the civil war.

The money raised from Live Aid probably killed as many as it saved. Mengistu used the aid to add to the problem in Ethiopia rather than be part of the solution. Geldof remains hypersensitive to any criticism, refusing to admit that the consequences of Live Aid were anything less than exemplary.

The roots of the French Revolution began in a far-off land called Mississippi. Capitalism funded empires, and private companies in Europe set out to conquer the world with the blessings of their governments. However, the French Mississippi Company was a financial fuckup of epic proportions that destroyed the French economy and led to a guillotine-o-rama of those deemed responsible.

The Mississippi Company had friends in the court of King Louis XV, and in 1717 sold shares on the Paris Stock Exchange to fund its colonization of the Mississippi Valley, because it's not like anyone else was using it (genocidal sarcasm font). The company did this thing called "marketing," which involves describing a land of alligators and swamps as one of amazing abundance and opportunity. Those French who had anything of value to invest shrieked, "Take my money!" The stock price soared.

But then some realized the stock was overvalued, and began a sell-off, creating a cascade of dumping shares that nuked the price. It was called the Mississippi Bubble, and it was one of the largest financial crashes in history. Many investors lost everything, and some said fuck it and shoved a musket in their mouth to bid the world *adieu.*

The French financial system couldn't recover; much of its empire was taken by the British. It was made worse by the French giving costly aid to the Americans in their revolution, coupled with a regressive tax system that focused on taxing peasantry and not the nobility or their luxury items. Meanwhile, the French crown was doing the eighteenth-century equivalent of getting high-interest cash advances from Visa to pay the Mastercard bill. By 1789, half the annual budget went toward paying just the interest on loans to various European banks and other lenders.

July 14, 1789

In June 1789, the middle class said these nobles are dipshits and they keep fucking us over, so we're creating a National Assembly and gonna make an actual for-real constitution so we can be proper capitalists. This prompted conservative elements of the aristocracy to seize control of the finance ministry on July 11, leading to growing unrest. The shitfuckery culminated in the storming of the Bastille on July 14, 1789, mostly because they saw the fortress as a symbol of royal tyranny. It only had seven prisoners in it at the time, four of whom were in for the heinous crime of forgery.

Thus began the French Revolution, not one of hungry poor, but of ambitious middle classes. It didn't go well. The country convulsed like a headless snake for decades before becoming a proper democracy. Now, July 14 is celebrated as France's National Day, with fireworks and wine and the whole bit.

The British Museum has one of the greatest collections of "Mind if we steal this?" in the world. For my visit, one such object stood out as most mesmerizing: the Rosetta Stone. But the Brits weren't the first to thieve it. Napoleon did that.

Aliens didn't build the pyramids, but Ancient Egyptian hieroglyphs were an alien language that no one had understood for fifteen centuries. On July 15, 1799, a key would be discovered that opened the book on a long-dead empire.

It wasn't just Europe that Napoleon terrorized. He had a three-year campaign in Egypt beginning in 1798. One thing Europe-

The Rosetta Stone

ans loved to do was study those they invaded, because the "It's for science!" proclamations made the subjugation and genocide of others seem more palatable. That's why Napoleon brought a team of 167 science-type folks on his military expedition.

Appropriately, the aforementioned stone was found while fortifying the port city of Rosetta, today called Rashid. Lieutenant Pierre* François Bouchard saw it and said, "Cool fuckin' rock, dudes." The British thought so too. They showed up in Egypt in 1801, kicked some French ass, and took the stone home. It's been in the aforementioned British Museum since 1802 on near-continuous display, and is the Royal Institute of We Stole That Shit's most visited object.

I mentioned a key. The stone was inscribed with three scripts: Ancient Greek, Demotic (Ancient Egyptian lowly peasant script), and hieroglyphs (Ancient Egyptian fancy priest script). It took some time to decipher it all, but experts were able to figure out the Ancient Greek by 1803, and since it was the same message in all three languages, the Egyptian scripts were figured out in 1822, allowing other Egyptian artifacts to be read. What did the stone say? It was a message from 196 B.C.E., a priestly decree saying thirteen-year-old pharaoh Ptolemy V is a righteous dude and we love him.

Egypt asked for it back in 2003, but the Brits were all "Ha-HA. Nope. Have this fake-ass one we made out of fiberglass instead."

*Fun Fact: Pierre means "stone" in French.

Prior to World War II there were fewer than 17 million Jewish people on Earth. More than a third of them were murdered in the Holocaust. To this day, over three-quarters of a century after the end of the fucking Nazi genocide, the world Jewish population has still not reached pre-war levels.

Antisemitism is alive and well in France (and everywhere, really). With roughly half a million people, France has the largest Jewish population in Europe. It's also the largest European source of Jewish immigrants to Israel; they're leaving a long history of being treated like shit by their countrymen.

In the spring of 1940, the German blitzkrieg rolled over France like they were a bunch of cheese-eating surrender monkeys. I stole that from *The Simpsons*. Anyway, the Germans didn't occupy all of France right away. They designated a "free zone" in the south. The leadership was based in the city of Vichy, so the region was named Vichy France. And they were an authoritarian puppet government of the fucking Nazis and totally complicit in the Holocaust.

Beginning on July 16, 1942, a terrible betrayal of French humanity took place called the Vel' d'Hiv Roundup. Paris was in the German-occupied zone, but the Vichy police state had some control there. The French police were ordered by the Vichy government to commit a mass arrest against Paris Jews and ship them to Auschwitz. And they did.

July 16, 1942

Vel' d'Hiv was an indoor cycling velodrome where many of the arrest victims were held in cramped quarters with little food or water, and no sanitation. During a two-day period, over 13,000 Jews, including 4,000 children, were rounded up by French police and sent off for extermination. Did I mention the police were French? Because they were French. Did I mention the French Vichy government was complicit? Because they were complicit as fuck. In fact, in the 1980s it was revealed that Vichy officials weren't just complicit in the genocide, they were enthusiastic about it. They were more than happy to order thousands of their fellow French citizens, fellow human beings, to Auschwitz to be murdered.

Assholes.

> To this day, over three-quarters of a century after the end of the fucking Nazi genocide, the world Jewish population has still not reached pre-war levels.

n Canada, depending on where you live, the drinking age is either eighteen or nineteen. But look southward to the United States and the drinking age is federally mandated: twenty-one across the board. So much for state's rights, amirite? Americans like getting fucked-up, and the American government likes setting restrictions on getting fucked-up.

July 17, 1984

In 1920 the Eighteenth Amendment said, "No booze!" Thirteen years later the Twenty-First Amendment said, "Okay, booze." Side note for the ammosexuals: Your Second Amendment isn't sacrosanct. You *can* ditch that shit. Or just follow the part about the "well-regulated militia."

Anyway, back in 1933, with the return to legal drunkenness, most states decided on twenty-one as the minimum age. Then in 1971 there was *another* amendment to the Constitution. See, for a long time in the United States it was legal for an eighteen-year-old to be drafted and sent off to die in some foreign land, but many of them couldn't even vote for representatives who opposed things like war or conscription. Then the Twenty-Sixth Amendment came along saying everyone who is eighteen or older can vote.

And a bunch of states were like, shit, if they can vote, they can drink. So, they lowered the drinking age to eighteen, nineteen or twenty, and that's how Nixon got a second term. Not really. Maybe.

For a time, people barely out of high school in twenty-nine states could boat-race and funnel beer and kill brain cells and even die of alcohol poisoning to their heart's content. They could also drive while drunk. Not legally. But they did anyway. I mean, the drinking was legal, but the driving while shit-faced wasn't.

And people got MADD. That stands for Mothers Against Drunk Driving, a charity that saw how the lowering of the minimum drinking age in several states coincided with more death from drinky-drinky/drivey-drivey/crashy-crashy. They were pissed, or mad, or whatever, and they let their representatives know.

And on July 17, 1984, Ronald Reagan, who was married to Just-Say-No Nancy, said fuck it. You want that sweet highway money? Up the age to twenty-one. Any state that didn't raise the drinking age to twenty-one would lose 10 percent of federal highway funding.

The coercion worked. Within a decade all states, and D.C., were in compliance.

Spain got to sit out World War II. The country was already fascist, so Hitler gave it a pass. And Spain remained fascist for another three decades after the end of the war, making it the longest dictatorship in modern European history.

In 1931, Alfonso Unlucky XIII was unlucky. He was deposed as King of Spain, a title he'd held for all of his forty-five years. The Second Spanish Republic was proclaimed. The elections in early 1936 saw victory for a left-wing coalition called Popular Front. The right-wingers felt like the Popular Front represented a bunch of dirty commies

Francisco Franco in 1930

running the country, and so the fascists stirred up some shit. Anarchy ensued, and six months later there was a series of assassinations of political figures on both sides. On July 18, 1936, the right-wingers said, "Fuck it. Time for a coup."

July 18, 1936

And the instigators of the coup, called Nationalists, or *pendejos,* or whatever, tried real hard, but failed to seize control of the country. Those loyal to the legitimate left-wing government, which some may be surprised to learn were called Republicans, retained most of their power. But that wasn't the end of it. Merely the beginning. Let's have a war, both sides decided.

And so, they did. Hitler helped out the Nationalists, and the Soviets sided with the Republicans. The war lasted three years and there were plenty of atrocities and purges and mass executions on both sides. Having the only big European war going at the time, volunteers poured in from all over to get in on the killing, including from the United States and Canada.

But by 1939, the Republicans were done for. Due to suppression, it's hard to say how many died. It might be as high as 2 million. The Nationalists were now in charge under no-longer-rebel-but-now-president-for-life Francisco Franco. He gave himself the title of *El Caudillo* (military or political leader) and ruled as dictator until his death in 1975.

Democracy was finally restored to Spain in 1978.

For all recorded history, we've treated women like shit.

Hunter-gatherer societies might have been different, but then the first agrarian revolution began around 10,000 B.C.E. That meant tending fields over hunting mammoths and shit. Settling down meant holding property. Holding property created a need for hands to work and inherit it. The steadier food supply also meant women could squeeze large babies out of small orifices more often.

July 19, 1848

Here are some fun stats. Prior to the twentieth century, fully a quarter of all babies died before their first year, and *half* of all children died before they reached fifteen. Across cultures and continents and millennia this was so; once born, you had only a fifty-fifty chance of living to your mid-teens. Only in the last century has child, and maternal, mortality plummeted.

Due in no small part to these realities, men have basically enslaved women as the breeding class, because to grow the population the average woman had to give birth at least five times in the hope that half the kids would survive to adulthood. And this was before epidurals. While Homo sapiens have given rise to a wide variety of cultures holding myriad beliefs, almost all had this one thing in common: fucking patriarchy treating women like property.

On July 19, 1848, the first women's rights convention began in Seneca Falls, New York, to "discuss the social, civil, and religious condition and rights of woman." Held in the Wesleyan Chapel, the convention was organized by Quakers, who are big on the whole equal rights thing, along with Elizabeth Stanton, who wasn't a Quaker.

Hundreds attended, including several dozen men. There was a heated debate about including the right to vote in their declaration. Famed social reformer Frederick Douglass, the only Black person in attendance, argued eloquently for its inclusion, and so it was.

The convention attracted much attention, and other such events began to spring up o'er the land by those [sarcasm alert] high-and-mighty women and the pussy-whipped men who supported them. Oh, wait. I forgot. Feminists don't like sex. The men weren't whipped. They were henpecked. Again, sarcasm.

Anyway, Stanton would later co-author (along with Susan B. Anthony and others) the six-volume *History of Women's Suffrage,* which would describe the Seneca Falls Convention as the beginning of the Women's Rights Movement in the United States.

Two years later the first National Women's Rights Convention was held, and by that time the right to vote had become a central tenet. It's a right that was finally won at the national level, mostly just for white women, in 1920, with the ratification of the Nineteenth Amendment.

Eunice Kennedy Shriver, sister to JFK, was close to her older sister Rosemary, who had an intellectual disability, causing her to have seizures and mood swings. In 1941, when Rosemary was twenty-three, her father Joe Kennedy decided to have her lobotomized. It didn't help, and she spent the rest of her life in an institution.

Influenced by this, Eunice became executive VP of the Joseph P. Kennedy Jr. Foundation in 1957 and shifted it from Catholic charities to focus on intellectual disabilities. Then, in 1962, a frustrated mother spoke with Eunice about her inability to find a summer camp that would accept her additional-needs child. Eunice decided to turn her own home into a summer camp that was free for children with intellectual disabilities.

Eunice had been disheartened at how such children were seen by many as a burden and focused Camp Shriver on what the children *could* do, rather than what they couldn't. In 1967, Anne McGlone (now Anne Burke, who is currently chief justice of the Illinois Supreme Court) was a physical education teacher with the Chicago Park District. After teaching disabled children, she came up with the idea for hosting a city-wide track meet for them, and contacted Shriver to ask for help.

July 20, 1968

Shriver was delighted with the idea, and opened the foundation's purse strings, transforming the event from a track meet to a full-on Olympics-style event. The first Special Olympics was held on July 20, 1968, in Soldier Field, Chicago. A thousand athletes attended from the United States and Canada. In her opening address Shriver said to the assembled athletes, "Many of you will win, but even more important, I know you will be brave, and bring credit to your parents and your country."

The Special Olympics World Games are now held every two years, alternating between summer and winter events, and attracts thousands of international athletes, supported by hundreds of thousands of volunteers and coaches.

The first Special Olympics was held on July 20, 1968, in Soldier Field, Chicago. A thousand athletes attended from the United States and Canada.

Scandals of teachers doing bad stuff in the classroom are all too common and usually full of ick. But sometimes a teacher breaks the rules and it's the right thing, such as with 24-year-old John Scopes, who decided Tennessee's law against teaching evolution was simian stupidity.

The law was named after an evangelical Christian. Let's not mention his name, because fuck that guy. Let's call it the Dumbfuck Act. So John Scopes was the football coach and only subbed in to teach when needed. In challenging Dumbfuck, he wasn't a lone rogue, but rather part of a test case prompted by the ACLU and local businessmen who thought a trial would bring some news coverage to their small town of Dayton.

Scopes wasn't even sure he *had* taught evolution. He agreed to say he had because the ACLU approached him and said, "This no-teaching-evolution law is bullshit and we want to challenge it. Lil' help?" and John said, "K."

John Scopes, shortly before the trial

The defense team included Clarence Darrow, the prosecution had William Jennings Bryan. And the defense lost. On July 21, 1925, after nine minutes of jury deliberation, Scopes was found guilty of teaching evolution and fined $100. Which is like $1,500 today. A lot for a teacher, because we don't pay them enough.

The Dumbfuck Act was upheld, prompting other states, such as Mississippi and Texas, to enact their own laws promoting ignorance and dumbfuckery regarding the teaching of evolution. The Tennessee Dumbfuck Act remained in effect until 1967, when it was finally repealed.

John Scopes suffered much public humiliation from religious zealots for his role in the trial, and he said fuck this hick town and did a master's degree at the University of Chicago, then became a petroleum engineer.

In 1968, the Supreme Court of the United States finally said laws against teaching evolution were contrary to the First Amendment, but that didn't stop the unintelligent trying to get "intelligent design" (lab coat creationism) bullshit taught in school alongside that heathen Darwinian stuff. One such case in Kansas in 2005 entailed "teaching the controversy" of intelligent design in science class. This prompted another 24-year-old hero to take a stand. Bobby Henderson, a recent physics graduate of Oregon State University, proclaimed that if the schools were made to teach intelligent design, they must also teach his equally valid creation story of the Church of the Flying Spaghetti Monster.

The internet loved the Spaghetti Monster, and this may have influenced the outcome. In 2007, the Kansas School Board voted 6–4 against amending science standards to include teaching intelligent design.

Colonization doesn't refer to literal colons, but it does involve assholes. It's when a bunch of people move to a new land and regardless of who already lives there say, "Yoink!" The unpigmented people were most effective at it, using this strategy to conquer a number of continents. But it didn't always go so smoothly for the invaders. One such colony just up and disappeared, and we're not sure what happened to it.

Sir Walter Raleigh had a habit of stealing land that didn't belong to him, starting with Irish-owned land in 1580. Four years later Queen Elizabeth gave him a royal patent to steal "remote, heathen and barbarous lands" in America and make them Christian, so he sent a military expedition to Roanoke Island on the outer banks of what is now North Carolina.

They arrived in 1585; it did not go well. They suffered food shortages and hostile relations with Native peoples. A year later Sir Francis Drake swung by and the Roanoke colonists were all "Get us the fuck outta here," and they hitched a ride home. But they brought tobacco and corn and potatoes back to England and limeys were like "Fuck yeah starch and cigarettes," and Raleigh decided to give this Roanoke colony thing another go.

It was a colonizing mission—meaning families—consisting of over a hundred people arriving on July 22, 1587. But then there was this pesky thing called the Spanish Armada harassing England, so it was three years before anyone came back to check on the Roanoke colonists, only to discover they were gone.

July 22, 1587

The only clue was the word CROATOAN carved into a post, referencing nearby Croatoan Island. The colony had been dismantled; it was assumed they'd peacefully relocated. The relief mission was going to check out Croatoan but shit happened and they never got around to it. It was over a hundred years before any European visited Croatoan, now Hatteras Island, to have a look. The colonists weren't there, but Native peoples were.

What happened? The mystery has been referred to as "the Area 51 of colonial history." They may have tried to sail back to England and been lost at sea. The Spaniards may have wiped them out. The Native populations might have massacred them all. Or, it is possible they assimilated with local Natives. As far as they knew, England had given up on them, and their only hope for survival would be to join with those whose ancestors had already lived there for thousands of years.

J
U
L
Y

215

By the end of World War I, half of all cars in America were the Model T Ford. Henry Ford did many great things. He also really hated Jews.

The Ford Motor Company was incorporated mid-June 1903. A little over a month later, on July 23, the company sold its first car. As a boy growing up in Michigan, Ford said fuck this farming bullshit and apprenticed himself to a machinist in Detroit, starting down a career path that would lead him to transform the assembly-line method of mass production.

Because of Ford, the motor vehicle went from being an expensive method of transportation for rich people to something the middle class could afford, which is why we have gridlock, pollution, and 3,700 global deaths a day from car accidents. Well, if Ford hadn't done it, someone else would have. But there are admirable things about the *way* he did it. He was committed to lowering manufacturing costs and the price of his cars, coupled with aggressive marketing, to grow the company into a behemoth. Ford became one of the richest men in America.

And he shared the wealth. Ford abhorred employee turnover, hiring and endeavoring to retain quality workers by paying them a generous wage that many considered exorbitant and coupling it with a shortened (five-day) workweek. The best mechanics flocked to his company. He also hired Black workers, women, and people with disabilities at a time when few others did.

He also launched the Ford Foundation, dedicated to improving human welfare. The foundation is one of the wealthiest charitable organizations in the world, donating to the arts, the fight for civil rights, microloans, and fighting the AIDS epidemic.

But yeah, that antisemitism though.

Ford bought an obscure newspaper from his hometown, the *Dearborn Independent*.

The 1910 Model T Ford

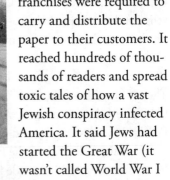

From 1920 to 1927, all Ford franchises were required to carry and distribute the paper to their customers. It reached hundreds of thousands of readers and spread toxic tales of how a vast Jewish conspiracy infected America. It said Jews had started the Great War (it wasn't called World War I yet), and that they basically ran a cabal that could be blamed for every imaginable ill in the world.

The antisemitic stories spread, given weight because they came from such a powerful man. Hitler was a big fan. Ford helped create a state of complacency in America regarding Germany's treatment of Jews; the United States turned away countless thousands of Jewish people fleeing Nazi extermination.

Welcome to another euphemism-o-rama to describe white people being shitty. If some bleached bastard so much as imagined a Black man had raped a low-melanin woman, the Black man's life would be at risk. And not just from lynching. In the not-too-old days, Black men could be sentenced to death by the state for sexually assaulting sunscreen slatherers.

The Scottsboro Boys were nine Black teenagers ranging in age from thirteen to nineteen. In 1931 Alabama they were falsely accused of raping two Wonder Bread women on a train. A racially mixed group of people was riding the rails on the train traveling through Tennessee. Some boys with a high degree of caucasity tried to push a Black boy from the train, proclaiming the car for the cauliflower crowd only. He and several other Black teens fought back, and the lads with the lotion-like skin ended up jumping from the train.

And then the toilet-paper teens had a sad, cuz embarrassed. So, they went full BBQ Becky and called the cops, saying they were assaulted by the Black boys. The sheriff got a posse together and stopped the train in Paint Rock, Alabama, and arrested the Black teens. Then two young mayosapien maidens on the train said the Black teens had raped them.

There was no sign or medical evidence of rape. The two women were suspected sex workers, and it's surmised they made false accusations to deflect attention away from them breaking the law by crossing state lines "for immoral purposes." Considering the time and location, they probably hated Black people too.

July 24, 1937

There was an attempted lynch mob, because of course, but the case was heard in Scottsboro, Alabama, and in three rushed trials with shit legal representation eight of the nine boys were found guilty and sentenced to death.

Communist Party USA and the NAACP got involved and launched appeals, during which one of the women recanted, saying none of the boys had touched either of them. But the cases weren't thrown out. Appeals dragged on for years. The end result was that none of them were put to death, but several were still found guilty in 1937 and received prison sentences ranging from 75 to 105 years, although they were all paroled within a decade.

On July 24, 1937, the four remaining Scottsboro boys, who had spent six years on death row, had the charges against them dropped. The cases are commonly cited as a prime example of a miscarriage of justice against Black people in the United States.

In 1912 the German kaiser reportedly asked what the Swiss militia, numbering only 250,000, would do if invaded by half a million Germans soldiers. The alleged Swiss reply was "Shoot twice and go home." Three decades later that attitude kept the country safe from Hitler's invasion.

July 25, 1940

"If you want peace, prepare for war" is an adaptation of the words of a writer named Vegetius in the Later Roman Empire. It can sound like bullshit, except when you realize nations have a long history of invading each other. During World War II the only thing that kept Hitler from conquering Switzerland was their promise that they'd make him regret it.

The beginnings of Swiss neutrality date back to the early sixteenth century, but it became official with the Treaty of Paris in 1815. Switzerland hasn't participated in a foreign war since, making it the country with the oldest military neutrality policy in the world. They're so neutral, they'd even let fucking Nazis use their banks to hide all that shit they stole from the Jews they murdered. But they had to keep up a fighting edge in order to enforce their neutrality so other countries would look at them and say, "Eh, not worth it. Keep your chocolate watches."

As WWII broke out, the Swiss decided they should do the unusual-for-them thing of putting someone in charge of the military by electing a general. Despite the guy being connected to an organization that didn't seem to mind the fucking Nazis too much, they chose lifelong military officer Henri Guisan. They didn't have the military equipment the fucking Nazis did, but they had a fighting spirit, and mountains.

On July 25, 1940, General Guisan delivered a historic address to his entire officer corps. He said no fucking way we're giving in to these fucking Nazis. You run out of bullets? You stab those fucking Nazi fucks with the pointy thing attached to the end of your rifle.

Switzerland had a decentralized political structure so there was no one person who could say, "We surrender!" Guisan told his officers that any proclamations of surrender, therefore, were to be considered fucking Nazi lies and to keep fighting. Go guerrilla. Hide in the mountains. Build a resistance. Kill those fucking Nazi fucks until there are no more left to kill.

At the peak of the war, Guisan mobilized 850,000 fighters out of a population of 4 million ready to defend their nation. The fucking Nazis took the hint, deciding to leave Switzerland alone.

Not everything was heroic, however. The Swiss accepted 27,000 Jewish refugees during the war but, even though they knew such people faced certain death, turned away almost as many more with a "Sorry. We're full."

In Dungeons and Dragons alignment terms, more like "Neutral Evil."

wonder how Che Guevara would feel about gringo trust-fund teens using Mom's credit card to buy T-shirts with his face on it from Amazon. For good or ill, Che and his buddy Fidel were an inspiration to those far beyond the Cuban shores, and the anti-communist cockstains in the CIA were not fucking having it.

July 26 is a big day in Cuba. The Batista regime was corrupt as fuck. Fulgencio Batista had been *el presidente* of Cuba from 1940 to 1944, then again beginning in 1952. He wasn't just corrupt, but also weak. Pretty fucking useless, really. That's important. But rebel leader Fidel Castro and brother Raúl were kind of useless at the beginning as well. On that July day in 1953, a little after a year into Batista's second term, the brothers led a strike against two military targets in Cuba and got their asses kicked. The Castros fled to the mountains, while many of their fighters were captured and later executed. Oops.

Fidel Castro and his guerrilla fighters

A couple of years later Che joined the rebel cause, and they went guerrilla. They called themselves the "26th of July Movement" because I guess getting fucked-up on the field of battle is inspiring. Anyway, years of fighting blah fucking blah, President Batista had an unhappy New Year because he knew he was done for, so he fled the country in the early hours of January 1, 1959.

Now, to summarize my master's thesis in as few words as possible.

People in a whole bunch of other Latin American countries languishing under corrupt right-wing regimes saw what happened in Cuba and said cool fucking *frijoles*. Let's do what they did. And so, they tried, but the CIA was like "Commies bad! Truman Doctrine! Contain that shit!" and they started intervening all over to bolster various fascist military dictators so they wouldn't be overthrown by their rebel movements.

July 26, 1953

Here is the thing: It's not so much the strength of the rebellion that leads to revolution, but the weakness of the regime in power. A strong regime can withstand decades of rebellion, even against a powerful insurgency. But the Batista regime was as weak as a kitten with long Covid. My thesis argued that the post-Cuba CIA interventions didn't really matter, because all those other Latin American countries had regimes strong enough to withstand their rebel movements from overthrowing them without CIA help. All but one: Guatemala.

The Guatemalan regime in the early '60s was Batista-like in its utter uselessness, and therefore ripe for revolution. Then the CIA came in and said quit fucking around and gave them money and guns and advisers and shit, so the rebels never stood a chance.

Didn't stop them from trying, though. Lotta genocide followed.

"**T**he sadness** will last forever." Those were the final words of Dutch Post-Impressionist painter Vincent van Gogh when he died at thirty-seven. He suffered through his life not just from mental illness, but poverty, malnutrition, alcoholism, and insomnia. His tortured genius made it onto over two thousand works of art, but he would not see commercial success in his short life.

July 27, 1890

Van Gogh was born to an upper-middle-class family and was fond of drawing as a child, but would always struggle as an adult. He drifted across Europe as a traveling art dealer, spent time as a Protestant missionary, and eventually moved back in with his parents and was supported by his younger brother after being such a financial failure.

In 1886 he moved to Paris, where he met and became friends and roommates with fellow artist Paul Gauguin, who influenced Vincent's work. The story of the ear is that he had a fight with Gauguin with a razor, and in a rage severed off part of his own left ear.

There has been both armchair psychiatry and fierce medical debate about Van Gogh's mental health. He has been posthumously "diagnosed" with everything from bipolar disorder to epilepsy to schizophrenia to syphilis to fucking sunstroke. He was subject to psychotic episodes and delusions. He forgot to eat and sleep, he drank heavily—being a big fan of absinthe—and ignored both his physical and mental health.

One indication of the artist having bipolar disorder is that most of Van Gogh's massive amount of work was done in the final two years of his life; he painted constantly, obsessively focused on his art, possibly due to being in a manic phase. Research has also shown a link between BD and creativity. It is a common disorder that has affected and still affects many artists, including Kurt Cobain, Demi Lovato, Nina Simone, Catherine Zeta-Jones, Russell Brand, Carrie Fisher, Jimi Hendrix, Sting, Kanye, Mariah Carey, and possibly Edgar Allen Poe.

The contribution of bipolar disorder to suicidal behavior is considerable. On July 27, 1890, life became too much for Vincent to endure. Although some claim he was murdered, it is generally accepted that he shot himself in the chest with a revolver and died two days later.

> **He has been posthumously "diagnosed" with everything from bipolar disorder to epilepsy to schizophrenia to syphilis to fucking sunstroke.**

On an episode of *The Simpsons,* for the 1984 Summer Olympics in Los Angeles, Krusty the Clown did a promotion that promised a free Krusty Burger when America won a gold medal in an event revealed on a scratch card. It was rigged because all the events were ones that "communists never lose." But then the Soviet Union and fourteen Eastern Bloc countries and allies decided not to play.

It was biting satire, because it's pretty much exactly what happened to McDonald's with its catastrophic 1984 Summer Olympics promotion. The Soviets decided it was payback time for the Americans (and dozens of their Western allies) who had boycotted the 1980 Summer Olympic Games in Moscow.

The 1980 boycott of the Moscow games was in protest to the USSR invading Afghanistan. In 1984, with the hawkish Ronald Reagan occupying the Oval Office, the Soviets said they feared for the safety of their athletes. There weren't legitimate security concerns, but that's why the USSR said they weren't coming, alleging "anti-Soviet hysteria." Most of the world saw the 1984 boycott for what it was: retaliation for 1980. Reagan tried to be accommodating in order to get the Soviets and Eastern Bloc to attend, but the USSR announced their boycott on May 8, three months before the games began. Other Warsaw Pact countries soon followed suit. Then other communist nations such as Mongolia, Laos, Vietnam, North Korea, and Cuba all said yeah fuck those capitalist pigs we're out too. Cuba's absence would be felt especially in baseball and boxing.

Although both boycotts were reflective of Cold War power politics, China said game on, muthafuckas, and decided to make an appearance. They'd split with the Soviet Union in 1961 over disagreements on how to do communism, and China likes winning Olympic medals and, having been part of the 1980 boycott, didn't want to miss out a second time.

The games opened on July 28, 1984, with some of the most competitive (and often pharmaceutically enhanced) athletes in the world sitting out. The 1984 games are considered the most financially successful of the modern Olympics, actually generating a profit. But from a competitive standpoint, a lot of gold medalists had to wonder if they truly were the best in the world that year.

Romania, despite being part of the Eastern Bloc, said fuck the Soviets and showed up anyway, coming in second place in the overall medal count, their most successful Olympics ever. That same summer, the USSR hosted the "Friendship Games" as an alternate competition for the Soviets and eight other boycotting nations.

People who love free Big Macs won big too.

I **n 2011,** I interviewed drummer Neil Peart for the *Los Angeles Times* and thought, *What a nice guy.* In 1974, the founders of the rock band Rush met Neil Peart when he auditioned for them and at first they thought, *What a weird guy.* He still got the job, and music history was made, changing the spirit of radio for decades to come.

July 29, 1974

To get the story of Peart's audition, I talked to the band's guitarist Alex Lifeson. Alex formed Rush in 1968 in Toronto with neighbor John Rutsey on drums; Lifeson's best friend, Geddy Lee, joined as bassist and singer a short time later. By 1974, with help from Cleveland radio DJ Donna Halper playing their music, Rush had a U.S. record deal and an American tour booked. But Rutsey's health wouldn't allow for the rigors of touring; the band needed to find a replacement, fast. Late in July of 1974 they auditioned three drummers; Neil was second. "We felt an obligation to audition the third guy," Alex told me. "We were being polite. We had already decided that Neil was absolutely the guy."

Sarcastically, Alex referred to himself and Geddy as "hip and cool" with waist-length hair and satin pants. Neil showed up driving his mom's Pinto. "He was a very nerdy-looking guy with short hair," Lifeson said. "But when he set up his drums and started playing, we were just blown away." The connection went beyond Peart's drumming prowess. "He arrived at noon and stayed until eleven at night and we just jammed

and then sat around, and we talked and laughed a lot. That was the thing that stood out, that we had camaraderie. We talked about books and social issues and then we'd jam for another hour then maybe smoke a joint and talk about more stuff. It was just an instant connection with him." Geddy Lee turned twenty-one on July 29, 1974. For a gift, he got a new band member.

At the time, Alex didn't understand how much Neil's joining would change the direction of Rush. "We were just excited to be on tour in America," he said. "It wasn't until we started writing material for *Fly by Night* [Rush's second album, the first with Neil] a couple months after he joined" that Lifeson realized the band was on a different path. That album, Alex explained, was written using acoustic guitars in the backs of cars. He described Neil as "very intelligent and well read" and so he was given the job of penning lyrics while they composed the tunes "bounding down highways on the way to the next gig."

"Our beginnings were bands like Cream and Zeppelin, but we wanted to grow out of that," Lifeson told me. "We wanted our own identity. I don't think that really happened until *2112* [the band's third album with Peart] that we felt we were our own band." The record company wasn't impressed with the previous two albums and told Rush to write some hits, but the band went in the opposite direction with *2112*, deciding to go down in a "blaze of glory," creating a dystopian-future-themed album that was not at all radio-friendly. And yet, word of mouth made the 1976 release into a massive seller.

Despite critics regularly excoriating the band, opining that Geddy Lee's voice sounded like "a cat being chased out the door with a blowtorch up its ass" and declaring Neil's lyrics "smug, hypocritical, pseudo-symbolic drivel," Rush would be awarded fourteen platinum and three multi-platinum albums in the United States, and was inducted into the Rock & Roll Hall of Fame in 2013. Their lasting legacy has been their influence on other bands, inspiring acts such as Foo Fighters, Nine Inch Nails, Rage Against the Machine, Smashing Pumpkins, and Metallica. Peart is considered one of the greatest rock drummers of all time, a drummer's drummer. Dave Grohl said of him, "His power, precision, and composition was incomparable. He was called 'The Professor' for a reason: We all learned from him."

Rush never stopped innovating in their music. "Neil was a great catalyst for that," Alex said. "He always had such a vision for the future." Neil Peart died of glioblastoma on January 7, 2020.

Neal Peart in 1977

Most kids, when they learn what "defenestrate" means, have a reaction of "Why do they need a word for that?" combined with "Haha, that's funny." As it turns out, defenestration—the throwing of a person from a window—has a rich history. The Czechs were big fans, doing it a few times in Prague between the fifteenth and seventeenth centuries. In the first one they chose a window quite high from the ground and attained the expected results of icky ground splatter. But there were additional consequences.

July 30, 1419

In 1415, Jan Hus, an influential Czech theologian and Church reformer, was burned at the stake because the Church don't need no reformin'. His followers, Hussites, were vexed. There was much discontent among Hussites because of the inequalities between Church leaders and the nobility, and the peasantry. Eventually they got pissed enough that on July 30, 1419, a crowd of Hussites marched to the town hall in Prague. Supposedly the Hussite priest leading the group was hit with a rock thrown from a window of the town hall, and it gave everyone a grand fucking idea.

They stormed into the building and threw the judge, the chief magistrate, and several members of the town council from the top window. They died, because those kinds of

Location of the First Defenestration of Prague

Czechs don't bounce. Mass death by defenestrating mob was now a thing. So was the civil war it started. Many more deaths came during the Hussite Wars, which would last for seventeen years.

Then the group did it again in 1483, except it was more symbolic, because the Prague politicians they were pissed at had already been killed in a coup, so they threw their corpses out a window as an additional fuck-you.

In 1618 was the Third Defenestration of Prague. Sometimes it gets called the second one, cuz throwing dead bodies doesn't count, or some shit. Anyway, it's the 1618 one, and it was a gooder. Although I guess that depends on your perspective.

In 1618 plenty of people were getting into this Protestantism thing that'd begun a century earlier when Martin Luther nailed a list to a church door of ninety-five reasons why the Catholic Church can fuck all the way off. The Protestants and Catholics in Prague weren't getting along so well, and some Protestants threw a bunch of Catholic governors out of the windows of Prague Castle and took over the government. None of them died, because they landed in a big soft pile of poo. Well, Catholics said they were saved by angels, but having their falls broken by a massive dung heap sounds more probable.

Anyway, that third bit of defenestration initiated the Thirty Years' War, in which 8 million people died. Fun times!

You know how you can go on Twitter, call some high-ranking politician a semi-sentient sack of otter snot, and then *not* go to jail? Relish that freedom. Historically speaking, it's a new thing.

Daniel Defoe, who wrote *Robinson Crusoe,* was a prolific English writer who dared to publicly insult the authorities in 1703, and they didn't take kindly to it.

Sixteen years prior to the publication of *Robinson Crusoe,* which is second only to the Bible in terms of number of translations, Defoe was a shill for the government. He was paid to write in praise of the administration, which was a practice admired about as much then as it is now. But unlike many mouthpieces, he played both sides. Where he got himself in trouble was the anonymous authoring of a satirical pamphlet titled *The Shortest Way with the Dissenters.*

The political situation at the time was one of upheaval. Queen Anne had recently ascended the English throne, and she launched attacks on "Nonconformists": Protestants who dissented with the established Church of England, including Presbyterians, Baptists, Calvinists, Methodists, Quakers, and others.

Defoe's satirical piece was written from the perspective of a High Anglican zealot. Intended as mockery, it declared that dissenters should be banished abroad, and their preachers hanged. Neither the authorities nor the dissenters were amused, an investigation was launched, and Defoe was discovered as the author. He went into hiding and wrote a "Hey, I was just kidding" pamphlet, but that didn't satisfy the crown. He was betrayed for the reward and part of his punishment for having been found guilty of "seditious libel" involved an hour a day in the pillory, for three days, beginning on July 31, 1703.

July 31, 1703

A pillory is that thing where you're locked in public with head and hands exposed so people can throw nasty shit at you. According to legend, the audience instead threw flowers. Defoe was then sent off to prison and couldn't pay his fine, so the First Earl of Oxford paid it for him in exchange for Defoe becoming a spy working against the earl's political opponents.

> **A pillory is that thing where you're locked in public with head and hands exposed so people can throw nasty shit at you. According to legend, the audience instead threw flowers.**

August

Remember when the *M* in MTV stood for "Music" and wasn't all Teen Jersey Catfish Mom "reality" crap? Pepperidge Farm remembers. Yet the station wasn't just about music, but how good you looked performing that music.

Despite numerous proclamations to the contrary, Christopher Cross, while not being a bassist–for–Duran Duran pretty boy, is NOT the radio star that video killed. Balding and portly, Cross didn't fit well with the new music medium and came to epitomize "MTV killed my career." Except it didn't. Cross's "Sailing" hit #1 on the *Billboard* Hot 100 in the summer of 1980 and won three Grammys the following year. And his "Arthur's Theme" also hit #1 and even won a fucking Oscar for Best Original Song in 1981. The song "Video Killed the Radio Star" seemed to be about the death of Cross's career, but it was first recorded by Bruce Woolley and the Camera Club in 1979, so unless they had a time machine . . .

Anyway, on August 1, 1981, MTV launched at 12:01 A.M. Eastern Time, and its first-ever video was a cover of "Video" by a British synth-pop band called the Buggles. It's worth noting that the Buggles' keyboardist, Geoffrey Downs, was a co-writer of the original song.

MTV wasn't carried everywhere, but where it was, it had an effect on music sales. Songs that didn't get radio play but were on MTV experienced rising sales-demand in record stores. There wasn't a plethora of American music videos yet, but the Brits had been making them for years and got lots of MTV airtime. The station was credited with launching the "Second British Invasion"—the musical variety; I've lost count of how many military/colonizing ones there were—by creating U.S. demand for bands such as the Human League, Billy Idol, Culture Club, Bonnie Tyler, Duran Duran, and people getting A Flock of Seagulls–style haircuts.

August 1, 1981

Early on, the station was criticized for its lack of inclusion of Black performers; there were only a select few getting limited play, including Michael Jackson, Donna Summer, and Prince. The success of Jackson's *Thriller* album helped "break the color barrier"—the one MTV had erected in the first place—leading to more airtime for Black artists. Although traditionally designed as a pop-rock station, MTV did begin to play rap and hip-hop as it emerged in the mid-'80s.

I heard "Sailing" on the radio a while ago and thought it hot garbage. Cross's debut album may have been a huge hit at a time when people thought yacht rock was cool, but afterward he languished in obscurity with all his follow-up efforts, and I don't think it can be blamed on his drunk-uncle looks. In the '80s, Phil Collins looked more like your friend's dad who sold life insurance than he did a cover–of–*Tiger Beat* heartthrob, and yet he dominated both MTV and radio for much of the decade.

Video didn't kill Cross's radio star, sucking did.

You know that "Find someone who looks at you the way . . ." meme? Fuck that. Find someone who, if you are murdered, will sell all their possessions to fund a mercenary fleet bent on revenge. Such is the story of Jeanne de Clisson, who swore vengeance upon the King of France for killing her husband, and turned murderous pirate.

August 2, 1343

Born in 1300 in western France to a noble family, Jeanne was married at twelve to nineteen-year-old Geoffrey and bore two children. After fourteen years of marriage, Geoffrey died, and she married a wealthy Breton named Olivier four years later. They had five children together. After eleven years of marriage to Olivier, the Breton War of Succession between the English and French began. Jeanne and Olivier sided with the French in favor of Charles de Blois as Duke of Breton.

Then, fuckery.

Olivier was a military commander defending the town of Vannes during the war, which was taken by the English in 1342. He was the only one ransomed free, for a surprisingly low sum, which led to de Blois alleging Olivier was a traitor.

The following year a truce was signed. Olivier and several other Breton lords were invited to a tournament on French soil, but King Philip VI violated the truce and had Olivier arrested. On August 2, 1343, with little evidence of treason, Jeanne's husband was found guilty, beheaded, and his corpse displayed in a grotesque fashion reserved for common criminals.

Jeanne was fucking pissed.

She sold everything, which was a lot, and used the funds to raise a force to attack the French in Brittany, a peninsula on the west coast of France. One such attack was against a garrison of de Blois's—her husband's accuser—where all but one was massacred. The survivor was purposefully left alive to tell the tale and spread fear.

With help from the English king, Jeanne outfitted three warships, the flagship being named *My Revenge*. She would hunt French ships and kill all aboard except a few witnesses to inform King Philip of what she'd done. For thirteen years she was a feared pirate in the English Channel, attacking not only French ships but towns in Normandy, putting them to the sword. Her viciousness earned her the nickname "Lioness of Brittany."

At the age of fifty-six she decided she'd had enough, married an English knight, and settled in Brittany for her remaining years.

Find someone who, if you are murdered, will sell all their possessions to fund a mercenary fleet bent on revenge.

Some consider athletes to be heroes; others believe them overpaid jocks; I think it depends. Historically, one of the greatest sports heroes ever was Jesse Owens, who issued a giant fuck-you to Hitler by winning four gold medals in the Berlin Olympics.

Fucking Hitler. What a piece of shit. He took over Germany in 1933 and wanted the 1936 Olympic Games to be a testament to the superiority of his nation and his race, because *that* is what the games are really supposed to be about. That dumbfuck fascist even hurt Germany's chances for medals by refusing to allow Jewish athletes, such as the high jump record–holding Gretel Bergmann, to participate.

Owens was already a track star leading up to the games; the previous year at the Big Ten meet in Michigan, in a period of only forty-five minutes, he set three world records and tied for a fourth. The United States almost boycotted the games, because fucking Nazis. I'm glad they didn't, because fuck Nazis.

On August 3 in the 1936 games, Owens won gold in the 100-meter dash. Then he went on to win the 200-meter dash, the 4 x 100-meter relay, and the long jump. He was the first American to win four gold track-and-field medals in an Olympics, a record not matched until 1984 by Carl Lewis, who did so in the same four events.

But it's not all a happy story. While Owens was the star of the games and stole the spotlight from *der fuckface führer,* Germany did take more medals than any other country, which was a big propaganda win for the Nazis, especially when you consider that these were the first-ever Olympics to be televised internationally. And then America, which was and is racist as fuck, screwed over Owens.

Jesse Owens winning gold in the long jump in the 1936 Olympic Games

August 3, 1936

The entire U.S. team was invited to compete in Sweden after the games, but Owens skipped that to return to America to take advantage of promised endorsements. Being Black, he had not qualified for athletic scholarships and instead had to work rather than attend school while training. The United States retaliated by yanking his amateur status, ending his athletic career.

The commercial opportunities didn't materialize in the harsh reality of being Black in America, and he was forced to take on menial jobs and race against horses for cash. Things turned around for Owens in the '50s when the United States appointed him a goodwill ambassador.

Additional acknowledgment must go to Ralph Metcalfe, a Black man who was Owens's teammate and friend. Metcalfe took silver in Berlin in the 100-meter dash that Owens won. Ralph went on to serve four terms in the United States Congress.

She was a fifteen-year-old Jewish girl, and she almost survived the war. Almost.

We know Anne Frank because of her diary, but there were so many others just like her. Girls and boys and men and women with lives and dreams cut short because many of their fellow humans saw them as less than.

August 4, 1944

Anne was born in Frankfurt, Germany, in 1929; her family relocated to Amsterdam in the Netherlands after Hitler's rise to power in 1933. Seven years later, the Nazi war machine steamrolled over the Dutch forces in four days, occupying the country. The family's flight from the Nazi regime had only delayed the horror.

The Franks tried to immigrate to the United States to escape the coming atrocities, but those efforts proved futile due in no small part to the United States being reluctant to accept Jewish immigrants because, well, they were assholes about the whole thing.

At first, there was segregation of Jews in the Netherlands, but before long came the deportations to concentration camps. On June 12, 1942, Anne received a blank book meant for autographs for her thirteenth birthday. It had a small lock on the front, and she decided to use it as a diary instead, with her first entry being on June 20. Sixteen days later Anne, her father Otto, her mother Edith, and her older sister Margot went into hiding in a secret annex above the company where Otto worked, aided by his most trusted employees.

The Frank family had left its apartment in disarray, along with a note, to make it appear they had fled to Switzerland. They had to leave Anne's cat, Moortje, behind, asking the neighbors to look after it. Soon after going into hiding the Franks were joined by the Van Pels, a Jewish family of three, and in the fall by a Jewish dentist named Fritz Pfeffer, making for eight people living in the cramped space for the next two years.

Anne passed the time by writing in her diary. She also kept up with her schoolwork, dreaming of being a journalist. Her final entry in the diary was on August 1, 1944.

It is uncertain who betrayed the family, but on August 4, 1944, the Gestapo raided the hiding place, and all were arrested and deported to Auschwitz. That fall Anne was relocated to the Bergen-Belsen concentration camp, where she died the following spring (probably from typhus), only a couple of months before the end of the war.

Anne's father, Otto, was the only one to survive. He found that his secretary had kept Anne's diary safe, and he saw it published in 1947.

Anne Frank

Ugh. Puritans. If you ever wondered why Americans are so damn hung up about sex, these folks had a lot to do with it. Don't wax poetic about the *Mayflower* traveling to America, because that was the Puritan invasion.

History now refers to the Puritans arriving in America—aka the New World that was just the regular world to millions of Native Americans for multiple millennia, but it's new to us and we're gonna fucking steal it—as "Pilgrims" who began the Plymouth Rock colony. But before they began with the land-stealing, they were being assholes back home in England, although I guess that interpretation depends on your perspective.

In the sixteenth century the English Reformation happened, which was the Church of England saying fuck you and adios to the Roman Catholic Church. The Puritans saw that and said, "Not fucking good enough" and broke away from the established church even further. They wanted to be even more "pure" in their worship of a book that was compiled and edited by a bunch of dudes in funny hats thirteen centuries previous.

Anyway, the Puritans weren't real popular in England, so many decided to fuck off to Holland first, and then to America, because who wouldn't want a bunch of colorless cocks taking over their continent? It was on August 5, 1620, that the *Mayflower* departed for America. But then, well, fuck. That stupid other boat with them, *Speedwell,* sprang a leak and they had to turn back almost immediately. They sailed again, another leak, and finally a fuck this and the *Mayflower* left

them behind, departing with 102 passengers and 30 crew. They spent a grueling ten weeks at sea before making landfall at the tip of Cape Cod.

August 5, 1620

They considered this their "Promised Land," but the land was all "Fuck you, have some winter." And half of them died before spring arrived. The local Native peoples taught the colonists food gathering and other survival skills, without which they all would have gone on to the Great Certainty the next winter. The following fall they celebrated the first harvest with the Native Americans via a massive feast, followed by the men unbuttoning whatever the seventeenth-century version of pants was as they slipped into a turkey coma while the women did all the cleanup muttering *motherfucker motherfucker motherfucker . . .*

As for the sex stuff, the Puritans loved and encouraged it, so long as it was within the confines of a heterosexual marriage. As colonization/genocide expanded, the Puritans were extremely influential on American culture and values, which is why so many see monogamous heterosexual intercourse solely between married couples as the only right and proper way to bump uglies.

You've heard of that icky purity culture and purity balls and purity rings bullshit? The Puritan influence on people's sex lives still dominates much of American society.

On **August 6, 1945,** for the first time ever, a nuclear weapon was used to vaporize a city filled with human beings. Many rationalizations have been made for doing so, but anyone who understands a modicum of American history shouldn't be surprised at the nation's willingness to commit such an atrocity.

August 6, 1945

The simplistic argument has been often presented that the use of the bombs saved lives, and perhaps they did. Many numbers have been thrown around over time, and they've grown in the telling. The basic argument is that nuking Hiroshima and Nagasaki—and killing a couple hundred thousand people in the process—brought a quick end to World War II, thereby removing the need for an amphibious invasion of the Japanese home islands, which allegedly would have cost significantly higher numbers of American and Japanese lives than were lost via the atomic bombings.

There is some logic to the argument, and the counterclaim that Japan was "ready to surrender anyway" is a subject of debate. Others contend that a naval blockade coupled with continued conventional bombing would have secured an unconditional surrender. Regardless, the decision to use nuclear weaponry on Japanese cities has another component that few know or understand. It involves the former Soviet Union.

The atomic mushroom clouds over Hiroshima (left) and Nagasaki (right)

> **If the United States could use their new fission-kaboom playthings to end the war quickly without Soviet assistance, they could thereby prevent Russia from having postwar influence in how Japan was administered.**

The United States and Russia were tenuous allies during WWII due to a common enemy, Germany. Russia was obligated by the 1943 Tehran Conference to enter the war with Japan after Nazi Germany was defeated. Said defeat was accomplished two months before the first atomic weapon was tested at the Trinity site in the New Mexico desert on July 16, 1945. Under the desperate conditions of 1943, the United States welcomed help in defeating Japan, even from the USSR, but seeing that first-ever atomic mushroom cloud created new possibilities: If the United States could use their new fission-kaboom playthings to end the war quickly without Soviet assistance, they could thereby prevent Russia from having postwar influence in how Japan was administered.

There is more. It is likely the United States also wanted to show off her new toys. There *was* motivation to send a "You guys really need to unconditionally give up" kind of message to Japan, but also relevant was the desire to broadcast to the Soviet Union what the bombs could do.

There were a number of reasons why the target cities were chosen, but an important one for Hiroshima was that it was a "pristine" target; it had not been hit with conventional bombs prior to its August 6, 1945, destruction via the airburst detonation of a 15-kiloton uranium nuclear device nicknamed "Little Boy." (The 21-kiloton "Fat Man" dropped on Nagasaki three days later was a plutonium weapon.) Choosing Hiroshima meant the United States could both see for themselves *and* display to Russia the full destructive power of these new weapons as a big "Whaddya think of that, you commie fucks?" As you likely know, Russia thought, *Holy Jesus Fuck Farts! We need to have those too!*

And so, Soviet agents stole the technology from the Americans a few years later, and the nuclear arms race began.

Listen to the fucking science. That's what Canadian American physician/ pharmacologist Frances Oldham Kelsey said regarding thalidomide, preventing a disaster for countless children in the United States.

In 1960, Kelsey was hired by the FDA to review drugs. Thalidomide was one of her first assignments. You know how people new to a job, especially women in the patriarchal-as-hell 1960s, might be afraid of making waves? Frances said fuck that.

Thalidomide was being used as a tranquilizer and painkiller, and the manufacturer was pushing it as a treatment for pregnant women with morning sickness. It had already been approved for use in Canada and almost two dozen European and African countries. The drug's German manufacturer, Grünenthal, pressured her to approve the drug for use in the United States, but she was concerned about it crossing the placental barrier, an area Kelsey had expertise in due to her previous work with malaria drugs.

And so, she told the company she needed more data to show the drug would not be harmful to the fetus of anyone who took it. This critical delay caused by Kelsey demanding further studies allowed time to see the horrifying effects of the drug in countries where it had been approved. Her instinct to withhold approval was correct, because the drug *did* cross the placental barrier and caused myriad serious birth defects.

It was estimated that approximately 10,000 people were affected by their mothers taking thalidomide, of which roughly 40 percent died at birth. The effects on those who survived included limb deformities, as well as problems with the heart, eyes, and urinary tract.

Kelsey was celebrated on the front page of *The Washington Post* for her tough stance. She said that her assistants and supervisors deserved credit for backing her up in her refusal to approve the drug. On August 7, 1962, she was awarded the President's Award for Distinguished Federal Civilian Service by John F. Kennedy.

Frances Oldham Kelsey with President Kennedy in 1962

"**O**urs is not a drive for power, but purely a non-violent fight for India's independence." These were the words of Mahatma Gandhi, given as part of his "Quit India" speech on August 8, 1942, in Bombay to the All-India Congress Committee. He explained that "a non-violent soldier of freedom will covet nothing for himself, he fights only for the freedom of his country."

Humans are shitty. It happens over and over that there are shitty leaders, and people look at them and say, "Those leaders are shitty. Let's fuck them up." And so, they violently overthrow those shitty leaders. And then once the overthrowers assume power, they start to behave in the same shitty way toward those they now rule as a method of maintaining their newfound power.

Gandhi knew that. He added in his speech that "the power, when it comes, will belong to the people of India." Too bad the caste system still exists.

India had been subject to the whims of Europeans since not long after Portuguese sailor Vasco da Gama first reached it in 1498 by sailing around the southern tip of Africa. Various European powers fought over the subcontinent for centuries, with Britain gaining dominance in the middle of the

nineteenth century. It was referred to as "the jewel in the British crown."

Gandhi's speech initiated a mass protest demanding what he called an orderly withdrawal of the British. He extolled that people should not hate the British, but only hate their imperialism. It's important to note that this was during the height of World War II. With its proximity to Japan, which was currently running rampant across the region, Gandhi feared India could end up exchanging one form of imperialism for another.

The British reaction was to imprison almost the entire Indian National Congress within hours of Gandhi's speech. There were many Indians who profited from British rule and were willing to help them maintain it. But there was support for change from the United States; President Roosevelt pressured Prime Minister Churchill to give in to some of the Indian demands.

The British weren't interested. They crushed the Quit India movement, basically saying, "Do fuck off. We're fighting a war." Two years after the war ended, in 1947, independence finally came to the region, but the process was not nonviolent, as the country was partitioned along religious lines between India and Pakistan, a controversial decision that Gandhi opposed. Millions were displaced, and several hundred thousand died. It is also estimated that 100,000 women were kidnapped and raped during this time.

Gandhi did not celebrate the independence, but rather spent all his efforts in appealing for peace.

Mahatma Gandhi (right) and Jawaharlal Nehru discussing Quit India; Nehru would later become India's first prime minister

Small spoiler warning for the 2019 film *Once Upon a Time in Hollywood*. It has a way happier ending than what really took place when members of the "Manson Family" murdered five people, including very pregnant actress Sharon Tate. Had Tarantino's vision been reality, there would have been no murders that night, or the following night.

August 9, 1969

What happened in the early morning hours of August 9, 1969, has dominated popular culture, but much less is known about the murders of the next night.

Cult leader Charles Manson, who wasn't there on August 9, thought his followers had done a shit job of the Tate murders; he was apparently displeased with how panicked the massacre had been. And so, he led them the next night "to show them how to do it."

He took the murderers from the previous evening, plus two other members of his fucked-up cult. The location chosen was fairly random. Manson had attended a house party on Waverly Drive the previous year and took them to the house next door. Inside were Leno and Rosemary LaBianca, owners of a grocery store chain. Their sixteen-year-old son Frank was supposed to be at home with his parents that fateful evening, but he'd been vacationing with friends at Lake Isabella and was having such a good time he asked to stay an extra night.

The news of the grisly Tate killings was all over Los Angeles, but the LaBiancas likely never imagined they could be next. Manson and his followers entered the home through an unlocked back door. Rosemary was already in bed; Leno dozed in a recliner in the living room; he was awakened when Manson shoved a gun in his face.

Manson brought Rosemary out from their bedroom and demanded all their cash, promising them they wouldn't be harmed. The murderers then tied them both up. With the LaBiancas still alive, Manson got in the getaway car and left the scene with three of his followers, leaving the other three behind to commit the murders and hitchhike home.

Which they did. It was horrible. Google the details if you must.

The LaBiancas are often referred to as "the forgotten murders."

> **The news of the grisly Tate killings was all over Los Angeles, but the LaBiancas likely never imagined they could be next.**

Oh, fuck. Oh, fuck! Oh, FUCK! Oh fucking fuck fuck. Oh Jesus Mother Christ fuck. Oh fucking shit we're so fucked fuck. Oh fuck I never even got the chance to fuck anyone fuck.

That's what I imagine the sailors of the Swedish warship *Vasa* were saying when it sank a mere twenty minutes into its maiden voyage. Oops.

King of Sweden Gustavus Adolphus was at war with Poland-Lithuania and launched a military expansion to meet the threat. The *Vasa* was built by private entrepreneurs beginning in 1626, and she was a beautiful clusterfuck of a ship. Richly decorated and heavily armored with sixty-four bronze cannons, *Vasa* had one of the greatest offensive capabilities of any ship of the time. She was also top-heavy as shit, making her dangerously unstable.

The Swedish king was in Poland at the time, demanding that his new flagship set sail to help in the war effort. The peons back home were reluctant to say, "Uh, King Gus, this ship might have some issues . . ."

And so, on August 10, 1628, *Vasa* set sail just south of Stockholm. The day had a light breeze. The gun ports were open to fire a sa-lute honoring the maiden voyage. But as the ship left the lee of the bluffs, a strong gust of wind filled her sails and the *Vasa* heeled rapidly to port. The sailors acted quickly to cast off the lines holding the sails (called sheets), and the ship righted. But a short time later an even stronger gust hit the sails, the ship heeled even more onto its port side, and the open gun ports submerged.

August 10, 1628

That's bad.

Water rushed into the gun deck, down into the hold, and the ship quickly sank in water a hundred feet deep, a mere four hundred feet from shore. The upper masts were still above the water, which survivors clung to. Ships were quickly dispatched in a rescue effort, but thirty sailors died in the sinking.

A crowd of several hundred people watched the debacle unfold. Upon learning what happened the king was, of course, ever so pissed. There was an inquiry, but no one was punished. The ship was recovered in 1961 and preserved as a museum. Today, it is the most visited museum in all Scandinavia.

'm not Austrian, so I didn't realize that Hedwig is something people would name a baby girl. I mean, a *Harry Potter* owl? Sure. But your daughter? Anyway, this Hedwig's last name was Kiesler, and she changed both first and last to become Hedy Lamarr: talented actress and brilliant inventor who helped develop a radio technology to guide Allied torpedoes to hit their targets.

August 11, 1942

Born and raised Jewish in Austria, she left a possessive husband in 1937 for Hollywood, and helped her mother escape to the United States the following year when the fucking Nazis annexed her homeland. Lamarr had been trained and worked as an actress in Europe, and soon found fame in America with MGM Studios head Louis Mayer promoting her as the "world's most beautiful woman."

Hedy Lamarr in 1944

She quickly became a big star, but fame wasn't something she embraced. It was reported that when asked for an autograph, she couldn't understand why someone would want it. To Hedy, her most interesting work was as an inventor. Despite having no formal training, she'd inherited a love of understanding technology from her father. While she dated business magnate Howard

Hughes, he encouraged her "tinkering" and made his scientists and engineers available to make anything she asked.

During the war, she learned of emerging radio technology that would help torpedoes hit their targets. But such technology was easy to jam by defenders. So Lamarr got to work with her friend George Antheil, a composer and pianist, to help develop a solution.

Together, they used a miniature player piano to synchronize radio signals to create FHSS, the frequency-hopping spread spectrum: a manner of sending radio signals that quickly changed frequency across a wide spectrum. The changes are known by a code in both the transmitter and the receiver, but not to eavesdroppers. The rapid hopping of frequencies prevented interference and interception. On August 11, 1942, the pair received a patent for their device.

At the time, it was difficult to implement, and the U.S. Navy wasn't keen on integrating technology that didn't come from inside the military. But a form of the technology was in use by the navy during the Cuban Missile Crisis in 1962. Today, a variety of spread-spectrum technologies are used in Bluetooth.

Hedy and George were posthumously inducted into the National Inventors Hall of Fame in 2014.

Do research on maternal death. Gather data. Compare data. Come up with a convincing hypothesis. Tell doctors to wash their hands. Get your ass fired. So much for the scientific method.

This is a story of two doctors. We'll begin with Hungarian Dr. Ignaz Semmelweis, who was working at a maternity clinic in Vienna in 1846. Back then, doctors still believed in air ghosts causing disease, or some equally stupid shit. Ignaz noticed that in the maternity ward where doctors delivered babies, there was *five times* the maternal death rate than when babies were delivered by midwives.

So, he compared several data points, ruling out all sorts of dumb shit like priests ringing bells, but when a colleague died from the same "childbed fever" the mothers were dying from, he got an idea. He realized that the doctors were doing autopsies, and the midwives weren't. He surmised there were cadaver particles present that were spreading disease.

He told doctors to wash their damn hands and instruments in a chlorine solution, and the death rate fell markedly. However, the doctors were miffed at being told *they* had been the ones causing maternal deaths. And Ignaz wasn't the easiest guy to get along with and was all JUST WASH YOUR FUCKING HANDS! Eventually he was fired, and the doctors went back to *not* washing their hands. Idiots.

Fast-forward nineteen years.

August 12, 1865

Joseph Lister was a British surgeon fascinated with reducing wound infections. Following the work of Louis Pasteur, he advocated the use of carbolic acid to sanitize instruments and wounds. In 1865, a seven-year-old boy suffered a compound fracture (that's when a bone breaks so bad it pops outside the skin—*ew*) when a cart wheel ran over his leg. On August 12, Lister worked on the boy at the Glasgow Royal Infirmary, and as part of his treatment sprayed his instruments, the wound opening, and the dressings in a solution of carbolic acid, having learned earlier that it was useful in preventing gangrene.

It was the first antiseptic surgery. Afterward, he was amazed at how well the wound had healed, and he went on to publish a series of six articles in *The Lancet* two years later documenting his results. It proved a turning point in the history of medicine, a critical juncture in the germ theory of medicine.

And if his name sounds familiar, it's where "Listerine" comes from.

Why is it that countries such as the "German Democratic Republic," aka the eastern part of Germany behind the Iron Curtain during the Cold War, felt the need to lie so blatantly by putting the word "Democratic" in their name? Looking at you, North Korea.

August 13, 1961

Anyway, it was East Germany that constructed the Berlin Wall, partially because leaders behind the Iron Curtain saw President Kennedy as weak and figured they could get away with it.

JFK was not a strong president, at first. He screwed the swine with the whole Bay of Pigs thing in April 1961—a U.S.-supported covert operation of Cuban exiles trying to overthrow Fidel Castro that failed miserably—and his reputation was hurting. Two months later at the Vienna summit, he met with Soviet leader Nikita Khrushchev and made the blunder of admitting that the United States wouldn't actively oppose the building of a wall. JFK further showed weakness by admitting to *The New York Times* that he'd fucked up by saying so. Sure, it's great to admit you made a mistake, but when you're jockeying for position with a brutal superpower dominated by an oppressive cockwaffle like Khrushchev (al-

An East German border guard leaps to freedom during construction of the Berlin Wall

though he wasn't near as bad as Stalin had been), revealing such weakness is inadvisable. It's what led to the Cuban Missile Crisis the following year.

German leader Walter Ulbricht was a good little commie, spending the Nazi years in exile. He was running East Germany in 1961, and in June of that year said, "You know what? I don't think we need a wall." Two months later he, along with Nikita, were both "Fuck it. Let's build that wall."

And so, they did.

At midnight on August 13, 1961, East German police and army closed the border between East and West Berlin, splitting families and friends apart, and construction of the wall began. In order to control it, the wall was built *inside* the East German border. It began with the stringing of many miles of barbed wire, but soon more permanent installations, including concrete walls and guard towers, were built to divide the city and the nation. The eastern PR campaign asserted that the wall protected them from western fascism.

Thousands successfully defected from east to west during the wall years using a variety of sneaky methods. Border guards were ordered to shoot all who attempted, even women and children. More than a hundred people were killed in attempted crossings between 1961 and November 9, 1989, when the wall finally fell.

There is only one uprising of enslaved people that led to the formation of a state that was not just free of slavery, but also ended up being ruled by former enslaved people and other non-whites. It is the nation of Haiti. The country's independence began with a Vodou ceremony.

Vodou is an African diasporic religion that began among slaves in Haiti in the sixteenth century. It evolved as a combination of West African religions merged with Roman Catholicism. Dutty Boukman was a man born in West Africa in 1767 who was captured and transported to Jamaica, then transferred to Haiti. While there, he became a Vodou *houngan* (priest). Alongside Vodou *mambo* (priestess) Cécile Fatiman, the daughter of an enslaved African woman and a white Frenchman, the two held a ceremony in a forest called Bois Caïman on the night of August 14, 1791, that was attended by about two hundred African enslaved people. It was at that ceremony the Haitian Revolution began.

Boukman prophesized that their fight would result in freeing them from slavery; Cécile sacrificed a pig said to have magical powers, and the attending enslaved people swore a pact in its blood that they would rise up and overthrow their white oppressors.

Many years of enslavement and brutal oppression had filled them with a hatred for whites. The revolt spread quickly and in a matter of days they had taken control of the entire northern province. The revolution was vicious, with the enslaved seeking revenge through rape, mutilation, and death. Within weeks, over 100,000 enslaved people had joined the uprising, making it the largest uprising of enslaved people since Spartacus in 73 B.C.E., and over the next two months they killed over 4,000 whites and burned over a thousand coffee and sugar plantations.

August 14, 1791

The surviving whites organized into a militia, fighting back and killing thousands of insurgents. One of those killed was Dutty Boukman. The French displayed his head in an effort to dispel his air of invincibility to the revolutionaries.

The war would rage for another dozen years, with both Spain and Britain getting involved. Jean-Jacques Dessalines, a Black French soldier who had become leader of the Haitian Revolution, declared Haiti a free republic on January 1, 1804, and immediately ordered a massacre of the remaining French in the country. Over the next few months soldiers went from house to house, torturing and killing entire families.

Dessalines made no apologies, saying he had saved his country and that "We have given these true cannibals war for war, crime for crime, outrage for outrage." The rebels' tenacity, along with their ability to organize and fight, filled many enslavers across the Americas with fear.

France, for its part, was a sore fucking loser. Haiti suffered political and economic isolation, and France, with warships ready to unleash hell, refused to recognize the country unless it paid the equivalent of $21 billion in reparations to former enslavers. That's right. France made former enslaved people pay their former slavers for the "crime" of freeing themselves. The payments had a devastating effect on the Haitian economy; they didn't finish paying off the debt until 1947.

Was Thomas Edison a dick? According to popular web comic *The Oatmeal* he was a giant dick, and not much of an inventor either, stealing ideas from others. The artist proclaimed Edison was a money-hungry motherfucker who profited from the labors of others. Historians tend to disagree with at least some of the comic, but there *is* one example of him plotting with Germans against the interest of the Allies in World War I. Because money.

It's called the "Great Phenol Plot." Technically, it wasn't against the law, but there was a cover-up, so it would seem Thomas Edison felt guilty about what he was engaged in. At the beginning of the war, most of the phenol in the United States was imported from Britain. The chemical has a number of uses, including for making acetylsalicylic acid, aka aspirin, as well as for making explodey things that create an Earth-shattering kaboom and can blow German soldiers into gooey bits raining down upon the Western Front.

What was Edison's role? He used a phenol-based plastic as the coating for the

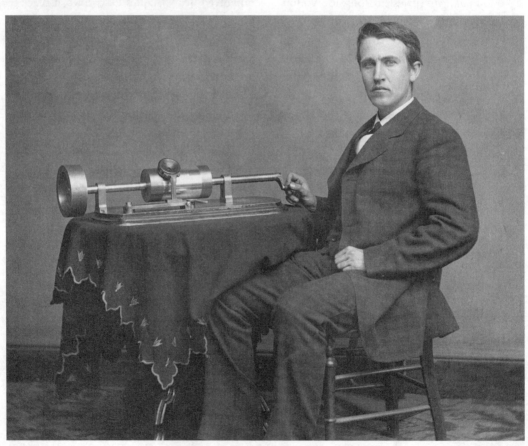

Thomas Edison with his early phonograph

manufacturing of his phonograph records. But by 1915, the British were all "Sorry, old chums, but we're afraid we can't be sending you any more phenol. Need it for sending those nasty Krauts off to German hell. Cheerio!" And Edison was all "Fuck. Records make me money, and I like money."

So, he began manufacturing the stuff himself. He made twelve tons of it a day.

The United States was neutral in the war at the time, although it was Ally-leaning, sending them lots of supplies, especially after a German U-boat sank the *Lusitania*. There were German agents in the United States tasked with undermining American industry. One of those agents was a former Bayer Pharmaceuticals employee named Hugo Schweitzer.

Bayer invented aspirin. Bayer needed phenol. Bayer is a German company. Britain sure as shit wasn't going to sell it to them, what with them being busy trying to kill the shit out of each other on the fields of France. So, Hugo set up a front company to funnel money from Germany and buy up a bunch of Edison's phenol—about three tons of the stuff a day.

Again, not illegal, but doing it in a secret and underhanded manner wouldn't look good. And when the U.S. Secret Service found a German agent's briefcase on a train containing details of the plot, they leaked the story to the press, which became front-page news on August 15, 1915. Both Bayer and Edison were humiliated, and public pressure ended the deal.

According to popular web comic *The Oatmeal* he was a giant dick, and not much of an inventor either, stealing ideas from others. The artist proclaimed Edison was a money-hungry motherfucker who profited from the labors of others.

There are myriad examples of humanity's ability to suck. One that often repeats is when a country is at war, and starts to run out of men, they send their children into battle.

Paraguay is a landlocked country in the middle of South America, and starting in 1864 it got itself into some deep shit with the beginning of the War of the Triple Alliance. Paraguay was in said excrement because it had no alliance. It was defending against countries on three sides: Brazil, Argentina, and Uruguay. It was the deadliest inter-state war in Latin American history, with the Paraguayans doing the majority of the dying.

Earlier in the nineteenth century the South American continent had fought for its independence from Spain and Portugal. Afterward, there were numerous territorial disputes between the various new nations. "This land is ours. That's the border." "No, THAT is the border. THIS is ours." "Says who?" "Says us." "Fuck you." "No, fuck *you*." Etc.

Anyway, the War of the Triple Alliance was about territory, and Paraguay, despite being a small country, had a significant military, but simply didn't have the numbers to win against the alliance. After five years of

> **"This land is ours. That's the border." "No, THAT is the border. THIS is ours." "Says who?" "Says us." "Fuck you." "No, fuck *you*." Etc.**

fighting, Paraguay was devastated and the capital city of Asunción was under enemy occupation, yet the Paraguayan president refused to yield. And so, on August 16, 1869, the nation sent her children to her defense at the Battle of Acosta Ñu.

The Paraguayan "force" of a mere 3,500 was poorly armed and mostly comprised boys aged nine to fifteen—many wearing false beards thinking it might frighten their opponents—along with some old men and injured soldiers. They faced 20,000 battle-hardened veterans of the Brazilian army.

Guess how that went.

The Brazilian commander, to his credit, told his emperor the war was militarily over and to let it go. The emperor wanted an official surrender, so he said fuck that kill them all. The commander resigned, and the emperor put his son-in-law in charge.

It wasn't a battle; it was a slaughter. Children clung to the legs of Brazilian soldiers, begging for mercy, only to be cut down. Many tried to flee, but the emperor's douche-in-law used his cavalry to cut off their retreat and set fire to the field, burning many of the children alive.

The war finally ended eight months later, with Paraguay having lost 40 percent of its territory. August 16 is commemorated as a national holiday in Paraguay, called Children's Day.

After Trump, getting a blowjob in the Oval Office doesn't seem like such a big deal. But two wrongs and all that. Bill Clinton has numerous allegations of sexual assault against him, and if he's guilty, he should absolutely go down. Go down. Heh. Anyway, in the case of Monica Lewinsky, it may have been "consensual," but it was also textbook sexual harassment.

He was forty-nine, she was twenty-two. No law against that. First issue is that he was and still is married. Hillary knew Bill had a wandering penis, and defended him, privately supporting the Clinton campaign's strategy of digging into the history of every accuser to discredit them. I don't believe it quite qualifies as "cheating" when she had his back like that. The issue is the constant falsehood, portraying him as a faithful leader unfairly maligned by lying whores.

Lewinsky was made to look like a lying whore.

In January of 1998, Bill went on TV and, while standing next to Hillary, said he "did not have sexual relations with that woman, Ms. Lewinsky." He also lied to a grand jury. That's where the "it depends on what the meaning of the word 'is' is" comes from. It's

what he was impeached for: perjury. The articles of impeachment were for *lying* about the blowjob, not receiving said fellatio.

August 17, 1998

The second issue is the sexual harassment. She was a White House intern; he was [checks notes] THE MOTHERFUCKING PRESIDENT! You're not supposed to do that. Imagine you're Monica, a young intern. How easy is it to say no when THE MOTHERFUCKING PRESIDENT wants a sexual relationship with you?

On August 17, 1998, Bill admitted he'd had an "improper physical relationship" with Monica Lewinsky that was "not appropriate." No fucking shit. I'm not going to say "to his credit" for coming clean, because fuck that guy. He lied about so much stuff and only told the truth because of the

> **She was a White House intern; he was [checks notes] THE MOTHERFUCKING PRESIDENT! You're not supposed to do that.**

blue dress with the Clinton DNA on it. FYI, "coming clean" is supposed to be an oxymoron. Moving on . . .

He bombed Afghanistan three days later. Just, you know, because.

The Nineteenth Amendment to the U.S. Constitution guaranteed women the right to vote. Mostly white women, that is. The suffrage movement was rife with racism; BIPOC women were left to fend for themselves. That's why it should not surprise you that a century after the amendment's ratification, roughly half of white female voters decided Trump deserved a second term.

August 18, 1920

Woman-suffragists had been struggling for the vote for many decades. Women were allowed to vote in certain states prior to 1920, but there was no national law to enforce it. World War I proved something of a turning point, as the National American Woman Suffrage Association (NAWSA) supported the American war effort and made the argument that it was hypocritical for the country to fight for democracy abroad yet deny it to half the population at home. The white half, I mean.

One argument made by suffragists involved stating the Fifteenth Amendment, ratified in 1870, demanded it. That amendment states voting rights cannot be denied "on account of race, color, or previous condition of servitude." They said being a woman, even a rich white one, qualified as servitude, but it didn't fly. In fact, it was debate over whether to support the Fifteenth Amendment that created a split along color lines in the suffrage movement; at the first-ever American Equal Rights Association convention in 1869, Elizabeth Cady Stanton and Susan B. Anthony made racist procla-

mations that Black men shouldn't get the vote before white women did.

In 1890, the aforementioned NAWSA came into being as a merging of two rival suffrage organizations. As the movement gained support, organizers came to the conclusion it could be even more popular, especially with Southern whites, if they punted the Black women and focused solely on getting the vote for white women. Mary Church Terrell, a Black woman, stayed within NAWSA to advocate for her people within the association, preaching strength through unity.

Lacking white support, in 1896 the National Association of Colored Women was formed as a merger of two other clubs at its first annual convention, where former enslaved woman and celebrated abolitionist Harriet Tubman was the keynote speaker. She and many other Black women would fight for decades to secure their voting rights. With the ratification of the Nineteenth Amendment on August 18, 1920, *all* women gained the right to vote, not just white women. But for most Black women the "right" was in name only. Loopholes in state constitutions prevented a whopping 75 percent of Black women from exercising this right. Black women were specifically targeted with long waiting lines, paying a head tax, undergoing tests, and being asked to interpret the Constitution before being allowed to register. In the South, it was also common for Black women to be physically attacked or thrown in jail for attempting to vote.

To this day, many American states use whatever methods possible to prevent Black women from voting.

Despite its prevalent beauty, unless you actually like oppressive theocracy, Iran ain't such a nice place to live.

As with so many other places, direct American interference in local politics did a lot to change the path of that nation for the worse. In this case, the hypocrisy was staggering, because the alleged pro-democracy U.S.A. overthrew a democratically elected prime minister to strengthen the power of the Iranian monarchy.

Didn't the United States come into being doing the *exact fucking opposite* of that? Isn't that the thing they're most proud of?

Mohammad Mosaddegh was elected prime minister of Iran in 1951 and implemented numerous social reforms, such as creating social security, land reforms, and striving to increase the power of the people over power held by the shah, the country's monarch. Where he really pissed off the West, however, was the nationalization of Iran's oil industry.

It's almost always about the fucking oil.

Mosaddegh wanted to limit the control that the British-owned Anglo-Iranian Oil Company (AIOC, which is now part of British Petroleum, those fucks who poisoned the Gulf of Mexico in 2010) had over Iranian oil reserves. The Brits wouldn't cooperate, so Iran said fuck you get out.

At the time, Clement Attlee was PM in Britain, and Truman was U.S. president. Ironically, the "Truman Doctrine" is about the containment of communism, but neither Atlee nor Truman favored direct military action, instead choosing to boycott Iranian oil. But then, good old Winston Churchill was back in as the British prime minister, and Eisenhower became president, and they saw what was going on in Iran and said, "Smells like some fucking commie bullshit," even though Mosaddegh certainly was no communist. He just wanted to better the lives of his people by fighting back against imperialism.

August 19, 1953

So, the United States struck a deal with the Brits. In exchange for helping with a coup d'état, the AIOC would end its monopoly and let American oil companies set up shop in Iran as well. The Brits agreed, and the CIA was unleashed to overthrow Mosaddegh on August 19, 1953, and put the shah back in as an authoritarian ruler, backed by well-bribed Iranian politicians and military brass, exacting a promise he'd be a good little boy to the Western capitalists.

It was the first such covert action by the United States—overthrowing a democratically elected regime during peacetime—but far from the last. Mosaddegh was arrested, sentenced to three years in prison, then spent the rest of his life under house arrest. Many of his supporters also received prison sentences, and several were put to death. Hundreds of others died in the coup.

Shah Mohammad Reza Pahlavi, viewed by many as an American puppet, would rule for another twenty-six years. The shah was overthrown by the Iranian Revolution in 1979, installing a new government that rules via religious tyranny.

AUGUST

247

Listen up you brainless, slack-jawed, truck-nutted, racist, shake-and-bake-meth-smoking, Confederate-flag-waving motherfuckers. You. Fucking. Lost. Asses kicked. Game fucking over. Traitorous troops capitulated. The official flag of the Confederacy forever shall be the waving white flag of "Please stop killing us we give up." Deal with it. Assholes.

August 20, 1866

Google "American Civil War" and the Wikipedia preview will tell you it went from April 12, 1861, to April 9, 1865. That is not entirely correct.

April 9 was the date the war "effectively ended" with the Ceasefire Agreement of the Confederacy commencing with the surrender of General Robert E. Lee, traitorous commander of the traitorous Confederate Army. But there were other traitors who kept on traitoring. It's a word.

The Confederacy didn't exist anymore, so every battle that took place afterward is considered a "postwar action." The last major land engagement was a month later, May 12–13, on the banks of the Rio Grande: the Battle of Palmito Ranch. The Union forces actually attacked the Confederates, possibly because the Union colonel, Theodore Barrett, had little field experience and wanted some of that kill-the-enemy glory for himself. But he actually lost the battle.

Multiple other surrenders followed after April 9 as word spread that Lee had given up, but one "commerce raider," the CSS *Shenandoah,* kept on capturing and/or sinking Union merchant vessels for another six months, finally surrendering on November 6, 1865. Some folks just didn't want to give up their glorious idea of the Traitorous States of Enslaving America.

But that slavery shit was still going on in Texas for many more months, because it was far south and it took a while for Union forces to arrive and lay down some law. Plenty of traitorous enslavers fled to Texas with those they enslaved as Union forces conquered the South, and there was much conflict between white and Black; the latter realized slavery was coming to an end elsewhere in the nation and resisted their continued bondage. Also, the Confederate authority had collapsed in the region yet Texas hadn't formed a new state government. By August 9, Texas finally got her shit together and formed a government with James Throckmorton, who had been a brigadier general for the Confederate army, as governor. *Finally,* on August 20, 1866, President Andrew Johnson proclaimed the *official* end to the Civil War, now that the Texas "insurrection is at an end and that peace, order, tranquility, and civil authority now exist in and throughout the whole of the United States of America."

Yeah, that was a crock of shit. But it was basically the final wrap-up. Too bad so many Confederate-flagged asspuddles have yet to get the goddamn memo. And the descendants of said asspuddles are still holding sway in the state; their school-approved history books are so whitewashed they belong in the fantasy section of the library.

My son and I are close, so I don't think he'd wage war on me to steal away my three-bedroom suburban empire and my fleet of two very used Japanese vehicles. Not so for King Stefan Uroš III of Serbia.

You know how in *Games of Thrones* Theon Greyjoy was kept as a hostage by Ned Stark? Keeping the child of a vanquished enemy to ensure the latter's good behavior was a common thing in history. Born in 1276, as a youth King Uroš III's name was Stefan Dečanski and he was sent by his father to live with Nogai Khan, a Turkish ruler, to maintain peace between the Turks and the Serbs. He stayed with them until he was twenty-three.

Like in *Game of Thrones,* his return home was less than glorious. He and his dad didn't get along that well, and in 1314 Dečanski and his dad had a fight and dear old dad exiled him to Constantinople with orders that he be blinded. The folks in Constantinople decided not to actually blind him. But still, dick move, Dad. Anyway, six years later his dad finally let Dečanski return home, and then Dad died the following year, in 1321, and Stefan Dečanski ascended the Serbian throne as Uroš III.

Considering his history, it may not surprise you that Dečanski's lack of a good fatherly role model impeded his ability to have a loving relationship with his own son, Stefan Dušan. After nine years of reign, Dečanski was involved in a war with the Byzantine Empire. In 1330 the Serbian forces had a decisive victory in the Battle of Velbazhd. But then Dečanski said, "You know what? I think we're good. Let's hold here."

August 21, 1331

And that pissed some people off.

Many nobles were all "No. Fuck that. Keep going. Expand. Give us more territory. Fucking wimp." And those nobles started to look to his son Stefan Dušan and say we like him better. The nobles whispered in Dušan's ear, and advisers whispered in Dečanski's ear, and fearing his was son moving against him, Dečanski ordered the kid to be seized and excluded from his inheritance. But his son was ready for him, and there was a father-vs.-son civil war.

The son won, capturing his father on August 21, 1331. Dušan imprisoned his father and had him strangled to death three months later. Dušan was named Stefan Uroš IV and as the nobles who supported him wished, he did indeed wage more war against the Byzantine Empire, eventually coming to rule it in 1346.

You know those fragile-as-fuck rectal abscesses who need to open carry an assault rifle just to get a goddamn latte? The wannabe warriors in their "tacti-cool" gear and empty-head-to-toe camo strolling the aisles of the Walmart battlefield? America's modern militia movement was born at Ruby Ridge.

August 22, 1992

White supremacist Randy Weaver failed to appear in court on firearms charges, and on August 21, 1992, six U.S. Marshals went to the Weaver compound to arrest him; it did not go well. During recon the marshals encountered Randy's friend Kevin Harris, Weaver's fourteen-year-old son Sammy, and their dog. There was a shootout. Sammy and one of the marshals, William Francis Degan, died. So did the dog.

A siege began, but the killing was not over. Sniper teams were deployed. The "rules of engagement" that law enforcement approved were later described as "severe" and "inappropriate."

Randy Weaver had taken his son's body and stored it in a shed near the family home. The day after the siege began, August 22, 1992, is when even worse shit went down. Randy went to the shed to visit his dead son. One sniper was Lon Horiuchi, a former U.S. Army officer and member of the FBI's Hostage Rescue Team. Horiuchi spotted Weaver and shot him in the back, wounding him. Weaver, his sixteen-year-old daughter, and Kevin Harris ran back toward the house. Horiuchi fired a second round at Harris as he entered the Weaver home. The bullet passed through Harris's chest, wounding him, and entered the body of Randy Weaver's wife, Vicki, who had been standing inside holding their ten-month-old daughter. Vicki Weaver died.

The siege would last another nine days.

A Department of Justice Task Force determined that the first shot met the criteria for "objective reasonableness" for use of deadly force, but the second did not because Horiuchi couldn't know if anyone was inside the door of the home.

In the aftermath, Randy Weaver and Kevin Harris were acquitted of all charges relating to the siege, and in a civil suit the Weaver family was awarded $3.1 million and Harris got $380,000. There was no admission of wrongdoing by the government.

Horiuchi was charged with manslaughter for the death of Vicki in 1997, but the charges were later dismissed. He was also present as a sniper at the Waco, Texas, raid in 1993, another law enforcement clusterfuck. Ruby Ridge and Waco provided the motivation for domestic terrorist Timothy McVeigh, another white supremacist, to murder 168 people in the 1995 Oklahoma City bombing. These events became ripe recruiting material for right-wing American militias. Tracking murders committed by domestic extremists revealed that between 2007 and 2016, 74 percent of all such killings were committed by right-wingers. Since then, they've been further emboldened with the election of Donald Trump to the presidency, and happily volunteered as his personal army in his failed coup attempt against the U.S. government on January 6, 2021.

There are no good guys in this tale. Heavily armed and racist militias are a threat to America, but the cops really fucked this one up, exacerbating the situation by being equally violent.

He tried to get away with some of that Swede cash but there was Norway he could Finnish the job. Because of Covid, many suffered stuck-home syndrome, but after a botched bank robbery in Sweden and subsequent hostage crisis, Stockholm Syndrome became a thing.

Enough dad jokes. Jan-Erik Olsson is a repeat offender, having committed numerous armed robberies. He was on parole when he entered the Kreditbanken in Norrmalmstorg, Stockholm, on August 23, 1973, intending to rob it.

They must have been at the meatball hut around the corner, because the cops got there fast, and Olsson shot one of them in the hand. He made the other cop sit in a chair and said, "Sing something." The cop sang what was likely a terrified rendition of Elvis's "Lonesome Cowboy." Olsson took four bank employees (three women and one man) as hostages and the siege began.

Jan-Erik demanded his friend and fellow criminal Clark Olofsson be allowed to join him. Being that criminals are often stupid, Clark thought that was a good idea. So now there were two bad guys holding the hostages, although the police used the excuse that Clark was their go-between.

The siege lasted six days. During that time, Olsson talked to the Swedish prime minister on the phone and said he was going to kill all the hostages if he didn't get money and a fast car. He had one of the hostages in a stranglehold while on the call and she was

> **They must have been at the meatball hut around the corner, because the cops got there fast, and Olsson shot one of them in the hand.**

heard to scream as he hung up. One of the hostages, Kristin Ehnmark, called the PM the next day and gave him shit saying he should just let the robbers go.

August 23, 1973

Afterward, Olsson wondered why none of the hostages had attacked him, and said, "There was nothing to do but get to know each other." The siege ended with tear gas; none of the hostages were seriously hurt. Afterward, no hostage would testify against their captors. Rather, they all helped raise money for the perpetrators' defense fund. Olsson got ten years' incarceration but Olofsson's conviction was quashed on appeal. Olofsson later became friends with hostage Kristin Ehnmark, although his crime-committing days were not over. Neither were Olsson's. After his release he also did more crime.

More recently, Stockholm Syndrome—the idea that hostages create an emotional bond with their captors—has been criticized as being a dubious diagnosis with little scientific support. The events of the robbery saw the media spread the term until it became a pop culture artifact, but the psychiatric community gives it little credence. Stockholm Syndrome has also been criticized as "riddled with misogyny and founded on a lie."

Exactly **1,404 years** after the sack of Rome, Washington, D.C., was likewise sacked. The White House got torched in the process.

August 24, 1814

The War of 1812 began because Britain, who had the world's largest navy, was restricting trade to its traitorous colonies. So, the United States declared war on Britain and immediately invaded Canada, which at the time was still a British colony. And the Americans got their asses kicked. Canada, fuck yeah!

After that, the war had mixed results, but on August 24, 1814, serious shit went down. Earlier in the day British forces handed a humiliating defeat to the Americans at the Battle of Bladensburg, only nine miles northeast of D.C. Knowing this, President James Madison, his top brass, and his government fled the capital, which turned out to be wise. Because the Brits then showed up in Washington and, in retribution for the damage Americans had done invading Canada, set much of the city on fire. This included not just the White House (then referred to as the Presidential Mansion) but several military and government buildings, including the

Capitol Building and the U.S. Treasury. At least it was a foreign power attacking the Capitol Building that time, and not that 2021 Civil War Redux bullshit.

Anyway, Americans are all "In God We Trust" and the Lord sent a mighty storm the next day to put out the fires. Or: random chance. One of those two.

A few weeks later, on September 11, the Americans won a naval victory against the British fleet, and the Brits retaliated the next day with a 25-hour naval bombardment of Fort McHenry in Baltimore. The next day the fort's defenders raised a large American flag as a fuck-you to the Brits, and Francis Scott Key wrote some song about bursting bombs and spangling stars. Perhaps you've heard it.

A treaty was signed the following December but tirades on Twitter weren't a thing yet, so it took a while for certain parties to get the memo, which is why the Brits attacked New Orleans in January and lost, leaving Americans with a finishing taste of victory even though precisely zero of their strategic aims for the war had been realized.

The war was basically a wash, but it must be noted that Native Americans played a major role, fighting on both sides, and suffering heavy casualties.

> **Anyway, Americans are all "In God We Trust" and the Lord sent a mighty storm the next day to put out the fires. Or: random chance. One of those two.**

Hugh Glass wasn't that breakable. DiCaprio won an Oscar for portraying him in *The Revenant,* but the original story of man vs. bear vs. dudes who abandoned him is a bit different from the movie. And by "different" I mean surprise ending!

I wrote "original" story rather than "real" because we're talking a backwoods tale from two centuries past, so who the fuck knows what really went down. Anyway, if you weren't aware and want to expand your vocabulary a bit, "revenant" means to return from the dead, and that part of the tale is the same.

In 1823, Glass was a fur trader along the Missouri River. In June of that year his party was attacked by a tribe of Native American warriors called the Arikara. Glass was shot in the leg during the battle, which was his first ouch, and the traders retreated downriver. They made it to Fort Kiowa, regrouped, and headed overland to the Yellowstone River. During that trip, on August 25, 1823, Glass was hunting game and surprised a grizzly with two cubs, and she went mama bear on his ass.

Glass and other members of the party managed to kill the bear, but not before she fucked his shit up real good. He was horribly mauled and was expected to die. The party built him a litter and dragged him behind them for two days, but he slowed their progress. The leader of the party asked for two volunteers to stay with Glass until he died and then bury him. John Fitzgerald and a man known as "Bridges" agreed.

Glass wasn't dying fast enough for them, so they said fuck it and left him, taking all the supplies and weapons. They returned to their party and said, "Oh, yeah. He totally died." But he was like a goddamn Terminator.

August 25, 1823

Glass woke up, set his own leg, let the maggots eat his ruined flesh so he wouldn't get gangrene, and fucking crawled to the Cheyenne River, surviving on berries and roots. There he built a raft and floated down to Fort Kiowa. The whole trip took him six weeks.

He recovered, then went in search of the two men who abandoned him to die, bent on murder. This is where the story departs from the movie. He found them, but didn't kill them. He found Bridges and decided not to kill him because he was so young. Then he found Fitzgerald, who had enlisted in the U.S. Army, and didn't kill him because the army would execute Glass for wasting one of its soldiers. Glass told Fitzgerald, "Better stay in that fucking army, bro, or I'll ghost your ass."

But it was the aforementioned Arikara warriors who did the ghosting. A decade after they first shot him in the leg, they finished the job when they attacked his trapping party along the Yellowstone River in 1833.

Half a century ago, women in America mostly had four career choices: secretary, teacher, nurse, or mom. And even though the Equal Pay Act was passed in 1963, women still earned only fifty-nine cents for every dollar a man made for similar work. And they were pissed.

August 26, 1970

In 1970 there were plenty of states where a woman couldn't have a credit card, make a will, or own property unless she had a husband. To celebrate fifty years of (mostly white) women getting the vote in the United States, feminist leaders said fuck this, we're going on strike.

The strike was led by feminist writer Betty Friedan, author of the 1963 book *The Feminine Mystique,* which is credited with launching "second-wave feminism" that went beyond mere enfranchisement. The goal of the protest was to focus on current battles faced by women in America, promoting free abortion on demand, equality in the workplace, and free childcare.

Sponsored by the National Organization for Women, 50,000 people, mostly women, gathered for a protest march on August 26, 1970. At the time, it was the largest-ever rally for women in the United States. Friedan sought permission from New York City to close Fifth Avenue for the strike, but was refused.

The strike began at Bryant Park at 5:00 P.M. to allow working women to attend, and spilled over into the streets. Police tried to keep protesters to one lane on Fifth Ave to prevent traffic from being blocked, but there were too many people. Other supporting strikes took place in Boston (5,000 people), San Francisco (2,000), and elsewhere.

The strike actions, asking women to cover their typewriters, stop waiting tables, and do no domestic work or cooking, gained less attention than the street protests, which garnered massive media coverage, both positive and negative. CBS anchor Eric Sevareid referred to feminism as an "infectious disease" and called the protestors a "band of braless bubbleheads." ABC anchor Howard Smith said women had nothing to be protesting over. In retaliation, the movement boycotted advertisers and ABC retracted Smith's statement. Smith, like a modern-day men's rights idiot, then said women were already liberated and were the ones really running things. Sure, Howard.

Interestingly, President Nixon acknowledged the movement positively. Betty Friedan said, "It exceeded my wildest dreams." Alas, of the three primary goals of the strike (access to abortion, childcare, and workplace equality), there is still much to be done to achieve them.

Lush Rimjob, I mean Rush Limbaugh, was a far-right fuckwipe who blamed global warming on volcanoes rather than humans. Turns out, like about most other things, he was full of shit. Krakatoa actually cooled the planet.

It wasn't quite Bugs Bunny levels of Earth-shattering kaboom, but it was a big one, and lots of people died. Seismic activity began years before, and steam and ash were coming out a few months beforehand. Explosions could be heard a hundred miles away in the two months previous. The Indonesian island of Krakatoa was letting those nearby know it was time to pack up their shit and GTFO.

Anyone who didn't listen had a bad day on August 27, 1883, when the Krakatoa volcano achieved critical fuck this and blew her stack with a force approximated at 200 megatons. For explodey-pow comparison, the largest-ever detonated nuclear device, which was a ridiculous Soviet experiment to see just how big a nuke they could detonate, was only a quarter of that. The eruption was roughly 10,000 times more powerful than the atomic bomb dropped on Hiroshima.

Over two-thirds of the island was obliterated in the eruption. It was heard 3,000 miles away. At a distance of 100 miles the volume was 180 decibels. FYI, 150 dB is enough to burst your eardrums, and sounds over 185 dB can actually fucking kill you. It wasn't just one explosion, but four, and each of them launched a tsunami 100 feet high, which, coupled with the ash and pyroclastic flows, killed 36,000 people.

The eruption sent a large amount of sulfur dioxide into the air, reflecting back incoming sunlight and causing a 0.72°F (0.4°C) global *decrease* in temperature the following year. The sky was darkened over much of the planet for years afterward, but the sunsets for the next few months were spectacular. Speaking of which, it is hypothesized that the explosion and the sunsets it created were the inspiration for Edvard Munch's painting *The Scream* a decade later.

August 27, 1883

And yet, Krakatoa is only the second most powerful volcanic eruption in recorded history. The premier explosive accolade goes to another Indonesian volcano named Mount Tambora, which erupted sixty-eight years before Krakatoa with far greater force, killing roughly three times as many people over a wide-ranging area. See, Tambora cooled the planet even more than Krakatoa, resulting in "the year without a summer," causing massive crop failures as far away as North Africa and Europe, adding to the death toll via starvation.

So why does everyone talk about Krakatoa in the #2 spot and not Tambora? Cuz telegraphs. When Tambora went boom, news traveled via slow-ass sailing ships and so it gained little notoriety as to why the weather sucked. But the Krakatoa news spread fast, becoming a well-known part of history.

He was a fourteen-year-old boy. He did nothing wrong. His name was Emmett Till. He was murdered solely for the crime of being Black in Mississippi.

Emmett was born and raised in Chicago and during the summer of 1955 was visiting relatives in the small town of Money, in the Mississippi Delta. This was Jim Crow–era South, a time when a Black man, or boy, even looking at a white woman could result in a severe beating or even death.

During his visit, on August 24, Emmett and his cousin Curtis Jones skipped church to go to Bryant's Grocery with several other Black boys. The store was owned by Roy Bryant. His 21-year-old wife, Carolyn Bryant, was running the store that day. What transpired is a subject of debate. Emmett may have wolf-whistled at Carolyn, or he may have whistled in general, as he was known to do to cover for his stutter.

When he learned of the whistle, Roy Bryant went nuts. He began to aggressively question several Black boys to find out who dared whistle at his wife. Roy and his half-brother John Milam tracked Till to his uncle's house, and in the early hours of

> **On the eighth anniversary of the murder of Emmett Till, Martin Luther King Jr. gave his "I have a dream" speech during the March on Washington.**

August 28, 1955, they used a gun to abduct Emmett. They brutally beat him, shot him, tied a heavy piece of farm equipment to his body, and threw him in the Tallahatchie River. The disfigured body was found three days later. Emmett's mother demanded an open-casket funeral so people would see what they'd done to her boy.

Bryant and Milam were put on trial for the murder. Carolyn Bryant testified before the judge that Emmett Till had done more than whistle. She said he had grabbed her and made sexual advances. The all-white jury never heard that testimony because the judge ruled it inadmissible. The jury acquitted the two men regardless; they even acquitted them of kidnapping despite the men admitting to having done so. The following year, with double jeopardy attached, Bryant and Milam admitted to *Look* magazine that they had in fact murdered Emmett Till.

Photos of the mutilated body of Emmett Till made international news and served as a catalyst for the next phase of the civil rights movement, with the Montgomery bus boycott later that year. On the eighth anniversary of the murder of Emmett Till, Martin Luther King Jr. gave his "I have a dream" speech during the March on Washington.

Many years later, Carolyn Bryant admitted that her testimony about Emmett grabbing her and making advances was a lie.

Charles Goodyear did not have many good years. He invented vulcanized rubber, but his patent was constantly infringed upon. While others made millions off his invention, he died hundreds of thousands of dollars in debt. At least the tire company decided to honor his name.

Born in 1800, Goodyear later became a partner in his father's hardware store, which went bankrupt in 1830. A self-taught inventor, he became interested in making temperamental natural rubber into something that was more useful. Through some fucking around and happy accidents, he created the process of vulcanization, getting his first patent in 1844. The fuck is vulcanization? It's a chemical-aided heating process that makes the rubber stronger, harder, less sticky, more durable and weather-resistant, and more elastic.

It was a major technological advancement that would change the world, so of course people stole the idea; Goodyear spent a lot of time in court fighting those who infringed on his patent. But he wasn't all that bitter, later writing that life wasn't measured just in money, and that "Man has just cause for regret when he sows and no one reaps." People sure reaped. In a sad end, in 1860 he traveled to New York to see his dying daughter, only to arrive and be told she had already passed. He collapsed at the news and died a short time later, at age fifty-nine.

Thirty-eight years later, on August 29, 1898, Frank Seiberling paid homage to the inventor by naming his new company the Goodyear Tire & Rubber Company. Based in Akron, Ohio, the company began with a focus on bicycle and carriage tires. As they became more popular, they focused on automobile tires.

August 29, 1898

The company grew into a multinational corporation. Today it has annual revenues exceeding $15 billion and employs 64,000 people. Goodyear kept its headquarters in Akron and is the only major American tire company. Its primary competitors are Bridgestone (Japan), Michelin (France), Pirelli (Italy), and Continental (Germany). And yet, in 2020 the soon-to-be-twice-impeached Donald Impotus Trump told Americans to boycott Goodyear because they wouldn't let employees wear MAGA hats.

The company released a statement saying, "Goodyear has zero-tolerance for any forms of harassment or discrimination." Employees are permitted to express support for equity issues such as Black Lives Matter or Pride, but Goodyear won't permit political campaigning of any type. So, no MAGA hats, but no Biden hats either. Trump thought that if you're not for him, you're against him, even though Goodyear tires are used on the presidential limousine.

In the week following Trump's call for a boycott, Goodyear's stock price was unaffected. As for Charles Goodyear, he was inducted into the National Inventors Hall of Fame in 1976.

While men were dying on the Somme during World War I, explorer Ernest Shackleton and his team were undergoing their own ordeal at the frozen ass end of the world.

There is something badass about traveling to Antarctica. Norwegian Roald Amundsen first reached the South Pole in 1911. Did you know it's 9,000 feet above sea level? So, not just a long-ass trip from the coast, but uphill the whole fucking way. Speaking of badass, in 2017 sixteen-year-old Jade Hameister skied from the Ross Ice Shelf to the South Pole, becoming the youngest person to do so. The previous year she'd done a TEDx Talk about her journeys, and trolls commented "make me a sandwich." So she did, and left it for them at her destination, saying, "Now ski 37 days and 600km to the South Pole and you can eat it." So badass.

In 1914, Sir Ernest Shackleton planned to be the first to do a land crossing of the entire Antarctic continent via the pole. It did not go as planned.

Shackleton was already an accomplished Antarctic explorer. In January 1915 his ship, the aptly named *Endurance,* became trapped in the sea ice. Eventually the ship was crushed by the ice and sunk, trapping twenty-eight men, sixty-nine dogs, and one cat on the ice. I'll rip off that Band-Aid now.

Endurance trapped in Antarctic sea ice

None of the dogs or the cat, named Mrs. Chippy, survived.

As the ice began to break up, the men were forced into their three lifeboats. It was a perilous and frozen six-day journey to the uninhabited Elephant Island. Knowing no one would find them there, they adapted one of the boats for a long sea voyage. Nine days after landing on Elephant Island, Shackleton and five of his crew departed on an 800-mile open-boat journey to South Georgia Island. I should mention that this was now fifteen months since *Endurance* became trapped, and near the start of winter in the southern hemisphere.

So, yeah. That trip sucked.

Sixteen days in the boat to South Georgia Island. Then a rest, followed by two days' journey across the mountains to the Stromness whaling station, which had been *Endurance*'s last port of call. Because Elephant Island had become encased in ice, three attempts at reaching those left behind failed. Shackleton finally begged the Chilean government to lend him a steam tug named *Yelcho,* and on August 30, 1916, the remainder of the crew of Shackleton's voyage were rescued, with no loss of (human) life.

The time from *Endurance* becoming trapped until the final rescue was over nineteen months. With the war still raging, about which the explorers knew almost nothing, their return to civilization received little attention.

There are plenty of conspiracy theories about the death of Princess Diana, which also happened on this day, but 109 years prior to that Mary Ann Nichols was definitely murdered. She was the first victim of the infamous Jack the Ripper.

Nineteenth-century England wasn't a happy place for most women, but the story of Mary Ann Nichols is an especially sad tale. Born Mary Ann Walker in 1845 to a working-class family, she married at the age of eighteen to a machinist named William Nichols. Together they had five children. They separated in early 1881, when Mary Ann was about thirty-six. She alleged her husband had an affair with the nurse who attended the birth of their fifth child. He said she was a drunk.

Her remaining years in the East London district of Whitechapel were not happy ones. People who lived in Whitechapel were generally not well-off, and Mary Ann struggled. She hired herself out as a housekeeper, lived in boarding houses and occasionally on the street, and supplemented her income via sex work, just to live.

In 1888 she worked as a domestic servant for the Cowdry family, but that lasted only a couple of months because she was an alcoholic and her non-drinking employer did not approve. In the late evening of August 30, she left a pub and sought a bed in a rooming house but was turned away for lacking the fourpence for the night's stay. Her last known words were her saying that she would go earn the money on the street. She was last seen alive in the early morning hours of August 31, 1888, standing on the corner of Osborn Street and Whitechapel Road.

August 31, 1888

Mary Ann's body was found by meat cart driver Charles Cross at 3:40 A.M. Although "found" is suspect, because it was later alleged that he was the one who actually murdered her by cutting her throat, and was interrupted by carman Robert Paul before Cross could finish mutilating her. Cross then did the basic "She was like that when I got here. Let's call the cops," to Paul.

Jack the Ripper would claim at least four more victims in the next few months, all of whom engaged in sex work. Six other murders have been linked to Jack. Dozens of suspects have been proclaimed over the years, but the killer's true identity remains uncertain.

She was last seen alive in the early morning hours of August 31, 1888, standing on the corner of Osborn Street and Whitechapel Road.

September

For China, World War II began in 1937 against Japan, and it was fucking horrible, with about 20 million Chinese deaths. The rest of the world considers the official start of the war to be September 1, 1939, when Germany invaded Poland. It was also fucking horrible. On a per-capita basis, more Polish people died than in any other independent country involved in the war.

The United States lost 0.32% of her population in WWII, and Canada lost 0.38%. Britain lost slightly less than 1%. The Soviet Union, which did the majority of the dying, and killing, in defeating the fucking Nazis, lost 13.7% of her population. By comparison, Germany lost 8.2% of her population. The two hardest-hit member nations of the USSR were Ukraine (16.3%) and Belarus, with a whopping quarter of its population killed.

A lot of people forget about Poland, which saw 17% of its population die during the war. Of the 6 million who died, only 250,000 were military and the rest were civilians. More than half of those civilians who died were Jewish. In all, Germany systematically murdered over 90% of Poland's Jewish population during the six years of occupation.

With Germany taking west Poland, then the Soviet Union invading east Poland a couple of weeks later, the country was fucked. Poland never officially surrendered, but despite brave resistance it was all over for them in little more than a month. Two days after the invasion began, Britain and France honored their agreement with Poland to protect its borders by declaring war on Germany, and the European theater of the war was off and running.

September 1, 1939

For countries like Canada and the United States that saw no invasion of their home territories, their casualties were almost exclusively military. It was the countries that had armies marching across their own lands and bombers flying through their skies that incurred massive civilian deaths.

Strategic bombing during the war lacked the accuracy to focus on military targets. Rather, there was a campaign of destroying cities from the air and killing millions of civilians in order to hamper a nation's war efforts. One of my favorite history professors sarcastically defined such "collateral damage" as "We killed some people we didn't intend to kill, but on the other hand, we killed a lot of them."

But what happened in many occupied nations during the war went far beyond collateral damage. It was hate-fueled atrocity after atrocity. It was genocide born out of a sense of superiority, seeing fellow humans as less than.

It was criminal, and few perpetrators were ever punished.

> "We killed some people we didn't intend to kill, but on the other hand, we killed a lot of them."

There is a reason Shakespeare wrote the story of *Antony and Cleopatra* as a tragedy. Things didn't end well for the pair. Their fortunes soured during one of the most important naval engagements in history: the Battle of Actium. It was one of those turning-point things.

September 2, 31 B.C.E.

In 44 B.C.E. Roman dictator Julius Caesar was repeatedly knifed. Yes, including by his good pal Brutus. That must have hurt not just physically, but emotionally. Anyway, Julius had adopted his grand-nephew Gaius Octavius and named him heir. With Julius gone there was a power vacuum, so Octavius became Octavian and formed a triumvirate with Roman politician Mark Antony and General Marcus Lepidus. Together they defeated Caesar's assassins and ruled as de facto dictators.

But the alliance would not last.

Shit went south, literally, when Antony, who was married to Octavian's sister, dumped her and moved south to Egypt to shack up with Cleopatra. Cleo had a son named Caesarion who had been born in 47 B.C.E., three years before the assassination of Caesar (remember to reverse the numbers in before-Jesus times). Cleopatra insisted Caesarion was the son of Julius Caesar, because they *had* rubbed slippery

bits, although Jules never acknowledged the kid. With Antony increasing his power in Egypt, Octavian saw the possible son of Julius Caesar as a threat to his rule. This was ancient Rome. You know how that goes.

It took time for shit to completely fall apart politically. Octavian stripped Lepidus of his power and sent him into exile, then made war upon Antony. The big naval battle took place on September 2, 31 B.C.E., in the Ionian Sea just west of Greece. A couple of things turned the tide. One of Antony's generals defected to Octavian just before the battle, bringing Antony's battle plans with him. Also, during the battle Cleopatra's fleet, which was on Antony's side, apparently said fuck this and sailed away without engaging Octavian's forces. It was a couple of millennia ago, so we're not sure, but it seems panic set in and what portion of Antony's fleet that could escape, did.

Back on land, a large part of Antony's army deserted him, and he became a fugitive. He fought on for a bit, but both he and Cleopatra took their own lives the following summer. Things also sucked for seventeen-year-old Caesarion, because Octavian had him killed a month after his mother's suicide.

Octavian used his victory to become Augustus Caesar, the "First Citizen" of Rome, ending the Republic and beginning the Empire that he would rule until his death in 14 C.E.

The man who freed the enslaved, President Abraham Lincoln, had 126 photos taken of him. A Black man who freed himself and became a powerful voice for the abolition of slavery, Frederick Douglass, had at least 160 photos taken of him, making him the most photographed man of the nineteenth century.

Born into slavery in 1818 on a plantation near Chesapeake Bay in Maryland, Douglass's birth name was Frederick Washington Augustus Bailey, and historians proclaim his father was "almost certainly white." Douglass later wrote it "was whispered my master was my father." That's a nice way of saying he was a child produced by an enslaver raping an enslaved person.

It was a large plantation and Frederick was separated from his mother as an infant, only seeing her on rare occasions prior to her dying when he was seven. He was first raised by his maternal grandparents, then separated from them at age six, and two years later was given to the Auld family in Baltimore.

Frederick Douglass

Douglass wrote of how Sophia Auld treated him "as she supposed one human being ought to treat another," teaching him to read. Sophia's husband, Hugh, disapproved, worrying that literacy led to yearning for freedom. Sophia adopted her husband's fears and stopped teaching him, hiding all written material. Frederick continued his education on his own, in secret.

Hugh Auld was right; as Douglass later often said, "Knowledge is the pathway from slavery to freedom." His self-education caused him to condemn slavery and teach other enslaved people to read. Once these lessons were uncovered, they were broken up by enslavers via clubs and stones.

September 3, 1838

In 1833, at the age of fifteen, Douglass was sent to a "slave breaker" named Edward Covey, who whipped the young man so often he would beat Douglass when the previous lashing's wounds had not yet healed. At sixteen, Douglass fought back, beating Covey savagely. Covey never whipped him again; Frederick said it was transforming, writing "a slave was made a man."

In 1837, Douglass met and fell in love with a free Black woman named Anna Murray, who encouraged and aided him in his quest to be free. On September 3, 1838, he wore a seaman's clothing provided to him by Anna to disguise his enslaved status and boarded a northbound train. By various trains and steamboats, he arrived in New York twenty-four hours later, a free man.

Anna followed, and they were married twelve days after his flight. Frederick would later drop his middle names and take the last name Douglass, becoming known internationally as an abolitionist, author, and preacher. He also supported the women's rights movement. He and Anna remained married forty-four years, until her death in 1882. While married he carried on a 28-year-long affair with a white woman.

The **1954** United States Supreme Court decision in *Brown v. Board of Education* may have been a win for desegregation, but it was far from the waving of a magic wand.

On the morning of September 4, 1957, more than three years after the landmark Supreme Court decision, nine Black students entered Little Rock Central High School in Arkansas for the first time. They did not receive a welcoming audience, and photographers were there to capture the moment. Chants of "Two, four, six, eight! We don't want to integrate!" echoed as Black student Elizabeth Eckford held her book and walked resolutely into the school. The iconic photo of the day showed a screaming girl behind her, Hazel Bryan, shrieking curses of "Go home, [N-word]! Go back to Africa!"

After the photo was published, Hazel received some critical attention, which didn't bother her but it caused her parents to pull her from school. She married and took the name Hazel Massery, starting a family. Later, as her photo became published in history books, she realized that her children might come to wonder about who that screaming girl was. Hazel felt guilty, and having changed her mind on integration and her attitude toward civil rights, contacted Eckford in 1963 and apologized. They then went their separate ways.

Forty years after the photo of "hate assailing grace" was taken, Massery, still feeling the damage to her reputation, hoped to settle accounts. The original photographer arranged for the two women to meet again, and for a time they became friends. But once the honeymoon was over, Eckford said that Massery "wanted me to be cured and be over it . . . so that she wouldn't feel responsible anymore." The friendship fizzled after a year under the realization that such painful slates don't wipe clean so easily. Forgiveness is not a right; it is a gift of the giver.

Today, segregation in the United States remains a harsh reality via economic means, with many white families choosing to send their children to private schools that Black, Indigenous, and People of Color (BIPOC) families often cannot afford, due to systemic racism that provides far more economic opportunities to white people.

Chants of "Two, four, six, eight! We don't want to integrate!" echoed as Black student Elizabeth Eckford held her book and walked resolutely into the school.

Hollywood has seen no shortage of scandals. The first big one involved the death of 26-year-old model and actress Virginia Rappe. It happened at a party hosted by famed comedy actor Roscoe "Fatty" Arbuckle, who would be falsely charged in her death.

The party was in Arbuckle's suite at the St. Francis Hotel in San Francisco on September 5, 1921, and despite Prohibition, everyone was drunk as fuck. Rappe suffered from cystitis, a condition aggravated by alcohol. She was known to party hard and suffer for it due to her condition. Additionally, the quality of alcohol during Prohibition wasn't the best. She got floor-licking drunk and went into the bathroom to blow violent chunks. A doctor was called, who said,

"She's drunk as fuck. Here is some morphine to calm her."

September 5, 1921

Two days later, she was in the hospital. Two days after that, she was dead from a ruptured bladder. Rappe's friend, Maude Delmont, cried rape and murder most foul to both the doctors and police, proclaiming Arbuckle the perpetrator. Maude told a tale of her friend screaming in pain when Arbuckle was alone with her, saying he crushed her bladder with his weight during a violent rape. But doctors found no sign of rape, nor any sign of sexual activity at all. And many other witnesses said Arbuckle was never

Arbuckle with his lawyers during his first trial

alone with Rappe, and that they heard no such screams.

It is worth noting Delmont had a record of both blackmail and extortion, and now she sought to profit from her friend's death via a false accusation. I mean, for fuck's sake, she sent telegrams to her attorneys in San Diego and Los Angeles that read, "WE HAVE ROSCOE ARBUCKLE IN A HOLE HERE CHANCE TO MAKE SOME MONEY OUT OF HIM." Nevertheless, Arbuckle was charged, and Randolph Hearst's newspaper chain ran wild with the story, portraying Arbuckle as a disgusting lecher who used his weight to overpower an innocent young woman. Roscoe's costars told a different tale, saying he was good-natured, shy with women, and would never hurt a fly.

A malicious prosecution by an ambitious prosecutor and the pressuring of witnesses to make false statements followed. Delmont's story changed repeatedly; she was never called to testify because prosecutors knew the only "witness" wouldn't hold up under cross-examination. The first two trials ended in a hung jury, but the third saw the defense rip the prosecution to shreds. The jury deliberated only five minutes. Four of those minutes were spent in writing an apology to Arbuckle that was read as they acquitted him.

The party was in Arbuckle's suite at the St. Francis Hotel in San Francisco on September 5, 1921, and despite Prohibition, everyone was drunk as fuck.

Arbuckle was financially ruined by the cost of the trials and, despite the acquittal, shunned by Hollywood in the aftermath. He retreated into the bottle for many years, and in 1933, on the eve of a comeback after signing a contract with Warner Bros., suffered a heart attack and died in his sleep, aged forty-six.

The rescue attempt of Israeli athletes taken hostage by Palestinian terrorist group Black September at the 1972 Munich Olympic Games was a colossal fuckup for which Germany deserves much blame. It's almost like that country has a history of not giving a shit about Jewish lives.

To begin the clusterfuckery, German intelligence had received a warning weeks earlier by a Palestinian informant in Beirut that an "incident" was being planned for the games, but security measures remained unbelievably lax. The head of the Israeli delegation even expressed concern at the lack of security for their athletes, and was assured extra security would be added, but none was.

In the early morning of September 5, the eight terrorists snuck over the fence of the Olympic Village while disguised in tracksuits to help them blend in with the athletes. They carried duffel bags filled with assault rifles, pistols, and grenades. The terrorists had received logistical assistance for their attack from German neo-Nazis, because of course. As the terrorists burst into the two apartments housing the athletes and coaches, two of the Israelis fought back and were murdered. The terrorists took nine other Israelis hostage.

The terrorists demanded the release of 234 mostly Palestinians held in Israeli prisons, as well as two West German militants held in German prisons. Although Germany denies it, Israel offered to send its special forces unit to Germany to handle the crisis, because they were expertly trained in how to deal with such a situation, as they would prove in the raid on Entebbe, Uganda, four years later. Germany declined, preferring to use its unqualified regular police officers to attempt a rescue.

September 6, 1972

Big surprise, that shit went sideways, and just after midnight on September 6, 1972, all nine of the hostages were murdered by the terrorists during the amateurish rescue attempt. One German police officer was also killed, as were five of the eight terrorists. The three terrorists who survived were imprisoned, but the German government LET THEM FUCKING GO a month later as part of a hostage negotiation when a Lufthansa flight was hijacked.

Like I said: colossal fuckup.

Anyway, the Israeli government was pissed, and launched Operation Wrath of God using the Mossad to track down and kill those responsible for the planning and execution of the massacre of their eleven athletes. And they had quite a bit of success over a lengthy period, including allegedly getting two of the three terrorists that Germany released. They also killed an innocent Moroccan man in Norway in 1973 via a case of mistaken, or perhaps misdirected, identity. Six Mossad agents were arrested and five convicted in the Norway killing but were released to Israel two years later.

He was born Lesane Parish Crooks and his name was changed to Tupac Amaru Shakur to honor the descendant of the last Incan monarch, who led a revolt against the Spanish in eighteenth-century Peru. After his rebellion failed, Túpac Amaru II was drawn and quartered and beheaded by the Spanish in 1781. Rapper Tupac Amaru Shakur also had an untimely death; he was killed by an "unknown" gunman in 1996.

September 7, 1996

Born in Harlem in 1971, Tupac's mother changed his name when he was one year old because she wanted him to have the name of a revolutionary; his music would prove it so. Tupac's family was involved in the Black Panther movement; his mother was tried and acquitted of conspiracy against the United States while eight months pregnant with him.

When he was thirteen, his family moved to Baltimore and he later enrolled in the Baltimore School for the Arts, studying poetry, acting, ballet, and jazz. He began his music career at seventeen and by twenty-one was a rising star. He introduced social issues into his music at a time when gangsta rap was the rage, and rapidly climbed to superstardom with his 1996 double-disc album *All Eyez on Me* achieving diamond sales status. He also acted in numerous films, to critical acclaim.

In 1993 Tupac nonfatally shot two drunken off-duty police officers, who, by the sound of things, had been acting like total dicks and were shooting at him. He was initially charged, then the prosecution said fuck this clusterfuck and dropped it. He spent a short time in jail in 1994 for beating another rapper with a baseball bat. That same year he was convicted of first-degree sexual abuse and sentenced to 1.5 to 4.5 years, but was released after eight months on a $1.4 million bond paid by Death Row Records CEO Suge Knight, pending judicial appeal. In 1994, Tupac was shot during a robbery attempt; he later blamed rappers P. Diddy and Biggie (and others) for setting it up as part of the growing West Coast vs. East Coast hip-hop rivalry.

On the night of September 7, 1996, Tupac attended a Mike Tyson boxing match in Las Vegas. After the match Tupac and his entourage were involved in a fight with Crips gang member Orlando Anderson. Later that evening, while driving to the Death Row Records nightclub, a white Cadillac pulled up next to Tupac's BMW and a Cadillac occupant shot Tupac four times with a .40-caliber pistol. Shakur died in the hospital six days later at the age of twenty-five. Anderson was the prime suspect, and probably did do it, but was never charged due to lack of evidence.

Conspiracy theories about the murder have run wild, as has Tupac's legacy. With his posthumous sales he is one of the best-selling musical artists of all time, with over seventy-five million records sold.

One day, perhaps, it won't matter. That day has not yet arrived. The LGBTQ+ community continually relies on people publicly proclaiming their sexuality or gender as a method of gaining acceptance that should already exist as a non-issue, by virtue of the fact that we are all human beings. Alas, a lot of said humans are bigoted assholes.

But things have improved significantly since September 8, 1975, when decorated Vietnam veteran Leonard Matlovich appeared in uniform on the cover of *Time* magazine with the headline "I Am A Homosexual" to protest the exclusion of gays in the military.

Born in 1943, Matlovich was the son of a career air force sergeant. He enlisted in the air force at age nineteen, served three tours of duty in Vietnam, and attained the rank of technical sergeant. During that time, he was awarded a Bronze Star for killing two Viet Cong soldiers attacking his post. He was also seriously wounded stepping on a land mine and received a Purple Heart, but remained in the military.

In 1973, at age thirty, he slept with another man for the first time. He came out to friends but hid his sexual orientation from his commanding officer. He then read an article by gay rights activist Frank Kameny and reached out with his dilemma of being gay in a military that wouldn't accept him. Kameny saw in Matlovich, a service member with a perfect record, a test case for challenging the military ban on gay people.

September 8, 1975

Matlovich, Kameny, and the ACLU planned for months. In March 1975, Matlovich hand-delivered a letter to his air force commander explaining his homosexuality, stating that "my sexual preference will in no way interfere with my Air Force duties." There was a hearing, and Matlovich was given an honorable discharge from the service. He sued, and in 1980 was ordered to be reinstated and promoted. The air force countered with a financial settlement, which Matlovich reluctantly accepted, knowing the air force would find some other way to kick him out.

Matlovich continued to work as a gay rights activist. He succumbed to complications from HIV/AIDS in 1988 and was buried with full military honors. His tombstone reads, "When I was in the military they gave me a medal for killing two men and a discharge for loving one."

> **His tombstone reads, "When I was in the military they gave me a medal for killing two men and a discharge for loving one."**

How does one crown a baby? I could barely get them to stop shitting, pissing, and puking long enough to change a damn diaper. Nevertheless, the Scots managed to make infant Mary a queen. They didn't have a lot of choice, because it was the sixteenth century and medicine sucked and everyone was fucking dying young all the time, including her dad.

September 9, 1543

King James V got sick and died of shit that would probably be fixed today by Tylenol and maybe some penicillin. Mary was six. Days. Six days old. James had Baratheon levels of bastards o'er the land, but only three legitimate children, two of whom died before their first birthdays, because, again, sixteenth century. Mary was the one that survived.

It takes time to plan a coronation, even for someone too young to know what the fuck is going on. On September 9, 1543, at the age of nine months, Mary's coronation as Queen of Scotland took place. Her first royal command was probably to barf up some breast milk.

Henry VIII, that pervy fuck, said Mary should marry his son, Edward, as a way to unify England and Scotland. One of the Scottish regents running things while Mary was shitting things, a Catholic cardinal, said fuck that Mary should marry a French dude because Catholic. Henry was pissed because he wanted to break the Scottish alliance with

France. He got militarily aggressive about the Mary marriage and the regents were all "Not winning too many hearts and minds here, Hank" and Henry II of France said, "Send Mary to marry my son and all shall be merry." And that's what happened.

Mary went to France at age five to get away from the English dick king. There, she was a favorite at court and educated in literature, languages, riding, music, and the all-important needlework. She married thirteen-year-old Francis, Henry II's son and heir, when she reached fifteen. That same year, Elizabeth I became Queen of England.

Henry II died the following year and Mary's husband became King Francis II. Then Francis died the year after that FROM A FUCKING EAR INFECTION because, again, medicine sucked. Mary returned to Scotland and, having lived in France since the age of five, was a fish out of water.

Okay, executive summary time. Six years of Catholic vs. Protestant fuckery. Queen Mary married her half-cousin and had a son, James. Her husband was murdered, and Mary married the alleged murderer. She was then forced to abdicate in favor of son James and fled to England asking cousin Liz for protection. Liz's "protection" basically meant fancy imprisonment, because lots of Catholics thought Catholic Mary should be queen instead of Protestant Elizabeth.

After eighteen years as a prisoner, Mary got involved in a plot to assassinate Elizabeth and put herself on the throne. The plot was uncovered, and Mary got her head chopped off in 1587.

Spying is dangerous business. Despite American revolutionary Nathan Hale only being a spy for a couple of weeks before being sent off to the eternal pushing of daisies by the British hangman, he remains a popular figure in U.S. history. Probably because of his badass last words.

It had been a couple of months since the white enslavers said all men are created equal so long as they're men and also white. Hale was born in Connecticut in 1755, graduated Yale, and became a schoolteacher. But in 1775 there was a war and young men often consider war to be glorious, so he was all sign me up. Being educated, he was made a lieutenant and before long a captain. Tall, strong, and handsome, he was popular with the ladies.

Early in the war the Americans were getting their asses kicked, but by August 1776 Hale had still not seen any combat and he was all thirst for adventure and shit. So, when General George Washington said he needed a spy for a dangerous mission, Nathan Hale was the only one to step forward. The date was September 10, 1776. Nathan Hale had twelve days to live.

He was tasked with determining where the British would invade the Island of Manhattan. He disguised himself as a Dutch schoolteacher seeking employment and did successfully gather intelligence. On September 20, New York was set on fire, possibly by rebels, and the Brits were on high alert. The next day, Hale was attempting to return to American-held territory when he was captured by the British. It's alleged his cousin, a British loyalist, saw him and ratted him out, but that was never substantiated.

September 10, 1776

Anyway, Hale had all sorts of incriminating documents on him, and he was ever so fucked. He admitted his name and rank, but the rules were the rules: You go behind enemy lines out of uniform, and you are executed for being a spy. Rumor has it he was very composed during his final moments on the gallows, saying, "I only regret that I have but one life to give for my country."

Considering who was hanging him, it's ironic he adapted those final words from the work of a British playwright, Joseph Addison.

He admitted his name and rank, but the rules were the rules: You go behind enemy lines out of uniform, and you are executed for being a spy.

Jet fuel melting steel beams wasn't the only bad thing that happened to Manhattan Island on this day. Four centuries previous, the white guy whom the river on the west side of the island is named for was looking for that Northwest Passage to India and encountered Manhattan and the people already living there.

September 11, 1609

Henry Hudson was an English explorer in the employ of the Dutch East India Company, a name which reveals *why* they were looking for that mythical shortcut to India, because going via South Africa sucked. So, he headed west and found the north was ice and shit and decided to see if there was a way *through* North America.

On September 6 his ship, the *Half Moon,* was anchored between Coney Island and Sandy Hook. A five-man crew in a rowboat was scouting the area when canoes of Native Americans attacked them with arrows, killing sailor John Colman and wounding two others. Hudson then took his ship into Upper New York Bay and on September 11, 1609, he was the first low-melanin man to see Broadway before it was Broadway.

For the next twelve days he ascended the river, reaching as far as modern-day Albany. During that time, he traded with Native Americans who weren't shooting them full of arrows, obtaining mostly furs. On September 23 he decided it was time to head home.

When he returned to England, the English authorities wanted to know what he'd found and were all "Let's see that captain's log stuff" and he was "Ew, gross. We throw that shit overboard." Meanwhile, the book form of the log was passed in secret to the Dutch ambassador to England, because Hudson was a loyal employee. The log was sent to Amsterdam and was used to lay claim to the region, creating a trading post on Manhattan Island five years later, followed by establishing "New Amsterdam" there in 1625.

For Hudson, in 1610 he was hired by the English to try that Northwest Passage thing again, and the crew was very excited when they found what would be called Hudson Bay, thinking it was the passage—shit, the dude got a river *and* a big-ass bay named for him? And then a company that makes really expensive blankets? Lucky.

Except, not so lucky. No passage to Asia was found. His ship and crew became trapped in the ice and wintered on the shore. Come spring, Hudson wanted to do more exploring and find that passage, but the crew was fucking done with that bullshit and wanted to go home. They mutinied, and Hudson, his teenage son, and seven loyal crewmen were set adrift in a small boat. They were never seen again.

Twice in two centuries the city of Vienna proved to be the location for a historical turning point in a war between Christianity and Islam. Jesus saved the day both times. Okay, maybe not, but hear me out.

In 1529 the Ottoman Siege of Vienna was led by Suleiman the Magnificent. Things started off shitty for StM, because the rains were unusually bad that year. Like, biblical flooding kind of bad. He had to leave a bunch of artillery and other material behind on his way to the siege. When he reached Vienna, his troops were not in good shape from months of trudging through the shit weather. And the rain just wouldn't fucking stop. Then, fucking snow. Fuck. Fuck this stupid fucking weather. FUCK!

Western European Christianity was saved from a Muslim invasion by nasty weather. Praise Jesus! Had to be him sending the right storm at the right time and not a lucky coincidence at all.

Fast-forward a century and a half. This time it's not the Siege of Vienna, but the *Battle* of Vienna. Same players, more Jesus to the rescue. The Ottomans had this major erection for capturing Vienna because of its important strategic location, making it the key to conquering the rest of Western Europe.

The Ottomans laid siege again for a couple of months, but then there was a big-ass decisive battle. I mentioned Jesus saving the day, but it was no climatological miracle this time. It was the power of belief. Or, at least, the power of shared belief in Jesus against those infidel Muslims, so let's work together and do some killin' of people who pray wrong.

September 12, 1683

For the first time ever, there was a Christian coalition involving the Holy Roman Empire led by the Hapsburg monarchy joining forces with the Polish-Lithuanian Commonwealth. They banded together to kick some Ottoman ass. The battle, which took place on September 12, 1683, included the largest cavalry charge in history.

The battle marked a major turning point in centuries of warfare between the Holy Roman and Ottoman empires. It sent the Ottomans running, and over the next sixteen years the HRE took back Eastern Europe from the Middle Eastern invaders.

And as legend has it, the croissant was invented in Vienna after the battle as a celebration of victory, with the pastry design referring to the crescent shapes on Ottoman flags. And it was introduced to the French a century later by Marie Antoinette, who was from, get this, Vienna. Yummy!

> **And the rain just wouldn't fucking stop. Then, fucking snow. Fuck. Fuck this stupid fucking weather. FUCK!**

Her name was Noor Inayat Khan, and she was a princess. Descended from renowned eighteenth-century Indian ruler Tipu Sultan, she was also a spy for the Allies during World War II.

Living in France at the outbreak of the war, her family fled to England. Although a pacifist, she was all "Fuck those Nazi fucks" and joined the Women's Auxiliary Air Force and was trained as a wireless operator. Her trainers considered her unfit both physically and mentally for the work of a spy, but her ability to operate the wireless equipment and fluency in French made up for it. The evaluation of her toughness would prove to be an error. In 1943 she would be the first woman sent to the mainland to serve as a wireless operator in enemy territory, sending and receiving information about sabotage operations, weapons drops for Resistance fighters, and helping airmen who had been shot down to escape.

She was flown into France and became "Madeleine." The job was especially dangerous because those Nazi fucks could pick up the transmissions and find their source location. After each transmission the operator had to change locations, which meant carrying the bulky wireless equipment from site to site. If they were stopped and searched, the radio was a dead giveaway, the carrier doomed.

The life expectancy of a wireless operator in 1943 France was six weeks.

Within a week of Khan's arrival all the other operators in her network were captured and sent off to a very bad place. London wanted to pull her out, but she refused because she knew she was the only link between Paris and London. By herself, she did the work of six operators for three months. One night, while stringing an antenna to a tree to make a transmission, she was questioned by a German officer. She charmed him by saying she wanted to listen to the radio. He then helped her hang the antenna.

Noor Inayat Khan

She was captured in October 1943 after being betrayed, possibly by a double agent. She twice attempted escape, almost being successful the second time. She was tortured for information over several months, but after the war the head of the Gestapo in Paris testified Khan never gave a single piece of information. After eleven months as a prisoner, on September 13, 1944 (a month after Paris was liberated), Khan was executed at the Dachau concentration camp by a gunshot to the head.

The final word she spoke was *Liberté*.

It took three U.S. presidents being assassinated before someone finally said, "Maybe we should put some actual effort into protecting these guys." Lincoln didn't get to see how the play ended. Garfield never made that train. William McKinley never got to finish shaking those hands. After McKinley was shot, the Secret Service got a new role and we got lots of Teddy Roosevelt quotes.

President William McKinley didn't like security coming between him and the people, which is likely a feeling he came to regret. On September 6, 1901, he was six months into his second term and attending the Pan-American Exposition in Buffalo, New York. Part of the attendance at the fair involved visiting the Temple of Music, where the president would meet with the crowd and shake hands. McKinley's secretary, George Cortelyou, worried there would be an assassination attempt at said music temple and removed it from the schedule. McKinley put it back on the schedule. Cortelyou removed it a second time. McKinley put it back on a second time. Cortelyou was all the fuck is wrong with you? and McKinley said (actual quote), "No one would wish to hurt me."

But Leon Czolgosz wanted to hurt him real bad.

After the financial crash of 1893, Czolgosz lost his job. Over the ensuing years he became involved with anarchism and was radicalized toward violence by believing that America was an unjust society where the rich exploited the poor and . . . Oh, wait. That's actually true. Anyway, he decided McKinley had to die.

September 14, 1901

In the Temple of Music, McKinley was doing the handshaking. When Leon's turn came, he slapped the president's hand aside and shot him twice with a .32-caliber revolver. One shot ricocheted off a button and lodged in McKinley's jacket. The other entered his abdomen. The crowd jumped Czolgosz and started beating the shit out of him like he'd just shot the president. McKinley said, "Go easy on him, boys."

It wasn't a fatal wound, except for the shit state of medicine at the time. Stomach wounds can be nasty, and McKinley got gangrene and died September 14, 1901. Afterward, the Secret Service, which had been around since 1865 protecting money, got the added job of protecting the president, Teddy Roosevelt got the job of president, and Leon Czolgosz got the electric chair.

You may have noticed that there is no shortage of criticism of a certain semi-sentient dayglo taint stain of a president in this book. Permit me to share one of those quotes from Teddy: "To announce that there must be no criticism of the President, or that we are to stand by the President, right or wrong, is not only unpatriotic and servile, but is morally treasonable to the American public."

It's okay to despise a little kid if he's just a cartoon, right? Because holy shit do a lot of people hate this sniveling little fuckstick. You think Canada Geese are evil? Canada's Caillou is like a four-year-old drank the souls of an entire flock of geese and was raised by Chernobyl wolves while fed a steady diet of meth and Monster Energy drinks. Having not ever heard of Caillou is a blissful state of ignorance akin to having never heard the Macarena.

September 15, 1997

A year before our first child was born, *Caillou* debuted on Teletoon on September 15, 1997. And because kids are a handful, yeah, we let him watch some fucking TV. Sue us. It was referred to as an "educational children's show," which I suppose it was, if the intent was to educate children on how to be the most annoying little shitnuggets of their generation.

Side note: Our kids turned out awesome, despite this fucking show.

Anyway, I'm pretty sure Quebec was pissed over the 1995 separation referendum narrowly getting voted down and this show, which was originally in French, was their revenge. The show was based on some books, which I think we can assume also suck. The show ran for thirteen godawful years and the *National Post* referred to it as "quite possibly the world's most universally reviled children's

program." Even John Oliver proclaimed, "Fuck you, Caillou!"

There was no educational component, no trying to teach math or colors or morality tales; it was completely lacking in teachable moments. Just a whining brat who regularly has meltdowns over the most minor of inconveniences. People try to get him to do things and he sucks, and he cries. He also regularly beats his little sister, Rosie, and is raised by parents who I'm certain have a hydroponic marijuana operation in the basement because no fucking way could anyone tolerate such a demon child without being baked out of their skulls 24/7.

Speaking of spawn of the underworld, where is he hiding the triple 6? His taint? Fucker's bald. Why is he bald? According to the show's producers it's because in the books he was way younger and so he had no hair, and when they made him older on the show adding hair made him unrecognizable.

Yeah, that's fucking bullshit. And it's not because Caillou has cancer. Caillou *is* cancer. He has no hair because he's the worst. His hair rejected him, said fuck you and noped out. Caillou was voiced by three different girls over the years. The voice actor for the first season referred to him as "quite a whiny character." No fucking shit. The second actor died in a car crash when she was only seventeen. Shit I almost forgot. The fucking theme song. It's the Macarena of children's show music.

John Oliver was right. Fuck you, Caillou.

A movie was made about Sully landing a plane on the Hudson; it's time for a movie about Shavarsh Karapetyan and the Miracle on Yerevan Lake. Like Captain Chesley Sullenberger, Shavarsh too is a man who used his training and courage to accomplish an amazing feat that saved many lives.

Born in 1953 in Armenia when it was still part of the Soviet Union, Karapetyan became a competitive swimmer at a young age, and later switched to finswimming, which is still swimming, but with fins. Some of the events involve lengthy breath-holding. He has broken eleven world records in the sport, winning numerous gold medals. And holy shit was he in the right place at the right time.

On September 16, 1976, when Shavarsh was twenty-three years old, he was at the end of his usual twelve-mile run with his brother Kamo . . . *with forty-five pounds of sand strapped to his back!* They were running alongside Yerevan Lake and heard the terrible sound of metal crashing through concrete as a crowded trolleybus with ninety-two people on board broke the barricade along the wall of the dam and hit the water, sinking in over thirty feet of water, eighty feet from shore. Shavarsh and Kamo dove, quite literally, into action.

The bus hitting bottom caused silt to explode; visibility was near zero. But Shavarsh found the bus and broke the back window with his legs. He grabbed people from inside, which contained a pocket of life-saving air, and brought them to the surface. There, Kamo, also an accomplished swimmer, ferried them to safety. Forty-six people died, but the brothers saved at least twenty lives that day while onlookers watched it unfold.

September 16, 1976

Shavarsh received multiple lacerations from the window shards, and because of the extreme cold and the presence of sewage in the water, he developed both pneumonia and sepsis. He was hospitalized for forty-five days. The lung complications that followed, along with psychological trauma, had a negative effect on his swimming career, but he still managed one more world record.

Because USSR, the story was hushed for years because apparently Soviet buses don't crash. After a Russian newspaper published the story in 1982, he became a national hero. Shavarsh's new wife had no idea until she read the paper; he never told her about it. True to form, in 1985 Shavarsh happened to be near a burning building and without a second thought ran inside to pull people out, receiving severe burns in the process that required another lengthy hospital stay.

> **Forty-six people died, but the brothers saved at least twenty lives that day while onlookers watched it unfold.**

For American soldiers and civilians alike, September 17, 1862, achieved peak levels of suck.

It stands out as the deadliest day in the nation's history.

In the Battle of Antietam, traitor Bob Lee, who later had a Dodge Charger named after him in a crappy TV show whose only cultural contribution was Daisy Dukes, took his traitorous Confederate Army of Northern Virginia fighting for the right to own people with more melanin onto Union soil in Maryland to face off against General George McClellan's Army of the Potomac.

I'll forgo a description of the battle and just say they beat the living shit out of each other over a creek called Antietam all day. The Union had twice the troops engaged in battle as the traitors did, but couldn't achieve "force concentration" so it wasn't a rout. Here is the murder by numbers: 2,108 Union deaths vs. 1,567 Confederate deaths, and 9,549 Union wounded vs. 7,752 Confederate wounded. And considering the shit state of medicine in the nineteenth century, it's a fair bet a lot of those wounded died at a later date. Oh, and there were 753 captured/missing Union vs. 1,018 captured/missing on the Confederate side.

By the way, in war where they use things that explode to inflict death, "missing" is often a more pleasant way of saying "blown to bits."

Tactically, the battle was a draw, but strategically the Union won because Lee abandoned his invasion of Union territory. President Lincoln was pissed at his general, however, for not pursuing Lee and fucking up those traitorous forces some more, and fired McClellan. Nevertheless, Lincoln considered the fact that they sent Lee packing enough of a victory that the timing was right for him to issue a preliminary Emancipation Proclamation five days later.

Now for the civilian deaths. In a completely unrelated event, but happening on the same day, same year, in Pittsburgh, there was an explosion at the Allegheny Arsenal. This was an important supply and manufacturing center for Union forces, and stuff that was intended to explode at a later date exploded when it wasn't supposed to. Seventy-eight workers, mostly young women, died.

> **By the way, in war where they use things that explode to inflict death, "missing" is often a more pleasant way of saying "blown to bits."**

In *The Hunt for Red October* Sean Connery, playing a Scottish-accented Soviet sub captain, learns that Alec Baldwin's character is CIA and proclaims "CIA!?" in shock and disgust. We're made to believe it's motivated by his Soviet distrust of an American intelligence agency. In reality, we should all be disgusted by the organization that was formed on September 18, 1947. Because its crimes are legion.

Created by President Truman's signing of the National Security Act a couple of years after the end of World War II, the CIA's "primary mission is to collect, evaluate, and disseminate foreign intelligence to assist the president and senior U.S. government policymakers in making decisions relating to the national security . . . The CIA may also engage in covert action."

Much has come to light about past covert actions and how the CIA fucked over so many different peoples. It's like, wow, these folks really suck at keeping secrets if they can't hide their atrocities for shit. News flash: They're not trying that hard to hide them. In a lot of cases, they don't give a shit except during the time of atrocity execution and for a short while afterward.

The CIA knows that its covert actions are going to eventually come to light and that most people won't care about them because by the time we learn what went down, it's history, and happened far away in a "shithole country." What the CIA and other intelligence agencies really care about keeping secret is the first part of the aforementioned

quote: the stuff about collecting intelligence and how it influences foreign policy. Since Trump didn't read, I doubt it made much difference while he was president, but historically much of American foreign policy has been directed by its spying. This is the boring part of spying. It's also what the CIA keeps the tightest lid on.

September 18, 1947

The budget for the James Bond shit is a small part of overall CIA expenditures, but that doesn't mean it hasn't used that money to stir up shit. The agency has conducted operations throughout Latin America and the rest of the world to support right-wing military dictators. Operatives have tortured suspected terrorists in black sites in violation of the United Nations Convention Against Torture. After WWII the CIA recruited over a thousand fucking Nazis to spy during the Cold War. And there are numerous allegations of CIA involvement in international drug trafficking.

And the shit CIA personnel did in Vietnam? Jesus Power-Bottoming Christ it was horrible. One example is the "Phoenix Program"; thousands of innocent Vietnamese were tortured and murdered solely on the basis of being ratted out by their neighbors. One method of torture used was rape, including raping people with eels.

The fuck?

Won't someone please think of the children? Twisted Sister is singing about how they aren't gonna take it and the album cover has scary men in makeup and David Lee Roth wants to have sex with his teacher and we need to get back to the times when the camera panned up so it wouldn't show Elvis's gyrations because Ben Shapiro's wife is right: Damp nethers are a medical condition!

September 19, 1985

The four "Washington Wives," called such because of their husbands' political power, included not-yet vice president Al Gore's wife, Tipper. In 1985 the women formed the Parents Music Resource Center because rock and roll is demon music that makes children sacrifice their parents to Satan while they sleep, and the only way to prevent that is by putting a sticker on the album cover.

The PMRC went after several songs it dubbed "The Filthy 15," targeting metal bands along with songs by Cyndi Lauper,

The Tipper Sticker

Prince, Madonna, and Sheena Easton. On September 19, 1985, the Senate held a hearing to discuss such "porn rock." The group wanted not just detailed warning labels, but album covers they deemed offensive hidden under the counter, and TV stations to not broadcast songs with explicit lyrics or videos.

At the hearing, opposing witness Frank Zappa said the proposal was "an ill-conceived piece of nonsense which fails to deliver any real benefits to children." John Denver spoke out against censorship, comparing it to Nazi book burnings. But it was Twisted Sister front man Dee Snider who stole the show.

In a later interview he said, "I ain't getting dressed up for nobody. I'm a dirtbag and I'm proud." He arrived at the hearing wearing tight and faded jeans, a sleeveless shirt, sunglasses, snakeskin boots, and his big hair. The PMRC proclaimed the Twisted Sister song "Under the Blade" was about sadomasochism, bondage, and rape, and Snider set them straight, explaining it was inspired by a band member's surgery and how it's about the fear one feels in the operating room. He said, "The only sadomasochism, bondage, and rape in this song is in the mind of Ms. Gore." Burn!

In the aftermath, a generic parental advisory label referred to as the "Tipper sticker" was put on "offensive" albums. Some stores, such as Walmart, refused to carry albums sporting the sticker. Other stores limited their sale to adults. But the pull of forbidden fruit is strong, and many believe the sticker actually increased sales of the albums that had it.

Bobby Riggs was a tennis player and a sexist douche. He was World #1 in tennis for three years back in the '30s and '40s, and in 1973 he referred to women's tennis as inferior and said that at the age of fifty-five he could still beat any woman. He was wrong.

Riggs challenged Billie Jean King and she told him to piss off. So, he then went after Margaret Court, a thirty-year-old about to win her seventh ranking as World #1. She said yes. And got her ass kicked in the match. (Don't feel bad for Margaret; she's a horrible bigot.) At the time of the match it got little attention, but the victory put Riggs on the cover of *Time* and *Sports Illustrated*. Riggs was magnanimous in his victory. Ha! JK. He was a total dick about it. He dragged female tennis players all the more.

King was all fuck this guy and then accepted his challenge, and the match became a major media event. It was dubbed "The Battle of the Sexes," and was held in the Houston Astrodome on September 20, 1973. It was watched by 90 million people worldwide as the pair battled for a purse worth over half a million dollars today. Over 30,000 were in attendance; it remains the largest audience to attend a tennis match in U.S. history.

The match was theater. King, whose tennis record was almost as impressive as Court's, arrived like Cleopatra in a litter carried by shirtless buff dudes. Riggs arrived via a rickshaw pulled by models. King gave Riggs a gift of a piglet as a statement about him being a "chauvinist pig." Riggs returned the insult with a gift of a giant "Sugar Daddy" lollipop.

September 20, 1973

King was behind at first, but she had learned from watching Court play him and adapted her game. She felt she "had to win" to defend women's tennis, saying "I thought it would set us back fifty years if I didn't win." Rather than play her usual aggressive game, she beat him at his own defensive style, making him run back and forth across the court. And yeah, she beat his ass.

Afterward, because sexist douches gonna douche, there were allegations Riggs threw the match because he bet against himself and needed the money. Those stories were unsubstantiated. Riggs's own son refuted the allegations, saying his dad was ashamed and depressed for several months after losing to King.

Billie Jean King and Bobby Riggs

Some people are just not to be fucked with. Empress Dowager Cixi began as a concubine to an emperor of the late Qing dynasty. She would come to rule China for forty-seven years, instituting numerous reforms. Later, she was scapegoated for an uprising that ended the Qing dynasty. She'd been dead three years, so it must have been her fault.

September 21, 1898

When Cixi was twenty-five, the emperor died, but she'd had a five-year-old son by him who became emperor. His dad had named regents in case of his death and Cixi was all fuck that and punted them, assuming the regency herself. Five-year-old boys have a tendency to do what their mom tells them, so she was effectively in charge of China.

The year was 1861, and China was in deep shit. The Second Opium War had recently ended and left the country in chaos. Cixi oversaw the restoration of the Qing dynasty, allowing it to survive another five decades.

Cixi's son died when he was only eighteen, and so Cixi threw the succession rules away, adopted her nephew, who was three years old, and got him installed as emperor

so she could be regent for him as well. In 1889, when the emperor was eighteen, Cixi "retired" but remained a powerful head of the family, with most government officials deferring to her rather than to the emperor.

But shit went down nine years later when the emperor decided to speed up the pace of change, launching his Hundred Days' Reform of politics, culture, and education. Cixi and more conservative members of government saw the reforms as too radical, fearing they would weaken the country. So, on September 21, 1898, she staged a coup d'état. She had the leaders of the reform movement executed and the emperor was exiled to house arrest for the remainder of his life.

Empress Dowager Cixi

Cixi would later implement reforms in China at a more moderate pace, but the Qing dynasty had problems that were beyond salvaging due to a combination of drought, civil unrest aimed at Chinese Christians, and foreign invasion by European, Russian, and Japanese powers. She died in 1908, and in 1911 the Xinhai Revolution brought an end to China's last imperial dynasty. Cixi was posthumously blamed, and history viewed her as a ruthless despot for many decades. More recent examinations determined she managed to maintain political order in a time of great turmoil.

The 2003 American invasion of Iraq may have been an epic clusterfuck done under false pretenses by war-profiteering ass monkeys, but there are still plenty of people who are happy that Saddam is dead. Kuwait wasn't the first nation he invaded in trying to establish Iraq as the dominant power in the region.

Revolutions rarely go smoothly, and Iran convulsed from the turmoil of the overthrow of the shah in 1979, an American puppet. With Iran being internationally isolated and facing sanctions, Saddam Hussein, who had officially ruled Iraq for only a year, saw an opportunity to seize territory and be the biggest bad boy on the Arab block, surpassing Egypt for dominance as a regional superpower.

Saddam had been vice president of Iraq since 1968, and a general of the military since 1976. He was *the* military strongman and had been investing heavily in the Iraqi military since 1975, when Iraq lost a border dispute with Iran over the Shatt al-Arab River, a strategically important waterway that provides access to the Persian Gulf. But in 1980, Iraq was now armed up the ass, and the Iranian military was in shambles. Egged on by both Saudi Arabia and Kuwait, who were enemies of Iraq, but I guess wanted to see a fight anyway because they also didn't like Iran, Saddam struck on September 22, 1980.

Iraq launched a full-scale invasion of its neighbor, beginning with a surprise air strike against Iranian air forces on the ground, hoping to copy the success Israel had with such a move in 1967 against its enemies during the Six-Day War. But it wasn't much of a success, and a ground invasion began the next day. Iraq captured 10,000 square miles of Iranian territory, but then the advance stalled. Saddam held the belief that Iran would collapse in the face of his invasion, but the opposite happened.

September 22, 1980

The people of Iran rallied around their nation and fought back with religious fervor. Quite literally. Iran is 95 percent Shia Muslim, and Iraq was ruled primarily by Sunni Muslims, and those two don't always get along so well. Bogged down, the conflict came to resemble World War I with trench warfare, barbed wire, machine-gun nests, and even the use of chemical weapons. As a bonus, Iran used lots of child soldiers too, because they were running out of adults. It's okay, though; those kids were given "keys to paradise" to gain them access to heaven if they died in battle.

Eight years of war and about a million dead later, the war came to an end. It was a stalemate with both sides claiming victory, but the only thing accomplished was massive death and destruction. Iranian Supreme Leader Ayatollah Khomeini, who hated Saddam and Iraq the way Trumpers hate it when Black people vote, referred to the United Nations Security Council ceasefire agreement as "taking poison." It was a bit slow-acting though. Khomeini died a year later.

When **Greta Thunberg** was fifteen, she was supposed to be in school learning to become a good little consumer of planetary resources. Instead, she was protesting the lack of action on climate change outside Swedish Parliament. And hordes of pasty penis-possessors from o'er the land collectively fudged their undergarments and unleashed the ALL CAPS fury, screeching like howler monkeys on a meth bender.

September 23, 2019

Born in Stockholm in 2003, by the age of eight Greta became obsessed over so little being done about an issue critical to the fate of humanity. In the spring of 2018, she won a climate change essay prize hosted by a Swedish newspaper, writing, "I want to feel safe. How can I feel safe when I know we are in the greatest crisis in human history?" Greta tried to organize a school strike, but when she couldn't get any takers, went ahead and did it by herself.

The following August, after Sweden experienced the hottest summer in 262 years, resulting in massive wildfires, Greta launched her protest. Rather than return to school, she protested alone outside Parliament every day until the September 9 elections, often in the rain, demanding her government follow the Paris Agreement on carbon emissions. On the first day, she posted a photo of her campaign on social media and the internet responded, sharing it widely.

After the election she returned to school but continued to protest every Friday. She

soon began attending demonstrations and speaking publicly across Europe while mobilizing her rapidly growing social media following to take action. At Greta's urging, over 20,000 students held similar climate protests in hundreds of cities around the world that December. The following spring, *The Guardian* wrote about "The Greta Thunberg Effect" and the young Swede made the cover of *Time* magazine as a "Next Generation Leader." Later that summer, she sailed across the Atlantic in a much-publicized carbon-neutral voyage to New York. The following month, on September 23, 2019, she addressed the United Nations Climate Action Summit.

"You have stolen my dreams and my childhood with your empty words, yet I'm one of the lucky ones," she spoke to them. "People are suffering, people are dying, entire ecosystems are collapsing." Holding back tears, she chastised world leaders for embracing "fairy tales of eternal economic growth." Toward the end she stabbed at them: "The eyes of all future generations are upon you. And if you choose to fail us, I say: We will never forgive you."

"How dare you?" she said to them. Four times during her four-and-a-half-minute speech she asked the same question about their lack of action: "How dare you?"

In the General Assembly Hall of the United Nations, to dozens of heads of state, business leaders, and senior representatives of civil society, Greta repeated those three words while being broadcast on live television to the world.

"How dare you?"

Just because you refer to polygamy as "plural marriage" doesn't make it any more palatable. Especially when you consider how one-sided it was/is among Mormons. Men could have lots of wives, but women were forbidden from having more than one husband. When it came time to officially end the sister-wife shit, it was done with great reluctance, and some didn't get the memo.

Joseph Smith talked to an angel and golden plates blah blah was founder of the Church of Jesus Christ of Latter-day Saints; he took over fifty wives. It's the women who suffer under polygyny, which is when polygamy is practiced by having multiple wives, not multiple husbands. A 2015 study of 171 countries found higher rates of violence toward women and children in polygynous societies. The authors stated that their research "clearly documents polygyny as a practice that constitutes a fundamental abuse of basic human rights and dignity."

By the late nineteenth century, the U.S. government had enough of the Mormons' shit and in 1887 passed an anti-polygamy law that disincorporated the LDS church and ordered the seizure of its assets. The church was all "No! Not the assets!" and fought back, but the law was upheld by the Supreme Court and in 1890, on September 24, the Mormons reluctantly issued the "Woodruff Manifesto," which officially advised against all future plural marriage. But if you and granddad already had a bunch of wives, you were "grandfathered" in. If you had five you could keep them but needed to cancel plans for turning that thirteen-year-old girl down the lane into #6.

Speaking of the term "grandfather clause," it has a racist history; it's related to preventing Black people from voting in Southern states for many decades following the Civil War and the passage of the Fifteenth Amendment. Briefly, it meant that anyone whose ancestors had the right to vote prior to the Civil War—meaning white people—were exempt from all sorts of new voting restrictions.

September 24, 1890

Anyway, it's important to note that at the time, polygyny was not uncommon, being practiced by approximately a quarter of Mormon families. Many were not pleased by the Woodruff Manifesto. You know how the South went to war over slavery? The Mormons once went to war over polygyny, with it being a major factor in the Utah War of 1857–58.

Many were pissed, proclaiming the manifesto would destroy their (misogynistic) way of life. And they continued taking multiple wives. The phasing-out of polygyny was a gradual process, but the United States decided they were doing a good enough job of it to allow Utah to become a part of the Union in 1896.

In 1904, with Mormons sneaking off to Canada and Mexico to add more wives, there was a second LDS manifesto banning new plural marriages worldwide. Nevertheless, there remain fundamentalist Mormon sects that believe polygyny is a requirement for "exaltation"—the highest level of salvation—and still practice it today.

Ruth Bader Ginsburg, may her memory be a blessing, said, "When I'm sometimes asked when will there be enough [women on the Supreme Court] and I say, 'When there are nine,' people are shocked. But there'd been nine men, and nobody's ever raised a question about that." This is the story of the first woman.

Reagan, despite the deification of him by many on the right, was not a good president. Trickle-down economics can inhale a big bag of dog farts. He did do one right thing, at least, and that was to finally get a woman as an associate justice on the Supreme Court of the United States: Sandra Day O'Connor.

Reagan had promised to appoint a woman to the Supreme Court as part of his election campaign, and in a rare show of good faith by a politician he followed through. He announced he would nominate O'Connor in early July of 1981, giving her one day's notice. She didn't know she was a candidate.

Reagan wrote in his diary that he caught shit from the pro-forced-birth religious wingnuts because they believed, correctly, that she would not be on board with over-turning *Roe v. Wade.* She said she found abortion personally repugnant but wasn't interested in changing the law. And so of course there was a big religious shitshow over the nomination, with Jerry Falwell and others stirring up much excrement over the choice. They didn't like her support for the Equal Rights Amendment either. Which, by the way, *still* has not been ratified.

Her confirmation hearing began on September 9, and for the first time the process was televised. Much of it focused on the issue of abortion. O'Connor was careful not to speak out in favor of abortion rights, because 'Murica. The judiciary committee approved her with seventeen votes in favor and one vote of "present." With one senator absent, she was confirmed by the Senate in a vote of 99–0. On September 25, 1981, she was sworn in.

Her voting record was very conservative, at least at first. Gradually it became somewhat less so, with her becoming more of a swing vote between conservative and liberal in more contentious decisions. Still, she didn't side against the conservative blocs all that often.

O'Connor retired in 2006 and was replaced by Samuel Alito. In 2009, President Obama awarded her the Presidential Medal of Freedom.

In **2016,** Donald Trump wore enough makeup during the presidential debates to decorate a clown college. But in 1960, Richard Nixon refused it, not understanding how the relatively new medium of television was going to make his undecorated face look the same as his soul: dead.

Nixon was vice president and had been serving under the popular war hero Eisenhower for the previous eight years. John F. Kennedy was a junior senator from a wealthy family. It was a closely contested election; Nixon held a slight lead going into the first-ever televised presidential debate on September 26, 1960. Many believe the results hinged on that single night.

Eisenhower probably would have destroyed Kennedy in 1960, but this was the first U.S. election post-ratification of the Twenty-Second Amendment: the one that says presidents can serve a maximum of two terms.

It was thought Nixon's knowledge of foreign policy and experience with radio debates would hand him victory, but image is important. Nixon had suffered a serious knee injury and spent the previous two weeks in hospital, losing significant weight. He looked drawn and his shirt was ill-fitting. His refusal of makeup made his five o'clock shadow visible against his pale face, and his tan suit blended into the background.

To the 70 million people tuning in, Nixon looked like shit. Conversely, Jack Kennedy had spent the previous two weeks campaigning in South Carolina and was sporting a tan. He wore a darker suit and had wisely taken the advice to wear makeup. He was also a handsome devil. Nixon next to Kennedy was like comparing those sarcastic "Nailed it!" baking fails against what it's supposed to look like.

September 26, 1960

Nothing more clearly displays the importance of image than the post-debate polling revealing that those who listened on the radio thought Nixon won, and those who watched the debate on TV said Kennedy was the victor. After the debate, Kennedy took a jump in the polls.

There were three more TV debates, and Nixon had learned his lesson. He regained the weight and wore makeup. Polls showed he won the second and third debate, and the fourth was declared a draw. But the number of viewers was far lower during the subsequent three than for the first debate, so for Nixon the damage was done.

JFK narrowly won the popular vote, garnering 49.72 percent to Nixon's 49.55 percent. More important, he took 303 members of the Electoral College to Nixon's 219. After his victory Kennedy himself said, "It was TV more than anything else that turned the tide."

> **After his victory Kennedy himself said, "It was TV more than anything else that turned the tide."**

In 1980 there was a TV miniseries based on James Clavell's novel of the same name titled *Shōgun*. The main character is an English sailor, and when he meets a Jesuit priest in Japan, he gets rather pissy. Being only twelve years old at the time, I didn't understand why the sailor would hate the priest so much. Later, I learned it's because Jesuits were dicks.

September 27, 1540

Jesuits are members of the Society of Jesus, and Jesus might think they were dicks too. The order was founded by Spanish Basque Catholic priest Ignatius of Loyola and six others. Ignatius's birth name was Iñigo, and like *The Princess Bride* character of the same name, he was known for poking holes in people with his sword. However, he was anything but honorable about it.

He was a punk, a womanizer, and often engaged in duels over the slightest insult. A military man, he fought in many battles without injury until a cannonball ricochet shattered his leg, ending his career. During his recovery, he turned to Jesus, and later began the Society of Jesus, which Pope Paul III confirmed on September 27, 1540.

The society's role is to travel the world and convert people to Catholicism because those heathens are just too fucking stupid and need to be evangelized toward the one true faith. The papal bull that began the order proclaimed the society "Government of the Church Militant"; the priests were considered "soldiers of God" in "defense and propagation of the faith," and Ignatius was named Superior General.

In addition to evangelizing Catholicism throughout the world, the order was known for power-seeking within the Church, and was linked to assassination attempts of both French and English kings. It also excluded Jews and Muslims who had converted to Catholicism from joining the order. The Goa Inquisition, which was Portuguese Catholics persecuting the shit out of Hindus, Jews, Buddhists, and even other Catholics in India, was initiated by Francis Xavier, a co-founder of the Jesuits. That inquisition lasted almost three centuries. Jesuits also basically gave us the term "the ends justify the means" by believing that it was just peachy to use dirty tactics to win a "righteous" battle.

But there was good with the bad. Jesuit schools were dedicated to the study of science, making significant contributions. Jesuits were also very opposed to Nazis and were viciously targeted by Hitler. The order was active in the rescue of Jews from the Holocaust, often hiding them in monasteries and schools despite the peril associated with doing so.

It remains a powerful and expansive order, active in over a hundred countries worldwide.

n 1901, President McKinley was shot in the guts and died from an infection. In 1981, President Reagan was shot, and the damage was far more dire than what McKinley suffered, yet he was saved. Part of Reagan's treatment involved multiple antibiotics, the first of which was discovered on September 28, 1928.

Cheese doesn't last long enough in our house to grow mold, but sometimes bread does. When I see that shit, I'm all ew gross and throw it out. Because mold is gross. And, as it turns out, also life-saving. Did you watch *Game of Thrones*? Badass Dothraki Khal Drogo died from a small cut that got infected. Throughout history people have died from ingrown fucking toenails. Mary Queen of Scots's first husband, the king of France, died from a goddamn ear infection. Prior to the twentieth century, once you were born you were just as likely to die before the age of fifteen as not, no matter where you were from or who your parents were. Bacteria kills motherfuckers, and it was important to find a way to kill the motherfucking bacteria first.

Alexander Fleming, a Scottish physician and microbiologist, had heard the rumors. As early as the late nineteenth-century researchers had posited that the mold *Penicillium* might contain antibacterial properties, but the process for it killing bacteria re-

mained elusive. It's possible that mold was known to kill bacteria long before, as there is evidence of ancient Egyptians using moldy bread as part of poultices for infected wounds. The way it works is that the fungi sees bacteria as competition and kills it.

September 28, 1928

Dr. Fleming was experimenting in the Inoculation Department of London's St. Mary's Hospital. He was not known for fastidiousness in his research, rather he was sloppy. Returning from vacation on September 3, 1928, and having left shit scattered around, he discovered that staphylococcus bacteria had accidentally contaminated a culture plate, and the plate was growing mold on it. And where there was mold, there was no staph.

He developed a hypothesis and tested it on September 28, 1928, confirming that the "mold juice" had the ability to kill a wide range of bacteria. He published his findings in the *British Journal of Experimental Pathology* the following year, but uptake was slow, as penicillin was difficult to isolate and manufacture on a massive scale. It would be more than a decade before methods were developed to mass-produce the drug, changing the course of modern medicine.

You know that *300* movie and how the sequel was about a big naval battle? I sure do, because I used to write about fitness for the *Los Angeles Times* and got to interview actors Lena Headey and Eva Green when *Rise of an Empire* came out. Surprise: The movie wasn't that historically accurate, but the naval battle was one of the most important turning points in ancient history.

September 29, 480 B.C.E.

That naval battle was during the second invasion of Greece by the Persian Empire. The first invasion was a decade previous and ended with a Greek victory at the Battle of Marathon and yeah that's why people now run marathons. Anyway, the second invasion began with the Battle of Thermopylae and the brave last stand of the 300 Spartans, but the math is off because it was actually about 7,000 various Greeks holding a choke point and killing the shit out of about 20,000 Persians. But the Persians still had another 80,000 soldiers, so the Greeks lost that battle. Around the same time as Thermopylae, the Greek navy was getting its ass kicked by Persians in the Battle of Artemisium; they retreated after suffering heavy losses. Things were not looking good for Greece.

Thermopylae, although a loss for Greece, showed how a small number of men could hold a narrow passage against a large army. Same deal with the Battle of Salamis, which took place about a month later, except on water. The Greeks were terribly outnumbered, but Athenian general Themistocles persuaded the various Greek allies to take their battered fleet into battle again, except this time being smarter about it.

Subterfuge won the day; Themistocles used a spy to convince the Persian navy he wanted to defect to their side and that the Greek command was fighting among itself. Considering this was a loose alliance, it wasn't hard to believe. Themistocles convinced Persian emperor Xerxes that if he sailed into the narrow straits on either side of the island of Salamis, he could block those ships seeking to flee and crush the alliance. While the Persians sought fleeing Greek ships, the defenders went on the offense.

The Greeks had fewer than 400 ships. The Persians had approximately 2,500. In the narrow straits their vastly superior numbers were a hindrance, making maneuvering impossible. On September 29, 480 B.C.E., the Persians were in nautical chaos as the organized and determined Greek fleet went on a sinking spree, winning the day. Xerxes said fuck this I'm bored and took a sizable chunk of his army home, leaving his general behind to mop up the Greeks on land and sea. He had every reason to believe that would be successful, because the Persians still had vastly superior numbers.

But it was not to be. The following year, on land at the Battle of Plataea and on sea at the Battle of Mycale, the Greeks sent the rest of Xerxes's forces packing. Well, not many of them. They killed most of the Persian soldiers and sailors, and only a small portion ever made it home.

That was the end of Ancient Persia invading Greece.

Americans have little knowledge of the atrocities they've supported across the world, so let's educate you about one few have ever heard of, even though it resulted in about a million deaths in only a year's time, making it one of the worst mass murders of the twentieth century.

This "on this day" begins by discussing the "30 September Movement" in Indonesia. The year was 1965, and the country was communist at a time when the good old U.S.A. had a real erection for killin' commies.

Indonesia is a new country. It was part of the Dutch Empire prior to World War II, during which it was invaded by Japan. With Japan's surrender, its people finally said fuck this we're running our own show now and declared independence, with Sukarno, which was his full name, as president in 1945. And he was president for a long time. By the early '60s he was veering the country to the left and the United States and Brits were using words like "liquidate" in reference to him because of his anti-imperialist foreign policy and development of ties with China and the Soviet Union.

Sukarno was in a perilous position. He'd placed many communists in positions of power, but the United States started backing right-wing factions within the Indonesian military. Realizing the country was a powder keg, the communists struck first. They formed their group on September 30, but the attempted coup d'état came the following day, and it did not go well.

September 30, 1965

In an effort to keep Sukarno in power, the communists assassinated six army generals and took the president under their protection, but by the end of the day the coup had failed, largely due to incompetent leadership and a swift counterstrike by right-wing military elements under Suharto (note: also his full name). Then everything went to even larger shit.

Suharto, in many ways, became de facto leader of Indonesia and began a purge of the country's communists. And by "purge" I mean massive fucking genocide, with the help of America. Those murderous cockgoblins in the CIA supported the killings, providing weapons, economic assistance, and training to over 1,200 senior officers to make them more efficient at dealing death. The CIA even created lists of communist officials to give to right-wing death squads for targeting. It is estimated that a million or more people were murdered over the following year. It wasn't just members of the Communist Party who were targeted, but atheists, "unbelievers," and ethnic Chinese people.

Suharto officially punted Sukarno in 1967 and assumed the presidency, remaining in power as a ruthless military dictator for the next three decades.

> **The CIA even created lists of communist officials to give to right-wing death squads for targeting.**

October

A hundred and fifty years after Xerxes and his Persians gave up trying to conquer Greece, Alexander the Great was all "Payback time, motherfuckers!" That payback culminated in the Battle of Gaugamela. And while the Persians didn't have much success with their attempts to conquer Greece, Alexander used his brilliant tactics to defeat a superior force and bring the Persian Empire to an end.

You know Aristotle? Of course you do. Dude was famous. Imagine having him as a teacher. Well, nowadays I'm sure he'd be spewing some shit we consider pretty fucked-up. But back then he was the pedagogical man, and he was responsible for Alexander's education. In 336 B.C.E. Alex's dad, Phillip II, was assassinated, and Alex ascended the throne at the age of twenty.

Phil had conquered and unified Greece, and Alex inherited a powerful kingdom with a strong and professional military. So, he wanted to play with it and do some conquering. Alexander would live to be only thirty-two, but he would spend the majority of his reign campaigning. Undefeated in battle, he is considered one of the greatest military commanders in history.

On October 1, 331 B.C.E., Alexander slept in. As was his habit, he ensured his soldiers were rested and well fed before battle. Conversely, the forces of the Achaemenid (Persian) emperor Darius III had been awake throughout the night, fearing an attack that never came. Darius had chosen the battlefield (in what is now northern Iraq), and the numbers are hazy because it was a long fucking time ago, but it is certain the Persians had a vastly superior force.

October 1, 331 B.C.E.

One brilliant tactic Alexander employed to defeat his enemy was a flanking maneuver that was actually a feint. He ordered his cavalry far to the right, making it appear as though he intended to attack the Persian forces from the side. Darius ordered his troops to match Alexander's cavalry to prevent them from being outflanked. Alexander moved them even farther right, and the Persians matched him, and the Greeks moved even further . . . and in so doing he pulled the Persian cavalry far enough out of position to create a gap that allowed the Greek troops massed in the center, led by Alexander himself, to attack with concentrated force, creating a wedge in the Persian lines, charging straight toward Emperor Darius.

Rumor has it that Alexander spied Darius on the battlefield and hurled a spear at him, missing the Persian emperor by inches. Frightened and seeing that his life was in personal peril, Darius fled the field and his troops quickly surrendered. The Persian Empire soon fell. To this day, Alexander's tactics are taught in military academies throughout the world.

In 1968 not a lot of Mexicans were excited for the Olympic Games set to be held in Mexico City that year, probably because their president spent the equivalent of a billion dollars on the Olympics rather than feed the people. When the people protested, murder happened.

October 2, 1968

The games were to begin on October 12, and the Mexico City summer was marked by growing protests. Social tensions were high, and President Ordaz suppressed labor unions and farmers who were pissed at, well, everything. Then university students got in on it, and the protests grew. Some of the protests were violent, but the one that took place on October 2, 1968, was peaceful.

Approximately 10,000 protestors arrived at the *Plaza de las Tres Culturas,* which I shouldn't have to translate, in the Tlatelolco district of the nation's capital, and the event began with speeches as they had oftentimes before. But the government was getting pissy about all this protesting stuff, what with the Olympics being only ten days away, and decided that high-velocity projectiles ripping through human tissue was a reasonable re-

> ## It wasn't just a short burst of fire, but a mass killing that went on into the night.

sponse to complaints about government corruption.

Troops were sent in. The official line, which was perpetuated via government-controlled media, was that the protestors shot at the troops first and those poor soldiers had no choice but to defend themselves. Of course, this was bullshit. You know who started the shooting? Fucking army snipers. They'd taken up positions on various rooftops and just began shooting into the crowd at a signal given by government helicopters dropping flares. This was planned murder. Then the soldiers on the ground joined in.

Protestors and passersby, journalists and children, were shot by government forces. It wasn't just a short burst of fire, but a mass killing that went on into the night. The government downplayed the number of deaths, but estimates are that hundreds were killed and many more wounded. Over a thousand were arrested. Thirty years later there was an official investigation, but no one was ever held accountable. In 2003 it was discovered the United States played a role in the massacre, providing weapons, training, and intelligence leading up to the events of October 2.

Y'all know that *Black Hawk Down* movie, in addition to being racist as fuck, contains a lot of bullshit, right? Although the Battle of Mogadishu technically achieved its aims by capturing the intended targets, it was a hollow victory that eventually led to the United Nations washing its hands of Somalia.

In the modern world, people don't starve unless someone wants them to, and like so many other wars, the Somali Civil War used hunger as a weapon. The UN became involved to provide food aid, then decided fuck it, let's bring in some good old Western democracy too. Except the warlord running the show in Somalia, Mohamed Aidid, wasn't keen on that.

In August, Aidid's militia had killed and wounded some American soldiers, so President Bill Clinton authorized payback. On October 3, 1993, Task Force Ranger, which was made up of Delta Force and Ranger operators along with Navy SEALs, launched what was intended to be a quick assault to take captive two of Aidid's high-ranking henchmen. The operation was supposed to take thirty minutes. But as nineteenth-century Prussian field marshal Helmuth von Moltke said, "No battle plan ever survives contact with the enemy."

It didn't go as planned because the Somalis fought back. The Delta team came in via helicopter to secure its targets and was to be extracted via a ground convoy. But citizens and militia, encouraged by Aidid's men on megaphones telling Somalis to protect their homes, blocked the roadways. The Somalis also used rocket-propelled grenades to shoot down not just one Black Hawk helicopter, but two. The American troops went in to rescue the downed flight crews, and the firefight began in earnest, lasting fifteen hours.

October 3, 1993

One thing the battle revealed is the value of training and superior weaponry. The Americans were badly outnumbered, but their "kill ratio" was a tactical victory. Nineteen U.S. troops died and seventy-three were wounded, but the force consisted of highly trained and well-equipped soldiers, fighting a ragtag militia. They killed several hundred Somalis and wounded several hundred more, many of whom would later die due to lack of proper medical aid. The kill ratio may have been as high as 50 to 1. America, fuck yeah!

But even such a tactical victory wasn't palatable to the American public, and the newly elected Clinton decided his nation shouldn't be acting as police for Somalia and withdrew troops over the next six months. Even more lawlessness followed in the country, transforming Somalia into a recruiting ground for anti-American terrorists. It inspired men such as Osama bin Laden because it gave the impression that if you bloodied America, it'd run.

Except it didn't run after 9/11. America created that Department of Homeland Acts of Patriotism thing and invaded countries and had more massively one-sided kill ratios in their favor, and they still lost those fucking wars.

Hell is other people while traveling coach, what with their seat yanking and terrible hygiene and dumbass luggage fuckery. *Stop doing goddamn pirouettes in the aisle and bashing me in the head with your oversized fucking backpack!* But at least we get to see the world. Back in "simpler" times, travel was such an ordeal that most people never went beyond a short distance from their home. It was usually only the very rich who went anywhere. And in 1883, the wealthy finally got to see Europe in real style with the opening of the Orient Express.

October 4, 1883

The first leg of the route opened in June, beginning in Paris, but the terminus was Vienna. Nice place. Lots of history. But not the Orient. It was October 4, 1883, when the rest of the route opened so people could travel from *la Ville Lumière* all the way to Constantinople, which wouldn't be called Istanbul for another half century.

It wasn't just one train, or even one route. The original trip required passengers to disembark in Romania to be ferried across the Danube to Bulgaria, where they would catch another train to the Bulgarian city of Varna, followed by a 150-mile ferry ride to Constantinople. The final leg of the train ride to Constantinople wasn't finished until 1885. Other routes were added through Switzerland and Italy in later years. Of course, all routes were shut down during the two World Wars, because people were rather busy killing each other across most of the continent.

The train was an inspired vision by a Belgian son of a banker named George Nagelmackers, who wanted to give (rich) people the opportunity to cross the continent in posh comfort, introducing luxurious sleeper cars for travelers. It took almost two decades and several false starts to bring the dream to fruition, and the inaugural voyage to Istanbul was a media event. Attendees marveled at how entering the train was like walking into one of the finest hotels in Europe. It contained intricate wood paneling and opulent leather furniture. During the eighty-hour trip from Paris to Istanbul, travelers slept on silk sheets.

Royalty traveled on and even drove the Express; the king of Bulgaria fancied himself an engineer and demanded he be permitted to drive the train through his country, which he did at a dangerous velocity. James Bond battled villains and bedded beauties on the Orient Express, but in the nonfiction realm the train was popular with real spies as well, because it made country-hopping both easier and more luxurious. It even gained the nickname "Spies' Express."

On November 11, 1918, one of the train cars was used for Germany to sign its surrender in World War I, and that car was proudly exhibited by the French until World War II. Petty douche that he was, Hitler had the French sign their 1940 surrender in the same car. As the war turned against Germany, Hitler had the car blown up because he didn't want the Allies to have it as a trophy yet again.

People forget just how fucking crazy the '70s were. Like, even Canada had a homegrown terrorist organization that was kidnapping diplomats and politicians, and they murdered one of them. But Justin's dad, Pierre, wasn't having it. He sent in the military.

The "October Crisis" began on October 5, 1970, with the kidnapping of British diplomat James Cross at his diplomatic residence in Montreal by the *Front de Libération du Québec,* which I expect you can decipher even if you don't speak French. The FLQ had been around since the early '60s and had detonated almost a thousand bombs. The group mostly targeted mailboxes in affluent anglophone neighborhoods such as the suburb of Westmount near Montreal. One bomb attack on the Montreal Stock Exchange in 1969 caused massive damage and injured twenty-seven people.

They financed their group via bank robberies, and stole dynamite from military and industrial sites. By 1970, twenty-three members of the FLQ were in prison. They took Cross from his home at gunpoint and told authorities they would exchange him for release of FLQ "political prisoners" and having the CBC broadcast their manifesto.

The CBC broadcast took place on October 8, and two days later the group kidnapped Quebec's deputy premier Pierre Laporte from his front lawn as he played football with his nephew. The military was then sent in to guard federal property in Montreal. CBC conducted a combative interview with Prime Minister Pierre Trudeau, asking how far he intended to take the military response. Trudeau replied with "Just watch me."

October 5, 1970

On October 16, Trudeau implemented the War Measures Act, suspending habeas corpus and giving far-reaching powers to police. Polls showed Canadians overwhelmingly supported the move. The next day, the FLQ announced they'd executed Pierre Laporte. His strangled body was found in the trunk of a car at a regional airport across the river from Montreal. The killers would be captured a couple of months later and charged with his kidnapping and murder.

James Cross was held captive for two months by a separate cell of the FLQ. He was finally released in exchange for the five kidnappers receiving safe passage to Cuba, which was approved by Fidel Castro. Shockingly, within a dozen years all convicted participants in the kidnappings and murder had been paroled, and those who fled to Cuba had all returned to Canada, some to serve short sentences.

In the aftermath, there was a significant loss of support for the use of violence by those seeking Quebec sovereignty.

Anwar Sadat was president of Egypt from 1970 to 1981, leaving office via assassination. He had been immensely popular, but in 1979 he signed a peace treaty with Israel that won him (and Israeli prime minister Menachem Begin) the Nobel Peace Prize. It also won him great enmity in the Muslim world. He signed the accord knowing it was likely the same as signing his own death warrant.

October 6, 1981

After ascending to the presidency, Sadat became popular for expelling the Soviet military from the country, opening up the economy, restraining the despised secret police, and reforming the military for another showdown with Israel. Egypt had lost the Sinai Peninsula in a war with Israel in 1967, and on October 6, 1973, Sadat, along with a coalition of Arab states, launched war against Israel to get some payback. It wasn't exactly a victory, but there were early successes in the war that restored Arab pride after the ass-kicking they took in '67. Sadat was a hero.

The peace process began in 1978, brokered by President Jimmy Carter. The terms were that the two countries recognize each other, making Egypt the first Arab country to acknowledge Israel, and ending the state of war that had existed between them since Israel declared statehood three decades earlier. It also saw the complete withdrawal of Israel from the Sinai Peninsula, which it had occupied for the previous dozen years.

The Arab and wider Muslim world was pissed. They saw the treaty as a betrayal of Arab unity against the "Zionist entity." Within Egypt many were pleased with the return of the Sinai, with the exception of the country's powerful Muslim Brotherhood who despised the thought of peace with Israel. Additionally, those on the left were vexed at Sadat for not holding Israel to the fire on the issue of Palestinian statehood.

Within two years of the signing of the peace treaty, things had gone to shit in Egypt. There was rampant inflation due to the country's isolation by other Arab nations, leading to rioting. Islamists in the country began to stockpile weapons and recruit officers in the military; an attempted coup in June of 1981 led to military crackdowns and imprisonments.

On October 6, 1981, there was a military parade in Cairo celebrating the initial victories of the 1973 war with Israel; Sadat was in attendance. A militant jihad cell that had been missed during the roundups disguised itself as part of the parade, and assassins leaped from a truck and attacked President Sadat with grenades and assault rifles, killing him and eleven others.

The assassination had been "approved" as a fatwā (a ruling under Islamic law) by Sheikh Omar Abdel-Rahman, who died in a U.S. prison in 2017 for his role in the 1993 World Trade Center bombing.

Mother Teresa was . . . not a saint. Well, technically she was, but in practice, not so much. How dare someone criticize a saint? It's easier if you realize that religion is a human construct, and that saints and miracles don't exist except in the minds of people who built one of the largest and most successful systems of control in human history.

Born Anjezë Gonxhe Bojaxhiu in 1910 in what is now North Macedonia, then later becoming Sister Teresa, she proclaimed that while visiting Calcutta (now Kolkata) she received an "order" as a religious experience to help the poor. Her missionary work received enough attention that on October 7, 1950, the Vatican okayed the Missionaries of Charity. She claimed its intention was to help "the hungry, the naked, the homeless, the crippled, the blind, the lepers, all those people who feel unwanted, unloved, uncared for throughout society . . ." Just how well she cared for such people became a subject of much debate.

Being she won a Nobel Peace Prize in 1979, and the Catholic Church canonized her in 2016, there has of course been much criticism of the criticism, but the criticism is based on direct observation and research, so here we go.

Dr. Aroup Chatterjee, a physician born and raised in Kolkata, spent years as an activist in the city's slums and worked in one of Teresa's charitable homes. Disgusted with what he saw, he conducted over a hundred interviews to write a book describing Teresa's "cult of suffering." Noted atheist Christopher Hitchens penned his own short polemical tome criticizing Teresa for using the wretched state of those she professed to help as propaganda pieces to promote fundamentalist Catholicism.

October 7, 1950

Tremendous amounts of money poured into the Missionaries of Charity, but most didn't appear to find its way to helping those in need. Rather, it went toward converting people to Christianity. Children were tied to beds. Those dying in agony were given little more than aspirin. Hypodermic needles were reused, and there was zero privacy even for defecation. People with no medical training administered long-expired medicines. Shit-stained blankets were washed in the same sink as dishes.

The editor for *The Lancet,* who visited Teresa's Kolkata hospice in 1994, described the care as "haphazard" and observed that many in the hospice weren't actually dying, but simply ill; yet there was no proper diagnosis or effort to save them. Pain management was practically nonexistent. And a 2013 academic study out of the University of Montreal revealed that her hallowed image was carefully constructed by the Catholic Church rather than earned via merit, and that the missions practiced "caring for the sick by glorifying their suffering instead of relieving it."

Mother Teresa said in 1981, "I think it is very beautiful for the poor to accept their lot . . . I think the world is being much helped by the suffering of the poor people."

That's fucked-up.

OCTOBER

World War I was almost over, and thirty-year-old Sergeant Alvin York originally didn't even want to fight in it for religious reasons, but then he did go, and killed a shit-ton of Germans, earning the Medal of Honor. Take that, God of nonviolence.

October 8, 1918

Raised poor in Tennessee, York was known as a drunken brawler, but in 1915, at the age of twenty-seven, he had a religious experience and vowed to cease his sinful ways. Two years later the United States finally said fine I guess we'll help defeat Germany and York registered for the draft as legally required. He claimed a religious exemption, writing "Don't want to fight." His conscientious objector status was denied, twice, and in 1918 he was off to Europe, handed a rifle, and told to go do some killing.

As a private he spent much time in conversation with his devoutly Christian company commander, who said it was fine to kill for Jesus if the cause was just. He prayed on it and decided he was ready to shut up and soldier, and did he ever.

Through the summer of 1918 he saw a lot of action and was promoted to corporal. In the last great push of the war, with only a month left in the fighting, York was part of the Meuse-Argonne offensive. On the morning of October 8, his company advanced into withering machine-gun fire. Many were killed or wounded in the first wave. York was part of the second wave, comprising seven-teen men, attempting to flank the machine-gun nest. The Germans weren't having it and killed or wounded ten men in a burst of fire. Of the remaining seven, six of them took cover, but York was all fuck this now I'm mad.

Skilled with a rifle, he picked off eighteen Germans with eighteen shots. "Every time one of them raised his head, I jes' teched him off," he later said. "I was shootin' pretty good." No shit. The Germans charged and he shot seven more with his pistol, bringing the tally to twenty-five enemy killed; others say he got even more than that. Inspired by York, his fellow soldiers started to attack the German force with vigor.

The German commander, realizing he was facing the fucking Grim Reaper in an American uniform (actually he thought he was under attack by a much larger force), surrendered. York and his men took the Germans prisoner. As they marched them back to Allied territory, they took additional prisoners, totaling 132 in all. York got a promotion to sergeant, a shit-ton of medals, and a movie made about him.

Some later claimed the story of York's heroics was exaggerated.

Sergeant Alvin York at the hill where he earned the Medal of Honor, 1919

f your god tells you to shoot a fifteen-year-old girl in the head because she promotes education for women, then your god is a fucking dick.

If you read any religious texts, most gods are dicks. Bunch of petty, slavery- and sexism-promoting vindictive assholes prone to fits of violent jealousy. But since they don't actually exist anyway, we can just blame asshole humans for inventing them as an excuse to be assholes. And the fucking Taliban sure are assholes.

Born in 1997 in Northwest Pakistan to a lower-middle-class Sunni Muslim family, Malala Yousafzai was educated mostly by her father, an educational activist. She began speaking publicly about education rights for women when she was only eleven, saying in a televised speech, "How dare the Taliban take away my basic right to an education?" And the Taliban was all, "Oh, yes. We don't have that right. Many apologies. We shall change our ways." Nah, they were gigantic cockwipes about the whole thing.

Early in 2009, Malala began blogging for the BBC. Meanwhile, the Taliban were terrorizing her part of the country and blowing up schools. Displaced by the violence, a *New York Times* documentary was made about her, and she continued to give numerous speeches and interviews, raising her profile markedly and winning her country's highest civilian honor. Death threats became a regular occurrence; they were published in newspapers, on her Facebook page, even slipped under her door.

The Taliban held a meeting about what to do about this terrible young girl they were so fearful of, and unanimously sanctioned an assassination. A spokesman said after the attack, "We had no intentions to kill her but were forced when she would not stop [speaking against us]." Yeah, real fucking heroes.

October 9, 2012

On October 9, 2012, two Taliban militants with previous assassination experience stopped her bus as she rode home from school. They asked which one was Malala, and the other girls would not say. Then they threatened to kill everyone, and Malala was identified. They shot her in the head, wounding two other girls on the bus in the process.

The international outcry was massive, including from President Obama and the UN secretary-general. That bullet sent from the would-be assassin's pistol propelled Malala from national treasure to international superstardom. After three days in a Pakistani hospital, she was transported to England for additional treatment; two days later she emerged from her coma.

Malala Yousafzai has continued her education and her activism, and in 2014 was co-recipient of the Nobel Peace Prize. As an additional fuck-you to the Taliban, in 2020 she graduated from Oxford University.

"**Panama**" by Van Halen is a great song. The Panama Canal is a great feat of engineering. And a pretty big fucking deal, because otherwise you had to go around an entire continent, and sailing around that southern tip had a tendency to kill people. Speaking of killing people . . .

October 10, 1913

The Isthmus of Panama was turned into a canal, no thanks to the French. They tried in 1881 but gave up thirteen years later because they kept having engineering problems and workers-dying problems. Not just from accidents, but the tropics are known for tropical diseases, and after 22,000 deaths the French said *putain* this and bugged out.

Nine years later the United States was all "We can do this no matter how many people have to die." And so they did. In order to make it happen they had to deal with the minor problem that Panama was part of Colombia and Colombia saying no fucking way. So, the United States sent in warships to support the Panamanian rebels who said, "We're gonna be our own fucking country, *pendejos*," and that's what they did. Panama declared independence in late 1903 and the United States was right there with the acknowledging "We got you, fam; strings attached tho."

President Theodore Roosevelt on a steam shovel at the Culebra Cut, 1906

The strings were a treaty that gave the United States control over building, indefinitely administering, and defending the canal. Basically, a violation of the new nation's sovereignty. But we're bigger than you so suck it. Panama was a U.S. protectorate until 1939.

The United States began construction and had learned from the French failures, implementing a massive sanitation and mosquito-killin' project to save workers' lives. Still, over the next decade another 5,600 died from disease and accidents, about 7.5 percent of the total workforce of 75,000. For comparison, about 2.5 percent of Americans who served in World War II were killed.

Over fifty miles long, the Panama Canal has been named one of the seven wonders of the modern world by the American Society of Civil Engineers. The big day for "this day in history" was October 10, 1913. That's when President Wilson sent a signal from the White House via telegraph that triggered a big kaboom. The explosion destroyed the Gamboa Dike—which is what it was supposed to do—and flooded the Culebra Cut, joining the Atlantic and Pacific Oceans together for the first time via the canal.

The canal was formally opened ten months later. To this day it remains one of the largest and most challenging engineering projects ever undertaken.

hree women publicly accused Brett Kavanaugh of sexual assault or sexual misconduct, and the Republican half of the Senate was all "He seems like a fine choice for the Supreme Court." To anyone who saw Clarence Thomas get the thumbs-up to be an SC justice in 1991, despite the withering testimony of Anita Hill, this does not come as a surprise.

President George H. W. Bush, who was accused by eight different women of groping them, nominated Clarence Thomas to the Supreme Court to replace Thurgood Marshall, who was the first Black man to occupy a spot on the top court in the land. Thomas had only been a judge for just over a year, and so the rationalization for his appointment was his allegedly outstanding character.

Initially, Thomas seemed a shoo-in, but a report of a private interview of Anita Hill by the FBI leaked to the press, and shit exploded. The hearings were reopened, and on October 11, 1991, Anita Hill testified before the Senate Judiciary Committee to tell the tale of how Thomas's character was anything but exemplary.

She testified that during her tenure as a lawyer at both the Department of Education and the Equal Employment Opportunity Commission, Thomas, her supervisor, repeatedly sexually harassed her. She said he asked her on dates over and over, and she always declined, asking him to stop, but he would not. She spoke of how he frequently talked about sex to her in descriptive detail, including talking about porn he watched. He talked about watching porn involving group sex, rape scenes, and women having sex with animals. He also often spoke to her about his own alleged sexual prowess.

October 11, 1991

Thomas responded that this was a racist smear campaign, despite the fact Hill is also Black and said it would have been "comfortable to remain silent," but when called to testify, felt it was important to tell the truth. Those who supported Thomas's nomination attacked Hill relentlessly, saying she suffered from a "delusional disorder." Four women who witnessed Thomas's actions were ready to testify to support Hill's accusations but were never called. So of course, Thomas was approved.

Joe Biden, who was chair of the Judiciary Committee at the time, called Anita Hill in 2019 to express "regret for what she endured." She said the call left her feeling unsatisfied, but in September 2020 Hill proclaimed that she would vote for Biden in the presidential election and work with him on gender issues.

In his tenure as an associate justice, Clarence Thomas is viewed as the most conservative member of the court.

Anita Hill testifies

On October 12, 1945, Desmond Doss became the first conscientious objector to be awarded the Medal of Honor for his actions during the bloodiest battle of the Pacific theater of World War II. And he never touched a rifle.

October 12, 1945

Doss was a religious man. I spoke with his only child, Tommy, who grew up hearing his father's story. We discussed a picture that hung on the wall of his father's childhood home in Lynchburg, Virginia. "It depicted the Ten Commandments," Tommy said. "Each commandment had a little drawing, and the sixth said, 'Thou Shalt Not Kill,' and it showed a picture of Cain after he killed his brother Abel." He would gaze at it again and again.

The defining moment for the rest of Desmond Doss's life arrived when the image of Cain killing Abel almost became real before his eyes. Desmond's father was a decorated veteran of World War I who suffered from PTSD, and he almost shot Desmond's uncle during a drunken argument. Desmond's mother grabbed the gun and told her son to hide it. Afterward, Desmond swore he'd never touch a gun again.

In 1942, with war ravaging the world, Doss registered for the draft and was called up. His shipyard work qualified him for a deferment, but he wanted to do his part. "I felt like it was an honor to serve God and country." His desire was not to take lives but save them.

He was classified as a conscientious objector, a designation he didn't want; he considered himself a "conscientious cooperator." The army tried to break him. Despite his designation, he was assigned to a rifle company; his request to be a medic was refused. Doss was abused by his fellow soldiers and given the worst duties.

In May 1945, despite suffering from tuberculosis, Doss was with the Ninety-Sixth Division as it attacked the Maeda Escarpment, nicknamed "Hacksaw Ridge," on Okinawa. After a vicious counterattack by Japanese forces, the Americans retreated back down a sheer cliff using cargo nets. Less than one-third of the men made it back down. Doss stayed behind.

Desmond Doss receiving the Medal of Honor from President Truman

Through the rest of that day and night, at constant risk of death from patrolling Japanese soldiers, Doss searched for his wounded comrades who were left for dead. He treated their wounds, dragged or carried them to the edge of the cliff, and fashioned a rope harness to lower them to safety. Without a weapon to protect himself, he repeated this more than seventy-five times.

When American forces went back up the ridge, Doss was with them. He was severely wounded in that action but survived and lived to be eighty-seven. One of the many lives Doss saved was that of his captain, Jack Glover, who had tried to get him transferred to a conscientious objector camp during training. Glover later said of Doss, "He was one of the bravest persons alive."

On October 13, 1908, Margaret Symons became the first woman ever to speak before the House of Commons in the U.K. House of Parliament. She was able to speak only a few words before being forcefully carried away, and she made them count.

Born Margaret Ann Williams in 1879, she accomplished through stealth what tens of thousands of others could not through mass gathering. In September of 1908, the Women's Social and Political Union printed and released a handbill with the title "Votes for Women," encouraging people to mass outside the House of Parliament on October 13 and "rush the House of Commons." In response, police issued arrest warrants for the three women who were leaders of the WSPU for inciting an illegal act.

As many as 60,000 massed outside in Trafalgar Square, but the police presence was overwhelming, and they prevented any rushing from taking place. Margaret Symons, however, worked as a journalist and had a friend who was a Member of Parliament. She knew that women were permitted within the building so long as they were escorted, and could even view the main chamber through a peephole.

As the crowd protested loudly outside, Symons escaped her escort and burst into the House of Commons where a debate was in progress. She yelled, "Attend to the women's question! Votes for women!" The men were frozen in surprise; the sergeant-at-arms recovered first and leaped toward Symons, grabbing her around the waist and carrying her from the room. As he did, she yelled again, "Votes for women!" The event was reported in major newspapers, capturing the tale of how history was made with her being the first woman to ever speak in the House of Commons.

October 13, 1908

It would be another ten years before women gained the right to vote in the U.K., so long as they were over the age of thirty. They did not attain voting rights equal to those of men for an additional ten years, in 1928. A woman did not speak in the House of Commons again until 1919, when Nancy Astor became the first woman to take her seat as a Member of Parliament, where she served until 1945.

As a consequence of her actions, Margaret Symons had her press permit to enter Parliament confiscated, although it was reinstated two years later. During and after World War I she worked as a journalist in Egypt.

You ever wonder how those Europeans developed their talent for just showing up in some already occupied land and saying, "This shit is ours now"? They practiced on each other a lot first. That's what the Battle of Hastings was in 1066, and the whole tale is way more complicated than just some dude who was king for less than a year getting an arrow in the eye.

October 14, 1066

Fucking hell, where to begin? How about Vikings? They went from mainland Europe to the British Isles and took a bunch of that shit starting in the eighth century. In the show *Vikings* there is a character named Rollo who kicked some French ass. Historically, there was a real Rollo who, after kicking some French ass, was granted lands in Normandy in 911. Basically, Vikings were killing and raping and stealing shit all over during this time, which leads us up to 1066.

At the beginning of that year the childless King Edward died in England and there was a succession crisis, proving yet again that inheritance is a shit system of governance. Harold, Earl of Wessex and brother-in-law to the dead king, was the richest and most powerful aristocrat so he got "elected" king. But Harald Hardrada, king of Norway, said no fucking way, that English crown was promised to me. William, Duke of Normandy and a direct descendent of Rollo, said no fucking way, that English crown was promised to *me*. Harold of Wessex said bring it on motherfuckers, and they did.

Hardrada attacked first, and after an initial victory got his ass kicked—and got dead—at the Battle of Stamford Bridge on September 25. So much for the Norwegian threat. But there was still William from Normandy. Three days later, while Harold and his forces were recovering from defeating Hardrada, William landed his forces in the south of England to establish a beachhead. Harold was all oh fuck we need to get our asses down there and kick those cocknockers off our island; they hurried south and arrived tired.

The two forces met in the Battle of Hastings on October 14, 1066. The opposing armies were of relatively equal size, but about a quarter of William's force was cavalry, whereas Harold had none such horsey soldiers. William was also a more skilled military commander. The battle raged for several hours, then Harold fell. Perhaps it was from an arrow in the eye, but others say four knights hacked him to bits. Dead is dead, and his troops fell apart after that.

William then marched across England, winning more victories, and was crowned king of England on Christmas Day. That's how he earned the name William the Conqueror.

> **Basically, Vikings were killing and raping and stealing shit all over during this time, which leads us up to 1066.**

She was born Margaretha Zelle in 1876 in the Netherlands but is known to history by her stage name: Mata Hari. She was an exotic dancer, a courtesan, and a spy. But that stuff about her spying for Germany during World War I is likely a pant-load. Didn't stop France from executing her though. They needed a scapegoat, and she was convenient.

At eighteen she married a wealthy army captain twenty years her senior in the Dutch East Indies (Indonesia), who had advertised his desire for a wife. He was a drunk who beat her and cheated on her. As a way to escape how shitty her life was, she studied Indonesian culture and dance.

The couple moved back to the Netherlands when she was twenty-four, and separated. Her husband basically abducted their one surviving child and Zelle had no financial means to get her daughter back, so she moved to Paris the following year, in 1903. Within a year she obtained fame as an exotic dancer. She was flirtatious and captivated wealthy men with her provocative nature. To appear more exotic, despite being white as white, she posed as a Javanese princess. Cultural appropriation for the win!

Her success spawned many imitators, but by 1912 she was getting older and you know how that goes for most dancing careers. Still, she remained popular among powerful men who wanted to sleep with her. Then, war.

As a Dutch citizen she was able to cross borders during the war because the Netherlands was neutral. Since she had performed for the German crown prince, France asked her to spy on him, thinking said prince had access to military secrets (he didn't). But then the Germans offered her money to spy for *them.* She took the money, but it is doubtful she did any actual spying for Germany. Overall, she was shit at being a spy, generating no intelligence for either side. Pissed off at the lack of results, Germany sent a "coded" message that was intended to be intercepted; it mentioned this awesome spy of theirs who was obviously Mata Hari.

October 15, 1917

The French intercepted the message as planned, and arrested Zelle in February 1917 and put her on trial to distract from the Great Mutinies of the French army. During her trial, prosecutors alleged she'd provided intelligence to the Germans that caused the deaths of tens of thousands of Allied soldiers, which was total bullshit; it was incompetent leadership that caused those deaths. The only "evidence" presented was to slut-shame her, saying her lack of morals meant of course she was guilty. The all-male tribunal quickly convicted her, and she was executed by firing squad on October 15, 1917.

Mata Hari performing in 1905

She never said, "Let them eat cake." The myth of a noblewoman uttering this phrase in reference to starving poor was around for about two centuries before Marie Antoinette, and it wasn't attributed to the French queen until five decades after her death.

Antoinette was a fish out of water and a political pawn used to cement a fragile alliance between her homeland of Austria with France. She was only fourteen when she was shipped off to marry the French heir to the throne, and before long became a victim of numerous lies that had the people of her new home despising her.

Marie was a homesick girl who sought escape in extravagance. In 1774, with the death of his grandfather, her husband Louis XVI ascended the French throne, and she became queen. Her husband was solitary, but Marie was a party girl. Living in luxury in the Palace of Versailles (I've been there, and all I can say is holy fucking shit), the royal couple was oblivious to the plight of the average French citizen.

Marie spent lavishly on dresses and jewelry and parties, but a comical scandal arose from the artificial hamlet created for her near the palace where she could escape court life by living in a fake gated village built solely for her and her close friends. Referred to as an "expensive pastoral comedy," it caused yet another uproar when the cost became known.

She became a target of ire among the people for her spending, and of course the criticism snowballed from there. She was called a whore, and it was said her children were not the king's, but bastards. Her reputation already suffering, it totally went to shit with the "Affair of the Diamond Necklace" in 1785. Marie was completely guiltless; con artists used her name to defraud the crown jewelers of an obscenely expensive necklace. But people didn't care about the truth; her poor reputation nosedived further and never recovered. People *hated* her.

Then in 1789 revolution began, and two years later the royal family attempted to escape France but were captured and returned to Paris. A year later Robespierre, a lawyer and statesman, was attaining power and gonna do his Reign of Terror thing and said fuck the monarchy, let's kill them.

The monarchy was abolished and Marie's husband the king was executed in January 1793. After a brief show trial Marie too was sent to the guillotine for crimes of treason, on October 16, 1793. She remained composed in front of the jeering crowd, and her final words were an apology to the executioner for accidentally stepping on his foot. She was buried in an unmarked grave but exhumed in 1815 during the Bourbon Restoration and was given a Christian burial in the Basilica of Saint-Denis.

Eight people died in the London Beer Flood, and since they're dead we can't ask them if it's better drowning in beer than drowning in regular water. I assume it still sucks.

It was called the Horse Shoe Brewery, and it had been in business in central London for half a century. On the afternoon of October 17, 1814, a clerk noticed a problem with one of the vats. Standing twenty-two feet tall and filled to the brim with thirty-three tons of ten-month-old porter, one of the vat's iron bands containing the behemoth of beer had slipped. The bands themselves weighed seven hundred pounds, and slipping was not uncommon. The clerk informed the supervisor, who told him to chill the fuck out. His exact words were "No harm whatsoever would ensue." Yeah, he was wrong.

The plan was to fix it later, but later wouldn't arrive. The band fell off, and with no warning the vat burst. This took out another vat to double the drunken drowning pleasure, and in all a few hundred thousand gallons of beer were released, destroying the back wall of the brewery and sending a fifteen-foot-high wave of suds down the street.

The deluge destroyed two houses and badly damaged two others. Five of the eight killed were attending an Irish wake for a two-year-old boy. Those inside the brewery survived but had to be pulled from the rubble.

Stories arose of hundreds of people gathering up the spilled beer, followed by much public drunkenness, but these were salacious rumors intended to slight the large Irish immigrant population in the neighborhood. No such revelry was reported by any credible source.

The brewery narrowly escaped insolvency, and the incident resulted in the phasing out of large wooden vats as beer containers.

Five of the eight killed were attending an Irish wake for a two-year-old boy. Those inside the brewery survived but had to be pulled from the rubble.

Phillis Wheatley, despite being immensely intelligent and talented, died young and poor, because America is only the land of opportunity for a select few.

October 18, 1773

She was born in West Africa around 1753 and sold into slavery when she was about seven years old. The little girl was chained for several weeks in the hold of a reeking, disease-filled ship crossing the Atlantic and fed only scraps, to become the property of another person. That's what she endured.

She landed in Massachusetts in 1761 aboard the slavery ship *Phillis,* from which her enslaved name was assigned to her. There, she was sold to a prosperous merchant named John Wheatley, and her enslaved surname was added.

John bought her as a servant for his wife, Susanna, "for a trifle," as she was "slender" and "frail." And as far as enslavers go, the family didn't completely suck as human beings. The couple's two children, Mary and Nathaniel, who were both in their teens, took on young Phillis's education. It was unheard of for a Black enslaved girl to learn to read, but by age twelve Phillis could read Greek and Latin classics in their original languages. They immersed her in studies of geography, astronomy, and history as well.

When she was fourteen, she wrote what was likely her first poem, "To the University of Cambridge, in New-England." The poem relayed a yearning for a life of academia and intellectual challenge.

She wrote several more poems, but American publishers were not interested in a book; many believed she could not have possibly authored them. And so, Nathaniel traveled with her to London to find a publisher. In 1773, when she was about twenty, Phillis met with prominent members of British society, and on September 1 her book *Poems on Various Subjects, Religious and Moral* was published. With publication the Wheatleys realized they could no longer keep her as an enslaved person, and on October 18, 1773, she was emancipated.

But that is where the "happy" tale ends. Despite Phillis's talent and intelligence, America was no land of opportunity for one of her color and gender. She married a free Black grocer when she was twenty-five, but they lived in poverty and two of their babies died. Her husband was sent to debtors' prison and she was left alone to raise a third child who was also sickly. To survive she worked as a scullery maid, but became ill and died at the age of thirty-one. Her infant child died soon after.

Modern Black scholars have proclaimed her poetry suffered from "Uncle Tom Syndrome"; it lacked awareness of her identity as a Black enslaved person. Other than the horrid trip from Africa, Phillis was not treated as other enslaved people were. She was molded by her owners to become a person they could control and display to white society as nonthreatening.

The Korean War might have been one of the stupidest ties of the twentieth century. Three years of death and destruction might have been avoided if the idiots in the UN had just said, a few months in, "Hey, we got all that lost territory back from North Korea's invasion. Let's just stop here." But no, they had to invade North Korea right back and then China said, "I don't fucking think so." Thus did a regional conflict transform into a battle between superpowers.

It began in June of 1950 with 75,000 commie North Korean troops pouring over the 38th parallel to conquer the evil capitalist-allied South Korea. And they damn near took all of it. The first military action of the Cold War, it would become a battle of titans with the Korean peninsula as proxy.

Within two months NK had taken all but a small portion of SK. The South Korea defenders were huddled behind a line called the Pusan Perimeter. The UN was all oh this will not do having commies take SK, and a coalition of twenty-one countries, with American troops making up 90 percent of the military personnel, launched a daring amphibious flanking maneuver at Incheon, which is in the northwest of South Korea, in mid-September, cutting off the NK troops that had invaded the South, turning the tables on those commie rats and taking back SK for the good guy capitalists. Go 'Murica!

But then, dumbassery.

The capitalist commanders said, "Those commie fucks need to be taught a lesson.

They crossed into our side, we're gonna cross into theirs." And so, they did. By October 17 they reached Pyongyang, the largest city in North Korea and its capital. Two days later, on October 19, 1950, the UN forces had captured the city. Forces were only a hundred miles from the border with China, and China wasn't fucking having it.

October 19, 1950

On that same day, China entered the war utilizing some linguistic fuckery. Linguistic fuckery? Yeah, get this. The regular armed forces in China are called the People's Liberation Army. But China was worried that if it sent those forces into North Korea, it could cause an official bigly war between China and the United States rather than a proxy war that wasn't nearly such a big deal because fuck Korea. So, China took a bunch of those PLA forces and changed the name to the People's Volunteer Army because adding the word "volunteer" meant Chinese and Americans could kill the shit out of each other in Korea without it snowballing into World War Fucking Three.

So, yeah, 200,000 Chinese PVA troops came pouring across the border screaming get the fuck out of North Korea, and they fought for another three years and lots of people died and everyone eventually ended up back where they started.

n March of 1942, as the Japanese forces surrounded American troops, General Douglas MacArthur was ordered by President Roosevelt to escape from the Philippines rather than be taken prisoner. Upon arriving safely in Australia, MacArthur said of having to flee the Philippines, "I shall return." This is the story of the men who permitted that return.

October 20, 1944

Just five months after fleeing the Philippines, the Americans were back on the offensive with the Battle of Guadalcanal in the South Pacific. Over the next three years the U.S. forces and their allies would gradually bite chunks out of Japan's new empire by taking back various islands one after another.

Over 15,000 Americans and 60,000 Filipino soldiers had surrendered in the Philippines and were taken as prisoners of war by the Japanese. It was the largest contingent of U.S. soldiers ever to surrender to an enemy force. The Americans going back to the Philippines wasn't only about reclaiming territory but rescuing those who had been kept for two and a half years in horrific conditions.

The Philippines is comprised of 7,100 islands, and the amphibious attack began on October 20, 1944, on the island of Leyte. On that day General MacArthur waded ashore and proclaimed, "I have returned." No word on if he then added, "Suck on that, motherfuckers."

The Americans arrived in overwhelming force. The battle for the single island would last over two months, during which 3,504

American soldiers would lose their lives. But the Japanese paid a much higher price, with 49,000 dead, more than three-quarters of them from starvation and diseases related to malnutrition, as they were cut off from supplies.

With so many islands occupied and such vicious resistance from the Japanese, the Americans would never fully retake the Philippine islands by the end of the war. There was still fighting taking place when orders from Tokyo were sent to Japanese commanders in the Philippines to surrender on August 15, 1945, six days after the second nuclear device was detonated over Nagasaki. Not all of them got the message. One Japanese soldier in the Philippines continued to fight on for another twenty-nine years.

Forty percent of American soldiers held by the Japanese in the Philippines died from either disease, starvation, or abuse. Some Japanese murdered their prisoners, as was the case with the Palawan Massacre of 139 Allied POWs in December 1944. These killings had the Allies saying holy Jesus shitsnacks we need to get those guys out of there. This prompted a series of rescue raids of POW camps to prevent further atrocities. One such rescue, at the Cabanatuan prison camp on January 30, 1945, became known as the Great Raid. Working with Filipino guerrilla fighters, American soldiers rescued over five hundred POWs from the camp who were in danger of being massacred.

It wasn't just in the Philippines that American prisoners were treated horrifically by the Japanese. Japan would not issue an official apology for its treatment of American POWs until 2009.

Colonialism fucked over Africa in every imaginable way. In his 1961 book *The Wretched of the Earth,* psychiatrist Frantz Fanon described colonization not only as a crime against humanity, but as having an overwhelming negative effect on the societal mental health of the colonized, who were viewed as little more than animals by the invaders. The author described violent uprising as a logical psychological response not just for attaining political freedom, but for improving national mental health. In 1950s Kenya, the Mau Mau Rebellion was one such display of extreme violence against the oppression of colonization. And while it failed as a revolution, it helped change western attitudes toward the thievery of the African continent.

The origin of the term *Mau Mau* is uncertain, and the rebels preferred the name "Kenya Land and Freedom Army." Kenya had been a British protectorate since 1895 and declared a colony in 1920. It was prized by the empire for its rich agricultural soils and a diverse geography with climates pleasing to European conquerors.

Resistance to the British invasion was immediate in terms of reaction to the settlers stealing their land, but the Mau Mau Rebellion took it to new levels of violence. The British were known for their divide-and-conquer method of rule, and so the rebels often struck against fellow Africans who were "loyalists" to the British Empire. Because they lacked the sophisticated heavy weaponry for mass warfare, they skillfully utilized guerrilla tactics, often striking at night fast and furious, then disappearing into the countryside. They were known to be well organized and careful in their planning, often hitting where their opponents were weakest. And while massacres of civilians were known to occur, the primary strategy was to avoid civilian casualties.

October 21, 1956

The British viewed the rebels as savages in need of extermination. They proclaimed the rebels wanted to take Kenya back to "the bad old days" before the Brits "civilized" it. Although the rebellion would continue for all of the 1950s, it was largely defeated as a military threat on October 21, 1956, when the British captured the Mau Mau leader, Dedan Kimathi Waciuri, and executed him four months later.

> **The British viewed the rebels as savages in need of extermination.**

The British committed numerous war crimes in suppressing the rebellion, using the familiar counterinsurgency strategy of collective punishment of innocent civilians to wean popular support away from guerrilla fighters. But the atrocities proved futile, and Kenyan home rule was established in 1960. The tenacity of resistance eventually resulted in the British population at home losing its taste for the amount of force it took to maintain their domination of the country.

Since the invention of the camera, we've enjoyed taking pictures of some catastrophic oopsie so the entire world can point at the image and say, "Ha-ha you fucked up." A prime example from the nineteenth century was this fucking train.

October 22, 1895

It happened on October 22, 1895, in Paris at the Montparnasse train station. A train from Granville, which is on the coast in the region of Normandy, was in just a wee bit too much of a hurry. You know when you're running late so you decide to drive faster to make up for lost time? That kind of shit kills people.

The train was several minutes behind schedule, so the driver was hitting the gas, or steam—howeverthefuck you make an old-timey locomotive go faster—and he also seems to have forgotten that the train possessed air brakes, because he failed to apply them and old locomotive #721 with its 131 passengers plowed through the bumper barricade, traveled across a hundred feet of station concourse, and crashed through a two-foot stone wall to nosedive into the street below.

No one died. On the train, that is. A woman in the street below took a train to the face. Actually, it was falling masonry that killed her, but dead is dead. Should have been her husband. It was her husband's newsstand where she was holding down the

> **You know when you're running late so you decide to drive faster to make up for lost time? That kind of shit kills people.**

fort while he went to get the evening papers to sell. He returned with what I'm sure was a what-the-fucking-fuck expression on his face, followed by "Ah! My precious newsstand!" Okay that's mean, I'm sure he was very upset about his wife but it's been over a century so I'm declaring it's not "too soon" to joke about.

The train driver got two months in prison and was fined the modern equivalent of about a thousand bucks. The train company paid a settlement to the family of the dead woman and agreed to pay for the education of her two children and even said hey when they grow up we'll give them jobs with our train company that killed their mom. Fuckin' sweet!

It was an ordeal to lower the train to the street, but once accomplished they discovered it had suffered remarkably little damage. In the meantime, plenty of photos were snapped, including the one shown here, which became one of the most famous images of transportation fuckups in history.

Speaking of laughing at fuckups, nowadays you can watch all the fail videos you can handle, even with Australian-accented sweary commentary for added comedic effect. Were there video of this particular incident, I expect "Ozzy Man's" review would sound something like *Oi the train's comin' in too fast and what the fuck are air brakes and ah shit through the barrier and through the fuckin' wall and ah Christ it's destination fucked!*

The Montparnasse train derailment

When I was a boy my father would pick me up at the Prince George Airport in British Columbia and drive us to his home south of Burns Lake. Along the three-hour drive we'd pass an ominous building on Fraser Lake called the Lejac Residential School. It was a place where the Canadian government sent Indigenous children to "kill the Indian in the child." But sometimes they just plain old killed the child. Either way, it was a literal ethnic cleansing.

October 23, 1966

Canada's Indian Residential School System began in 1874 and comprised 130 schools across the nation. They were run by Christian churches and took Indigenous children from their families in order to assimilate them into white culture. Over the network's existence, approximately a third of all Indigenous children in Canada were placed in such schools. The schools were rampant with physical and sexual abuse, as well as death. Several thousand children died over the years. Notable for the Lejac school was when four boys, eight and nine years old, ran away on New Year's Day, 1937. Dressed in only light clothing against the Canadian winter cold, they made it six of the seven miles back to their home before they froze to death.

Chanie Wenjack was another boy who died fleeing a residential school. He was a twelve-year-old Ojibwe child who fled the Cecilia Jeffrey Indian Residential School in Ontario where he had been forced to live for three years. He intended to walk back to his home on the Marten Falls Reserve, almost four hundred miles away.

He had been sent to the school with his two sisters; the administrators changed his named to "Charlie." On October 16, 1966, he and two friends fled the school. They made it twenty miles to his uncle's place, where they stayed for four days. Chanie then left on his own, lightly dressed, following the railroad to make his way home. He made it another dozen miles before he collapsed and died from hunger and exposure on October 23.

A coroner's inquest the following month stated, "The Indian education system causes tremendous emotional and adjustment problems for these children." No shit. In February of 1967 *Maclean's* magazine published an article with the misnaming title "The Lonely Death of Charlie Wenjack." It brought the tragedy of Canada's residential school system to national attention.

But it would be another three decades before the last residential school would close in Canada.

It was a place where the Canadian government sent Indigenous children to "kill the Indian in the child." But sometimes they just plain old killed the child.

Magicians know best that there is no magic, nothing supernatural; it's all a combination of preparation and trickery. Alas, Harry Houdini couldn't prepare himself enough to trick his way out of a ruptured appendix, and the non-magical science of 1926 medicine wasn't up to saving him.

Houdini's exploits made him a household name. Born Erik Weisz in Budapest in 1874, the dude performed mesmerizing tricks that had the audience wondering how in the three-in-one-shampoo-conditioner-body-wash-fuck he did that. He was a great escape artist and debunker of bullshit whose work captivated millions. At age twenty he was performing with his brother, "Dash," at Coney Island when they met Bess Rahner, who was part of a song and dance act. Dash pursued Bess but she was wild about Harry. They married and Bess became Harry's magic assistant for the rest of his life, which would be only another thirty-two years.

It was October 22, 1926. Harry was fifty-two and about to perform in Montreal, but he had a broken ankle. Prior to the show a number of people were in his dressing room, including students from McGill University. Witnesses proclaim one student, 31-year-old J. Gordon Whitehead, asked Houdini about his ability to withstand punches to the midsec-

Harry Houdini in 1905

tion, to which Harry replied he could endure a lot.

Houdini was reclining due to his ankle, and Whitehead, who was just an ordinary dude and not some boxer as later reported, hit him several times. Houdini stopped him and said he'd not had time to prepare for the blows. If his ankle had not been broken, he would have stood and clenched to prepare.

He performed that night in pain. He ignored the increasing pain for two days, until he saw a physician who diagnosed acute appendicitis. The doctor advised immediate surgery, but Houdini ignored him and performed another show in Detroit on October 24, 1926, which would be Houdini's last performance. He had a fever of 104°F, and passed out during the show, but was revived and continued. Afterward he was taken to a hospital, where he died a week later from peritonitis due to a ruptured appendix.

It's unclear if the punches were to blame, and Whitehead was not charged, but Bess fought with the insurance company to have the dressing room incident labeled the cause of his death in order to get a double payout on his life insurance.

Imagine this. It's 1936 and you're a teenager in Hitler's Germany. Membership in the Hitler Youth has just become mandatory, but you say no fucking way because fuck that Nazi bullshit. What do you do? Answer: You become a pirate.

October 25, 1944

At the time, you were allowed to leave school at age fourteen, but if you were seventeen you were going to get conscripted. If you stayed in school, you'd be forced into the Hitler Youth in order to be indoctrinated into Nazism and work to convert others into the murderous cult. Many young people quit school and formed their own resistance group called the Edelweiss Pirates, and they loved to punch Nazis.

In addition to all the allegiance-to-Hitler stuff, being in the Hitler Youth sucked. It was highly regimented fascist paramilitary bullshit and totally the death of fun. Hitler Youth was boys only; girls were made to be part of the League of German Girls. Edelweiss Pirates were all about freedom of expression and growing long hair and mixing genders and fucking up those Nazi punks.

They numbered in the thousands, and in addition to just enjoying being teens and playing that "degenerate" jazz and blues

> **The pirate slogan was "Eternal War on the Hitler Youth."**

music and exploring their sexuality, they'd hunt down Hitler Youth patrols and beat the shit out of them on a regular basis. The pirate slogan was "Eternal War on the Hitler Youth."

Before the outbreak of World War II the pirates were seen as little more than an irritation by the Nazi government, but during the conflict they did things such as gather up Allied propaganda dropped by airplanes and push it through people's mailboxes to spread the word that Hitler was bad. They also helped German army deserters disappear. They added sugar to the gas tanks of Nazi vehicles, pulled down Nazi flags, and even derailed munitions trains.

On October 25, 1944, the Nazis finally took them seriously and Heinrich Himmler, Hitler's right-hand man, ordered a crackdown. The following month, thirteen people, many of them Edelweiss Pirates, were publicly hanged in Cologne.

The Nazi regime kept up the pressure on the Edelweiss Pirates, imprisoning many and even sending some to concentration camps, but their spirits would not be broken. History was unkind to the pirates, viewing them as criminals rather than a true resistance group. But efforts have been made to rehabilitate their image and view them as an important part of resistance to fascist authority during WWII.

He was a hero who went through a trial by media that fucked him over and put him through hell. Richard Jewell's attention to detail saved many lives during the Centennial Olympic Park bombing in 1996, but many were quick to imagine he was the one who planted the bomb in the first place.

The bombing took place on July 27, 1996, during the Summer Olympic Games in Atlanta. The bomber was Eric Rudolph, a terrorist who would later bomb abortion clinics and a lesbian nightclub. Rudolph created a fragmentation pipe bomb, placed it inside a green backpack, and left it under a bench in the park where thousands were gathered for a concert.

Jewell saw the backpack and became suspicious. He contacted the police and worked with other security to clear the area so the bomb squad could investigate. Then it exploded. One person was killed and more than a hundred others injured. Had it not been for Jewell, it would have been far worse.

At first Jewell was seen as a hero, but then public opinion quickly turned against him when *The Atlanta Journal-Constitution* reported the FBI was treating him as a possible suspect. Then other media jumped on it and shoved an electron microscope up Jewell's ass looking for any scandal they could spin into a story. They latched onto him being overweight and living with his mother and portrayed him as a loser: a failed law enforcement officer who planted the bomb in the first place in order to "find it" and become lauded as a hero. A federal agent gave him the nickname "Unabubba" and Jay Leno referred to him as "Una-doofus."

October 26, 1996

But he really was a hero. He actually did deserve to be lauded. He didn't plant the fucking bomb. He saved a lot of lives that day.

He was never charged, but the FBI searched Jewell's home, twice, and did a thorough investigation of him, questioning his colleagues and keeping him under 24-hour surveillance. On October 26, 1996, after putting him through three months of torment, the state attorney sent Jewell a letter saying he was no longer a suspect in the investigation. No apology was offered at the time, but the following July, Attorney General Janet Reno expressed regret for the leak that led to the media shitfuckery, saying, "I think we owe him an apology." No, really?

Afterward, Jewell filed several libel suits and received a number of settlements. He continued to work in law enforcement until his death in 2007 at the age of forty-four. The actual bomber, Eric Rudolph, is serving four consecutive life sentences.

Vasily Arkhipov was a handsome fellow. He's also the reason the world isn't currently being run by intelligent cockroaches. I mean, that might be an improvement, but he is a prime example of how one person can literally save the world by saying, "Wait a fucking minute. What if we decided to *not* be psychopathic dicks and start a nuclear fucking holocaust?"

October 27, 1962

Many don't realize just how fucking close we came to nuclear annihilation during the Cuban Missile Crisis. One such example of the levels of dumbfuckery was that Cuba had a hundred short-range "tactical" nukes on the island, and local Soviet officers were *pre-authorized to use them* in case of an invasion by the United States. President Kennedy was encouraged by his military advisers to invade the island, which would have resulted in the American forces being vaporized, which would have snowballed into the cockroach scenario I mentioned earlier.

Kennedy saved us by deciding not to invade, even though he had no idea about the tactical nukes. That wasn't the only near-miss during those tense thirteen days where a cooler head kept humanity alive.

Arkhipov's personal history may have contributed to him keeping his cool. The year prior to the missile crisis he was executive officer on *K-19,* the USSR's first nuclear-powered ballistic missile submarine. Soviet technology being not the best, the boat almost suffered a meltdown in its reactor.

Arkhipov, who was played by Liam Neeson in a 2002 film version of the event, witnessed twenty-two of his fellow sailors get a lethal dose of radiation. Perhaps the experience made him personally leery of the negative potential of nuclear reactions.

During the missile crisis Americans implemented a naval blockade of Cuba, and the Soviets tested their resolve with an oceanic confrontation. Arkhipov was aboard the submarine *B-59* when the U.S. Navy detected it on October 27, 1962, and dropped signaling depth charges to force it to surface and identify itself. The sub had been too deep for any communications with the outside world for days, and the captain thought war had already broken out and decided to launch a nuclear torpedo, which is the same as a nuclear bomb, just put inside a torpedo. It still has a mega-radioactive-explodey-pow. If they launched it, it would have triggered World War We Are So Fucking Fucked.

To authorize a launch, the captain, the political officer, and executive officer Arkhipov all had to agree. The other two did, but Arkhipov said what are you totally fucking bugshit? No! Arkhipov had a solid reputation from his *K-19* days, and he convinced the captain to surface and ask Moscow the fuck was going on.

Planetary destruction was averted, and Arkhipov was eventually promoted to the rank of vice-admiral, retiring from the Soviet Navy in the mid-1980s. He lived to be seventy-two, dying from kidney cancer that may have been caused by radiation exposure on *K-19.*

Perhaps it's burning love, perhaps it's burning fever. You can prevent all sorts of nasty illnesses, including ones that cause a spike in body temperature, by getting vaccinated. Elvis knew this and used his fame to get the anti-vaccine fuckwaffles to STFU by having the new polio vaccination injected into his arm on television.

Sometimes polio was like a mild case of the flu: fever, sore throat, body aches, etc. Other times, the girl next door would no longer go a-walking. In only about 0.5 percent of cases did it affect the central nervous system, leading to permanent disability and even death. But considering how virulent the disease is, that was still a lot of people.

Jonas Salk and his team at the University of Pittsburgh created the first effective polio vaccine in 1952. Prior to that, as many as 20,000 Americans were paralyzed annually by the disease, most of them children. Salk first tested the vaccine on himself and his family. It was declared safe in the spring of 1955, but in the rush to produce it vaccine protocols were not strictly followed by two manufacturers, and more than two hundred people ended up getting paralytic polio via their vaccines, because the solution had not been properly inactivated. Eleven people died. The government took immediate steps, and those were the only incidents of a tainted polio vaccine.

Because the disease mostly affected children, they were the focus of the vaccination program. Teens and adults were choosing to opt-out, believing they weren't at risk. Tell that to President Roosevelt, who contracted the disease when he was thirty-nine. The vaccine was working, but herd immunity wasn't being reached because adults weren't getting vaccinated.

October 28, 1956

Public health officials reached out to Elvis, whose star was on the rise, to see if he would be willing to get publicly vaccinated to promote Salk's life-saving discovery. He agreed, and on October 28, 1956, he received his shot on television by Dr. Harold Fuerst and Dr. Leona Baumgartner in the CBS studios in New York. Over the next six months, the polio vaccination rate among teens went from less than 1 percent to 80 percent. Within four years, rates of polio declined by 90 percent. Elvis wasn't always the greatest guy, but he is credited with playing a major role in this success.

It's worth mentioning that Salk refused to patent his vaccine, giving it away instead. It's estimated he gave up about seven billion dollars in wealth with this act of generosity. To both Elvis and Salk, I wish to say thank you. Thank you very much.

> Elvis knew this and used his fame to get the anti-vaccine fuckwaffles to STFU by having the new polio vaccination injected into his arm on television.

In October of 1929, the bear took the bull by the horns and drove it right into the fucking ground. That was actually a thing they did in California in the nineteenth century, having fights between grizzlies and bulls.

Those fights wiped out California grizzlies, and also inspired the terms "bear" and "bull" markets on Wall Street. During the '20s, things were very bullish. If you're an investor, that's good. It means stocks are on the rise. The Dow Jones index that measures stock performance increased sixfold between 1921 and 1929. Due to speculation, many regular working-class folk who knew little of investing wanted to get in on it and purchased stocks "on margin." That means they were buying stocks on credit, putting down as little as 10 percent of a stock's value. Such credit purchasing was one of the things that contributed to the crash. Another contributor was that people were just too Pollyannish; they believed the stocks were worth more than was realistic. There was also an agricultural recession affecting the country's economy.

And then, the panic selling.

The first big crash was on October 24, with the market losing 11 percent of its value. The mass volume of trading delayed the ticker tape, so many brokers didn't know what stocks were actually trading for. The trading floor was in a panic. October 28 saw more panic selling as investors faced "margin calls," which translates to the lender saying to the borrower "your stock ain't worth shit, fucking pay me."

On October 29, 1929, shit went down, and so did the stock market.

Some rich folks, including the Rockefellers, tried to bolster the market by buying up stocks to show faith in the investments, but it was too late. There was a mild recovery, because stock prices were so low, they had nowhere to go but up. But by 1932 most stocks were worth about a fifth of what they had been in the summer of 1929.

The stock market crash was a major contributor to the Great Depression of the 1930s. Those hardest hit were Black people because companies had a "last hired, first fired" policy regarding Black employees. One thing the Depression did was help bring about an end to Prohibition, as it was felt that legalizing alcohol would help stimulate the economy.

On October 29, 1929, shit went down, and so did the stock market.

You're surprised that people are stupid enough to embrace that QAnon bullshit? Guess you forgot about how some thought the *War of the Worlds* radio broadcast was real and Martians were invading and bringing their extra-large anal probes. It wasn't a *mass* panic, however, but rather a small panic that grew in the telling due to nefarious capitalistic maneuvering. It was enough of a thing that the police showed up at the CBS studios and tried to halt the broadcast though.

The show, part of the radio drama series *The Mercury Theatre on the Air,* wasn't even listened to by that many people. Broadcast on October 30, 1938, the one-hour program began by explaining it was an adaptation of the 1898 H. G. Wells novel *War of the Worlds;* they *told* listeners it was fictional. For the first twenty minutes it was presented as a typical evening radio broadcast that was regularly interrupted with increasingly dire news bulletins about the alien invasion of Earth.

Oh, no! Martians! Our mighty American military cannot stop it. We're doomed. Fuckin' doomed I tells ya. Except lots of listeners weren't necessarily paying that close attention, and didn't think "Martians," but imagined the news of the "invasion" and "poison gas" meant those Nazi fucks were landing on American shores. It was 1938, after all. People were getting worried about that Hitler douchenozzle.

The broadcast was just approaching its midway break—with actor Ray Collins pretending to choke to death on air from alien poison gas—when the CBS supervisor received a phone call telling him to cease the broadcast. Then the police arrived and there was a struggle in the offices between cops and CBS producers trying to prevent them from bursting into the studio and stopping the show from continuing. In the aftermath, the media went wild with the story of mass panic.

October 30, 1938

Yes, there was some panic, but the extent was overblown, and it took many years to reach a consensus that it was "greatly exaggerated." Rather than panic, most called local news outlets or police to ask dafuq was going on, only to be told the broadcast was fictional and to un-bunch their underwear.

Why did the story of mass panic gain such traction? Likely the newspapers were to blame. Always seeking a story to exploit, this one had the added benefit of making radio look bad, look unreliable as a news source. You can't trust those dirty radio broadcasters, but you can trust us, the newspapers. Extra! Extra! Turn off your radio and buy our newspaper!

Orson Welles being interviewed the day after the broadcast

After the German Blitzkrieg steamrolled France in a matter of weeks, things were looking pretty bleak for poor, isolated Britain. Repelling the Nazi invasion of the islands would rely upon the bravery of a handful of skilled aviators, observation, wing design, silk, and Hitler's dumbfuckery.

October 31, 1940

After the evacuation at Dunkirk, which the Royal Air Force *did* provide air cover for,

despite the prevailing myth, the Battle of Britain began. The attacks by the Luftwaffe (Germany's air force) were intended to force Britain into either an armistice or full surrender. But the British weren't having it. Because fuck Nazis.

The German plan was to first wipe out Britain's air power, and then consider an amphibious invasion. But that operation never came about, because the RAF kicked some Luftwaffe ass. How? First, the RAF fighter pilots were well-trained volunteers. To become an "ace" you needed to shoot down five enemy aircraft. Almost two hundred air-

Supermarine Spitfire

men achieved that distinction during the battle, and four pilots became aces in a single day of fighting. These dudes were badass.

Second, they had the home-field advantage. Any German aircrews who were shot down and parachuted to the ground spent the rest of the war in a prison camp, but a British pilot making his silky landing had some farmer drive him back to his base so he could jump in another fighter plane and shoot down more Germans.

Another was that the Spitfire, a primary fighter craft of the RAF, had a tighter turning rate than the German Messerschmitt, due to a curved wing design. The latter had some other advantages, but the Spitfire had a slight edge in a dogfight. While Spitfires engaged in dogfights with enemy fighters, RAF pilots in "workhorse" Hurricane fighters focused on destroying German bomber aircraft.

More important was who saw whom first, and this is where the Observer Corps came in. Using a combination of rudimentary radar and a chain of people with binoculars scanning the skies, they could report enemy locations to RAF pilots in their fighters so they could dash in and send the Luftwaffe invaders off to Nazi hell.

Then, a "fortunate" accident. During one engagement a German bomber, apparently unintentionally, dropped bombs on civilian areas of London. The Brits were all "Blow up our civilians, will you?" and retaliated with a not-terribly-successful bombing raid on Berlin to do the same. Hitler was pissed—how dare those limey fucks bomb his capital!—and shifted strategy away from attacking RAF airfields and aircraft manufacturing, and toward blowing up Londoners for some payback. Beginning on September 7, 1940, Germany bombed London for fifty-seven days in a row. Prior to this, the RAF was on the verge of obliteration from the constant German onslaught focused on wiping them out, but Hitler's shift to bombing London gave the RAF the few weeks' respite they needed to get more pilots and planes ready to counterattack.

No longer being a primary target, the RAF quickly bounced back and before long were shooting down German bombers faster than they could be replaced. Having lost the opportunity to attain air superiority over Britain, any chance of a German amphibious invasion of England was lost. Victory in the Battle of Britain was declared on October 31, 1940.

No longer being a primary target, the RAF quickly bounced back and before long were shooting down German bombers faster than they could be replaced.

November

The most immediate threat faced by humanity is *still* nuclear obliteration. Yeah, climate change is a clusterfuck, but that's a slow apocalypse that we might get our shit together enough to ameliorate and even recover from. Nukes, though? They could fly today, because fascist fucknuts have control over enough of them with sufficient radioactive explodey power to render much of the planet a glow-in-the-dark wasteland.

Anyway, on August 6, 1945, there was a pretty big kaboom over Hiroshima, but the scientists at Los Alamos, New Mexico—where they created the first atomic bomb—knew they could build something way bigger. They called it "The Super," and it was a fusion bomb built by a dick. He was a Hungarian-born scientist named Edward Teller, and yeah, he was totally a dick with a volatile personality who stabbed "father of the atomic bomb" Robert Oppenheimer in the back. They'd worked together on the Manhattan Project, and in 1954, during the height of the anti-communist Second Red Scare, Teller testified at a hearing of the Atomic Energy Commission that Oppenheimer collaborated with communists and shouldn't be given back his security clearance. It was a baseless accusation, yet it contributed to the loss of Oppenheimer's clearance and the death of his career.

In turn, Teller was ostracized by the scientific community for being a fucking rat, but the government still liked Teller's style. See, Teller was the one pushing for creation of a "thermonuclear" weapon—the aforementioned Super—because fusion goes boom much bigger than regular ol' fission. And the United States was all oh hey that sounds awesome please make us one of those.

November 1, 1952

And so, Teller did make such a bomb, leading the team that created "Ivy Mike," the first-ever thermonuclear device to be tested. They blew up the Enewetak Atoll in the Marshall Islands on November 1, 1952, with over 10 megatons of big-ass kerblammo. That's about five hundred times more powerful than the bombs dropped on Japan.

Teller was in California at the time of the test, and knew it was successful because he detected it via a seismometer. In celebration he decided to send an unclassified telegram to his colleague Liz Graves, a group leader at Los Alamos, letting her know of the success hours before any word came from the test site. The telegram was only three words: "It's a boy."

> In turn, Teller was ostracized by the scientific community for being a fucking rat, but the government still liked Teller's style.

D. **H. Lawrence** had been dead thirty years when his book *Lady Chatterley's Lover* launched a shitstorm of an obscenity trial in his homeland, creating a watershed moment for the liberalization of publishing in England regarding writing about fucking, including use of the word "fuck" to describe said fucking.

November 2, 1960

David Herbert Lawrence wrote some things that vexed some people and he said fuck you England and exiled himself to mainland Europe after World War I ended. In 1928, when he was forty-two, he privately published *Lady Chatterley* in Italy, and the following year it was published in France. Because Italians and French were okay with artistic depictions of fucking, it didn't stir up much controversy.

Long story short: She's a young woman married to an upper-class man who was paralyzed in the Great War. He can't perform physically and ignores her emotionally, so she says fuck this and fucks the gamekeeper and it's all thrusting buttocks this and awakening orgasms that. Plus some other stuff happens, including analysis of class divisions. Anyway, Lawrence died from tuberculosis two years after its first publication. Drag.

A censored version of the book was published in England two years after his death, but people wanted the rest of it, because it was sexy, what with her coming to adore this gamekeeper with all of her physical being 'n' shit. It would take another twenty-eight years, but Penguin had the guts to publish the uncensored version in 1960, and then was promptly put on trial under the 1959 Obscene Publications Act.

One of the issues with the book, besides the sex scenes, was how often the word "fuck" appeared in it. I guess back then I would have been fucked for the way I write. Anyway, the Act had an escape clause for conviction if the publisher could prove the work had literary merit. And that's what the trial focused on: the merit of the book as a work of literature. After a diverse array of experts testified, Penguin was found not guilty on November 2, 1960.

The case was heavily publicized, and Penguin quickly sold three million copies of the book because it turns out Brits have dirty minds. Alas, English lawmakers still have twisted undergarments regarding coverage of what's under those garments. As an example, in 2014 the country banned the display of female ejaculation in porn, but showing male ejaculation is fine. Go figure.

One of the issues with the book, besides the sex scenes, was how often the word "fuck" appeared in it.

November 3, 2020, was fucking tense, and it stayed tense for another four days before the U.S. presidential election results were confirmed. It was the same day Trumpanzees thought the "silent majority" was gonna rise up and vote en masse to keep the apricot assmonkey in power so he could usher in the apocalypse. Interestingly, exactly fifty-one years before, the term "silent majority" was popularized by another shitty president.

During the run-up to the 2016 election, when the fascist fuckwipe was holding his racist rallies, many held up signs saying, THE SILENT MAJORITY STANDS WITH TRUMP. This was prompted by Trump saying at one such rally in the summer of 2015, "The silent majority is back, and we're going to take our country back." Turns out, those alabaster assholes were right. There were more of them than we knew, and Eric's dad became president by a margin of negative three million votes. Fucking Electoral College bullshit.

On November 3, 1969, the term came into popular usage when President Nixon was giving a live television address asking for support for his actions regarding the war in Vietnam. He said, "To you, the great silent majority of Americans, I ask for your support." It was a not-so-subtle way of speaking directly to the "patriotic" Americans who weren't currently protesting the shit out of the war. It was painting the antiwar crowd as unpatriotic, being purposely divisive to rally his right-wing base. It was classic divide-and-conquer.

The term "silent majority" refers to those who hold certain beliefs but do not express them publicly. With his speech, Nixon alleged that most people *did* support him and his actions regarding Vietnam, and that the antiwar group was just a loud minority and we should just ignore those traitors. And that's what Trumpers believed: Those traitors who vilified their orangutan oligarch were but small in number, and most were silently supportive and going to deliver him a landslide victory.

November 3, 1969

Considering all the gun-totin', truck-drivin', horn-honkin', slur-spewin', traffic-blockin', dictionary definition of "loud and obnoxious" brainless invertebrates we witnessed, I'm taking issue with their use of the word "silent."

Over and over since Nixon said it, the term has been used by right-wing politicians to convince people to ignore dissent, to make their critics seem a deranged and vocal minority that doesn't represent the "true" beliefs of the majority. I've seen it from the bootlicking Trump-lovers invading my social media pages. The silent majority was frequently referenced to proclaim Trump's impending victory. It's a continuation of the divide-and-conquer that, sadly, has often been very effective. Nixon was reelected in 1972 in a landslide.

But Trump's supporters weren't right in 2020. People voted as if their lives depended on it, and Biden/Harris won the popular vote 51.3 to 46.9 percent and took the Electoral College 306 to 232. Alas, the Trumpers were just as obnoxious in defeat.

don't give a shit if you don't like the guy. Comparatively speaking, Barack Obama was fucking awesome, and his election filled many with hope that America wasn't irrevocably fucked. And yet, for four years, America was ever so fucked.

November 4, 2008

First, we need to talk about Jeri Ryan, who many know as "Seven of Nine" in the *Star Trek* franchise, and her unwillingness to take her husband's shit. Wait, what? Yeah, she played a significant if indirect role in the election of Barack Obama.

Back in 2004, Jeri's ex-husband, Jack Ryan, was a likely winner for election in the Illinois senate race. But then Jack's divorce records were made public, revealing that he'd pressured Jeri to have public sex in various swingers' clubs. But resistance is not futile, and Jeri said fuck that noise and divorced him instead. Jack denied the allegations but dropped out of the race a few days later and was replaced by the unexciting MSNBC host Alan Keyes. Obama, who had only been a state senator up to that point, annihilated Keyes in the election and became senator, and then four years later became the Democrat nominee to be president, narrowly beating Hillary Clinton.

The 2008 election was the war hero sup-

porting the war in Iraq that had been going on for five years vs. a man opposing the war who proclaimed a need for change in Washington. McCain was hindered by being tied to George Bush, and a lot of people were sick of eight years of Republicans in power, especially since the economy imploded right before the election. I don't think Sarah Palin as a VP choice did McCain any favors either.

Conversely, a lot of people were wondering if a Black man could win the presidency in the United States of Racist America. When Obama did win by a wide margin on November 4, 2008, many were elated. They felt this represented a hopeful future for their country. The massive attendance at Obama's inauguration was a love fest. His supporters were overjoyed.

Of course, there was a substantial portion of the American population that was just fucking seething over the Obama victory. How dare a Black man occupy the White House? The Tea Party, aka the American Taliban, became a thing only a month after President Obama assumed office, and Republicans made every effort to block Obama's policies no matter what they were. For eight years the racism festered like an infected wound, becoming a major contributor to the election of the blatantly racist and vocal Obama critic Donald Trump to the presidency in 2016.

Guy Fawkes wasn't the leader of the plot to blow the ever-loving shit out of the House of Lords and send them all off to meet their version of the Lord. Guy was the explosives guy. He was doing it because his version of the Lord wasn't being tolerated, so have a few dozen barrels of kaboom-powder, you Protestant fucks.

In 1603, James I became king of England, succeeding the childless Elizabeth I. James's mom was Mary Queen of Scots, whom Elizabeth had executed in 1587 for trying to have her assassinated. That's called regicide, FYI. Anyway, Mary had been a devout Catholic, and English Catholics, who had been treated like shit by Elizabeth, were hopeful the new king would be more tolerant of them as an homage to his mom, or something, but James was all nah fuck you guys.

The leader of the Gunpowder Plot was a prominent English Catholic named Robert Catesby, and he was pissed at James for not being nicer to Catholics, so he decided to blow some shit up. Charismatic and influential, he brought several other conspirators into the plot, including Fawkes, who had ten years of military experience and knew how to make things go boom.

The plan was to blow up the House of Lords on November 5, 1605, during the State Opening of Parliament, which would be followed by a popular revolt in middle England and then they'd install James's nine-year-old daughter as a puppet queen and tell her Catholics = good even though we regicided your dad so be nice.

November 5, 1605

It didn't work out.

One of the conspirators didn't want one of the lords, Monteagle, to die, so he sent him a vague letter that basically said yo, skip this parliament cuz bad shit's gonna happen. That prompted a search of the House of Lords and lo and behold who is this mustachioed mofo guarding these thirty-six barrels of aristocrat-explode waiting to a light a fuse? Guy Fawkes was arrested, the plot thwarted.

Fawkes was tortured for a few days to get him to reveal the nature of the plot and the names of his co-conspirators. On November 8, Catesby went down in a blaze of glorious gunfire, refusing to be taken alive. Fawkes and other conspirators were executed the following January in typical messy, painful, seventeenth-century English fashion. As a fuck-you to Catesby, the authorities dug him up and put his head on a spike outside the House of Lords.

> **Fawkes and other conspirators were executed the following January in typical messy, painful, seventeenth-century English fashion.**

President Reagan was shot in 1981 and it kind of fucked him up. So, asking the question "Was he aware?" regarding the Iran-Contra scandal that began four years later isn't really fair when I'm not sure he was even aware that he was president at the time. I jest. Maybe.

What the fuck was Iran-Contra? I'm not sure most people who lived through it can describe the convoluted shenanigans, so let's break it down.

It began in the summer of 1985. Despite the Reagan government having a "we don't negotiate with terrorists" policy, they totally negotiated with terrorists. Because militant theocracy, there was an arms embargo against Iran, which was currently bogged down in a brutal war with Iraq. Iran is mostly Shia Muslim, and at this time there were seven American hostages being held in Lebanon by the Shia group Hezbollah. What happened was the Americans sold weapons to Iran, in violation of the embargo, and then Iran agreed to use its influence to get the Hezbollah in Lebanon to release their hostages.

But wait, there's more!

At the time, there was a socialist government in Nicaragua, and if you're a Republican the word "socialism" gives you twisted knickers. As was really fucking common, the Americans decided to give money to some far-right fucksticks to overthrow said government. Said terrorist fucksticks were called the "Contras," which derives from *la contrar-*

revolución. As the name implies, it was a "Fuck your revolution" revolution. Well, technically a rebellion, because they failed. It's only a "revolution" when you win.

Anyway, the United States had been sending money to the Contras for a while, but then there was this thing called the Boland Amendment passed by Congress that said they couldn't do that anymore. And so, Marine Corps Lieutenant Colonel Oliver North, who was working for the National Security Council in Washington, D.C., takes some of the money gained by selling arms (illegally) to Iran and gives it (illegally) to the Contras. They took the money made from negotiating with terrorists illegally to give it to some other terrorists illegally.

Early November in 1986, a Lebanese magazine revealed the dirty details of how the United States was selling arms to Iran in violation of the embargo. Three days later, on November 6, 1986, the U.S. intelligence services owned up, saying yeah, we did that shit. And then it was all over the news.

Reagan denied knowing anything. A whole bunch of people were indicted in the ensuing scandal, but when Reagan's VP George H. W. Bush became president he went on a pardon-o-rama. Oliver North was convicted, but this was overturned on appeal.

Later, there were accusations the CIA was directly involved in dealing cocaine as part of financing such shenanigans, but that's probably not true. More likely is that they knew the Contras were dealing drugs to help finance the conflict, but the CIA conveniently ignored such illegal activity by their allies.

A lot of people only know which month the Russian Revolution took place because of the movie *The Hunt for Red October*. Except it didn't happen in October. Well, not *our* October. Because back then the Russians were old-style. I mean Old Style . . . calendar. The Russians hadn't yet caught up with using the New Style calendar, so Lenin and his Bolsheviks began their assault on what they said was October 25, 1917. Much of the rest of the world, however, was calling that day November 7.

It was actually a follow-up. There had been something of a revolution the previous February, I mean March. Fuck. Whenever. Anyway, *earlier in the year* they'd overthrown the tsars, and things were being run by a provisional government, but it was pretty fucking useless, and the people were still good and pissed. So, the workers formed councils called "soviets," which is a word I expect will sound familiar.

Throughout the summer there were shortages of food, and unrest grew. Peasant uprisings were common. Also, there was a fucking war going on with the rest of Europe; the end of World War I was more than a year away and the Russians were getting their asses kicked and the people were all like "Why are we still fighting this bullshit war?"

Germany was on the other side in the war, so it decided to help Vladimir Lenin get back home from exile in Switzerland so he could stir up shit in Russia and ease things on the Eastern Front for Germany. Smart. And the plan worked. On November 7/October 25, a bunch of pissed-off Soviets attacked the Winter Palace, the official home of Russian emperors, in Petrograd, which is now called St. Petersburg, except between 1924 and 1991 it was called Leningrad. My head hurts.

November 7, 1917

So, yeah, Lenin and his Bolsheviks charged the Winter Palace and it was . . . kind of a nothingburger. The soldiers were like, nah, we're sick of this bullshit provisional government too. We don't want to fight Germany or the Bolsheviks. Fuck this, we're changing sides. Those guarding the palace decided to join the revolutionaries rather than fight them.

The transition was pretty peaceful, for about five minutes. The Russians quickly noped out of the rest of World War I, but then there were six years of civil war between Lenin's Red Army and the White Army, which was more about monarchism, capitalism, and social democracy. If you know anything about history, you know the "Reds" won and established the Soviet Union.

Also, it sucked to be a tsar. In July 1918 the Romanoff family, which had ruled Russia for three centuries, was executed in a basement in Yekaterinburg.

Have you ever been a kid who broke their ankle and the X-ray tech was twisting your broken limb into a painful position to get just the right picture and you revealed just how much profanity a thirteen-year-old knew? Just me? Anyway, getting X-rays can suck, but they were a massive leap forward in medicine.

This high-energy electromagnetic shit that can see your bones is called Röntgen radiation, because German physics professor Wilhelm Röntgen discovered it by accident.

You could say Nikola Tesla accidentally discovered X-rays a year before Röntgen did, except Tesla didn't realize it at the time. Tesla was playing around with some vacuum tubes that created electrical discharge in the form of cathode rays. You know how us old-timers would refer to television as "watching the tube?" Same idea. Anyway, Tesla took a photograph of his pal Mark Twain using such a vacuum tube. The photo didn't turn out, and Tesla didn't realize until after Röntgen's discovery was made public that the blotchy photo that looked nothing like Samuel Clemens *or* Mark Twain was actually an X-ray that revealed the internal screw used to adjust the camera lens.

As for Röntgen's discovery, he had his lab notes burned after he died because crazy-ass scientist, I guess, and his biographers had to reconstruct how he first figured it out. So, who fucking knows? Let's make some shit up. Okay not really, but as famed historians

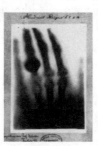

First X-ray:
"Hand with Rings"

Will and Ariel Durant said, "Most history is guessing, and the rest is prejudice."

On November 8, 1895, Röntgen was investigating cathode rays and wrapped a vacuum tube in black cardboard to cut the visible light from getting through. But he noticed that a screen a few feet away was giving off a green glow, and that *some form* of light *was* getting through the cardboard. What Tesla missed the year previous with his accidental X-ray photograph, Röntgen investigated further.

Röntgen began experimenting like mad, and six weeks later, on December 22, he took the first-ever "medical" X-ray, of his wife's hand. She looked at it and said, "I have seen my death." Nice. Six days later he submitted his first paper on the subject, referring to the images as "X" rays to indicate that this was an unknown type of radiation. When the term caught on, he was all no goddammit that's not what I want to actually call them, but it stuck.

It wasn't just the name that caught on, but the technology. Immediately. Röntgen saw the medical applications right away and sent letters to physicians across Europe saying, "Check out this cool shit I discovered" and they were like "Yeah that is cool shit ima use it." And just two months after his discovery a doctor in England used X-rays to find a needle stuck in the hand of an associate, the first clinical application.

Röntgen won the first-ever Nobel Prize in Physics for his discovery. And me? I've broken several bones and had a half dozen root canals, so my corpse is probably gonna glow in the dark.

She was in court in Los Angeles as a witness for the prosecution to testify against two men who burglarized her home. But Helen Hulick wore pants, and the judge sent *her* to jail instead.

You know how some people, me included, hate the word "moist"? I'm the same way with referring to pants as "slacks." But that's what they called them back then. Except fuck that, let the anachronisms run wild. So, yeah. A couple of assholes broke into Helen's home. On November 9, 1938, she showed up in court to testify wearing pants. The judge was all heavens to Betsy goodness gracious no won't someone think of the children.

Judge Arthur Guerin rescheduled the case, telling Hulick that when she returned, she better be wearing a dress. Hulick was interviewed by the *Los Angeles Times* and was quoted in the paper the following day: "You tell the judge I will stand on my rights. If he orders me to change into a dress, I won't do it. I like slacks. They're comfortable." That's pretty badass.

Helen Hulick was a kindergarten teacher and used to dealing with obstinate children like the judge. She returned to court on November 15 and was all check out these pants, motherfucker. Like a typical five-year-old, the judge had a hissy fit. He said to her,

"You drew more attention from spectators, prisoners and court attachés than the legal business at hand." Then he spewed some bullshit about "orderly conduct" because he apparently didn't have the ability to control his own courtroom when a woman wore pants in it. He told her to return the next day in a dress or prepare to be punished.

November 9, 1938

She showed up again in pants, prepared to be punished. The judge held her in contempt, sentencing her to five days in jail. Women weren't allowed pants in jail either; her prison garb was a denim dress. She was ready to serve her time, but her attorney got her out with a writ of habeas corpus to take the matter before the appellate court to determine if her detention was legal.

The higher court said fuck that Judge Guerin guy. Let the woman go. She was free to return to court to testify, wearing pants. Except she didn't. As a final fuck-you to the judge, after winning the right to wear pants, she went hard in the other direction, overdressing in the fanciest attire she possessed.

Because sometimes a woman wants to wear pants, and sometimes she wants to wear a fancy dress.

> **"You tell the judge I will stand on my rights. If he orders me to change into a dress, I won't do it. I like slacks. They're comfortable."**

Can I say **"fuck"** in a piece about *Sesame Street*? Why the fuck not?

Created by the Children's Television Workshop and broadcast on PBS precursor National Educational Television, *Sesame Street* aired its first episode on November 10, 1969. And unlike fucking *Caillou,* it has cool characters and actual education. Like, learning numbers and shit from a vampire, a big-ass bird promoting vaccination, and normalizing homosexuality with Ernie and Bert.

November 10, 1969

I know some are gonna take issue with that last one. But imagine it's true. Would it matter?

Anyway, the goal was to both entertain and educate, and it worked. A lot of effort went into the show's production behind the scenes, involving pedagogical researchers and psychologists to help kids to not grow up to be psychopaths or vote Republican. Well, bit of sarcasm there, because I'm sure plenty of kids grew up to use the numbers the Count taught them to justify trickle-down Reaganomics. Regardless, *Sesame Street* was big on displaying empathy, tolerance of diversity, and nonaggressive methods of conflict resolution.

The show also regularly lampooned "Donald Grump" as a greedy landlord who tried to evict Oscar. Grump bragged that he owned more trash than any other grouch.

Interestingly, a 2015 study revealed that the show works just as well for early-childhood education as going to preschool, a boon for low-income households. The show has a diverse cast of characters with their own sets of flaws to help kids understand themselves and others better. As an example, the Cookie Monster isn't just fun to laugh at because he shoves cookies in his face like the apocalypse is imminent. He's also an example of someone with impulse-control issues who struggles to focus, and who tries and fails frequently, but also experiences successes.

Because of its progressive nature, not everyone has been a fan. In 1970 a station in Mississippi (of course) refused to air the show because it had a "highly [racially] integrated cast." It wasn't always smooth sailing; early on the show came under fire for its depiction of Latinos and women, and rather than be dicks about it the producers hired a more diverse cast of actors and writers to do a better job of representing a variety of groups. The show has been lauded for how it responds positively to criticism.

Sesame Street was born out of the civil rights movement, and the creators were ambitious about helping make the world a better place. It has had episodes that confront racism, normalize breastfeeding, feature a boy with Down syndrome as a recurring character, another whose dad is in jail, an HIV-positive character, a girl singing about the parts of her wheelchair, and more.

In celebration of the anniversary of this wonderful show, I do believe that I'll bake some cookies and be unrestrained in my eating of them.

How many times do you have to take communion before you've consumed an entire Jesus? How many Jesuses have been consumed since people started the practice? I'm sure some math whiz could figure it out, but we need to begin at the beginning.

Christianity is weird. It has zombies and embraces the symbol of its savior's torture. And the dude who speared Jesus to death? They made him a saint. Like, the fuck? Imagine explaining that shit to Jesus. Pope: "Hey, JC. Remember the soldier who coup-de-grâced your ass? We thought that was awesome so we gave him the highest honor we could." JC: "The fuck is wrong with you?"

Anyway, right after Jesus got sent off to meet his dad/himself people didn't automatically go "Hey let's start pretending to eat the guy." At least, not officially. That didn't happen until November 11, 1215, at the Fourth Council of the Lateran in Rome.

Prior to that, it all started at the Last Supper with Christ telling his pals this bread is me this wine is me so down the hatch with that shit, and apparently they didn't think that was weird. It's called the Eucharist and it caught on as a ritual among Christians so that a dozen centuries later the Church figured they should formalize some rules around it, affirming it as official dogma.

The Eucharist was cemented under Pope Innocent III, and if I know anything about popes, I doubt he or any of the others who took that name were all that innocent. Anyway, it was a big ecumenical council with a ton of patriarchs and bishops and abbots and shit. The council decided a lot of stuff, including stamping out heresy, calling for yet another crusade against those infidels in the Middle East, plus a bunch of other housekeeping bullshit. But a big one was about transubstantiation—that's where it became official Church doctrine to accept that some wafer and cheap wine are for-real transformed into the body and blood of Christ by a priest during the Mass, so be a good Christian and go cannibal on the Lord.

November 11, 1215

How does it work? The answer is simple, and one often used among various religions to explain myriad phenomena: God did it; "the bread being changed (*transubstantiation*) by divine power into the body, and the wine into the blood," they said.

A few hundred years later Martin Luther was all "Are you fucking kidding me?" about the Eucharist, and Protestants created their own version that was more a "memorial," going through the motions with no magical transformations into flesh and blood. Alas, the ensuing disagreements between Protestants and Catholics over the right way to pray to Jesus would lead to centuries of rending and spilling of literal flesh and blood.

"Thar, she blows!" Except this wasn't a case of a whale expelling water and air from its blowhole; it was a dead sperm whale rotting on an Oregon beach that some genius thought the best way to dispose of was to use a thousand pounds of dynamite. To say things did not go as planned would be a gross, and I mean really fucking gross, understatement.

November 12, 1970

It should come as no surprise that 16,000 pounds of dead whale left to rot in the sun for three days doesn't smell so good. People in the small city of Florence, Oregon, wanted something done. Oregon didn't have a Department of Rotting Whale Carcass Removal, but they did have the Oregon Highway Division, and apparently beaches fell under the jurisdiction of highways because dune buggies or some shit. I don't know. Anyway, the highway guys talked to some navy guys and they decided, "Let's blow that fucker to Neptune." The planet? The Roman god of the sea? Who knows? But they wanted to explode that cetacean, and so they did. Kind of.

> **It should come as no surprise that 16,000 pounds of dead whale left to rot in the sun for three days doesn't smell so good.**

The idea is that they would blow it to literal bits that would be small enough for scavengers such as seagulls to come along and say oh wow thanks bits of exploded rotting sperm whale is my favorite, and eat it all up and smelly problem solved.

That is not what happened.

The whalesplosion, which took place on November 12, 1970, was a media and spectator event. I mean, if you heard the gubmint was gonna blow the shit out some mega sea creature nearby, you'd go watch, wouldn't you? Of course you would, and you'd regret the fuck out of it. Because they did the kaboom, and it did not neatly blow the whale into little bite-sized chunks. Rather, it threw massive chunks as far as three hundred yards, raining stenchy whale gore down upon the crowd. One piece the size of an NFL offensive lineman destroyed a car in the parking lot.

And it didn't even get rid of the whale. They blew a fair-sized chunk out of it, but most of the carcass remained right where it was. What wasn't around anymore was a single fucking seagull.

The world's deadliest invention is the nuclear bomb, potentially. Tomorrow, those devices could kill billions. Except they haven't. Yet. Hopefully they won't. But when it comes to the single military invention that has killed more people than any other, that was created by a Soviet tank mechanic shortly after the end of World War II.

Born in the small town of Kurya in southern Russia, Mikhail Kalashnikov was the seventeenth of nineteen chil—Oh my god his poor mother. Mikhail was a sickly boy who enjoyed working with machinery, but also a poet who would author six books.

He was drafted into the Red Army in 1938, and because of his small size and mechanical skills they made him a tank mechanic, and later a tank commander. He was wounded in October 1941 in a tank battle with German forces, and while in hospital heard fellow soldiers complain about how shitty their rifles were and that they jammed all the time.

He got to work and came up with several designs, but on November 13, 1947, he completed what he would name the *Avtomat Kalashnikova* Model 1947. Aka the AK-47. Within two years it became the standard-issue assault rifle for the Soviet Army.

The design was so effective, everyone wanted one. Approximately 100 million AK-47s and variants have been manufactured in ensuing years. It became a symbol of revolution in countries around the world, including Vietnam, Afghanistan, and nations throughout Africa and Latin America. But it's also popular in the United States; in 2012, Americans bought as many AKs as the Russian military and police.

November 13, 1947

Why is this weapon so popular? It's inexpensive to produce, short, light, simple to use, the recoil isn't bad, it works well in a variety of harsh conditions, doesn't require much maintenance, and it rarely jams. For his invention, the Russians awarded Kalashnikov just about every medal they had to give.

How many people have been killed by bullets fired from AK-47s? Many millions. Kalashnikov, who died in 2013 at the age of ninety-four, said we should blame the Nazis for his becoming a gun designer; he had wanted to design agricultural equipment. He also blamed politicians for how his weapon was used, saying, "I sleep well." However, in his final year the lifelong atheist wrote a letter to the head of the Russian Orthodox Church that proclaimed, "The pain in my soul is unbearable."

When **Nellie Bly** was eight, Jules Verne published a book about a man named Phileas Fogg who traveled *Around the World in Eighty Days.* Seventeen years later, Bly said Phileas was a slacker. I shall do it faster. People thought she was crazy, but she'd already spent time in a mental institution, so why not?

November 14, 1889

Born Elizabeth Cochran near Pittsburgh in 1864, when she was sixteen she read a column in the *Pittsburgh Dispatch* titled "What Are Girls Good For?" and the answer the author provided was basically "making babies and doing housework." Nellie was all oh fucking hell no and wrote a response and the editor was impressed with her prose and gave her a job. She took on the pen-name Nellie Bly.

She began with investigative writing about the harsh lives of working women, and when factory owners complained about

Nellie Bly in Mexico, 1888

being exposed as douchebags the paper moved her to writing about fashion. Bly said fuck you and went to Mexico and spent six months writing about that, publishing it in a book. What made her really famous was when she was twenty-three, Nellie pretended to be insane to get locked up in the Women's Lunatic Asylum on Blackwell's Island (now called Roosevelt Island) in New York as an undercover assignment. She wrote about the deplorable conditions for *New York World,* which was owned by that Pulitzer guy, and *Ten Days in a Mad-House* became a book that caused a massive sensation, and the asylum was forced to implement reforms. Her heroic stunt launched a new form of investigative journalism.

Ready for another adventure, on November 14, 1889, with two days' notice, she left Hoboken on a steamship headed for Europe to prove that Verne's circumnavigation could be completed in under eighty days. One of her stops was in France where she met the inspiring author Jules Verne himself. She sent telegraphs along the way to report on her travels.

She traveled across Asia mostly by rail; in China she visited a leper colony and in Singapore she bought a pet monkey that she took back to the United States with her. She completed her trip around the world in seventy-two days and wrote yet another book about her adventures, although some dude couldn't abide a woman being a world record holder and beat it a few months later, but Nellie was first to do it in under Verne's eighty days.

In 1998, Nellie Bly was inducted into the National Women's Hall of Fame. The New York Press Club has a journalism award named after her.

Seems to me the city of Berlin has a history of people getting together and deciding to do things that involve a lot of other people dying. You know how Las Vegas is a popular conference destination for modern businesses and associations? Berlin was that in 1884, except the business was how European powers were going to conquer and exploit Africa.

Late in the nineteenth century there was a "New Imperialism," which saw various powers seize land that was already occupied by other people. One example of such colonial fuckery was the "Scramble for Africa."

There was a brewing conflict, and Belgian King Leopold II, who fucked over the Congo in every way imaginable, said hey, rather than fight, let's have a party and set up some rules. And Otto von Bismarck, who was running the show in Germany, said that sounds awesome, I'll host. And so, a dozen European countries, plus the United States and the Ottoman Empire, got together starting on November 15, 1884, in the city of Berlin to determine exactly how they would work together to rape an entire continent. But they didn't want it to seem like they were dicks about the whole thing, so to put lipstick on the pig of mass colonization they said they'd end slavery while they were at it.

A common myth about the conference, which lasted almost four months, was that it was various powers hovering over a map with rulers and pencils to sketch dividing lines regarding who owned what. But that wasn't what happened. What really happened was much worse.

What they did was establish the rules of the game of how they would conquer the continent. First was that they wouldn't even consider that any of the lands in Africa had a sovereign right to self-government. They were on a "civilizing mission" to "save Africa from the Africans." And in the process, they would turn it into a personal playground and steal as many of their natural resources as they wished. There was no African representation at the conference, because their opinions didn't matter.

November 15, 1884

To add religious legitimacy, the General Act of the conference, which was signed and ratified by almost all the participating countries (the United States signed but did not ratify it), declared the rules for their thievery were made "In the Name of God Almighty."

Cartoon depicting imperial powers carving up Africa

Historians originally called it the Battle of Cajamarca, but upon closer examination many realized "Battle" wasn't the best descriptor and changed the word to "Massacre." It's when Spanish conqueror Francisco Pizarro slaughtered the Incan leadership to kick off the destruction of the Incan Empire.

November 16, 1532

The guile of these motherfuckers. Ten years earlier, Spanish conquistador Hernán Cortés landed in what is now Mexico and said yo we're like all peaceful and stuff. Take us to your leader. And so, they took him to see Moctezuma II and the Spaniards slaughtered his bodyguards and took the Aztec emperor hostage. Cortés and his men then used this paralysis of the Aztec leadership to break apart the empire, which ruled over 5 million people, and conquer it.

Ten years later Pizarro said well shit that worked out great. I'm gonna do the same to these Incans. And so, he did.

Arriving with fewer than 200 men in what is now Peru, Pizarro did the whole "peaceful emissary of the king of Spain" bullshit line and requested a diplomatic meeting with the Incan ruler Atahualpa. Atahualpa felt he had little to fear from this small group of Europeans, because he had a battle-hardened army of 80,000 behind him.

The Incan ruler invited Pizarro and company deep into his territory for a meeting, and they arrived on November 15, 1532.

Atahualpa had no idea of what had happened with Cortés and the Aztecs, so he was fatefully incautious in his dealings with Pizarro. The following day, November 16, he left his army outside the city and he and his retinue did not bring much in the way of weapons to the conference—a sign not only of peaceful intent, but of confidence in their superior numbers. Yeah, that was not smart. They misjudged how murderous these Spaniards could be.

With their Indigenous quarry lacking sufficient weapons, Pizarro and his men ambushed the Incans. The Spaniards used cavalry, cannons, and guns to devastating effect, murdering thousands of commanders, counselors, and attendants. They took Atahualpa prisoner.

Atahualpa's army was about a mile away, and the Incans who fled the massacre told the horrific tale. Despite outnumbering their foe about 400 to 1, they were shocked and demoralized at the loss of leadership and scattered.

Just as Cortés had done in what is now Mexico, Pizarro used Atahualpa to control the Incan Empire and loot the shit out of it. Eight months later he decided the deposed Incan ruler was a liability, so he conducted a sham trial, found the emperor guilty of various crimes, and had him strangled to death.

On **May 25, 1977,** *Star Wars* premiered and blew our minds. Eighteen months later, the *Star Wars Holiday Special,* complete with interspecies virtual-reality porn, was broadcast on CBS, and it blew minds in a totally different way. What was responsible for such a televised atrocity? Answer: Cocaine. Mountains of it.

Holy shit where to begin? Chewbacca travels to his home planet for Wookiee Christmas and Han Solo tags along. And because it's *Star Wars* they get chased by Imperial Star Destroyers, but for once the stupid hyperdrive on the Aluminum Falcon works and they escape. Meanwhile, on Planet Wookiee, or whatever the fuck they call it, Chewie's dad, whose name is Itchy—really, his dad's name is the same as the homicidal mouse from *The Simpsons*—is being a dick to Chewie's son, whose name is Lumpy. Jesus Christ. Or hairy space-Jesus birthday celebration. I don't know. And no one knows what the fuck anyone is saying because it's just endless Wookiee wailing without a single subtitle.

Anyway, Chewie's wife is making a fancy dinner and worried that her husband, who has been busy blowing up Death Stars and *not* getting a fucking medal for it, won't make it on time so she calls Luke and asks where the fuck are those guys and oh my god who fucking cares this catastrophe was ninety-eight minutes long.

One of the presents Itchy gets for Wookiee Christmas is a VR porn set. And he tries it out right there in the living room and things get *real awkward* as he . . . maybe you should just google that part. It's not a sheepdog-looking critter he's cerebrally jerking it to, but a very human Diahann Carroll.

November 17, 1978

Somehow, they managed to reunite the entire cast for this catastrophe, and you can tell they don't want to be there. Ford has an expression that says he's ready to murder his agent and Fisher is obviously chemically altered. It aired on November 17, 1978, and didn't even crack Nielsen's Top 10 for the evening. It was panned by . . . everyone. I mean, shit, they admitted it was inspired by *Donny & Marie* to give it a variety-show flavor. In one scene, Bea Arthur sings in the Mos Eisley Cantina, for fuck's sake. I was a ten-year-old *Star Wars* geek at the time and I bailed after half an hour.

One reviewer for *The A.V. Club* said the show was "written and directed by a sentient bag of cocaine." George Lucas, upon seeing the horror he had wrought (except not really because he was pretty hands-off), thought it was so bad he never permitted it to be replayed or released in any format ever again. This is the guy who gave us Jar Jar.

Of course, it *is* on the internet. So, go find it, you sick fuck.

> **What was responsible for such a televised atrocity? Answer: Cocaine. Mountains of it.**

We should probably stop using the phrase "drink the Kool-Aid." First off, it was cyanide-laced *Flavor* Aid that took the lives of almost a thousand people in Guyana, not Kool-Aid. And second, it wasn't so much a mass suicide as it was a mass murder. People say drink the Kool-Aid to refer to people who *voluntarily* embrace their doom. Most of those in Jonestown didn't want to die.

November 18, 1978

Jim Jones was a cult leader, a self-professed faith healer, and an all-around murderous piece of fucking shit. Born in 1931 in Indiana, childhood acquaintances referred to him as a "really weird kid" who obsessed over both God and death.

Jones became a communist in the era of McCarthyism in the 1950s. He decided a way to spread communism was to "infiltrate the church." Later, he realized that running your own church was a great way to make money to achieve one's aims, so he studied none other than Adolf Fucking Hitler to learn how to manipulate his cult members.

Anyway, for a couple of decades he enjoyed growing influence and media attention due to his supportive stance regarding racial integration of his "church." Aside from that bit of progressiveness, he was the fucking worst. Outwardly he was seen as a humanitarian, but he abused his followers and made them sign over all their possessions to him.

By 1977, people were starting to ask questions and Jones said fuck this we're moving to another continent, and about five hundred of his followers went off to Guyana to set up a cult commune, with many more arriving a short time later, bringing the population to almost a thousand people. It was not a good place to be. Congressman Leo Ryan was concerned about how American citizens were being treated there and flew down with a delegation to investigate. While they were there, a bunch of people said get us the fuck out of here and he said okay I have an airplane. As they tried to leave, they were ambushed by cult members with guns who killed Ryan and four others, and wounded eleven. Side note: One of the wounded, Jackie Speier, was hit five times and almost died. She later served as a Democrat in Congress from 2008 until 2023.

Jones knew he was in deep shit and wanted to take everyone down with him, so on November 18, 1978, immediately following the murders at the airstrip, he called for "revolutionary suicide." He said the U.S. intelligence services were going to parachute in and torture them all, so drink this poison. A lot of people didn't want to and were forced to drink or were injected with cyanide. Over 900 people died in the massacre, 304 of them children. By the way, it was not an easy death. It took several minutes and was horrifyingly painful.

Jones, that cowardly piece of shit, shot himself in the head.

t's fewer than three hundred words, and as part of the speech President Lincoln said, "The world will little note, nor long remember what we say here." He was wrong about that. The Gettysburg Address is one of the most famous speeches in history, but initial reaction was muted, and media opinions divided.

The Battle of Gettysburg took place in the first three days of July 1863, and it was a horror. Traitorous general Robert Lee led his traitorous Confederate Army against Union general George Meade. After three days, the combined casualties numbered approximately 50,000. It was a Union victory, and Lee dragged his traitorous ass back to Virginia in defeat. Many consider the battle a turning point in the U.S. Civil War because it halted Lee's plans to invade the North and force an early end to the war. The Union victory reinvigorated the North and turned the tide against the slavery-supporting shitnuggets.

Immediately following the battle, the fallen were buried where they lay, many in poorly marked graves. A local attorney, David Wills, launched a campaign to have Gettysburg designated a national cemetery. The dedication took place on November 19, 1863. The featured speaker was Edward Everett, a leading orator in the nation who was a former senator, former secretary of state, and former head of Harvard University. Everett gave a lengthy speech on the day of dedication, but afterward he wrote to President Lincoln, saying, "I wish that I could flatter myself that I had come as near to the central idea of the occasion in two hours as you did in two minutes." Lincoln replied that he was pleased his address was not a "total failure."

November 19, 1863

Witnesses to Lincoln's address said the reaction to his speech was quiet, the clapping delayed, scattered, and "barely polite." And the media was of course divided along partisan lines. Lincoln, a Republican back when Republicans weren't the fucking worst, was praised for his speech in Republican-leaning papers such as *The New York Times.* Conversely, the Democrat-leaning *Chicago Times* proclaimed the speech shameful, with "silly, flat and dishwatery utterances."

Lincoln's closing statement in the short speech was "that government of the people, by the people, for the people, shall not perish from the earth." I would say that "We can only hope" but this would not be true. We, the people, can fight to make it so.

> **The Union victory reinvigorated the North and turned the tide against the slavery-supporting shitnuggets.**

Some say you shouldn't punch Nazis. Fuck that. Punch them in the head until your fucking hand breaks. After World War II we didn't punch Nazis; we hanged the bastards.

November 20, 1945

I'm torn about the whole death penalty thing. If someone killed a member of my family, I'd want the fucker to die. Hell, I might do it myself. But at the societal level, it just doesn't work. Using the United States as an example, there are many problems with it. It's unfairly applied to poor people and people of color. Because of the lengthy appeals process, it's more expensive to execute someone than to put them in prison for life. It is proven to not be a deterrent to crime. It breaks the social contract of a society that respects life. Mistakes are made, and you can't make someone undead. Etc.

But those Nazi fucks had it coming.

They murdered millions and the West put them on trial. The first and best known of the Nuremberg trials began six months after the war ended, on November 20, 1945. But they'd been planned for over three years. Representatives from countries occupied by Germany began meeting in 1942 to plan

> **Desiring vengeance is not a healthy emotion, but considering their crimes I'm having a difficult time feeling bad about that.**

how they'd one day hopefully hold those Nazi cockwaffles accountable. Nuremberg was chosen for the trials because the Palace of Justice was still intact after the Allied bombing, and because the city was also the birthplace of the Nazi Party, so it was another fuck-you to fascism.

The trials lasted over ten months, exposing the crimes of twenty-four of the most notorious political and military leaders of the Third Reich. Twelve of them were sentenced to the eternal dirt nap. One of the dozen condemned was Hermann Göring. Göring was one of the most powerful leaders in the Nazi Party. Someone smuggled cyanide into his cell for him and he killed himself the night before his scheduled execution. Asshole.

Another seven war criminals got sentences ranging from ten years to life; three were acquitted; and two ended up not being charged. When it came to the executions being carried out, they didn't go that smoothly. Accusations were made that the drop for the hanging was too short, and a number of them, rather than have their necks broken for a quick death, died slowly and painfully over several minutes from strangulation.

Desiring vengeance is not a healthy emotion, but considering their crimes I'm having a difficult time feeling bad about that.

We're entering the season of getting Christmas rammed down our throats. But what's Hanukkah about? It started more with ramming swords into throats.

The Jewish people have been attacked and oppressed since, well, forever. So, it shouldn't be surprising the holiday is tied to a war. Specifically, the Maccabean Revolt, which began in 167 B.C.E. After the death of Alexander the Great in 323 B.C.E., his Greek Empire split up into several smaller ones. One of those became known as the Seleucid Empire, which took control of Judea in 198 B.C.E., and the Greeks were total dicks about it; they wanted to convert Jews to the ways of Greek culture and religion. But the Jews were all fuck that we got our own culture and religion that we're pretty happy with so piss off.

Persecution of the Jewish population grew via various laws designed to oppress them, and after three decades they'd had enough. Specifically, a Jewish country priest named Mattathias was done with this bullshit. In 167 B.C.E. a Seleucid officer tried to force Mattathias to sacrifice an animal to an idol. If you've seen the movie *The Ten Commandments* you know he wasn't keen on that, so he ghosted that motherfucker, tore down the idol, and said, "Let's fuck their shit up!" More or less.

Mattathias and his family led the rebellion and became known as the Maccabees, meaning "The Hammer." They went on a guerrilla warfare campaign of destroying Hellenistic (Greek) altars and launching devastating attacks on the Seleucid army using hit-and-run tactics.

November 21, 164 B.C.E.

Mattathias died a year into the revolt, and his son Judah took over. Over the next two years there were many battles, yet the badly outnumbered Jewish forces managed to prevail, due in no small part to Judah's brilliance as a military commander.

The first Jewish Temple of Jerusalem was built in approximately 1,000 B.C.E., then destroyed by Babylonian king Nebuchadnezzar II in 587 B.C.E. It was replaced with a second temple in 516 B.C.E. When Judas Maccabaeus and his forces retook Jerusalem, they found the second temple defiled and destroyed, and they were pissed. But they restored and rededicated the temple on November 21, 164 B.C.E. And it is that restoration and rededication that Hanukkah celebrates.

Why is Hanukkah eight days? Because of the miracle of the oil. Upon reclaiming the temple, they found the ritual olive oil used to light the temple defiled. There was only enough to last a single day. But legend proclaims it lasted eight days, just long enough to press more oil. And that's what Hanukkah is about.

Nichelle Nichols of *Star Trek* fame, as awesome as she was, was not the first woman to be part of an interracial kiss on television. But the episode initiated a catalyst event that helped change the world for the better.

November 22, 1968

Exactly when the first interracial kiss happened on television is a contested subject. As context, the U.S. Supreme Court didn't approve interracial marriage until 1967. In the U.K., the first interracial kiss involving a Black person on TV dates back to 1959. In the 1950s in America, Lucy and Desi, who were married in real life, kissed on *I Love Lucy,* and even though he was a white Cuban, people at the time still considered them an "interracial couple." But this wasn't considered close to the same thing as a Black person kissing a white person in racist-as-fuck America.

Nichols's smooch wasn't even the first interracial kiss on *Star Trek.* In October 1967, William Shatner, playing Captain Kirk, kissed Filipino actress BarBara Luna. And earlier that year Ricardo Montalbán, a Mexican playing an Indian, kissed one of Kirk's white officers, played by Madlyn Rhue.

But a Black woman and a white man kissing on television in the United States back then was a Big Deal, and it was broadcast for the first time on November 22, 1968, between Nichols as Lt. Uhura and Shatner as Captain Kirk.

The episode was called "Plato's Stepchildren," and this is the cool part. NBC execs were being overly cautious cocks about airing the kiss because of certain even-more-racist-than-average states. They wanted two versions: with a kiss, and without. But Nichols and Shatner deliberately fucked up the "no kiss" scene again and again so there was no no-kiss version, and the executives had no choice but to air the episode with the kiss.

The effect of the kiss, once it aired, was overwhelmingly positive. Fan mail poured in, with almost no one considering it offensive. That doesn't mean there weren't a bunch of snowflakes out there who couldn't handle people with varying degrees of melanin in their skin touching lips, but perhaps they weren't *Star Trek* fans.

NBC execs were being overly cautious cocks about airing the kiss because of certain even-more-racist-than-average states.

The Soviets called it Operation Uranus, which was appropriate because it involved handing the Nazis their asses at the Battle of Stalingrad. The deadliest battle of World War II, Germany and their allies suffered close to 900,000 casualties, and the Soviets had about 1.2 million casualties. It was a horrific shitshow and you definitely didn't want to be there, because the odds of surviving it were almost nonexistent.

The German invasion of Stalingrad (now Volgograd, because fuck Stalin) began in August 1942. Stalin was all hell fucking no that city is named after me and launched a massive counterattack. Operation Uranus was a plan to encircle the Germans (and Italians, Hungarians, and Romanians, who were all fighting on the side of the Axis) and cut them off from resupply or retreat. And it worked. The northern arm of the Red Army launched on November 19, 1942, and the southern arm attacked the following day.

The plan was to hit the Axis's northern and southern flanks where they were weak, because they were protected not by Germans, but by Romanian forces. These soldiers were simply not as tough, and both flanks quickly collapsed. Germans sent in their reserves to protect their southern flank, but it wasn't enough. They couldn't stop the encirclement. They were F U fucking fucked.

Soviet soldiers during the Battle of Stalingrad

It took three more days to complete the encirclement, but it was a done deal on November 23, 1942, and then over a quarter million Axis troops were trapped in Soviet territory, cut off and with only the impending Russian winter for company. Sucks to be them. The remaining Italians and Romanians surrendered, but Hitler said no fucking way we superior German specimens shall surrender. I know! I'll promote the commander to field marshal. No German field marshal has ever surrendered. That will solve the problem!

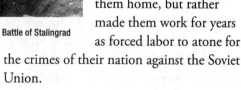

November 23, 1942

Except it didn't. Starvation and cold took as many German lives as did Soviet bombs and bullets, and on January 31, 1943, newly promoted Field Marshal Friedrich Paulus waved the white flag. Only 90,000 Germans were left at this point to surrender. They were sent to Soviet prison camps and let's just say the Russians didn't feel much like being nice to them. Even after the war ended, they didn't send them home, but rather made them work for years as forced labor to atone for the crimes of their nation against the Soviet Union.

Only 6,000 ever saw home again.

Oh God he is such a fucking piece of shit. He *did* mock a disabled reporter and then he lied his ass off about it. Of course, the Trumpanzees believed the lies. That's what happens when you're in a fucking cult.

The reporter's name is Serge F. Kovaleski and he is a Pulitzer Prize–winning investigative journalist for *The New York Times.* Kovaleski has a congenital condition called arthrogryposis, which restricts joint movement. And at one of Trump's hate-filled rallies in South Carolina on November 24, 2015, the Fanta Menace did something that should have cost him the election. The fact that it didn't—and that numerous other displays of his reprehensible character were likewise waved away by those who voted for him—reveals just how fucked-up many in the United States are.

The background is that Trump had oft-repeated a myth of "thousands" of "Arabs" cheering and dancing as the World Trade Center collapsed, saying he personally witnessed them doing it. When called on his bullshit, Trump referenced a piece written by Kovaleski in *The Washington Post* as evidence it was true, but, being a complete fucking dumbass, he misrepresented the shit out of what Kovaleski wrote. Kovaleski's 2001 story said only a few people were "allegedly" seen celebrating, and that there were no reports at all, even unsubstantiated ones, of hundreds or thousands cheering and/or dancing.

Kovaleski then released a statement to news organizations confirming what he actually wrote, exposing Trump as a lying fucking liar in the process. Caught out, Cheeto Benito tried to make the reporter appear stupid and confused. "You've got to see this guy: 'Uh, I don't know what I said. Uh, I don't remember.'" Trump said this to a crowd while doing a blatant imitation of Kovaleski's disability.

Revealed once again as a garbage human, two days later Trump released a statement saying, "I have no idea who this reporter, Serge Kovalski [sic], is, what he looks like or his level of intelligence . . . I merely mimicked what I thought would be a flustered reporter trying to get out of a statement he made long ago. If Mr. Kovaleski is handicapped, I would not know because I do not know what he looks like."

How do we know this is a steaming pile of bullshit? First off, it's Trump. Lying is what he does. Second, he said, "You've got to see this guy" followed by a disgusting and obvious imitation of his disability. Also, we have the words of Kovaleski himself, who said, "Donald and I were on a first-name basis for years. I've interviewed him in his office. I've talked to him at press conferences. All in all, I would say around a dozen times, I've interacted with him as a reporter while I was at *The Daily News.*"

Such a piece of shit.

Bart Simpson to cop: "Can I see your club?" Cop: "It's called a baton, son." Bart: "Oh. What's it for?" Cop: "We club people with it." In the sixteenth century, Finnish peasants didn't call them clubs either, but cudgels. And they used these cudgels to club the shit out of the nobility.

It was called the Cudgel War, and it was doomed from the start because they brought clubs to a gun fight. It took place in what is now Finland, but at the time it was part of the Kingdom of Sweden. Sweden had been in a lengthy scrap with Russia, which was not at all uncommon, and wars cost money so the rich folks said hey let's tax the poor folks, and the poor folks started bashing rich folks in the head.

Wars don't just cost money, but lives, and peasants weren't just sick of the exorbitant taxes, but also of being pressed into becoming cannon fodder. There was a short uprising before Christmas in 1595, but the Swedish cavalry quickly crushed that. Eleven months later, on November 25, 1596, the Cudgel War officially began with a peasant uprising in what is now northwest Finland. The leader of the uprising wasn't a peasant, however. They'd elected wealthy landowner Jaakko Ilkka to run the rebellion. That's not uncommon in history, FYI. Rebellions are usually led by wealthier and more educated members of society. The French Revolution was led by an ambitious middle class that was sick of the nobility hogging all the money.

Anyway, they also had some swords and a few guns, but mostly the peasants used blunt instruments that also included the mace (a stick with a spiky metal ball on the end) and flail (a stick with a chain on the end, and at the end of that chain is a spiky metal ball). I've never been smoked in the head with a spiky metal ball, but I expect it could ruin anyone's day. And the peasants ruined a lot of people's days with their various instruments of brain-bashing. For a time, northwest Finland was not a good place to be a rich person.

November 25, 1596

The peasants laid waste to manorial estates and slayed the gentry, especially the tax collectors. Those tax collectors had an especially bad time of it. Then the professional, disciplined, well-armed, battle-hardened Swedish army was sent in. And holy shit, even though they were outnumbered the peasants still kicked some ass. Initially. The peasants were obviously pissed, and it was a case of "size of the fight in the dog, not the size of the dog in the fight." Alas, they fought to a truce that demanded the handing over of Jaakko. Jaakko said oh shit time to fuckity bye and noped out of there, but he was caught and executed. Other rebel leaders kept fleeing or getting killed, and the peasants were soon leaderless.

Come February of 1597 there was a big open battle with the Swedish army, and the peasants got fucking shit-mixed and that was that.

You don't get "the Impaler" added to your name by being a nice guy. Vlad Dracula may not have been an actual vampire, since those don't exist, but he did kill plenty of folks. He's also one of the most important rulers in the history of what is now Romania, and considered a national hero. Probably not by the people who got giant stakes shoved up their asses, though.

November 26, 1476

What a life this guy led. His dad, Vlad II Dracul, was ruler of Wallachia, and the Ottomans held Vlad Jr. (who was the second oldest son) hostage, along with Jr.'s younger brother, so that Dad Vlad would remain loyal. But Dad Vlad and his oldest son were murdered in 1447, and there was a scramble for the throne. Vlad Jr. had a second cousin named Vladislav, because people liked that name, who wanted the throne, and there were armies running this way and that, and Vlad Jr. seized the throne in Wallachia with Ottoman support while his cousin was away fighting other Ottomans, becoming Vlad III aka Vlad Dracula and yeah later Vlad the Impaler. Anyway, Vladislav got his ass kicked by the Ottomans and then learned Dracula had just stolen the throne and was all "That motherfucker!" and took the remnants of his army back home and Dracula ran away. Confused yet? I am.

> **Vlad Dracula may not have been an actual vampire, since those don't exist, but he did kill plenty of folks.**

Dracula's first rule lasted less than two months. Eight years of exile followed, then Vlad III Dracula said fuck that cousin-douche Vladislav and invaded his homeland again, this time with Hungarian support, and killed Vladislav. Then he went medieval on some asses. He did a purge of the nobility who he suspected of plotting against him, and attacked the Transylvanian Saxons for supporting his opponents, plundering their villages and taking captives back to Wallachia for a nice little bit of impaling and earning of a nickname. We're talking tens of thousands of men, women, and children. If you google that, there are various methods of shoving a long sharp pole through parts of a human body that really aren't supposed to have poles inserted into them. None of them are pleasant.

Then Vlad, having earned "the Impaler," six years into his second rule went after the Ottomans in 1462, lost, and spent fourteen years as a prisoner. Third time wasn't the charm either. Vlad the Impaler, after having rallied supporters, once again fought and reclaimed the Wallachian throne on November 26, 1476. But he had to fight to retain power and a month later was killed in battle with the Ottomans who supported his rival. They hacked Vlad's body to pieces, and his burial site is unknown. Maybe he turned into a bat.

The common belief regarding the assassination of San Francisco politician Harvey Milk is that he died because he was gay. That may have played a role, but it was more about political grievances the murderer had. The media said the shooter blamed his desire to kill on eating Twinkies.

Milk was the first openly gay elected official in California's history, serving on the San Francisco Board of Supervisors beginning in early 1978. He'd be dead less than a year later, but not before becoming a popular icon in the city's gay community. In his short tenure as a city official, Milk sponsored a law banning discrimination based on sexual orientation for housing, employment, or use of public accommodations. It passed 11–1, with the one dissenting vote being Dan White's, the man who murdered him.

White was a Vietnam veteran, and a former police officer and firefighter. He won as a Democrat to become a city supervisor at the same time as Milk, who was a U.S. Navy diving officer during the Korean War. The pair initially worked well together, despite White representing a conservative neighborhood and seeing himself as a defender of "family and religious life against homosexuals." White was a contradiction, because his vote helped defeat the anti-gay Briggs Initiative that sought to ban gay people from working as teachers. He also invited Milk to attend his child's baptism.

The antagonism began when Milk voted in favor of a group home for youth offenders in White's district, which White strongly opposed. It's possible White's subsequent dissent against Milk's gay rights ordinance was revenge for this. Pissed off that he couldn't get his way, White resigned his seat on November 10. Rather than hold an election, Mayor George Moscone appointed a liberal replacement for the seat. People in White's former district were pissed and told White to rescind his resignation, which he did, but the mayor said "no backsies." One of the people who lobbied the mayor not to take White back was Harvey Milk.

November 27, 1978

On November 27, 1978, Dan White showed up at City Hall carrying his old service revolver, entering via a first-floor window to avoid the metal detectors. He confronted Mayor Moscone in his office, asking again to be reinstated. When Moscone refused, White emptied his gun into the mayor, killing him. He reloaded, then went in search of Milk, found him, and killed him too.

White was later captured and tried for murder, but his defense team claimed diminished capacity due to depression. The defense presented a change in diet as evidence of said depression, which the media then misrepresented as a high-sugar diet being his excuse for the murders. They called it the "Twinkie defense." It worked, and White was convicted only of voluntary manslaughter and given a light sentence. The city was enraged, and the White Night Riots followed.

White served only five years, then took his own life less than two years after his release from prison.

American presidents and British prime ministers aren't overly welcome in Iran these days, but in 1943 Tehran was host city for the meeting of Allied superpowers to discuss how they were going to beat the Axis in World War II.

The Tehran Conference—a meeting of Stalin, Churchill, and Roosevelt—began on November 28, 1943, and lasted four days. Why was it held in Tehran? Well, because the Soviets and British had invaded it a couple of years earlier. They wanted to secure a corridor to get Allied supplies to the Soviets, who were busy doing the lion's share of the killing and dying in fighting the fucking Nazis. They also wanted Iran's oil for the war effort. Neutral Iran's opinion was basically yeah sure come on in and take our oil it's not like we can stop you, dicks.

Anyway, the primary purpose of the conference was for Stalin to say will you two fucknuts hurry up and open a western front on those Nazi assholes so we don't have to do ALL the dying? And Roosevelt and Churchill were like yeah we're fuckin' working on it, saying it would be a May 1944 invasion and Stalin was actually pleased with that. The Western Allies were only a little bit

Stalin, Roosevelt, and Churchill at the Tehran Conference

Anyway, the primary purpose of the conference was for Stalin to say will you two fucknuts hurry up and open a western front on those Nazi assholes so we don't have to do ALL the dying?

late, launching Operation Overlord to invade Normandy on June 6.

Other important shit went down too, including discussions regarding the creation of the United Nations. There was this rather useless thing called the League of Nations that had been around since 1920 for maintaining world peace, but obviously it had done fuck all to prevent WWII. Roosevelt said hey Stalin why don't we try that again so we don't have to worry about Germany pulling this kinda shit for a third time and Stalin was like yeah we could probably do that. The idea was for Britain, the United States, the USSR, and China to act as "four policemen" to maintain world peace. Of note is that the name "United Nations" was coined by Roosevelt, and although he died prior to its creation in October of 1945, the American president considered the plans for the UN "the crowning act" of his career.

As you know from the August 6 entry, this conference was also when the Soviets said yeah we'll help America beat Japan once Germany is toast and that was something that contributed to the nuking of Japan to quickly end the war in the Pacific because 'Murica no longer wanted Soviet help. Regarding Germany, there were also discussions of how they were gonna divide that shit up once Hitler did the fascist dirt nap, but nothing was agreed to except that they were gonna neutralize Germany's ability to wage war ever again.

One foreboding instance was when Churchill asked Stalin, yo what are your postwar "territorial ambitions" and Stalin said, "There is no need to speak at this present time about any Soviet desires."

If it was a movie, that would be where the music switches to a minor key.

"**Chattel**" is personal property other than land. It is a thing that is owned that the owner can do with what they please. Chattel slavery treated people as things with no rights at all, and the owner could not only murder them with no legal consequences, such as toss them off a slavery ship to drown, but could also collect on the insurance.

November 29, 1781

Luke Collingwood was a murderous piece of shit. He'd been the surgeon on the slave ship *William,* and apparently didn't give a shit about the Hippocratic Oath, because on his very first command, of the British slavery ship *Zong,* he decided to murder over a hundred human beings he considered mere cargo.

As a surgeon his job had been to select enslaved people in Africa for transport based on perceived health. Often, when a surgeon rejected an enslaved person deemed too weak, the African enslaver murdered the person right in front of the surgeon. Saying no, as surgeons often did, was sentencing the enslaved to death. Humanity did not exist in the slavery trade; it was only about the money.

Collingwood was a shit navigator and had taken on too many slaves for transport, and over fifty had already died from sickness due to overcrowding and malnutrition. The ship got lost on the trip from Africa to the Americas, and ran low on drinking water. To "solve" the problem of not having enough water, they threw 132 enslaved overboard beginning on November 29, 1781. Another ten leaped to their drowning deaths in acts of defiance.

Once it arrived in Jamaica, one of the ship's owners, James Gregson (another piece of shit) filed an insurance claim for the loss of "cargo" on the voyage. The insurance underwriter disputed the claim and there was a trial that found for the enslavers. But then there was an appeal and the enslavers lost. The trials gained much public attention, and British abolitionist Granville Sharp referred to the event as the "*Zong* Massacre."

Sharp tried to have charges brought against the crew for murder, but John Lee, Britain's solicitor general, refused, saying, "What is this claim that human people have been thrown overboard? This is a case of chattels or goods. Black people are goods and property; it is madness to accuse these well-serving honorable men of murder . . . The case is the same as if wood had been thrown overboard."

That statement tells you all you need to know about such people.

Ouch, quit it. Imagine this. It's 1954. You're a thirty-four-year-old woman living on a farm in Alabama, which . . . probably wasn't super exciting. Anyway, you're taking a nap. And then a fucking meteorite the size of a goddamn cantaloupe crashes through the roof and smacks into you.

Considering how small the populations of prehistory were, and how big the planet is, it's not that likely some troglodyte was sleeping off a mammoth feast and got bonked by a space rock at any time before we started writing such shit down. And so, it is quite probable that the events of November 30, 1954, represent the first time a hominid took a meteorite to the face . . . Oh, wait. It hit her on her side . . . and she lived to tell the tale. There is a 1677 Italian manuscript that tells an unverified story of a monk who was *killed* by a meteorite, describing his death as "equally terrible and unexpected." And there are unconfirmed reports that in 1490 in China "stones fell like rain" and killed over 10,000 people, but many experts question if they came from space. There were rumors of people getting hurt in the shockwave from the Tunguska event in Siberia in 1908 as well. But the woman in Alabama was the first verifiable recorded instance of a known person surviving being hit by a space rock.

Her name was Ann Hodges, and some named it the Hodges meteorite, whereas others call it the Sylacauga meteorite, after the name of the nearest city to where Hodges lived. I prefer the former, because she's the unfortunate woman who got hit, and I can't pronounce the other one. Ann lived because it wasn't a direct hit, but a ricochet. She was snoozing on the couch and, after traveling through the roof, the meteorite hit the large console radio next to her, then caromed into her lower left side. She was badly bruised but could walk.

November 30, 1954

Michael Reynolds, an astronomer and meteorite expert at Florida State, said of the odds of a person being struck by a meteorite: "You have a better chance of getting hit by a tornado and a bolt of lightning and a hurricane all at the same time."

The rocky fireball was visible in three states as it streaked across the sky. If it hadn't been slowed down by both the roof and the radio, it would have ghosted Ann's ass. With Cold War paranoia running hot, the police chief confiscated the meteorite and gave it to the air force. Ann's landlord said it hit my property, so it's my rock. Ann eventually got it back, then donated it to the Alabama Museum of Natural History in 1956. Ann's husband said the stress of the international attention of the story put his wife in an early grave. She died aged fifty-two from kidney failure.

> **"You have a better chance of getting hit by a tornado and a bolt of lightning and a hurricane all at the same time."**

December

With all due respect and well-deserved adoration for Rosa Parks, she wasn't the first. More than eight months before Rosa, fifteen-year-old Claudette Colvin courageously refused to give up her seat to a white person on a bus in Montgomery, Alabama, but then Claudette got pregnant and civil rights leaders who'd planned to thrust her into the limelight worried over the optics of doing so with an unwed teen mother. Because 1950s America.

Yet there was a silver lining for Claudette in not becoming a well-known face of the civil rights movement. In March of 1955, when Claudette was arrested for refusing to relinquish her seat, Dr. Martin Luther King Jr. was a relatively unknown Montgomery preacher. But in the ensuing months his star rose significantly, allowing him to take charge of presenting Rosa Parks to the world as an icon of civil rights for Black people and launch his own world-changing career at the same time.

Black women have always shouldered the brunt of the labor in advancing civil rights, stepping into harm's way no matter the cost. On December 1, 1955, Rosa Parks decided it was her time. She was seated at the front of the "Colored Section" of the bus. But when more whites got on the bus than were seats available in the "White Section," the bus driver moved the sign for the Colored Section further back and told her and three other Black people to move to the re-designated Colored Section. The others complied, Rosa did not.

December 1, 1955

Years later Rosa said in an interview, "When that white driver stepped back toward us, when he waved his hand and ordered us up and out of our seats, I felt a determination cover my body like a quilt on a winter night."

Rosa was arrested, and the forty-two-year-old woman, who had already been active in the civil rights movement for over a dozen years, became a leader of the Montgomery bus boycott, earning such honorifics as "the first lady of civil rights" and "the mother of the freedom movement." Despite much adversity and threats of death, Rosa Parks remained active in the Civil Rights Movement for the rest of her life. She died in 2005 at the age of ninety-two. Her casket lay in state at the Rotunda of the U.S. Capitol, the first woman to receive such honors, where it was viewed by over 50,000 people.

> **Black women have always shouldered the brunt of the labor in advancing civil rights, stepping into harm's way no matter the cost.**

Benazir Bhutto was the first woman to be democratically elected as a head of state for a majority Muslim country. She was liberal-minded and favored separation of religion and politics, which, along with being a woman, led to her later assassination.

Born into an aristocratic family, she studied at both Oxford and Harvard. Her father had served as Pakistan's prime minister from 1973 to 1977 on a socialist platform. He left office via coup and assassination.

Benazir joined her father's party and moved it from the political left closer to the center, and on December 2, 1988, Bhutto became prime minister of Pakistan. Her attempts at reform were frequently blocked by more conservative members of government and the military. Her tenure lasted less than two years because the 1990 election was rigged for the conservative opposition to win. She became leader of the opposition and then was elected PM again in 1993, and stayed in the position for over three years.

Bhutto made efforts to modernize the country, including on the matter of women's rights, but was plagued by things like a coup attempt in 1995, and a bribery scandal that led to the president—the country has both a prime minister and a president—dismissing her government the following year. In 1998, Bhutto went into self-exile in Dubai and didn't return until 2007 to once again run for the leadership of her country. But the fundamentalist fucknuts who don't think women should have any say in society weren't having it.

On December 27, 2007, Bhutto was leaving a political rally in the city of Rawalpindi. She was traveling in a bulletproof vehicle but used the sunroof to stand half out of the car and wave at the crowd. That's when a young Taliban terrorist shot her three times from less than ten feet away, then detonated an explosive vest loaded with ball bearings. Twenty-two people died in the attack, including Bhutto. Al-Qaeda took responsibility, gloating at having terminated "the most precious American asset."

Riots followed the assassination, leading to another fifty deaths.

At my first-ever concert in 1984, I rushed to get near the front to see Iron Maiden up close. I tripped and went down. I was stepped on only once before my friend Don grabbed the back of my leather jacket and hauled me to my feet. Considering eleven people died in a similar manner at a concert by the Who only five years previous, I can't explain why the practice of rush seating still flourishes.

On December 3, 1979, the Who was in the middle of the U.S. portion of their world tour, playing at the Riverfront Coliseum in Cincinnati. The Who is awesome, and the concert sold out, with almost 15,000 of the more than 18,000 tickets sold being unassigned seats; it was the deadly "first come, first served" for seating choices. Getting prime real estate at a major concert event is never pure and easy.

The crowd had been waiting for hours outside. The doors were all supposed to open simultaneously, but only a pair at the end of the main entrance opened. People began going mobile, pushing toward them. Then a sound check by the band was interpreted as the concert having started, and some kids slipped; they weren't all right. Some were trampled, others were crushed against the building. Eleven people died from asphyxiation, and twenty-six others were injured.

December 3, 1979

The concert went ahead as planned. No one told the band about what happened until after the show.

You better bet people were pissed. There was a class-action lawsuit against the band, the promoter, and the city of Cincinnati. The city enacted a ban on unassigned seating for a time, but later repealed it. Two months after the tragedy, the show *WKRP in Cincinnati* did an episode titled "In Concert" that gave a fictionalized account of the events.

Over forty years later the Who planned to return to Cincinnati for the first time since 1979. It was scheduled for April 2020 but was delayed for two years due to Covid. They wouldn't be fooled again into putting their fans at unnecessary risk.

You better bet people were pissed. There was a class-action lawsuit against the band, the promoter, and the city of Cincinnati.

Just so we're clear, the Pacific theater of World War II fucking sucked. The Allies faced a tenacious enemy who refused to give up and didn't subscribe to the Geneva Conventions; they considered anyone who wasn't Japanese a member of an inferior race and treated them as such. Add in nasty jungle diseases and it was a whole lot of not fun. The Marines' fight against entrenched Japanese all began in a place called Guadalcanal.

December 4, 1942

Eight months after Pearl Harbor, the United States launched its first major land campaign against the Japanese forces that had swarmed across a multitude of Pacific islands. Guadalcanal is part of the Solomon Islands, only a short distance from Australia. The American offensive on the island, which also included a naval battle, would last six months, and by the time it was over Japan would be on the defensive for the rest of the war.

This is the story of one patrol.

It was called "Carlson's Patrol," named for its leader, Lieutenant Colonel Evans Carlson. It was a 2nd Marine Raider Battalion of seven hundred men, tasked with preventing a Japanese force more than three times its size from escaping the American encirclement of the island to rejoin the Imperial Japanese Army. On November 6, the patrol landed their boats thirty miles behind enemy lines and headed into the jungle to kick some ass.

The Raiders went in blind, knowing almost nothing about enemy positions, numbers, or movements. Carlson's Raiders went guerrilla, breaking the battalion into smaller companies and utilizing Native islanders as scouts to fan out and seek the enemy so they could fuck their shit up.

And fuck up their shit they did. For an entire month. The other name for Carlson's Patrol is the "Long Patrol." Utilizing repeated hit-and-run tactics against the Japanese over twenty-nine days, Carlson's group killed a total of 488 enemy soldiers while only losing 16 of their own.

The patrol ended on December 4, 1942, when Carlson's Raiders made their way back into friendly territory, looking like scarecrows. They were emaciated, unshaven, and covered with sores. The jungle had taken a toll; half the men were suffering from malaria, dysentery, ringworm, or jungle rot. The Marines within the American-held perimeter cheered their return.

Who likes getting fucked-up? Answer: lots of people. Beginning in 1920, the United States tried to get people to stop drinking with the Eighteenth Amendment, prohibiting alcohol. And everyone was immediately all "Oh, booze is against the law? As good citizens we shall refrain!" Yeah, no. They kept right on punishing those livers, and after thirteen years the government said fine fuck it have your damn booze.

Alcohol overindulgence is no joke. In the United States about 90,000 people die each year from over-imbibing, and roughly a quarter *trillion* dollars is lost each year, mostly in terms of hindered workplace productivity; I know I've put in some lackluster days due to day-after drain bamage. It's also costly in terms of health, domestic violence, criminal behavior, and vehicle crashes. Temperance movements were well aware of the societal costs of getting fucked-up, and they wanted to fuck up everyone's good (and bad) times by making the devil's drink illegal. And they succeeded.

But freedom tho.

With the implementation of the no-more-booze-for-you amendment, most people were no fuck you don't take my booze. Actual consumption of alcohol wasn't against the law, but the problem was getting your hands on the stuff, what with production, transport, and sale being illegal. The amendment had a modest effect in decreasing alcohol consumption, mostly in rural areas. But in cities it was all "Let's motherfuckin' partay!" like Republicans during Covid. And this was a boon for organized crime. Many historians assert Prohibition created the Mafia. Oops.

December 5, 1933

In 2015 in Canada, one of Prime Minister Justin Trudeau's election platforms was legalizing weed, and we voted for that handsome mofo and he kept his promise. In 1932, Franklin Roosevelt included in his platform bringing back the booze. It was the Great Depression, and people were depressed, and they were all fuck yeah let's guzzle depressant by the gallon. Well, it was more about job creation and taxes, but whatever. FDR kept his promise too, and eight months after taking office, on December 5, 1933, the Twenty-First Amendment saw the repeal of the Eighteenth, the only amendment to be completely repealed.

Hey, Second Amendment–loving ammosexuals. Just FYI that altering/repealing amendments is a thing that can be done. Cry about it.

Anyway, FDR acted even faster than that. He took office on March 4, 1933, and by March 22 he'd repealed the Volstead Act prohibiting sale of booze. But the highest-concentration beer you could get until the Eighteenth Amendment was actually repealed was 3.2%, which was a percentage someone pulled out of a posterior orifice. And that's where all those jokes about American beer being like making love in a canoe come from.

Ten seconds earlier Joseph Goebbels, Hitler's minister of propaganda, was all smiles to have his photograph taken. Then Goebbels was informed that the man taking his picture, Alfred Eisenstaedt, was Jewish. The Nazi's demeanor changed to an evil scowl in an instant. Unwavering, Eisenstaedt snapped another photo. He named the resulting image "The Eyes of Hate."

December 6, 1912

The exact date the photos were taken is uncertain, but it was during a three-day meeting of the League of Nations in Geneva in late September/early October 1933. For this world-changing "shit went down day" I've selected Eisenstaedt's fourteenth birthday, December 6, 1912, when he received his first camera as a gift from his uncle.

Goebbels was a murderous piece of shit known for his "homicidal antisemitism." But he didn't want just Jews to die. On May 1, 1945, the day after Hitler killed himself, Goebbels and his wife murdered their six children before killing themselves. Fuck that guy and fuck all Nazis. Let's talk about the photographer.

Eisenstaedt was born in 1898 in Dirschau, West Prussia, then part of Germany. As mentioned, he received a camera for his birthday, but quickly lost interest in it. He was drafted into the German army at eighteen and served on the Western Front of World War I as a cannoneer. In December 1917, a year before the war officially ended, it was over for Alfred when his artillery unit was hit by a British shell. The rest of his unit was killed, and Eisenstaedt nearly lost both his legs.

The postwar depression in Germany ruined the family business, and Alfred struggled to make ends meet. During the 1920s his interest in photography renewed, and in 1927 he sold his first photograph, of a woman playing tennis, for three dollars to a German weekly publication. His talent would win him many clients and his star as a photographer rose. In regard to taking the "Eyes of Hate" photo, Alfred said of Goebbels: "He looked at me with hateful eyes and waited for me to wither. But I didn't wither. If I have a camera in my hand, I don't know fear."

Alfred moved to the United States in 1935 and became well known for his celebrity photography. He photographed Marilyn Monroe, Bob Hope, Eleanor Roosevelt, Winston Churchill, and the Kennedy and Clinton families. Eisenstaedt's most famous photo is one you likely have seen. It's during the Victory over Japan celebration in Times Square taken on August 14, 1945, of a U.S. Navy sailor grabbing a dental assistant and kissing her. It was several decades before the woman in the iconic photo was (most likely) identified as Greta Friedman, who said of the assault sixty years later, "It wasn't my choice to be kissed . . . The guy just came over and grabbed!"

Lots of shitty things happened on December 7. Pearl Harbor was attacked in 1941. A windstorm killed 9,000 people in Britain in 1703. An earthquake took 50,000 lives in Armenia in 1988. Insta-Douche Dan Bilzerian was born . . . And it is also the date that Cicero of Rome was assassinated. A respected statesman, Marcus Tullius Cicero tried in vain to uphold Rome as a republic, but imperialists said nope, fuck you, and ghosted him.

Rome was founded in 753 B.C.E. as a kingdom, but a couple hundred years later the people were all fuck these kings and overthrew them to establish the Roman Republic. It wasn't a democracy but an oligarchy, where power rested in the hands of an elite few. Still, it's usually a better system than a solitary tyrant ruling an empire via whim. And that's what Cicero was fighting against.

In addition to being a noted politician, Cicero, who was born in 106 B.C.E., was a celebrated orator and author. Fully three-quarters of surviving Latin literature from the time period covering Cicero's adult years were authored by him. His influence on Latin, and European languages as a whole, is immeasurable.

Okay, so Julius Caesar was a dick. All that stabbing, including being stabbed in the dick? Totes deserved it. He basically destroyed the republic and sent it on the path to empire. And Cicero was no fan of Caesar, but he wasn't involved in his assassination. Nevertheless, the conspirators figured he would have approved of the stab-fest, and afterward Brutus lifted his blood-dripping dagger and called out Cicero's name, asking that he restore the republic. Afterward, Ci-cero wrote a letter to one of the conspirators that basically said why the fuck didn't you invite me to the Caesar stab-o-rama? That must have been fucking awesome!

December 7, 43 B.C.E.

Anyway, after Caesar was decorated with dagger-shaped holes, Cicero and Mark Antony—another wannabe dictator and leader of the Caesarian faction—were the two leading men in Rome, and Cicero was using his powerful oratory skills to denounce the shit out of Antony. Cicero was all like: Yeah, Antony, fuck that guy. Except, you know, way more eloquent.

But in this case, the sword was more powerful than the pen, or voice, and Antony allied himself with Caesar's adopted son Octavian and Roman general Lepidus, and went on a killing rampage of the opposition. Soldiers attacked Cicero on December 7, 43 B.C.E., as he left his villa with the intention of fleeing to Greece. It is believed his final words were "There is nothing proper about what you are doing, soldier, but do try to kill me properly."

Going stabby on Cicero

You are likely familiar with the term "Immaculate Conception" regarding the Virgin Mary, the mother of Jesus. However, "Immaculate," in this case, doesn't refer to a lack of semen-stained sheets; it has nothing to do with her being a virgin.

December 8, 1854

I guess you can't create a god by lots of grunting and sweating and spurting of DNA and only one person having an orgasm. It's just too ignoble. According to Christian theology written in the gospels of both Matthew and Luke, Mary was a virgin who was impregnated not by Joseph, but by the Holy Spirit. I believe adult sites have an entire genre of that kind of thing. So, yeah, no sticky man-chowder involved. Got it. But Immaculate Conception doesn't refer to any seminal lacking, but rather a dearth of sin.

On December 8, 1854, Pope Pius IX put forth an "apostolic constitution," which is the most hey-I'm-really-fucking-serious-about-this solemn religious legislation a pope can make. It was called *Ineffabilis Deus,*

which means "Ineffable God." In it, he defined the Immaculate Conception of the Blessed Virgin Mary.

Take note: This was not about the conception of Jesus, but the conception of *Mary.*

It means that from the time *she* was conceived, Mary was free of original sin—that whole thing about how humans are tainted from birth and destined to disobey God and woe is us do we ever suck please punish us for being wretched kind of shit. Anyway, it wasn't just no sexy time allowed, Jesus needed a *clean vessel* in order to enter the world. That's why they made up this story about how Mary wasn't born with that sin that was made up in a different story about some guy having sex with his own rib and eating an apple. Between the Virgin and the Immaculate Conception stuff, Jesus was like the extra-virgin olive oil savior.

If Catholic Hell is real, I am ever so fucked. So are Protestants, because they were all like come on that sounds like bullshit to us. Eastern Orthodoxy, which reveres Mary, wasn't too keen on the proclamation either. But the Catholics went hard on it, and they have an annual feast day about it on December 8 and everything.

> **Between the Virgin and the Immaculate Conception stuff, Jesus was like the extra-virgin olive oil savior.**

n late nineteenth-century France, Marguerite Durand was tired of your shit. And if you didn't like that her pet lion took a shit on your carpet, that was too damn bad. She launched a feminist newspaper that was staffed solely by women, except for the janitor. He was a man. Someone had to clean up the lion poop.

Durand was born in 1864 in Paris to an unwed mother and sent to a convent for her early education, then she went on to the Paris Conservatory to study performing arts before joining the famed theater group Comédie Française at the age of seventeen. Seven years later she gave up her acting career to marry a lawyer who introduced her to the world of politics, getting her involved in writing pamphlets. The marriage wouldn't last, but her passion for writing would.

She took a job writing for the leading Parisian paper, *Le Figaro;* in 1896 they sent her to cover the International Feminist Congress with the intention that she would pen a humorous take on it. Instead, it radicalized her, because the idea that women are equal to men still

Marguerite Durand with "Tiger"

seems a radical idea to many, even though an entire fucking century has gone by since then. Jesus. The fuck is wrong with us? Anyway, the following year, on December 9, 1897, Marguerite Durand launched her own daily feminist publication called *La Fronde,*

which meant "slingshot," referring to a mid-seventeenth-century rebellion against the French monarchy. The paper advocated for women's rights across a multitude of areas, including not just voting rights but admission to the bar association and acceptance into a men's-only art school.

December 9, 1897

A brash and audacious woman with a background in public performance, Durand took no shit. She became known for walking the streets of Paris with her pet lion, named "Tiger." One journalist said of Tiger, "She is at once a great spoiler of carpets and a symbol." The lion, coupled with Durand's beauty, which she admitted she used as a weapon to spread her message of equal rights for women, made her a force that could not be ignored.

Her publication, her persona, and her activism raised feminism's profile in France to new heights. Besides all of her employees at the paper being women, they were paid the same wages as men for the same work. The paper changed many attitudes regarding women's capabilities in various areas previously believed to be solely the dominion of men.

Use caution with whom you proclaim a hero. Most people have a dark side. For some, it's darker than others. Way fucking dark. Genocidally dark.

Winston Churchill was a man who in his long life did many great and terrible things. During World War II his leadership played a vital role in maintaining a defiant morale in the face of impending defeat at the hands of the fucking Nazis. In 2002 a nationwide poll of over a million voters proclaimed Churchill the greatest Briton to ever live, because I guess they didn't mind all the awful things he also did.

December 10, 1953

Churchill was a big fan of imperialism, seeing it as an act of altruism. He said, "By conquering and dominating other peoples, the British were also elevating and protecting them." I believe the conquered may have held differing opinions regarding this. He was a big fan of racial hierarchies and eugenics, and saw nothing wrong with the genocidal treatment of Indigenous persons in the various nations the British Empire conquered.

His greatest crime was his role in the Bengal famine of 1943. Bengal is a region of India, which at the time was a British possession, and Churchill let approximately 3 million Bengalis die of starvation. On his or-

ders, 170,000 tons of wheat from Australia bypassed those starving in India to head to Europe and . . . go into storage. Churchill's rationalization was that he anticipated the need for the wheat to feed Europeans once the war was over. During the famine he also demanded India export rice to feed the war effort. In 1943 that was his only concern: defeating Germany; it was his sole priority no matter how many Bengalis had to die. He even blamed India for the famine, saying, "They breed like rabbits." His racism made people blanch even at a time when being racist as fuck was totally the norm.

Despite the racism, Winston was one helluva writer. Both talented and prolific, on December 10, 1953, Churchill was awarded the Nobel Prize for Literature "for his mastery of historical and biographical description." So yeah, the guy could write, and he really hated Hitler even before hating Hitler was cool. But we must not whitewash the nasty shit he did.

Everyone is flawed. Some aren't just flawed, they're evil. We should not praise people as heroes, because we will always find reason to be disappointed, crushed, or aghast. However, we can praise heroic acts. Admire the deeds you deem worthy rather than the person behind them. Alternatively, feel free to say fuck them and cancel them from your life. No one is owed your admiration. No one.

do declare, war. Because . . . reasons? That's the puzzle in why Nazi Germany declared war on the United States. I mean, fucking Nazis were bugshit bonkers to begin with, but Hitler's decision to pick a fight with America while already fighting a bunch of other countries remains a mystery.

After Japan bombed Pearl Harbor, the United States logically reacted with "You motherfuckers! We're gonna war the shit out of you." But relations between the United States and Germany at that point, while far from amicable, were not in a state of war. Most Americans wanted to remain out of the actual fighting in Europe, because war sucks and the United States doesn't have the greatest record when it comes to trying to stop genocide. Rather, they . . . actually, that's a whole 'nother story.

Anyway, Japan and Germany were allies, but Japan didn't provide Hitler with any advance warning that it was gonna bomb the shit out of Hawai'i on December 7, 1941. And according to their agreement, Germany only had to come to Japan's aid if another country attacked Japan, not if Japan attacked another country first. Germany's foreign minister, Joachim von Ribbentrop,

reminded Hitler that Germany was under no obligation to declare war on the United States, but Hitler was all yeah fuck it lets spread the horror. He didn't seem to care that it would add another substantial enemy force to what Germany was already fighting, and this was six months after Germany had invaded Russia, where things were definitely not going well for the fucking Nazis.

December 11, 1941

It's believed Hitler didn't think much of American military resolve, seeing it as corrupt and "Jewish dominated." And so, without much consultation or preparation, at 3:00 P.M. on December 11, 1941, Hitler gave a speech declaring war on the United States. The American reply was bring it on, motherfucker; they declared war back later that day.

English historian Sir Ian Kershaw said of Hitler's declaration that he was "attempting to seize the initiative." However, "it was a move from weakness, not strength. And it was more irrational than any strategic decision taken to that date."

Germany's foreign minister, Joachim von Ribbentrop, reminded Hitler that Germany was under no obligation to declare war on the United States, but Hitler was all yeah fuck it lets spread the horror.

---

t was over a month since the election and we still didn't know who the fucking American president would be, because hanging chads or some shit, and Ralph fucking Nader, that dick. Then the Supreme Court called it for another dick: Dick Cheney. We know he was the one who ended up running things. Into the fucking ground.

December 12, 2000

The 2000 U.S. presidential election was as close as you could get, with Al Gore winning the popular vote by 0.5 percent, but anyone who was around for 2016 knows that doesn't matter for shit what with the "Black people only count as three-fifths of a person" Electoral College being the final arbiter of who got to decide if they'd blow up Iraq or would do anything about the planet being on fire. Anyway, it was down to a single state: MethGatorLand. Why is Florida the crazy shit state? Not sure, but in 2000, the meth gators were running loose.

Okay, so, fucking Florida. It was close. George W. Bush got 2,912,790 votes, and Gore got 2,912,253: a difference of a mere 537 votes. The Florida Supreme Court called for a recount, but on December 12, 2000, the U.S. Supreme Court ended that recount in a vote of 5–4 along partisan lines, giving the presidency to dumbass Dubya with 271 Electoral College votes to Gore's 266. Fuck. Not that the recount would have given Gore the election anyway. But we would have seen a President Gore if that arrogant assbucket Ralph Nader had stayed the fuck home. He doesn't get nearly enough hate for the loss. Let's rectify that.

Ralph led the Green Party on an everyone-gets-a-pony platform. In Florida he got 97,488 votes. He knew in advance that he was a potential spoiler but ran anyway. I've read articles from people who suck at math saying, "Not all those who voted for Nader would have voted for Gore!" They quote polls reporting only 60% of Nader voters would have gone to Gore if Nader wasn't on the ballot; having 40% go for Bush seems unlikely but I'll allow it. More important is that those articles didn't run the fucking numbers. Sixty percent of 97,488 = 58,493. Add that to Gore's total and it = 2,970,746. Then give Bush the other 40% and he ends up with 2,951,785, *still* losing to Gore by almost 19,000 votes. Hell, assume half of the Nader voters stayed home and Gore still handily wins Florida. Shit, even if only a mere 25% of Nader voters showed up and did the 60/40 split, it still goes to Gore by over 4,000 votes. Yet Nader refuses to admit he cost Gore the election.

In short, fuck Ralph Nader.

In 1984 a young Patrick Swayze and the mom from *Back to the Future* and even Jennifer Grey, a few years before she and Patrick were *Dirty Dancing*, went guerrilla warrior against commie invaders of 'Murica in a jingoistic rah-rah we're so badass movie titled *Red Dawn*. Nineteen years later Operation Red Dawn found a dirty and pathetic Saddam Hussein hiding in a hole in northern Iraq. And yeah, they named the operation after the fucking movie.

When the United States invaded Iraq for the second time in 2003 because of a bunch of weapons of mass destruction that never existed/George Jr. wanted to finish Daddy's job for him, Saddam went into hiding because he was pretty sure 'Murica wasn't fucking around this time and wanted him deader than a betrayed Kurd in 1991. That's a little history joke for you, except not really a joke, because in the 1991 invasion of Iraq the United States encouraged the Kurdish people to rebel against Saddam, then stood back and watched as Saddam mercilessly crushed that rebellion. It wasn't the only time the United States fucked over Kurdish people, but that's another tale.

Saddam was "High-Value Target Number One," and the United States launched a massive manhunt to track the fucker down. In the preceding six months Task Force 121, which was a combined special operations group that included Rangers and Delta Force, had conducted a dozen raids and hundreds of interrogations to find Hussein. A few dozen of those interrogations involved

his family members, and by mid-December they learned Saddam was hiding on a farm south of his hometown of Tikrit.

December 13, 2003

In the *Red Dawn* movie, the guerrilla fighters called themselves "Wolverines" after the high school football team, because teenage football players are more than a match for trained soldiers from the Soviet Union and Cuba because freedom > commies. On December 13, 2003, TF121 launched its raids on two sites they named Wolverine 1 and Wolverine 2, but Saddam couldn't be found. Psych!

The American soldiers were just about to leave when one kicked a piece of flooring, exposing a "spider hole" (a military term used to describe a small, one-man foxhole). At first the soldier thought it might be the beginning of an enemy tunnel system and was about to toss in a grenade, but then Saddam popped out. Despite the deposed dictator not offering any resistance, the soldier brained Saddam with the butt of his rifle. Maybe not a bad idea though, as Hussein did have a Glock pistol on him. Also, fuck that guy. Clobber away. The Iraqi Special Tribunal put Saddam on trial, finding him guilty of crimes against humanity and sentencing the totalitarian from Tikrit to death. The execution was carried out on December 30, 2006.

Queen Victoria ascended the throne in 1837 at the age of eighteen and ruled for over sixty-three years. It was during her tenure that Britain became the empire upon which "the sun never set." Of course, the conquered peoples mostly weren't too thrilled about that, so let's focus on the love story instead.

December 14, 1861

In twenty-four U.S. states it is against the law to marry your first cousin, but in Britain it's just fine, legally speaking. From a social perspective it's come under fire, but royalty did it all the time. Queen Elizabeth II was married to her third cousin, but Vicky went for the first-cousin lovin' when she married her mom's brother's son.

She met Albert when she was sixteen and wrote in her diary of how handsome he was. After becoming queen, she lamented that she believed she would never marry, because she liked being in charge and didn't want no man telling her what to do no how. But two years after her coronation, Albert paid another visit and she was ready for sum fuk. Being queen, the protocol was that Victoria had to propose to him, and so she did just five days into his visit. They repeatedly did Shakespeare and chill, having nine kids, and

Queen Victoria, Albert, and their nine children

> **But Victoria never got over the loss of her beloved cousin Albert and wore black for the rest of her life—another forty years—as a representation of her mourning.**

to the best of my knowledge none of them had flippers, just a bit of hemophilia.

Albert was a devoted husband and father, and Victoria relied on him as an adviser in matters of state. But then, on December 14, 1861, at the age of only forty-two, Albert died. At the time it was believed to be of typhoid, but later supposition based on his chronic stomach pain suggested it was more likely Crohn's disease, renal failure, or abdominal cancer.

Victoria was devastated and secluded herself in her castle, earning the nickname the "Widow of Windsor." She turned to food for comfort, gaining much weight, which made her even more reluctant to appear in public, but eventually she would reemerge.

After her husband's death she became close friends with a Scottish servant named John Brown. Due to the amount of time they spent together there were rumors that Brown became familiar with the sound of a queenly queef. Recently surfaced evidence indicates that, yeah, she probably was rubbing slippery bits with the guy, and I say good for her. But Victoria never got over the loss of her beloved cousin Albert and wore black for the rest of her life—another forty years—as a representation of her mourning.

America, fuck yeah! Gonna carry all the guns and be a muthafuckin' HEE-RO!

On December 15, 1791, the date that the Second Amendment to the United States Constitution was ratified, the state of firearms technology was, comparatively speaking, still in its toddler phase. In the eighteenth century a well-drilled trooper could reload a single shot in a musket in about twenty seconds. Today's modern ammosexual is usually not all that well-drilled and neither are they part of a militia, well-regulated or otherwise. And yet he—it's almost always a he—can take out dozens at a school, place of worship, or shopping mall single-handedly without so much as a background check.

December 15, 1791

But there is much money to be made dealing in fear.

All those times over the decades when some 'Murican shouted "They're gonna take our guns!" . . . did they? Nope. But the panic caused massive gun buying. It's almost like there is a profitable weapons industry with a vested interest in making you imagine their product is about to be made illegal, so buy a bunch more! Don't be concerned that you're more likely to die from a gunshot if you have a firearm in your house; there are murderers on every block trying to steal your eight-year-old 47-inch Sanyo TV. Stand your ground!

What was on the minds of the Founding Fathers when they came up with the Second Amendment? Well, they were big fans of militias. Alexander Hamilton referred to them as "the most natural defense of a free country." Others said the militia is "the bulwark of a free people." At the time, many believed *all* citizens should be part-time soldiers, because those citizens just finished gaining freedom for their country from the British. They were opposed to the idea of a standing army, seeing it as a threat to freedom. And if everyone had guns and was ready to soldier, there would be no need for that standing army.

But now there is a standing army, a large and expensive one that has the power to kill billions by pushing some buttons. I know you've watched a lot of action movies and you *really* want to prove how much of a bad-ass you are, but your AR-15 isn't gonna do shit against an Apache helicopter with a 30mm chain gun or a Hellfire missile launched from a Predator drone.

Additionally, the idea of gun + colonial complexion = patriot, while Black person + gun = criminal is nothing new. The 2A has not been equally applied throughout history. Free Black people were often legally restricted in gun ownership, as were Native Americans. Back then, white Americans were armed in order to be able to maintain control over non-whites. Nowadays, however . . . Oh, wait. Shit.

You know the guy who did an amazing job playing Dumbledore in the first two *Harry Potter* films, but then he died and got a comparatively mediocre replacement? That actor—the dead one—was in a 1970 film as English "Lord Protector" Oliver Cromwell. When we lost Richard Harris, many were devastated. Conversely, when England lost Cromwell, they later dug him up and "posthumously executed" him, because fuck that guy.

Between 1642 and 1651, England was at war with itself. On one side were the Parliamentarians, who fought to achieve a constitutional monarchy. On the other were the Royalist forces of King Charles I, who were all about that "divine right of kings" absolute monarchy bullshit. There had been other civil wars in England's history, but those were more about *who* should rule. This one was more about *how* the country should be ruled.

Cromwell was a Puritan, ugh, who believed God was totes on his side. A longtime member of Parliament, he climbed through the officer ranks to become a general and won a series of battles to play a critical role in the Parliament army's victory over the forces of the Royalists.

After kicking some Royalist ass, they put King Chuck (played by Alec Obi-Wan Kenobi Guinness in the film) on trial and decapitated his ass. Cromwell was one of the signatories of the death warrant; it was the first time an English king had been executed, but it wasn't over. Dead Chuck had a son, Charles II, who was currently king of Scotland, so the fight continued on with the Royalists having the son of their dead royal to rally behind. Two years of more fighting, during which Cromwell also went genocidal against Catholics in Ireland, and Chucko Numero Dos was defeated and exiled.

December 16, 1653

And for a short time, there was a thing called the Commonwealth of England, in which Cromwell played a leading role. But he got pissed at how the government was being run, considering it useless, and dissolved Parliament by force. Then, on December 16, 1653, he became what he loathed, a de facto king as "Lord Protector" of England. And just like a king, when he died in 1658 from natural causes, his son took over. But the second Lord Protector was short-lived, although not literally. The Royalists surged back into power, and Cromwell Jr., who unlike his dad was a total wimp, fled to France and lived a long life mostly in exile.

On the twelfth anniversary of his dad being executed, the restored monarch King Charles II wanted some payback on his father's killer. He had Oliver Cromwell dug up, hung in chains, and beheaded. Cromwell remains a controversial figure in English history.

When you take a commercial flight, your chances of death are at the opposite end of the spectrum from your chances of extreme annoyance. Because your fellow air travelers are obnoxious assholes, every last one of them, and so flying coach may have you cursing the Wright brothers. But powered flight had to start somewhere, and even though there was a much higher risk of death back then than there is now, at least Orville Wright had the seat all to himself.

December 17, 1903

Although it wasn't really a seat—Orville flew while lying prone—and it was also cold as fuck.

Wilbur was the older Wright brother, born in 1867. Orville was born in 1871, and only got to go first because of a coin toss. Growing up in Dayton, Ohio, the brothers attained a variety of mechanical skills via working with various machinery, including a printing press when they launched a weekly newspaper in 1889. But then there was a bicycle craze when people realized that old-timey design with the big-ass front wheel was stupid as fuck, and the Wright brothers got in on building bikes with the new design that we still (mostly) use today. The success

The first powered flight

of their bike shop helped fund their interest in powered, heavier-than-air flight. Not only that, but seeing how bikes could be balanced and controlled gave them ideas about how to do the same with an aircraft.

Gotta learn to glide before you can fly, though. And the brothers tested several gliders to get a better idea of how to control them. The Wrights knew of the myriad examples of other attempted aeronauts who would glide, crash, and die; they became obsessed with learning how to steer and land the fucking thing in one piece, so as to not die. Observation of birds gave them the idea of "wing warping"—changing the shape of the wing to control the aircraft.

In 1903, after four years of research, including relying on the work of others and testing with gliders, as well as building their own wind tunnel to test nearly two hundred different wing designs, the pair consulted with the U.S. Weather Bureau to choose a suitable location for their world-changing flight attempt, and selected Kitty Hawk, North Carolina.

On December 17, 1903, in front of five witnesses, one of whom had a camera to snap a photo of the first flight, Orville flew for twelve seconds into a freezing headwind for a distance of 120 feet. Each brother did two flights that day, with the final one being flown by Wilber and lasting fifty-nine seconds, traveling 852 feet, although his landing was a bit of a crash.

Of course, there were others who claimed to have done it first, but history has largely proclaimed those guys to be full of shit.

On December 17, 1903, in front of five witnesses, one of whom had a camera to snap a photo of the first flight, Orville flew for twelve seconds into a freezing headwind for a distance of 120 feet.

In over two centuries of the U.S.A. being a thing, three presidents have been impeached. And Nixon wasn't one of them; he resigned before impeachment. But Donnie Dumbfuck was, and he should have been convicted too, but presidents don't get convicted in 'Murica, because then people would have to admit they fucked up in choosing the guy. And just like with Vietnam, Americans have a hard time admitting they've made a terrible mistake.

December 18, 2019

Being impeached is like being indicted. It means enough evidence has been brought forth that prosecutors believe they have a case against you, and you get charged and put on trial. The first president to be impeached was Abraham Lincoln's VP. After Abe got dead, Andrew Johnson took over as president; Johnson was racist and generally a shit human being. In 1868 Congress impeached him for firing and replacing the secretary of war, whom he disagreed with regarding postwar Reconstruction, without first making sure Congress said it was okay. He escaped conviction by a single vote in the Senate. Nineteen years later the Supreme Court said Johnson's impeachment was unconstitutional, having been politically motivated, and changed the rules so impeachment had to be more about "treason, bribery, or other high crimes and misdemeanors."

In 1998, Bill Clinton was impeached not for getting a blowjob from Monica Lewinsky, but for lying about that bit of fellatio;

the articles of impeachment were for perjury and obstruction of justice. He got off too, pun intended. The Senate decided that while he'd been a bad boy, his crimes weren't at the level of high crimes and misdemeanors.

Then, on December 18, 2019, Orange Julius Seize Her became IMPOTUS the Third when the House voted to impeach the motherfucker. The official charges were abuse of power and obstruction of Congress. This stemmed from a phone call with the President of Ukraine in which Trump withheld approved military aid to Ukraine in order to coerce that country's leader into investigating Joe Biden's son, who sat on the board of a Ukrainian energy company. In short, Trump used the office of the president to pressure a foreign power to interfere in the 2020 U.S. presidential election so he could win it. And then he interfered with Congress trying to investigate his crime. Fuck. That. Guy.

The trial was a sham that suppressed a shit-ton of evidence. A depressing wow-the-Senate-is-fucking-broken fact about the vote: The 48 Democrat senators who voted to convict Trump represent 18 million more voters than the 52 who let him go on with being the worst fucking president in U.S. history.

Thirteen months later Trump became the only president to be impeached twice, this time for incitement of insurrection. Seventeen Republican senators were needed to side with Democratic Party senators to convict the motherfucker, but only seven members of the GOP found enough spine to do so, and Trump was acquitted a second time.

When a head of government dies, especially while still holding office, there is usually a big show of national mourning and a fancy funeral. But what if there is no body? What if the popular leader of the nation just . . . disappeared?

His name was Harold Holt, and as far as Australian politicians go, he wasn't a total dick. He had some progressive ideas. In 1966 he took over as head of the Liberal Party of Australia when his predecessor, Robert Menzies, retired. That made him prime minister without having been elected, but there was an election a few months later and Holt's party won in a landslide.

One of the cool things he did was amend the constitution to further dismantle the "White Australia" policy and promote equal rights for the country's Aboriginal population. But he also expanded the country's involvement in the Vietnam War, proclaiming he was "all the way with LBJ," referencing his support for U.S. president Johnson. People at home weren't thrilled about that.

Holt was an avid swimmer and spearfisher. On December 17, 1967, he was with four friends at Cheviot Beach in the state of Victoria in southern Australia. The conditions were rough, but he proclaimed to "know this beach like the back of my hand." Only one of the other four joined him in the rough water, staying close to shore. But Holt, having more courage than brains, did

Harold Holt in 1966

a "hold my Foster's Lager," swam into deep water, and was caught in a rip current that carried him out to sea.

December 19, 1967

Kinda fucked up for his buddies. "Hey, there goes our friend Harold, who also happens to be the leader of our nation, being washed out to sea." By the way, Aussie readers, I know most of you think Foster's is piss.

A massive search was launched, but Holt was never seen again, his body wasn't recovered, and he probably became fish poop.

Two days later, on December 19, 1967, Prime Minister Harold Holt was declared dead.

Of course, there were conspiracy theories. Some said he used the water to take his own life. Others said he faked his death, or was murdered by the CIA, or was picked up by a submarine so he could defect to China. On a sort-of personal note, the name of Holt's widow's first husband—the guy she divorced to be with Holt—was James Fell. Creepy. Maybe she should have stayed with James, because in my experience guys with that name are faithful husbands, and Harold had allegedly cheated on his wife, Zara, with dozens of women.

Anyway, because Australians have a fucked-up sense of humor, they named a public swimming pool after the guy.

Her name was Palestina Isa, but she went by Tina. She was born in Brazil in 1972, but her family moved around, and she wound up in St. Louis and became a U.S. citizen. Her father was a Palestinian Muslim, her mother a Brazilian Catholic. When Tina began to behave the way most other American teenagers do, they murdered her, calling it an "honor killing." Because some people use their religion as an excuse to be dicks.

December 20, 1991

"She was so American," one of her classmates said. She was a high school honor student who wanted to study aeronautics in college. Tina enjoyed listening to hip-hop and chatting with her friends about boys they liked. Her parents tried to keep her on a short leash, forbidding her from playing sports or going on school trips. She wasn't allowed to date or to work, and her father said she was going to be married to a Palestinian man from the West Bank that he would choose for her.

Tina wouldn't follow the oppressive rules and snuck out to go to the prom. Pissed at the disobedience, her parents tracked her down at the school and hauled her home. During Tina's senior year they decided to remove her from school for not doing as she was told. In a meeting with the school guid-

> In the middle of the argument her father, Zein Isa said, "You are going to die tonight," and he grabbed a knife from the kitchen.

ance counselor her mother, Maria Isa, referred to her daughter as a "tramp" and a "whore."

On November 6, 1989, Tina was late getting home. She'd just taken a job at a local Wendy's against her parents' will and was walked home from her first shift by a boy she'd been dating, also against her parents' will. When she came in the door of her home her parents raged at her, calling her a bitch and a she-devil. They accused her of fornication. In the middle of the argument her father, Zein Isa, said, "You are going to die tonight," and he grabbed a knife from the kitchen.

Tina pleaded with her mother for help, but instead her mother pinned her down and yelled at her to "Shut up!" while her father repeatedly stabbed her in the chest, saying, "Die! Die quickly!" We know exactly what was said because the FBI was recording it. The FBI had the house bugged because Tina's father was part of a jihadist terrorist cell they were investigating.

The next morning the FBI listened to the tape recordings in horror and gave them to the St. Louis police. The parents were convicted of Tina's murder and on December 20, 1991, were sentenced to death. Zein died in prison from diabetes in 1997 before his sentence could be carried out, and Maria's sentence was later commuted to life in prison. She died in prison in 2014 at age seventy.

Assholes.

t was called the Santa María School Massacre, but it wasn't just students who died. It was miners and their families who were on strike to protest for better working conditions. But the Chilean government wasn't interested in listening to their grievances and sent in the army, murdering thousands.

It happened in the port city of Iquique in northern Chile. The country had been in turmoil for some time over terrible working and living conditions for the country's miners. The nation's worker movement started with the nitrate miners; there had been several strikes over the previous five years, beginning in 1902.

The nitrate mines were mostly owned by British and German companies. The strike began on December 4, 1907, and by December 13 work in all nitrate mines had stopped. Several thousand workers, who were made up not just of Chileans, but also Peruvians, Argentinians, and Bolivians, marched with their families to the port of Iquique. There, the maritime workers joined them in the strike.

The strikers and their families had been camping at the Santa María School for a week when President Pedro Montt sent in the army under the command of Colonel Roberto Silva Renard. Renard ordered the gathered to disperse and return to work, but they replied with a hearty go fuck yourself.

He gave them an hour, saying if you don't move, we're going to open fire. They said fuck you again. Once the hour was up, the killing began.

December 21, 1907

The soldiers started with killing the strike leaders, but it quickly turned into a murderous frenzy where they hunted down and machine-gunned anyone they saw, including women and children who were begging for mercy. The death toll was estimated to be over 2,000 people; the exact number is unknown because the government would not permit an investigation and buried the victims in a mass grave.

As a reward for the mass murder, Colonel Renard was promoted to brigadier general. However, seven years later he was walking down the street to his office when he was confronted by Antonio Ramón, the brother of a man who had died in the massacre. Seeking revenge, Ramón repeatedly stabbed Renard, but was interrupted when bystanders came to the general's aid. Renard survived the attack but was blinded and partially paralyzed from the stab wounds; he lived another six years mostly as an invalid. Chilean workers raised money for Ramón's defense fund, and he served only five years in prison.

Alfred Dreyfus was Jewish, making it a lot easier for people to railroad him into getting a life sentence for a crime he didn't commit. A French artillery officer, his 1894 conviction for treason was a public spectacle that had crowds chanting "Death to the Jew!"

How did an innocent man's life take such a turn? There was a French spy at the German embassy in Paris, and in a garbage can in the embassy he found a ripped-up letter with handwriting that resembled that of Dreyfus. Captain Dreyfus was accused of passing secrets to the enemy and was court-martialed; there was a closed trial. On December 22, 1894, he was convicted of treason and sentenced to life in prison. After the conviction, there was a public ceremony where his insignia was ripped from his uniform and his sword was broken in half. That's where the chants for his death happened.

Dreyfus was deported across the Atlantic Ocean to the penal colony on Devil's Island, off the coast of northeast South America. His family believed Alfred had been wrongly convicted and worked to see him freed. Fifteen months after the conviction Colonel Georges Picquart, who was French head of counterespionage, discovered that the real traitor was not Dreyfus, but Major Ferdinand Esterhazy. When Picquart brought this information to his superiors, they said shut

Alfred Dreyfus incarcerated on Devil's Island

the fuck up and reassigned him to Africa.

But the family would not give up. They worked with journalists including Émile Zola to *"J'Accuse . . . !"* government officials and expose the evidence against Alfred as paltry and reveal this Esterhazy fuckstick as the real traitor. With the accusations of Esterhazy made public, he had a closed trial in 1898 but he was found not guilty. People were pissed, and Esterhazy quickly retired and fled to the U.K., where he remained the rest of his traitorous fucking life.

But what about poor Alfred? His ordeal was now very public, and the country was divided. Antisemitic riots broke out. Eventually, there was a thorough investigation and the Supreme Court quashed Dreyfus's conviction. But it wasn't over. The wank socks in the French military didn't want to admit they had the wrong guy and put him on trial and convicted him *again.* This time he was sentenced to ten years' hard labor, but the sentence was commuted due to the extenuating circumstances, and a few days later the French president pardoned Dreyfus. Seven years later, in 1906, Dreyfus was officially exonerated, reinstated in the army, and promoted to the rank of major. He fought in World War I when it broke out eight years later.

The rampant antisemitism the Dreyfus Affair engendered was a catalyst for Zionism, convincing many Jewish people they needed their own state away from Europe where they could protect themselves from those seeking to kill them solely for being Jewish.

There's not a better match for an organ transplant than from your identical twin. And considering the history of kidney transplant attempts prior to 1954, it was a good thing for brothers Ronald and Richard Herrick that they shared the same DNA.

Doctors had been playing around with transplanting kidneys for half a century, with little success. In 1902 researchers in Vienna had success with animals, and in 1909 in France a doctor tried giving a rabbit kidney to a child suffering kidney failure, but the kid died two weeks later. In 1933 in Ukraine the first human-to-human transplant took place, but the surgeons didn't realize that their blood groups weren't compatible, and the recipient died two days later.

In 1950 a somewhat successful transplant was conducted on a woman in Illinois who had polycystic kidney disease, but anti-rejection drugs didn't exist yet, and ten months later her body rejected the donated kidney. However, that ten months gave her remaining kidney time to recover and she lived for another decade. Another transplant attempt was made in 1952 in Paris, but the kidney failed after three weeks.

On December 23, 1954, success would finally be found with the Herrick brothers in Boston. Ronald, who I assume was a swell fucking guy, was the donor, and Richard the recipient. The brothers were only twenty-three years old and Richard was dying; without the transplant he would have had no chance. Because they were identical twins, no anti-rejection medication was needed. Richard lived for another eight years. The success of the operation ushered in a new era of organ transplantation. Today, close to 20,000 kidney transplants are performed in the United States each year. More than 80 percent of kidney recipients live at least another five years.

The lead surgeon for the Herrick trans-

December 23, 1954

plant, Dr. Joseph Murray, received the Nobel Prize for Medicine in 1990.

And if you haven't yet, please sign up to be an organ donor. You won't need those things after you die, but someone here on Earth could definitely benefit from them. Think of it as a form of afterlife.

In 1933 in Ukraine the first human-to-human transplant took place, but the surgeons didn't realize that their blood groups weren't compatible, and the recipient died two days later.

---

s it just me, or is eggnog kinda fuckin' gross? I can definitely understand the desire to booze the shit up to make it more palatable. And on Christmas Eve 1826 a bunch of West Point cadets did exactly that, and they got so fucked-up they rioted. One of the rioters was the future president of the treasonous Confederate States of We Want to Enslave People, Jefferson Douchebag Davis.

December 24, 1826

Small dairy farms were all over the place in nineteenth-century America, and people drank their milk; eggnog was popular for adding booze to. Not just rum, but they put sherry, brandy, and whiskey in the stuff. President Washington was a fan of the alcoholic nog.

At West Point Military Academy possession of alcohol was forbidden, and drunkenness was a big no-no, even at Christmas. But young men can be ingenious when it comes to breaking the rules for the purposes of getting hammered. After failing to get booze at a local tavern, two days before the party cadets secured the cooperation of a security guard to take a boat across the Hudson River to a more cooperative tavern owner who sold them whiskey and rum.

They smuggled the booze back to the North Barracks and hid it for the December 24 festivities. The day before Christmas the party started late, at 10:00 P.M. By 2:00 A.M. on Christmas Day, things were getting rowdy, and the party had spread to the South Barracks as well. At 4:00 A.M. Captain Hitchcock, a faculty member, showed up at the North Barracks and literally read the Riot Act. They said fuck you Hitchcock and a fight broke out. In the South Barracks, Lieutenant Thornton attempted to control the raucous revelry and for his troubles was knocked unconscious.

Then shit got crazy. Windows were smashed and a pistol was fired in an attempt to kill Captain Hitchcock. It turned into an actual riot of approximately seventy cadets fucked-up on boozy eggnog. Then the arrests started, with some of the cooler-headed cadets helping officers in restoring order.

Reveille sounded at 6:05 A.M., and it was still a shitshow of random gunfire, profanity, sounds of breaking glass, and moans of hungover pain. Some cadets were still in their rooms getting hammered, while others dragged their disheveled and drunken asses to parade.

The officers used the term "mutiny," and there was hell to pay. There were nineteen courts-martial resulting in numerous expulsions. Jefferson Davis spent over a month confined to barracks for his role. Two of those expelled (Benjamin Humphreys and Hugh Mercer) later became traitorous generals in the traitorous Confederate Army.

Merry Christmas. Try not to riot.

December 24: "Let's kill the shit out of each other." **December 25:** "Let's take a break from blowing each other to bits and play football." **December 26:** "Okay, back to the killing." Close to 10 million people died in World War I, but they were mostly doing what they were told by people who never got near a battlefield. For one day of the horror, soldiers on both sides proved they were merely pawns in the murderous games of their leaders.

It was the first year of the war, waged since the summer. This was a new way of making war, and hostilities quickly devolved into a stalemate, with soldiers huddled in trenches on both sides fighting back and forth over the same patches of ground. The situation resulted from advances in killing technology and the fact that there was almost an entire continent at war, which made flanking one's enemy almost impossible.

After only five months of fighting, the soldiers hadn't grown to really despise each other quite yet. And so, on Christmas Day of 1914, there was a series of unofficial truces up and down the Western Front. Soldiers from both sides spontaneously wandered into "No Man's Land"—named so because on any other day if you took a stroll out there someone machine-gunned your ass—to greet and exchange pleasantries with their enemies.

British, Belgian, and French soldiers put down their weapons and met with their German adversaries to exchange souvenirs and food, sing carols, and even play games of football. The Americans wouldn't arrive on the front for another two and a half years, so it's not right to call it soccer.

December 25, 1914

The pope had called for a Christmas truce a few months earlier, but the leaders were all nah fuck that guy. It's uncertain how it all started, and not everyone participated. In some areas there were still hostilities, and in others the truce only allowed for burial details for the corpses rotting in No Man's Land. One hypothesis is that carol singing on both sides is what prompted the sudden truce and peaceful meeting of enemies on the battlefield, but it remains a subject of debate. As many as 100,000 men participated up and down the line.

> The pope had called for a Christmas truce a few months earlier, but the leaders were all nah fuck that guy.

The following Christmas, truces were explicitly forbidden by high command; they worried soldiers would come to view their enemy as actual human beings and adopt a "live and let live" mentality. By 1916 the two sides hated each other so much that any thought of a Christmas truce was impossible.

In June 1987, President Reagan gave a speech in West Berlin where he said, "Mr. Gorbachev, tear down this wall!" And no one, including Soviet leader Mikhail Gorbachev, paid attention. But then, two and a half years later, people started tearing down the wall and Americans were all "Our president! Our president made that happen!" Yeah, bullshit.

December 26, 1991

They called it the "Cold War" because the two greatest superpowers to arise out of World War II, the United States and the USSR, never directly confronted each other. That's because they constructed and pointed at each other a metric shit-ton of intercontinental boomsticks that could obliterate the planet. So, they fought smaller proxy wars through nations like Korea, Vietnam, Israel, and Afghanistan instead. The rivaling superpowers spent countless billions on weapons, until the Soviets finally said okay we're out of money so we're done now.

In 1989, President Gorbachev began loosening the yoke of control on various Soviet satellite states in Eastern Europe. Bush Sr. was president at the time and basically sat back and watched it happen. Gorbachev's actions were prompted by bankruptcy. The military expenditures needed to control their empire destroyed the economy, and so they pulled back. Lacking Soviet military support, the communist leaders in Eastern Bloc countries were all like "Oh wow are we ever fucked."

And fucked they were, because the removal of troops resulted in an organic, democratic momentum that swept many Eastern European nations, leading to the fall of the Berlin Wall in November 1989. The overthrowing of communist governments was largely peaceful, with the exception of Romania. That was a violent revolution that saw the execution of the president, who by the way was a murderous cock who had it coming.

The fun wasn't over yet. Gorbachev began the democratization process at home, allowing for multiparty elections. Commies didn't like the "parade of sovereignties" spelling the death of their once-mighty empire, and in August 1991 they tried a coup against Gorby, but it failed. At that point the writing was on the wall for the old USSR. Everyone was like fuck this "union," we're out. By December the collapse of the empire was complete. Gorbachev resigned on Christmas Day, and on December 26, 1991, the Soviet Union officially dissolved.

Boris Yeltsin was president of Russia, which was the largest republic in the former USSR, and he led the formation of the "Commonwealth of Independent States" as a cooperative entity among many former Soviet republics. Boris also took control of the launch codes for their several thousand nukes.

Internationally, Gorbachev is mostly celebrated for ending the Cold War. At home, many Russians were pissed at him for letting their great empire collapse, precipitating an economic crisis. Make no mistake, Gorby still controlled a massive military and could have fought to keep the Soviet Union together. It would have been ghastly, with countless deaths. But he just let it go, earning him the Nobel Peace Prize. Nevertheless, the loss of empire created a vacuum filled by crime, corruption, and right-wing nationalism.

t is a beautiful bit of architecture called the Hagia Sophia, located in Istanbul, and it's almost 1,500 years old. Considering those who built it didn't have all sorts of fancy machinery, it's pretty impressive that it was constructed in only five years.

In 532 the city was named Constantinople and Justinian I was the Eastern Roman emperor. Islam wouldn't even exist for another century, and Justinian had the Hagia Sophia, which means "holy wisdom," built as an Eastern Orthodox Christian cathedral, the largest one in the empire. Completed on December 27, 537, at the time it boasted the world's largest interior space, as well as the largest pendentive dome. I'm not sure what that is, some kind of impressive architecture thing I'm sure you could google.

The reason Justinian had it built was because the previous church on that spot was destroyed earlier that year in the Nika Riots, where half the city burned and tens of thousands died. The riots began because of high taxes; Justinian used his army to put down the riots and then said fuck you I'll build an even bigger church with your tax money. The structure is said to have changed the history of architecture and was the largest cathedral in the world for a thousand years until the Seville Cathedral was completed in Spain in 1520.

But it wouldn't remain a cathedral forever. Constantinople fell to the Ottoman Empire in 1453, and the conquering Muslims were all nice church I think we'll use it to pray to our version of the same god instead. And so, after nearly a millennium of Jesus-and-his-dad worship, the prayers switched over to Allah worship.

December 27, 537

They had to do some major renos; they weren't gonna just start using it as a mosque without first purging or covering much of the Jesus and Mary and saints and angels–type decorations and architecture, then replacing it with their own Islamic decorations and architecture. It was *Extreme Makeover: Religious Edition.*

It remained a mosque for almost five centuries, but in 1935 it was changed to a museum under the secular Republic of Turkey. However, in July 2020, with Turkey slipping back toward religion-influenced authoritarian fuckery, the building was once again reclassified as a mosque.

The Hagia Sophia, 1900

In 1900, as she spoke her wedding vows, Constance Markievicz notably omitted the part about obeying her husband. She wasn't a big fan of obeying British law either, being a guerrilla fighter against the imperialists.

She was born Constance Gore-Booth in 1868, and her father was an Irish landowner who wasn't a dick. During the famine of 1879–80 her father provided free food to his tenants, instilling in Constance a concern for the less fortunate. She was a painter who became radicalized toward Irish nationalism and women's rights in 1907 when she engaged in that perilous and mind-altering practice of . . . reading books.

A countess in fancy clothes, she was not initially welcomed by the Irish working class fighting for self-rule, but she won them over through years of effort, urging outright rebellion. Skilled with firearms, she began a training camp to teach boys how to shoot so they could kill British soldiers.

After years of failed efforts at diplomacy, the 1916 Easter Rebellion took place in Dublin, with Irish attacking British and taking over much of the downtown. By this time, Constance was a leader in the movement and a sniper in the rebellion, shooting at Royalists from rooftops. The uprising failed; British forces overwhelmed the rebels, and she and her compatriots were arrested. They were sentenced to die, but Constance's sentence was commuted to life in prison on account of her gender. This pissed her off. She said, "Why didn't they let me die with my friends?"

The mass executions turned public opinion against the British, and Constance and many others were soon released. She was only out of prison a year when she was sent back in 1918 for anti-conscription activities (the Irish weren't keen to fight in World War I). During that time, on December 28, 1918, Constance was elected MP for Dublin St. Patrick's, winning 66 percent of the vote, making her the first woman elected to the U.K. House of Commons. Even if she hadn't been in prison, she would not have taken her seat, as the Sinn Féin party of which she was a member had a fuck-you abstentionist policy where winning politicians refused to take their seats. She was named minister of labor in 1919 but left government in 1922 because she was pissed about the new Anglo-Irish Treaty.

She kept on fighting for Irish independence, serving more prison time and going on a hunger strike in the process, until her death in 1927 from appendicitis. Her final act was to give away the last of her wealth to those in need.

Constance Markievicz with a Colt revolver

Fuck you if you think it was a battle. Wounded Knee was a mass murder of nearly 300 Lakota people, including many women and children. That didn't stop the U.S. government from awarding twenty soldiers the Medal of Honor for their participation in the massacre, however.

In previous years the government had seized Lakota lands in what is now South Dakota. By then the bison on which Lakota relied had been hunted to near extinction. The government had promised to protect reservations from gold hunters and settlers, but of course the fuckers reneged on that, because they'd proven they were fine with genocide of America's Native populations again and again.

Despair led to the embracing of the "Ghost Dance" religion on the reservation, which told of how their ancestors would return and bring back the time of abundance, and the white invaders would disappear. Of course, encroaching settlers saw the Ghost Dance performed and because of their ethnocentrism freaked right the fuck out and figured the Lakota were going to murder them all. In mid-December 1890, U.S. officials reacted by attempting to arrest Chief Sitting Bull and killed him in the process.

Ghost Dance practitioners were deemed "hostiles." Fearing for their lives, members of the Miniconjou band of Lakota Sioux fled the reservation toward the Badlands to escape. The 7th Cavalry pursued them, and on December 29, 1890, surrounded the Lakota at Wounded Knee Creek and demanded they relinquish all their firearms. One Lakota, Black Coyote, was deaf and spoke no English. When ordered to give up his rifle he didn't understand, and was resistant when someone tried to take his rifle that he'd paid a great deal of money for and needed to feed his family. A struggle ensued and the rifle discharged into the air. This initiated the mass murder on the now-disarmed Lakota by the U.S. Army, using not just their rifles, but cannons with exploding shells.

December 29, 1890

Some of the Lakota were able to retrieve confiscated weapons and return fire. Twenty-five U.S. soldiers were killed, but much of that was from friendly fire from their own rifle crossfire and cannons. Most of the Lakota fled and were hunted down and murdered. Bodies of women and children were found as far as three miles from the camp, having been stalked and killed by the soldiers as they ran away in terror. The bodies of the slain were buried in a mass grave at the site of the massacre.

> **In mid-December 1890, U.S. officials reacted by attempting to arrest Chief Sitting Bull and killed him in the process.**

Despite all this, the site of the mass murder is officially referred to as the Wounded Knee Battlefield. And here I thought a battlefield was a place where armies fought each other, not where soldiers murdered unarmed men, women, and children.

f you're my age, there is a fair chance the first you ever heard of Rasputin was the 1978 Boney M. disco song. Apologies if it's in your head now. That fucking song. If you haven't heard it, do NOT google.

December 30, 1916

Born a lowly Siberian peasant in 1869, Grigori Rasputin became a self-proclaimed holy man even though the Russian Orthodox Church was all nah fuck that guy he's not one of ours. He had a religious experience at age twenty-eight and started preaching all sorts of fucked-up shit that of course gained him cult followers because humans are stupid and that's how it works.

Around 1904 he traveled to St. Petersburg, the center of Russian power at the

Grigori Rasputin

time, and charmed his way into high society, befriending Emperor Nicholas and Empress Alexandra. Their son, Alexei, had hemophilia and Rasputin was all hey I have magic powers and I'll heal the little rapscallion for ya. The kid had some bleeding events and Grigori prayed and Alexei got better so of course it was Rasputin's magic that did it.

As a result, over the next ten years Rasputin's power in the Russian court grew. Being a dick, he used it to accept bribes and sexual favors. There was a myth that he controlled Russia and Nicholas and Alexandra were his puppets, but that's a gross overstatement. He *was* influential, and plenty of other people didn't like that, seeing him as a danger to the country and the monarchy, but he wasn't running the show. But things came to a head after 1915 when Nicholas left St. Petersburg to lead Russian troops on the Eastern Front during World War I and Rasputin had increased influence over Alexandra back home. A while later the nobles decided they'd had enough and resolved to waste his hairy ass.

Prince Yusupov invited Grigori to his palace for some feasting. Allegedly the food was poisoned but Rasputin just refused to fucking die, so they shot him a bunch of times and he still didn't die so they threw him in the freezing cold river and he finally drowned, the fucker. Except that's most likely a fairy tale. There was no poison, and he died from a close-range adios-motherfucker shot to the head in the early morning of December 30, 1916.

He *was* thrown in the butt-ass cold Malaya Nevka River though; his body was found three days later.

Libertarians. These brainless inverte-brates make me want to start swearing like a mom with a red-wine hangover walking barefoot through a LEGO-filled living room. "Oh, the free market will regulate itself." Yeah fucking bullshit. If you permit capitalism to run amok, it sure as shit will, and the British East India Company was the epitome of greed gone fucking bugshit bonkers, trafficking in human misery.

Formed on New Year's Eve, 1600, the British East India Company grew to become the most powerful company the world has ever known. How did they do it? Ruthlessly violent exploitation, muthafuckas! And Queen Elizabeth I was totally behind it. She gave the English businessmen who started the company a royal charter and said go forth and conquer and exterminate and be wealthy and all that cool imperialist shit.

They sailed to India and set up shop, trading tea, spices, silk, cotton, and dyes. Sounds perfectly capitalistic and utterly aboveboard, doesn't it? Oh, forgot about the opium. Opium was a big one. And if you didn't want to buy it, well, they had a big navy and army and they'd fucking *make* you buy it. You've heard of the Opium Wars? That.

Eventually they got tired of just having trading posts and decided, you know what, we should just own this place. It's ours now. Suck it, foreigners. Oh, and pay us taxes too. They'd evolved from merchants into empire builders, taking over most of the Indian sub-continent, parts of Southeast Asia, and Hong Kong. At its height it had an army numbering more than a quarter million soldiers to control its stolen lands. They also traded in enslaved people, because when you're that fucking evil of course you do.

December 31, 1600

After almost three centuries of fuckery, the company eventually came to ruin and dissolution toward the end of the nineteenth century, not because of any moral outrage at home over the atrocities committed, but because English political and business interests realized they were getting fucked out of opportunity by the British East India Company having a monopoly.

To this day, the world's global economic-political structure remains influenced by the actions of the British East India Company. Its toxic legacy of corporate exploitation remains ever-present.

Formed on New Year's Eve, 1600, the British East India Company grew to become the most powerful company the world has ever known.

March 14—Jack Ruby shooting Lee Harvey Oswald
Date: 1963
Author: Robert H. Jackson

March 21—Virginia Hall
Date: 1945
Author: CIA

March 26—Louis Riel (center) and the Provisional Métis Government, ~1870
Date: ~1870
Author: Believed to be Joseph Langevin

March 27—Sergeant Reckless and U.S. Marine Sergeant Joseph Latham
Date: ~1953
Author: USMC Photographer

March 29—Julius and Ethel Rosenberg, 1951
Date: 1951
Author: Roger Higgins

April 1—1974 AMC Gremlin
Date: 1978
Author: Bob DuHamel
License: https://creativecommons.org/licenses /by-sa/2.5/deed.en
Notes: Photo was altered from color to black and white

April 4—Dr. Martin Luther King Jr. in 1964
Date: 1964
Author: Marion Trikosko

April 7—Violet Gibson after her arrest for attempting to assassinate Mussolini
Date: 1926
Author: Italian Ministry of the Interior

April 11—The Stone of Scone in the Coronation Chair at Westminster Abbey
Date: ~1875
Author: Unknown

April 12—Yuri Gagarin in 1961
Date: 1961
Author: Arto Jousi

April 17—Hannie Schaft
Date: Unknown
Author: Unknown

April 20—Marie and Pierre Curie in their lab
Date: ~1904
Author: Unknown

April 21—The remains of Richthofen's plane after it was looted for souvenirs
Date: 1918
Author: Unknown

April 24—Annie Oakley
Date: 1899
Author: Richard Fox

April 27—No Kum-Sok meeting Vice-president Nixon
Date: 1954
Author: Unknown

April 30—Albert Einstein, age 25
Date: 1905
Author: Lucien Chavan

May 7—The *Lusitania* on her maiden voyage in New York, 1907
Date: 1907
Author: Maritime Quest

May 8—Londoners celebrate the end of the war in Europe
Date: 1945
Author: Unknown

May 10—Nelson Mandela, age 19
Date: 1937
Author: Unknown

May 12—Florence Nightingale in 1858
Date: 1858
Author: Henry Hering

May 18—Aimee Semple McPherson preaching at Angelus Temple in 1923
Date: 1923
Author: *Los Angeles Times*

May 21—Amelia Earhart in 1936
Date: 1936
Author: Harris & Ewing

May 25—Oscar Wilde (left) and Alfred Douglas
Date: 1893
Author: Gillman & Co.

May 28—Ontario premier Mitchell Hepburn with the Dionne Quintuplets
> Date: c. 1934
> Author: Unknown

May 31—A newspaper clipping that contributed to the Tulsa Race Massacre
> Date: 1921
> Author: *Tulsa Tribune*

June 6—U.S. soldiers approaching Omaha Beach on D-Day
> Date: 1944
> Author: Unknown

June 16—George Stinney's mugshot
> Date: 1944
> Author: State of South Carolina

June 19—Juneteenth celebration in 1900
> Date: 1900
> Author: Grace Murray

June 23—Robert the Bruce addressing his troops at the Battle of Bannockburn
> Date: c. 1906
> Author: Edmund Leighton

July 3—A mujahideen fighter with a surface-to-air missile launcher
> Date: 1988
> Author: Unknown

July 4—*The Death of Epaminondas*
> Date: 1812
> Author: Bartolomeo Pinelli

July 6—Louis Pasteur in his lab
> Date: Unknown
> Author: Unknown

July 11—The duel between Burr and Hamilton
> Date: 1901
> Author: Henry Davenport Northrop

July 15—The Rosetta Stone
> Date: 2007
> Author: Hans Hillewaert
> License: https://creativecommons.org/licenses/by-sa/4.0/deed.en
> Notes: Photo was altered from color to black and white

July 18—Francisco Franco in 1930
> Date: 1930
> Author: Unknown

July 21—John Scopes, shortly before the trial
> Date: 1925
> Author: Watson Davis

July 23—The 1910 Model T Ford
> Date: 1910
> Author: Harry Shipler

July 26—Fidel Castro and his guerrilla fighters
> Date: 1956
> Author: Unknown

July 29—Neil Peart in 1977
> Date: 1977
> Author: Fin Costello

July 30—Location of the First Defenestration of Prague
> Date: 2014
> Author: Øyvind Holmstad
> License: https://creativecommons.org/licenses/by-sa/3.0/deed.en

August 3—Jesse Owens winning gold in the long jump in the 1936 Olympic Games
> Date: 1936
> Author: Unknown
> License: https://creativecommons.org/licenses/by-sa/3.0/de/deed.en

August 4—Anne Frank
> Date: 1940
> Author: Unknown

August 6—The atomic mushroom clouds over Hiroshima (left) and Nagasaki (right)
> Date: 1945
> Author: George Caron (left image) / Charles Levy (right image)

August 7—Frances Oldham Kelsey with President Kennedy
> Date: 1962
> Author: Unknown

August 8—Mohandas Gandhi (right) and Jawaharlal Nehru discussing Quit India; Nehru would later become India's first prime minister
> Date: 1942
> Author: Unknown

August 11—Hedy Lamarr in 1944
Date: 1944
Author: Unknown

August 13—An East German border guard leaps to freedom during construction of the Berlin Wall
Date: 1961
Author: Peter Leibing

August 15—Thomas Edison with his early phonograph
Date: 1878
Author: L. C. Handy

August 30—*Endurance* trapped in Antarctic sea ice
Date: 1915
Author: Frank Hurley

September 3—Frederick Douglass
Date: 1856
Author: Unknown

September 5—Arbuckle with his lawyers during his first trial
Date: 1921
Author: Unknown

September 13—Noor Inayat Khan
Date: 1943
Author: Government of the United Kingdom

September 19—The Tipper Sticker
Date: 1990
Author: Recording Industry Association of America

September 20—Billie Jean King and Bobby Riggs
Date: 1973
Author: Unknown

September 21—Empress Dowager Cixi
Date: 1900
Author: Yu Xunling

October 8—Sergeant Alvin York at the hill where he earned the Medal of Honor, 1919
Date: 1919
Author: Pfc. F.C. Phillips

October 10—President Theodore Roosevelt on a steam shovel at the Culebra Cut, 1906
Date: 1906
Author: Unknown

October 11—Anita Hill testifies
Date: 1991
Author: R. Michael Jenkins

October 12—Desmond Doss receiving the Medal of Honor from President Truman
Date: 1945
Author: U.S. Federal Government

October 15—Mata Hari performing in 1905
Date: 1905
Author: Unknown

October 22—The Montparnasse train derailment
Date: 1895
Author: Studio Lévy and Sons

October 24—Harry Houdini in 1905
Date: 1905
Author: Unknown

October 30—Orson Welles interviewed the day after the broadcast
Date: 1938
Author: Acme News Photos

October 31—Supermarine Spitfire
Date: 1943
Author: U.S. Air Force

November 8—First X-ray: "Hand with Rings"
Date: 1895
Author: Wilhelm Röntgen

November 14—Nellie Bly in Mexico, 1885
Date: 1888
Author: Unknown

November 15—Cartoon depicting imperial powers carving up Africa
Date: 1884
Author: François Maréchal

November 23—Soviet soldiers during the Battle of Stalingrad
Date: 1942
Author: Unknown

November 28—Stalin, Roosevelt, and Churchill at the Tehran Conference
Date: 1943
Author: U.S. Signal Corps

December 7—Going stabby on Cicero
Date: 1880
Author: Unknown

December 9—Marguerite Durand with "Tiger"
Date: Unknown
Author: Unknown

December 14—Queen Victoria, Albert, and their nine children
Date: 1857
Author: Caldesi and Montecchi

December 17—The first powered flight
Date: 1903
Author: John T. Daniels

December 19—Harold Holt in 1966
Date: 1966
Author: Australian News and Information Bureau

December 22—Alfred Dreyfus incarcerated on Devil's Island
Date: 1898
Author: Unknown

December 27—The Hagia Sophia, 1900
Date: 1900
Author: Achille Samandji

December 28—Constance Markievicz with a Colt revolver
Date: 1915
Author: Unknown

December 30—Grigori Rasputin
Date: Unknown
Author: Unknown

Acknowledgments

No book is the work of a single person.

I want to begin by lauding the efforts of three amazing women, giving a heartfelt thank-you to my friends Ryane Chatman, Carrie King, and Michelle Szpilzinger. Often in the writing of the daily "Shit Went Down" column on Facebook, I tackled difficult subjects, and these three women gave patient advice that shaped my writing in ways beyond measure. If I failed in any of these pieces to show due compassion or understanding, the fault lies with me for not listening adequately. I also owe much thanks to the many thousands of Facebook commenters who provided insights, corrected errors, noticed typos and (unintentional) grammar mistakes, as well as offered suggestions for subjects to write about.

Prior to the version you hold in your hands, this book was first self-published. I could not have done that without the help of Karen Durrie, Avery Olive, Stephani Finks, Sonia Simpson, Jennifer Theroux, and Mark Leslie Lefebvre. And with the success of that version, I must thank my wonderful agent, Peter Steinberg of United Talent Agency, for getting me the republishing deal.

On that note, many thanks to my brilliant editor, Mary Reynics of Bantam, for her "Atlantean" efforts to make this work the best it could be. Every page of this book has her mark on it. I'm also grateful to Lawrence Krauser; I cannot imagine that copyediting such a work was an easy task. Additional thanks go out to other members of the Bantam team for their production and design work: Emily Hartley, Andy Lefkowitz, Mark Maguire, Ralph Fowler, and Victoria Allen.

I must express special gratitude to media historian Donna Halper for helping me secure the interview with Alex Lifeson for the July 29 story, thereby fulfilling my dream of interviewing all three members of my favorite band, Rush. That story was too close to my heart to limit to a single page.

The year 2020 was a fucktacular shitnado of ass, what with Covid and lockdowns and a real fear of a Trump reelection. And yet, my kids managed to not drive me totally bugshit while cooped up as I wrote the column that became this book. So, thanks for that. And thank fucking science for vaccines, too.

And finally, thank you to my lovely wife, my biggest fan for all these years, without whose ongoing support I never would have been able to make it as an author. I love you.

Index

Page numbers in *italic* print indicate illustrations.

Indonesia, 291
Ineffabilis Deus (Pius IX), 366
infant mortality, 212
Innocent III (pope), 337
Inquisition, 288
insulin, 13
integration, 145, 264, 359
"intelligent design," 214
International Feminist Congress
    (1896), 367
International Ladies' Garment
    Workers' Union, 89
interracial marriage, 173
inventions. *See also* nuclear weapons
    aircraft, *376,* 376–77
    AK-47s, 339
    aspirin, 243
    penicillin, 289
    printing press, 57
    radio technology to guide
        torpedoes, 237
    steam engine, 194
    vulcanized rubber, 257
    whisky, 161
Iran
    overthrow of Mosaddegh, 247
    overthrow of shah, 283
    scandal with Contras, 332
    war with Iraq, 28, 169, 283
    during World War II, 354
Iraq
    Operation Red Dawn, 371
    war with Iran, 28, 169, 283
Ireland
    Bloody Sunday, 202
    Easter Rebellion, 388
    independence, 388
Irish Republican Army (IRA), 202
Iron Curtain, 185
Isa, Palestina, "Tina," 380
Isa, Zein, 380
Isaacson, Walter, 127
Islam
    Abbasid Caliphate's Golden Age,
        44
    extremist murders of *Charlie*
        Hebdo staff, 9
    Hagia Sophia and, 387, *387*
    Muhammad, 169
    Russians in Afghanistan and,
        195
    Siege and Battle of Vienna, 273

in Spain, 4
Sunni-Shia split within, 28, 283
Isla Vista, California, massacre, 151
Israel
    antisemitism and, 143, 382
    attack on athletes from, at 1972
        Olympics by Black September,
        267
    Balfour Declaration, 143
    peace treaty with Egypt, 298
Italy, 41, 103
Ivan IV, "the Terrible," 18, *18*
"Ivy Mike," 327
"I Will Always Love You" (Parton),
    53

J'Accuse . . . ! (Zola), 382
Jackson, Michael, 227
Jack the Ripper, 259
Jacobs, Seth, 172
James, Jesse and Frank, 99
James, LeBron, 122
James I (king of England), 84, 331
James V (king of Scotland), 270
Japan, 5, 38. *See also* World War II
Jaws (movie and book), 181
Jeanne de Clisson, 228
Jenner, Edward, 142
Jennings, Waylon, 37
Jerusalem, 168
Jesuits, 288
Jewell, Richard, 319
"The Jewish Question," 139
Jews. *See also* antisemitism;
    Holocaust; Israel
    Black Death and, 11
    during First Crusade, 168
    Henry Ford and, 216
    Hanukkah, 347
    in Spain, 4
    Women's March leaders, 23
Joan of Arc, 126
John (king of England), 175
Johnny Cash at Folsom Prison, 14
Johnny Cash at San Quentin, 14
John Paul II (pope), 141
Johnson, Andrew, 248, 378
Johnson, Lyndon, 32
Jones, Curtis, 256
Jones, Jim, 344
"Jubilee Day," 180, *180,* 248

Julius Caesar, 12, 262
Juneteenth, 180, *180,* 248
Jung, Carl, 110
Justinian I (Eastern Roman
    emperor), 387

Kaasen, Gunnar, 36, *36*
Kalashnikov, Mikhail, 339
Kameny, Frank, 269
Kandel, Lenore, 16
Kansas Territory, 152
Karapetyan, Kamo, 277
Karapetyan, Shavarsh, 277
Kavanaugh, Brett, 186, 303
Kelsey, Frances Oldham, 234, *234*
Kendrotas, Giorgios, 104
Kendrotas, Theodoros, 104
Kennedy, John F.
    assassination of, 78
    Berlin Wall and, 240
    Cuban Missile Crisis, 320
    election of, 287
    Kelsey and, 234, *234*
    photograph of Đức, 172
    presidential debate (1960), 287
Kennedy, Joseph, 213
Kennedy, Robert, 32
Kennedy, Rosemary, 213
Kent State Massacre, 132
Kenya, 313
Kershaw, Sir Ian, 369
Key, Francis Scott, 252
Keyes, Alan, 330
Khaalis, Hamaas Abdul, 75
Khalid Sheikh Mohammed, 60
Khan, Noor Inayat, 274, *274*
Khomeini, Ayatollah, 283
Khrushchev, Nikita, 69, 240
Killen, Edgar, 8, *8*
Kim Jong-il, 47
Kim Jong-nam, 47
Kim Jong-un, 47
King, Billie Jean, 281
King, Martin Luther, Jr., 32, 100,
    100, 359
King, Rodney, 67
Kira (Japanese official), 38
Kirov, Soviet Union, 98
Kleiss, Norman, 164
Klug, Aaron, 112
Knight, Suge, 268

James wanted to be a history professor, but chose love instead. He didn't wish to make his physician wife uproot a practice time and again while he did a PhD then searched for a tenure-track position fuck knows where. So, after the master's degree in history, he got an MBA and worked as a marketroid, but he hated that so he became a fitness columnist for the *Los Angeles Times* and the *Chicago Tribune,* and he was pretty good at it.

A decade later the COVID-19 pandemic was beginning, which freaked him out, and he had a sudden inspiration to write about history instead of fitness and holy shit it worked out. Speaking of working out, the terror of a possible Trump reelection and perhaps coughing himself to death from the plague rampaging o'er the land caused Fell's exercise regimen to take a hit. Beer consumption also went up and he gained the Covid "19" plus a few more pounds.

But career success, getting vaccinated, and the world pulling back from the brink of going full fascist were wonderful stress

PHOTO: © LORI ANDREWS

relievers so he got mostly back into shape and now he can pose his 55-year-old ass in the mirror and say dumb shit like "Still got it."

This whole bio was a lead-up to saying that James Fell is a history buff.

I'll see myself out.

JamesFell.com

About the Type

This book was set in Garamond, a typeface originally designed by the Parisian type cutter Claude Garamond (c. 1500–61). This version of Garamond was modeled on a 1592 specimen sheet from the Egenolff-Berner foundry, which was produced from types assumed to have been brought to Frankfurt by the punch cutter Jacques Sabon (c. 1520–80).

Claude Garamond's distinguished romans and italics first appeared in *Opera Ciceronis* in 1543–44. The Garamond types are clear, open, and elegant.